$24.95

Programming Concepts
and Problem Solving

The Benjamin/Cummings Series in Computing and Information Sciences

E. G. Booch   *Software Engineering and Ada*   (1983)

H. L. Capron, B. K. Williams   *Computers and Data Processing*   (1982)

D. M. Etter   *FORTRAN for Scientists and Engineers*   (1983)

P. Linz   *Programming Concepts and Problem Solving: An Introduction to Computer Science Using Pascal*   (1983)

T. N. Norman   *UCSD Pascal*   (1984)

Programming Concepts and Problem Solving

An Introduction to Computer Science Using Pascal

Peter Linz

University of California, Davis

The Benjamin/Cummings Publishing Company

Menlo Park, California • Reading, Massachusetts
London • Amsterdam • Don Mills, Ontario • Sydney

Sponsoring Editors: Susan A. Newman and John Noon
Production Coordinator: Susan Harrington
Copy Editor: Susan Harrington
Interior and Cover Designer: Nancy Benedict
Technical Artist: John Foster
Chapter Opener Artist: Constance Romweber

Figure 1-3 courtesy of Apple Computer, Inc.
Figure 1-4 courtesy of Burroughs Corporation.

Library of Congress Cataloging in Publication Data

Linz, Peter.
  Programming concepts and problem solving.

  Includes bibliographies and index.
  1. PASCAL (Computer program language)   I. Title.
QA76.73.P2L56   1983   001.64′24   82-14699
ISBN 0-8053-5710-6
ABCDEFGHIJ-DO-898765432

The Benjamin/Cummings Publishing Company
2727 Sand Hill Road
Menlo Park, CA 94025

preface

the discipline of programming

The first programmers were, by necessity, recruited from various disciplines. Engineers, physicists, and mathematicians learned how to use the computer through self-study or by listening to informal instructions from manufacturers' representatives. Being highly trained in mathematics and other scientific disciplines, they saw programming not as a new discipline requiring careful study and practical experience, but as something that an educated person could learn in his or her spare time.

This attitude was passed on to succeeding generations of scientists and persists in some circles to this day. For many years, the teaching of programming centered around courses that did little more than give students a detailed description of the features of a particular programming language. Even computer science majors, whose needs were quite different, were subjected to such introductory courses. This perfunctory approach produced a lot of bad programmers and contributed to what is now called the "software crisis."

the introductory course

Education in computer science, like education in nuclear physics, is a lengthy process that involves both formal training and practical experience. The starting point for this learning process should be an introductory course in which the student learns the fundamentals of the discipline. The course should include some general ideas of computer organization, but should stress problem solving, with the associated ideas of programming languages, data structures, and algorithms. This provides some basic skills, but, more important, lays down a solid foundation for further study. One of the most influential of the many curricula suggested for undergraduates in computer science, the ACM Curriculum '78, has as its fundamentals two such classes (CS1 and CS2), which deal with concepts of programming and problem solving. This text contains all the material needed to teach these courses.

use of pascal in the text

In an introductory course, it is important to stress the importance of concepts over the details of the particular language being used. The temptation to use a pseudolanguage is hard to resist. But with a pseudolanguage, students still have to learn an actual language so that they can write programs suitable for the computer. Thus they learn two languages, one of which is of no permanent value. The second and more profound disadvantage is that one cannot easily talk about such important topics as programming style, efficiency, selection of data structures, and so on.

Fortunately, Pascal is an excellent teaching tool. Its syntax involves a number of conventions, but they are natural and easy to remember. In essence, it is not much harder to learn than a reasonably complete pseudolanguage. Having taught many introductory courses in several languages, including FORTRAN, BASIC, and PL/I, I am enthusiastic about Pascal, and expect it to become the standard teaching language of the future.

teaching the course with pascal

However, since the book does devote a great deal of space to the description of the syntax and semantics of Pascal, some students may get the idea that the language is the most important aspect of the course. It is the instructor who must provide the right emphasis and guidance. He or she must establish a dialogue with the students, and give them the benefit of his or her experience. A book can only provide a background for such a dialogue. Consequently, I have tried to keep the text simple, and to explain the ideas in the simplest way possible. I have tried to avoid complicated examples and minor technical points, and have made no attempt to anticipate all imaginable questions. It is the responsibility of the instructor to deal with these questions, if and when they are asked.

features of the text

examples

Most of the examples in the text follow a four-part format, the parts of which are indicated in the text by the use of four puzzle pieces:

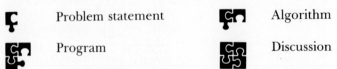

	Problem statement		Algorithm
	Program		Discussion

The examples are usually short—illustrating at most a few points—so that they demonstrate a concept as simply and effectively as possible rather than obscuring the point by excessive length. (In my experience, few students read programs that are much longer than a page.) In any case, the programs that students are asked to write will generally be quite a bit longer.

exercises

Exercises range from very simple to quite complex, so that they can fill a variety of pedagogical needs. Short exercises provide students with a quick test of their grasp of a particular concept; intermediate exercises include some that give practice in the important task of editing and adapting existing code; other, longer exercises provide a valuable introduction to complex programs.

appendix

The appendix gives a relatively complete summary of Pascal syntax, including a list of reserved words, standard identifiers, and operator precedence rules, as well as a complete set of syntax charts for the Pascal used in the text.

other features

Several other helpful pedagogical features have been integrated in the text, notably the *key terms* appearing in boldface italic in the text and in the text margins. Other important terms also appear in italic. *Further Reading* sections at the end of each chapter direct students to sources for further information on the chapter's topic—and most of the entries list specific chapters for students' convenience.

supplementary transparency package

To enable the instructor to discuss programs and concepts from the text readily in the classroom, a supplementary transparency package is available. It contains all the programs and figures from the text that are most likely to be of help to the individual instructor.

courses for which the book is suitable

The text was designed for a full-year course with two lectures per week (60 hours). Only a very fast class will be able to cover all the material in this time. For a more moderate pace, some of the material in the later chapters will have to be covered selectively. A full-year course meeting three times a week (90 hours) will be able to cover all the material at a leisurely pace. In fact, there will probably be enough time to cover additional material—perhaps another language, such as FORTRAN. If this is done prior to the study of Chapter 7, the second language can be used in a comparative study of style in Chapter 7.

The book may also be used for shorter courses, with the following typical examples:

1. A one-quarter course meeting three times a week, or a one-semester course meeting twice a week (30 hours). Coverage might include a brief discussion of Chapter 1, a full treatment of Chapters 2–5, and an introduction to functions and procedures, omitting recursion.
2. A two-quarter course meeting twice a week, or a one-semester course meeting three times a week (40–45 hours). It should be possible to cover

all of Chapters 1–8, with a brief treatment of the data structures in Chapter 9.

Acknowledgments   The material in this book was developed from notes on a course that I have taught for a number of years at UC Davis. Many students, too numerous to mention by name, have contributed indirectly by often teaching me as much as I taught them. I am grateful to all of them. I am also indebted to those who have reviewed my manuscript at various stages. The comments and suggestions of Joseph Autin, Grady Booch, Laurian Chirica, John Gillespie, Marc Kerstetter, Rod Southworth, Louis Steinberg, Ronald Suprenant, Elizabeth Unger, and Dorian Yeager have greatly influenced me and helped in improving my original effort. Finally, my thanks go to the people at Benjamin/Cummings, particularly to Susan Newman and Susan Harrington. Their efforts and expertise in putting this book together have been remarkable.

Peter Linz

special notes to the instructor

contents of the text

The material in the text divides easily into several different sections: Chapter 1, which introduces the study of computer science; Chapters 2–10, which cover, in sequence, the simplest ideas through the relatively advanced concepts of stacks, files, and trees; and Chapters 11, 12, and 13, which cover sequential files and algorithm analysis.

chapter 1

Those who consider it important to get the student on the computer fast can cover Chapter 1 in parallel with Chapters 2 and 3. However, I do not consider it a drawback to delay the writing of programs. Students need to become familiar with the system, learn about text editing, or perhaps run some "canned" programs. They should not be rushed; students should be thoroughly familiar with the system before they are allowed to run their own programs. Also, while there is no substitute for practical experience, an undue rush to get students on the computer will leave them with the impression that they can learn only when they are "plugged in." This is one of the worst things that can happen. Students should be taught to think away from the computer.

chapters 2–10

The material in Chapters 2–10 is essential and was written to be covered in sequence. Because it is essential that students be introduced to effective programming and debugging techniques as early as possible, I have included short discussions of these topics in the earlier chapters. These ideas are summarized and expanded in Chapters 7 and 8. At least some of this important material can be covered simultaneously with Chapters 3–6, but a review should be made after the completion of Chapter 6. Some may consider Section 8.4, on proving correctness of programs, an esoteric subject and skip the section. The deletion would not entail any loss of continuity, but I feel that the material, if presented in the right spirit, teaches the student that close reasoning about a program is worthwhile. Students ought to be encouraged to use this approach as a complement to debugging.

chapters 11–13

The material in Chapter 11 does not depend on Chapters 9 and 10, so some rearrangement can be made here at the instructor's discretion.

Algorithm analysis, covered in Chapters 12 and 13, is somewhat mathematical, and may be difficult for those with inadequate mathematics training. But even someone programming for business applications will need to know that using a bubblesort to sort a file with 100,000 records is not a good idea. It is unfortunate that many programmers learn only too late that mathematics is as essential to programmers as it is to engineers and physicists. Perhaps the simple analyses of Chapters 12 and 13 can get students started in the right direction.

exercises

As was mentioned briefly earlier in the preface, exercises in the text range from very simple to quite complex. The student can use short exercises as an immediate test of understanding, and short exercises can also be used in in-class tests. One type of problem of intermediate difficulty deals with the modification or extension of programs given in the text—very valuable practice, as it requires the student to analyze and modify someone else's code. No practicing programmer can escape this chore. Finally, there are traditional programming exercises, in which the student is asked to find an algorithm, write a program, test and debug it, and submit the solution. In normal circumstances, students will be assigned one of these each week. In exercises of this kind, I have generally given the overall description, but have not specified every detail, so that the instructor can adapt the exercises to meet specific needs. Some instructors may want to provide very explicit requirements (including standard test data), while others will prefer that the students draw up the final specifications and select the test examples.

A few programming exercises are quite long and will take a great deal of time if they are carried out completely (an example is the "mini-information system" in Section 11.5). The instructor may not feel justified in asking the students to complete such exercises, but the student may benefit greatly from being required, for example, to prepare initial specifications, give some high-level description of the algorithm, or decide what data structures to use. Although in general students should be discouraged from writing complex codes, it is important that they be introduced to complex programs at this early stage. In writing programs, however, students should be encouraged to use the top-down design method as an ideal tool with which to maintain simplicity and brevity.

It will help the student greatly if some classroom time can be devoted to discussion of the programming exercises, such as the instructor's solution or the best student programs, if only once or twice a quarter or semester.

system dependency problems

In addition to the text material, the instructor will have to cover various topics that are system-dependent. This will include the text editor, file storage, and any possible unusual features of the local Pascal compiler. The programs in the text were checked and run with a Unix Pascal compiler on a PDP 11/70 computer. The compiler is fairly standard, but there may be occasional problems in running programs on other systems, such as restrictions on sets and the handling of sequential files, or, obviously, problems with the differing internal accuracy of the machine.

brief table of contents

Chapter One — 1

fundamental concepts of computer science

Chapter Two — 23

programming and problem solving

Chapter Three — 57

writing simple programs

Chapter Four — 79

repetitive computations and control structure

Chapter Five — 97

data types

Chapter Six — 133

subprograms

Chapter Seven — 163

effective program design and implementation

Chapter Eight — 201

testing and debugging programs

Chapter Nine — 219

data structures and their implementation

Chapter Ten — 253

more on data structures

Chapter Eleven — 281

file processing

Chapter Twelve — 309

algorithm design and analysis

Chapter Thirteen — 327

some important algorithms

Appendix — 365

summary of pascal syntax

Index — 385

complete table of contents

Chapter One

fundamental concepts of computer science   1

1.1 Information Processing Systems   3
Exercises 1.1   5

1.2 Data Representation   7
The Binary System   7
Data Storage   9
The Floating Point System   10
Characters and Symbols   12
Exercises 1.2   12

1.3 Computer Organization   13
The Central Processing Unit   13
Main Memory   14
Secondary Storage   14
Machine Languages   14
EXAMPLE 1.1   A Simple Computation   16
EXAMPLE 1.2   A Computation with Alternatives   17
Computer Classification by Size   18
Exercises 1.3   18

1.4 System Software   19
The Operating System   19
Other Software Programs   20
Exercises 1.4   20

1.5 Programming Languages   20
Exercises 1.5   21

Further Reading   22

Chapter Two

programming and problem solving   23

2.1 Algorithms and Their Construction   24
Flowchart Language   27
EXAMPLE 2.1   Computation of Weekly Pay   31
EXAMPLE 2.2   Counting Items   32
EXAMPLE 2.3   Testing Pairs of Numbers   33
Structured Problem Solving   34
EXAMPLE 2.4   Test Score Analysis   35
Exercises 2.1   36

2.2 Statements, Variables, and Expressions   37
Conventions for Writing Programs   37
Identifiers   38
Constants   39
Variables   40
Expressions   41
Arithmetic Expressions in Pascal   41
Boolean Expressions in Pascal   43
Exercises 2.2   44

2.3 Assignment Statements   45
Exercises 2.3   47

2.4 Input and Output   48
Input   48
Output   50
Exercises 2.4   54

Further Reading   55

Chapter Three

writing simple programs   57

3.1 The Structure of a Simple Program   58
The Puzzle Solving Approach in This Text   59
EXAMPLE 3.1   Interest on a Savings Account   60
EXAMPLE 3.2   Computing the Roots of a Quadratic Equation   61
EXAMPLE 3.3   Change-Making Program   63
Exercises 3.1   65

3.2 Alternative Computations 65
Selection of One of Two Alternatives 66
EXAMPLE 3.4   Payroll Computation 68
Selection of Many Alternatives 70
EXAMPLE 3.5   Date Conversion 73
Exercises 3.2 75

3.3 Good Programming Habits 76
Exercises 3.3 77

3.4 Testing and Debugging Programs 77
Exercises 3.4 78

Further Reading 78

Chapter Four

repetitive computations and control structure 79

4.1 Loops 80
Counted Loops 80
Conditional Loops 82
EXAMPLE 4.1   Course Grade Assignment 85
Exercises 4.1 88

4.2 The Goto Statement 89
Exercises 4.2 91

4.3 Programming with Complicated Decisions 92
EXAMPLE 4.2   Data Validation 92
Exercises 4.3 96

Further Reading 96

Chapter Five

data types 97

5.1 Unstructured Data Types 98
Constants 98
Type Declarations 99
Variables with Restricted Ranges 99

Enumerated Data Types   100
Exercises 5.1   101

5.2 Sets   102
EXAMPLE 5.1   Test Classification   104
Exercises 5.2   106

5.3 Arrays   107
One-Dimensional Arrays   107
EXAMPLE 5.2   Detection of Duplicates   108
EXAMPLE 5.3   Sorting Numbers   110
Multidimensional Arrays   113
EXAMPLE 5.4   Business Sales Figures   114
Exercises 5.3   117

5.4 Processing Character Strings   118
EXAMPLE 5.5   Translating from English into Pig Latin   120
Exercises 5.4   122

5.5 Records   123
EXAMPLE 5.6   Inventory Updating   127
Exercises 5.5   130

Further Reading   131

Chapter Six

subprograms   133

6.1 Functions   135
EXAMPLE 6.1   A Simple Function   137
EXAMPLE 6.2   The Mean of a Set of Numbers   138
Exercises 6.1   139

6.2 Procedures   139
EXAMPLE 6.3   A Procedure for Some Statistical
Computations   140
Exercises 6.2   142

6.3 The Structure of a Program with Subprograms   143
EXAMPLE 6.4   More Statistical Computations   145
Scope of an Identifier   150
Exercises 6.3   152

6.4 Communication between Subprograms 152
    Exercises 6.4 154

6.5 Recursion 155
    EXAMPLE 6.5 Recognizing Well-Formed Expressions 156
    Exercises 6.5 160

Further Reading 161

Chapter Seven

effective program design and implementation 163

7.1 Programming Style 165
    EXAMPLE 7.1 Maximum of Three Values 166
    Variable Names 168
    Comments 169
    Physical Layout 170
    Exercises 7.1 171

7.2 Program Structure 171
    Exercises 7.2 173

7.3 Modular Structure and Top-Down Design 174
    Exercises 7.3 175

7.4 Program Design 176
    Problem Specification 176
    Algorithm Design 177
    Coding 177
    EXAMPLE 7.2 Plotting a Bar Graph 177
    EXAMPLE 7.3 A Game-Playing Program 183
    Exercises 7.4 185

7.5 Input/Output Handling 186
    Exercises 7.5 187

7.6 Program Modification 188
    Exercises 7.6 190

7.7 Writing Efficient Programs 190
    Execution Time 191

Storage Space   195
Exercises 7.7   195

7.8 Documentation   197

7.9 Summary   199

Further Reading   199

Chapter Eight

testing and debugging programs   201

8.1 Error Types   202
Exercises 8.1   204

8.2 Program Testing   204
Exercises 8.2   209

8.3 Debugging   209
Exercises 8.3   212

8.4 Proving Program Correctness   212
EXAMPLE 8.1   Error in SIMPLESTAT   213
EXAMPLE 8.2   Roots of a Quadratic Equation   214
Exercises 8.4   216

Further Reading   217

Chapter Nine

data structures and their implementation   219

9.1 Structure and Relation in Data   220
Exercises 9.1   222

9.2 Stacks and Queues   222
Stacks   222
EXAMPLE 9.1   Pascal Implementation of Stacks and Stack Operations   224
EXAMPLE 9.2   Evaluation of Postfix Expressions   228
EXAMPLE 9.3   Translation from Infix to Postfix Notation   231

Queues   233
   EXAMPLE 9.4   Implementation of Queue Operations   234
   Exercises 9.2   235

9.3 Lists   237
   Exercises 9.3   244

9.4 Some Applications of Linked Lists   245
   EXAMPLE 9.5   Manipulation of Polynomials   246
   EXAMPLE 9.6   Text Editing   247
   EXAMPLE 9.7   Sparse Tables and Matrices   248
   Exercises 9.4   251

Further Reading   252

Chapter Ten

more on data structures   253

10.1 Trees   254
   Preorder Traversal   257
      EXAMPLE 10.1   Printing Labels of a Binary Tree in
                     Preorder   258
      EXAMPLE 10.2   Recursive Procedure for Printing Labels of a
                     Binary Tree   262
   Postorder and Inorder Traversal   263
   Exercises   263

10.2 Dynamic Memory Allocation   265
   EXAMPLE 10.3   Implementation of a Stack with Pointers   269
   EXAMPLE 10.4   Implementation of Linked Lists with
                  Pointers   271
   EXAMPLE 10.5   Implementation of Binary Trees with
                  Pointers   273
   Exercises 10.2   274

10.3 Criteria for Selecting Data Structures   275
   EXAMPLE 10.6   Representation of Sets   276
   EXAMPLE 10.7   Symmetric Tables   277
   EXAMPLE 10.8   Text Editing Revisited   278
   Exercises 10.3   279

Further Reading   279

Chapter Eleven

file processing 281

11.1 Characteristics of Secondary Storage Devices   282
   Magnetic Tapes   283
   Magnetic Disks   284
   Magnetic Drums   286
   Floppy Disks   286
   Exercises 11.1   287

11.2 Files and Their Structure   287
   Exercises 11.2   289

11.3 Sequential Files in Pascal   289
   EXAMPLE 11.1   Splitting a File   292
   EXAMPLE 11.2   Extracting Information from a File   293
   EXAMPLE 11.3   Data Editing   296
   Exercises 11.3   298

11.4 Information Retrieval   299
   Exercises 11.4   301

11.5 File Organization   301
   Directories   302
   Hashing Functions   303
   Indexed Sequential Organization   304
   Inverted Files   305
   Exercises 11.5   306

Further Reading   307

Chapter Twelve

algorithm design and analysis   309

12.1 Algorithm Discovery   310
   Exercises 12.1   314

12.2 Efficiency of Some Algorithms   314
   EXAMPLE 12.1   Searching   314
   EXAMPLE 12.2   Searching with Several Keys   316

EXAMPLE 12.3   Sorting   317
EXAMPLE 12.4   Packing Objects into a Bin   319
Exercises 12.2   321

12.3 Analysis of Algorithms   321
Exercises 12.3   324

Further Reading   325

Chapter Thirteen

some important algorithms   327

13.1 String Manipulation   328
Concatenation   328
EXAMPLE 13.1   Concatenation with a Special Linked List   329
Extracting Substrings   331
Pattern Matching   331
EXAMPLE 13.2   A Pattern Matching Program   331
Exercises 13.1   334

13.2 Searching   335
Sequential Search   335
EXAMPLE 13.3   Retrieving Records with Different
Activities   336
Binary Search   337
EXAMPLE 13.4   Recursive Binary Search   338
Binary Search Trees   339
Hash Addressing   343
Exercises 13.2   345

13.3 Merging and Sorting   346
Merging of Two Sorted Files   346
Sorting   349
EXAMPLE 13.5   Recursive Mergesort   350
Bucket Sort   352
EXAMPLE 13.6   Comparison of Various Sorting Methods   352
Exercises 13.3   352

13.4 Combinatorial Problems   353
EXAMPLE 13.7   Solution of the Bin Packing Problem   355
Exercises 13.4   361

13.5 The Complexity of Problems   361
Exercises 13.5   364

Further Reading   364

Appendix

summary of pascal syntax   365

A. Reserved Words and Standard Identifiers   366
Reserved Words   366
Standard Identifiers   366

B. Operator Precedence Rules   367

C. Syntax Charts   367

D. An Indentation Convention   383

Index   385

Programming Concepts and Problem Solving

Chapter One

fundamental concepts of computer science

Nowadays the word "computer" is being heard with increasing frequency. There is a widespread feeling that computers are causing a fundamental and revolutionary change, not only in our technology, but also in our personal lives. Some look upon this situation with fear and awe; others welcome it; but most agree that the impact of computers on our lives is already significant and will become more pervasive in the future.

Calculating aids and devices have been used throughout most of recorded history. One of the oldest, the abacus, has been used in China and Japan for many centuries. In the western world, the slide rule, dating back to the seventeenth century, has long been a favorite tool of engineers and scientists. Of more recent origin are mechanical devices such as tabulating and adding machines. All of these helped in making routine calculations a little less laborious, but had little effect on society as a whole.

The history of the computer, however, is quite brief, dating back to about 1945. In the late 1940s, the process of computing was automated by means of electronic circuitry and thereby speeded up to a point where the calculating machine could not only aid in computation, but could perform tasks previously considered utterly beyond the capabilities of a machine. The first computers were experimental machines in university laboratories, but commercial models soon followed. They quickly became central in the ongoing process of automation which, for better or worse, is reshaping our world.

Virtually everyone who lives in today's industrialized nations is affected in some way by computers. Billing, banking, and weaponry and defense systems rely on computers, and data banks often hold detailed personal information on many people. Yet few laymen have more than a vague understanding of what computers are all about.

Two mistaken views of computers enjoy a certain amount of popularity among the general public. The first, created by science fiction writers and encouraged by overly optimistic computer scientists, sees the computer as a superbrain capable of feats of intelligence well beyond the ability of any human being. Soon, they hypothesize, these marvellous machines will do all our work and thinking for us, and we will all retire to lives of complete leisure. The opposing view sees the computer as a menace, rigid and inflexible, that increasingly regiments our lives and robs us of personal freedom. Here, the computer represents technology out of control, its function totally unrelated to human values and needs.

While there is a grain of truth in these positions, they are both quite exaggerated. Though computers can perform specific tasks that we would find tedious, they are not and never will be even comparable to the human brain; the fear of a "computer takeover" stems primarily from our sense that we don't always use constructively the tools science has given us. Yet the inability to use technology wisely is by no means confined to our application of computers.

It will not be our aim in this text to discuss the design, use, or social implications of computers. Our scope will be much more limited. We will come to understand a little about computers by learning how to use them.

programming

Using a computer involves communicating with it and instructing it to carry out some task by ***programming*** it. As we shall see shortly, to program a computer, we need to express our wishes so that the computer can deal with them—in a language the computer can understand. Therefore, most of our effort will involve programming methods and programming languages.

In principle, it would be sufficient to study a computer language and learn to use it. As long as we have a clear understanding of what a computer can do and know how to give it instructions, we might not need to be concerned with the actual mechanism by which the instructions are carried out. But such an uncritical approach is not always satisfactory. In practice, a general knowledge of what goes on in computers can help us in understanding their potential as well as their limitations. In this first chapter, therefore, we will study some of the basic concepts of computer science and introduce the terminology that will be used in the rest of the book. In actual practice, though, there are considerable differences in detail from one computer to the next. In reading this material, you should be sure that you not only learn the concepts, but that you understand how they are applied in the particular computer that you are using.

1.1

information processing systems

One dictionary defines a computer as "a mechanical or electronic apparatus capable of carrying out repetitious and highly complex mathematical operations at high speeds." While this definition conveys a correct impression, it does not adequately describe a modern computer. A modern computer is more than a machine for performing arithmetic operations. In fact, the more appropriate and expressive terms "information processing system" or "data processor" are often used instead of "computer." In everyday usage, ***data*** and ***information*** are essentially synonymous.

data
information

Computer scientists, however, make a distinction: "data" refers to a representation of some fact, concept, or real entity. Data may be in various forms—for example, written or spoken words, numbers, and pictures. "Information" denotes organized and processed data. "System" is defined as a set of connected and interacting components having an overall unity and purpose. An information processing system, then, transforms raw data into organized, meaningful, and useful information.

Figure 1.1 illustrates the three components of an information processing system: *input, output,* and *processor.* The processor, which can be

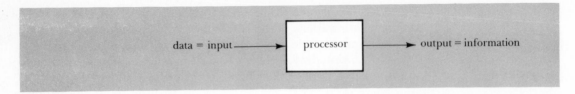

data = input ⟶ processor ⟶ output = information

FIGURE 1.1

Schematic
diagram of an
information
processing
system

quite complicated, is represented by a simple box. It can accept data, called input. The input is then transformed to produce output.

Based on this scheme, a great many devices or organisms can be considered information processing systems. A thermostat controlling a building's temperature is a very simple information processing system. The input is the measured temperature, and the output is a signal controlling the furnace or the air conditioner. The processor itself can be understood with a knowledge of some elementary physics. In contrast, the brain of an animal or a human is a very complicated information processing system. The input and output are impulses originating in the sensory organs and in turn controlling various muscles. The processor is so complex that it is beyond our complete understanding for even the simplest organisms.

Both examples, although different in nature and complexity, fit the general pattern. What distinguishes them from each other and from other examples of information processing systems are (1) the kind of input that can be accepted, (2) the kind of output that can be produced, and (3) the decision process that transforms the input to output. In both examples, too, the decision mechanism can be changed. The setting on a thermostat can be altered manually so that the thermostat acts differently at different times. In a brain, changes occur, for example, with learning and aging. In either case, the decision process is not fixed. In a computer, such a

program
software

changeable decision mechanism is called a ***program***. The set of programs that direct a computer's operation is called ***software***.

Adding a few details to Figure 1.1 gives us a schematic representation of a computer (Figure 1.2). From it, we can identify a computer's major

hardware

physical components, called ***hardware***.

1. The Central Processing Unit (CPU). The CPU consists of electronic circuitry capable of performing some simple computations, such as adding or multiplying numbers. The repertoire of the CPU is quite limited—not much more extensive than that of a pocket calculator. The operations are, however, carried out accurately and at high speed. The power of a computer stems entirely from the CPU's speed and reliability.
2. Main Memory. The information processed by the CPU usually has to be stored in main memory until computations are completed. A computer's programs are also stored in main memory.

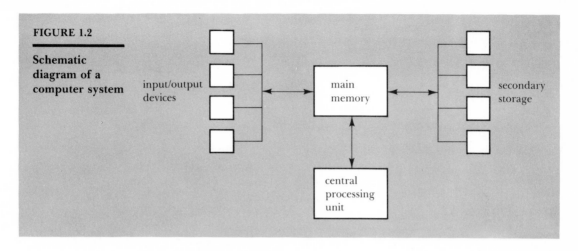

FIGURE 1.2

Schematic diagram of a computer system

input/output devices

main memory

secondary storage

central processing unit

3. Secondary Storage Devices. Various devices, such as magnetic disks and tapes, are used to store large amounts of information. To be processed by the CPU, the data stored on the secondary storage devices have to be brought first into main memory.

4. Peripheral or Input/Output (I/O) Devices. These devices allow the human user to communicate with the computer. Some typical I/O devices are typewriter or video terminals, punched card readers, and printers. A large system may have several hundred peripheral devices attached to it.

In practice, a large computer installation may have several CPUs, each with its own memory as well as shared main memory; a variety of secondary storage devices; and peripherals located in various parts of a building, across town, or even elsewhere in the country. Figure 1.3 shows a small "home" computer. Figure 1.4 shows a somewhat larger system, which may perhaps be used in a business firm or an educational institution.

EXERCISES 1.1

1. Find other examples of information processing systems. Classify them according to their input and output and the complexity of the processors. Are their decision mechanisms fixed or variable? What are their mechanisms for program modification?

2. Find out the components of your computer. In particular, find out what peripheral and secondary storage devices are attached to it, then draw a diagram like Figure 1.2 for your system. (To get the necessary information, ask friends, computer consultants, your instructor, or whoever else may be familiar with your system.)

FIGURE 1.3

A small
computer system

FIGURE 1.4

A larger
computer system

1.2

data representation

the binary system

A computer receives data in the form of words or numbers, which are typed into the machine in a sequence of characters. After the data are processed, the information is returned in the same form. But information is not necessarily stored in the same form in which the user sees it.

Data storage and processing in computers are greatly simplified by the use of so-called *bistable* circuit elements. These are devices that have only two possible states, denoted by 0 and 1. For example, a switch can be open or closed, voltage can be positive or negative, or a magnet can be magnetized in one of two directions. When bistable elements are used, the circuitry of the computer needs to distinguish between only two alternatives, an approach so advantageous that it is employed in virtually all computer design. The numbers 0 and 1 are called **binary digits,** or **bits** for short. All information stored in the computer is processed in binary form, that is, as strings of 0s and 1s. When we give data to the computer in any other form, the computer must first convert it to binary form.

binary digits
bits

To see how numbers can be represented in binary form, consider what we really mean when we write a decimal number, say 32.5. When we write 32.5, we employ a positional number system in which the value associated with each digit depends not only on the digit itself, but also on its position with respect to a reference point, called the decimal point. Thus, 32.5 is shorthand for

$$30 + 2 + \frac{1}{2}$$

or

$$3 \times 10^1 + 2 \times 10^0 + 5 \times 10^{-1}$$

To get the value of any number represented in decimal form, we multiply each digit by a power of ten, non-negative and increasing to the left of the decimal point, negative and decreasing to the right. The number ten is said to be the *base* of the representation, hence the term decimal system. In the decimal system the allowable digits are 0, 1, . . . , 9.

It is possible to use a similar idea to represent numbers in another base, say B. When we choose base B, we can use all digits 0, 1, . . . , $B - 1$, but none larger. For $B = 2$, the allowable digits are 0 and 1—the binary numbers. The implied multiplier is a power of two, because two is the base. In the binary system, the reference point is called the *binary point,* and, as in the decimal system, positive powers are to the left and negative powers to the right. For example, the binary number 1101.01 stands for

$$1 \times 2^3 + 1 \times 2^2 + 0 \times 2^1 + 1 \times 2^0 + 0 \times 2^{-1} + 1 \times 2^{-2}$$

or 13.25 in decimal form. In short, conversion from binary numbers to decimal numbers is quite straightforward: we simply write down each bit, multiply it by the appropriate power of two, then add.

Perhaps the simplest, although not the most efficient, way to convert from decimal numbers to binary numbers is to find the powers of two that must be added to get the required value, using a table of powers of two (Table 1.1). In such a table, we get positive powers by successive multiplications by two and negative powers by successive divisions by two.

To convert a decimal number like 27 into binary form, we write

$$27 = 16 + 8 + 2 + 1$$
$$= 1 \times 2^4 + 1 \times 2^3 + 0 \times 2^2 + 1 \times 2^1 + 1 \times 2^0$$
$$= 11011 \text{ in binary}$$

The same process can be applied to fractional values. For example:

$$0.3125 = 0.25 + 0.0625$$
$$= 0 \times 2^{-1} + 1 \times 2^{-2} + 0 \times 2^{-3} + 1 \times 2^{-4}$$
$$= 0.0101 \text{ in binary}$$

Now try the same pattern on the decimal number 0.3.

TABLE 1.1

The powers of two

2^n	n	2^{-n}
1	0	1
2	1	0.5
4	2	0.25
8	3	0.125
16	4	0.0625
32	5	0.03125
64	6	0.015625
128	7	0.0078125
256	8	0.00390625
512	9	0.001953125
1024	10	0.0009765625
2048	11	0.00048828125
4096	12	0.000244140625
8192	13	0.0001220703125
16384	14	0.00006103515625
32768	15	0.000030517578125
65536	16	0.0000152587890625

$$0.3 = 0.25 + 0.05$$
$$= 0.25 + 0.03125 + 0.01875$$
$$= 0.25 + 0.03125 + 0.015625 + 0.003125$$

The first three terms are powers of two, but the last is not. We can continue, but we will never end up with an exact power of two (try it). We can write that the decimal number 0.3 is approximately 0.010011 in binary form, but in fact, no finite sequence of bits can represent 0.3 exactly. Therefore, when *conversion* such a number is converted into binary form by the computer, a ***conversion*** *error* ***error*** will be made. If the computer gives 0.29999999 when you expect the number 0.3, remember that the difference could stem from a conversion error.

data storage

Let's consider how information is organized in the computer, particularly in main memory. Main memory consists of bistable elements, such as tiny magnets, each capable of storing one bit. A number of bits are grouped *word* together, making up a ***word.*** In general, all words in memory have the same number of bits, say n, where typical values for n are 16, 32, 48, and 64. (Often n is chosen so that it is a power of two, but 48 is an exception here.)

Every number stored in the memory occupies one word. This determines what numbers can and cannot be represented. For example, take $n = 32$ and assume that all numbers considered are integers. This in effect means that we think of the binary point as being located to the right of the *integer* right-most bit and fixed there. We use the term ***integer representation*** for *representation* this convention. For most computations, though, provision is made for negative as well as positive numbers by making one of the bits, say the left-most, the *sign bit*. Zero is used to denote a positive number and one to denote a negative number (Figure 1.5). The largest number that can be represented in this way is the number in which all bits, except the sign bit, are one, or

$$2^{n-2} + 2^{n-3} + \cdots + 2^0$$

This sum is surprisingly easy to compute. It is a fact that for any positive number p,

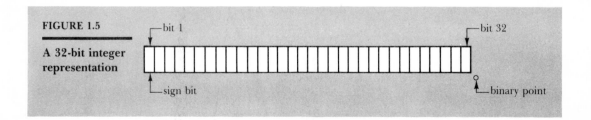

FIGURE 1.5

A 32-bit integer representation

bit 1   bit 32

sign bit   binary point

$$2^p + 2^{p-1} + \cdots + 2^1 + 2^0 = 2^{p+1} - 1$$

This important identity can easily be proven mathematically, but you can convince yourself that it is true by trying it on a few cases (say, $p = 4$ and $p = 5$). Using it with $p = 30$, we see that

$$2^{30} + 2^{29} + \cdots 2^0 = 2^{31} - 1$$

Because we are accustomed to working in decimals, let us develop some rules of thumb for conversion. Table 1.1 shows that 2^{10} is approximately 10^3, so that three decimal digits correspond closely to ten bits. Therefore, $2^{31} - 1$ approximately equals 2×10^9, and a 32-bit word allows us to represent integers between roughly -2×10^9 to 2×10^9. It's quite a respectable range, but not always large enough.

One problem with this representation is that we cannot restrict calculations to integers but must allow for noninteger numbers. Going back to Figure 1.5, we could change convention and consider the binary point to be located somewhere in the middle of the word, say between bits 15 and 16. We then would have 15 bits for the integer part of a number and 16 bits for the fractional part. This represents decimal numbers from about 0.000015 to 32,000, certainly an insufficient range for many applications.

To extend the range of numbers that can be represented, we could increase the number of bits per word, but this would increase the cost of the hardware. Furthermore, even doubling the number of bits would not solve the problem.

the floating point system

A much better way is to adapt exponent notation, which is often used in physics and chemistry to express very large and very small numbers concisely. Using exponent notation we write, for example,

$$\text{speed of light} = 3.0 \times 10^8 \text{ meters/second}$$

$$\text{mass of an electron} = 9.108 \times 10^{-31} \text{ kilograms}$$

In computers, we use *floating point* representation. In this system, each number is represented by a *mantissa* (m) and an *exponent* (e). Its value is given by

$$m \times 2^e$$

Note that two is used instead of ten because of the binary nature of the computer. A word in memory is composed of two parts, one representing e, the other m, each of which is a signed quantity expressed in binary form.

Exactly how this is done differs from computer to computer. For the purpose of discussion, let us consider the pattern depicted in Figure 1.6. Here, we take the exponent to be an integer. We also assume that the binary point for the mantissa is located to the left of the mantissa and that the left-most mantissa bit is always one. (This is called a *normalized floating point*

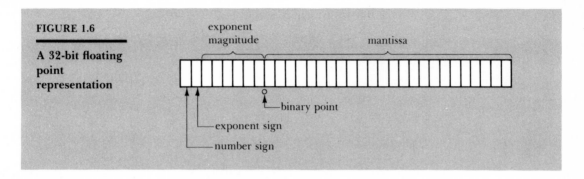

FIGURE 1.6

A 32-bit floating point representation

system.) This implies that $\frac{1}{2} < = m < 1$ and that the representation is unique. For example, the bit pattern

0 1 0 0 0 0 1 1 1 0 1 0 0 0 0 0 0 0 0 0 0 0 0 0 0 0 0 0 0 0 0 0

is to be interpreted as

$$\text{number sign} = 0; \text{ the number is positive}$$
$$\text{exponent sign} = 1; \text{ the exponent is negative}$$
$$\text{exponent magnitude} = 3$$
$$\text{mantissa magnitude} = 0.625$$

Therefore, our bit pattern represents the decimal number

$$0.625 \times 2^{-3} = 0.078125$$

The range of numbers that can be represented in floating point depends both on the total number of bits per word and on the way in which words are divided into the exponent and mantissa fields. In our case, the largest possible exponent is $2^6 - 1 = 63$, and the smallest is -63. The largest mantissa is essentially one, while in magnitude the smallest is 0.5. Thus, the range of possible numbers is roughly

$$0.5 \times 2^{-63} \text{ to } 1 \times 2^{63}$$

or

$$5 \times 10^{-20} \text{ to } 9 \times 10^{18}$$

Many computers have even larger ranges. Also, the mantissa has 24 bits, which, according to our rule of thumb, corresponds to slightly more than seven decimal digits. Thus, our floating point numbers have about a seven decimal digit accuracy.

Most computers provide both integer and floating point representation—and there is a corresponding distinction in programming. Most programming languages allow both integer and noninteger numbers, with integers stored internally in integer format and noninteger numbers in floating point.

In floating point, each value has the same number of bits in the mantissa, that is, the same number of significant digits. If we add or multiply two such numbers, we may get a result that has more than the permitted number of bits. To make the result fit into the floating point format, we normally discard the least significant bits, perhaps rounding the result. The small error created this way is usually ignored. Nevertheless, it does exist,

roundoff error

and is called the **roundoff error.** When only a few computations are involved, roundoff error is usually insignificant, but in large computers that perform thousands of individual operations, the accumulation of roundoff error may cause difficulties, especially in complicated scientific computations. For our discussion, we will simply note that conversion and roundoff errors may affect computations slightly.

If a number is so large that it requires an exponent larger than can be accommodated in the computer, we say we have an *exponent overflow*. If a number is so small that it requires a negative exponent smaller than can be accommodated, we say we have an *exponent underflow*. When an overflow or underflow condition arises, the computer will usually terminate the computation.

characters and symbols

To represent alphabetical characters and special symbols, we assign a distinct group of bits—typically, six, seven, or eight bits—to each character. One popular code is the seven-bit ASCII (American Standard Code for Information Interchange) code. Because seven bits are available per character, we can have a maximum of 2^7, or 128, different characters. The ASCII code includes all lower- and uppercase letters of the alphabet, the digits zero through nine, and all the special characters that can be found on a typewriter or terminal keyboard. The ASCII code for A is 1000001, for B, 1000010, and so on.

Because eight is a power of two, groups of seven bits are not as convenient for computer design as groups of eight. Therefore each charac-

byte

ter is stored in an eight-bit field called a **byte.** It is useful for programmers to remember that one character generally takes eight bits of memory.

EXERCISES 1.2

1. Convert the following binary numbers to decimal form: 1011, 11.00101, 10.00111011.
2. Convert the decimal number 29.875 to binary form.
3. Can the decimal number 0.01 be represented exactly in binary?
4. Express the decimal number 85 in base three.

5. Using the convention shown in Figure 1.6, what does the bit string

   00001100101010000000000000000000

   represent?
6. If the bit string in Exercise 5 is considered an integer, what value does it represent?
7. Using the convention of Figure 1.6, give the floating point representation for 29.875.
8. Using the convention of Figure 1.6, what is
   a. the smallest value for x so that x^2 will produce an exponent overflow
   b. the largest x so that x^2 will give an exponent underflow
9. If in a 32-bit word we use ten bits for the exponent magnitude and 20 bits for the mantissa, what is
   a. the range of representable numbers
   b. the approximate number of decimal digits accuracy
10. Find out how integers, floating point numbers, and alphabetical characters are represented in your computer.

1.3

computer organization

the central processing unit

The CPU is logically the most complex part of a computer system. It takes data from main memory, processes them, and later returns them to main memory. Basically, the CPU can perform addition, subtraction, multiplication, and division; it can test the contents of its own temporary storage system; and it can compare numbers and alphabetical characters and, based on the outcome, make some simple decisions on its next steps of operation. Finally, it can perform some very primitive input and output operations. All of the CPU's operations are carried out at extremely high speeds. A CPU that can perform one million instructions per second is no longer a rarity; there are some larger computers with speeds nearly 100 times this rate.

registers   Most CPUs have storage cells, called *registers,* in which information is stored temporarily while the CPU operations are in progress. Some CPUs
accumulator   have one special register, called the *accumulator,* which stores the results of individual operations, and which may in turn serve as an operand in various computations. For example, to perform an addition, the contents of the accumulator may be added to the contents of a memory word and the result put back in the accumulator. Many manual calculators operate on the same principle, the contents of the accumulator being displayed by means of lighted numbers. While the use of accumulators is not universal in CPU design, it is common and will serve as model for further discussion.

main memory

address

The information the CPU needs is stored in main memory. The memory is divided into a number of words, each having a fixed number of bits. With each word is associated an integer number $1, 2, \cdots, n$, where n is the total number of words in memory. The CPU uses this ***address*** to refer to a particular word. The size of a memory can vary from a few thousand to several million words; a memory size of 64,000 words is typical for a small-to-medium computer.

access time

The size of main memory is a crucial factor affecting the capability of the system. Often an installation starts with a small memory, with additional capacity added as the workload increases. Another factor that greatly influences the power of the system is the speed of the main memory. Memory speed is measured by ***access time,*** which is the time required to transfer one word of information between the memory and the CPU. These transfer speeds are normally quite high; an access time of one microsecond (one millionth of a second) is considered reasonably but not extremely fast.

secondary storage

magnetic disk

If a computer has a main memory of 64,000 words of 32 bits, and each character is stored in an eight-bit byte, then it has the capacity to store $64,000 \times 4$, or 256,000 characters in main memory. This is about the size of a small book, and is totally inadequate for a good many tasks that even the smallest computers may be called upon to perform. Consequently, main memory is supplemented with secondary storage, where the bulk of the data will be saved until the CPU needs them. Secondary storage devices can accommodate many millions of characters, but access to this information is much slower than to information in main memory.

magnetic tape

One very popular secondary storage device is the ***magnetic disk,*** a device similar in appearance to a phonograph record. Information is stored on the surface of the disk and read from it as the surface revolves past a magnetic sensing device. Disks with a capacity of several million characters are common. Another widely used storage medium is the ***magnetic tape.*** This venerable device, although slow in access, is inexpensive and is easily removed from the computer, and thus provides a method for storing data for months or years.

machine languages

The main memory also stores programs that control CPU operations. A program is a set of instructions giving the sequence of steps to be performed by the computer. Starting at a certain address, successive instructions are carried out until the end of the program is reached. The steps have to be specified in *machine language*. Unfortunately, almost every computer model has its own version; for our purposes, we will make up a simplified machine language to represent machine languages in general.

The repertoire of our mythical machine will contain the following instructions:

memory location

1. INPUT i: read a data item from the input device (such as a card reader) and store it in **memory location** i, that is, in the word whose address is i.
2. OUTPUT i: send the information contained in memory location i to the output device (that is, the printer).
3. LOAD i: copy the contents of memory location i into the accumulator.
4. STORE i: copy the contents of the accumulator into memory location i.
5. ADD i: add contents of memory location i to the contents of the accumulator and place the result in the accumulator.
6. SUBTRACT i: subtract the contents of memory location i from the accumulator and place the result in the accumulator.
7. MULTIPLY i: multiply contents of memory location i by the contents of the accumulator and put result in the accumulator.
8. DIVIDE i: divide the contents of the accumulator by the contents of memory location i and put the results in the accumulator.
9. JUMP i: start a new instruction sequence at memory location i.
10. JUMPNEGATIVE i: if the contents of the accumulator are negative, start a new instruction sequence at memory location i.
11. HALT: Stop the computations.

Usually there are many more instructions, but these will suffice for our examples.

Our instructions are just verbal descriptions of operations. When stored in memory, though, a program has to be in a suitable form, that is, in bits. Consequently, we associate with each operation a binary code. In our example, the codes will be as follows:

```
0000   INPUT       0110   MULTIPLY
0001   OUTPUT      0111   DIVIDE
0010   LOAD        1000   JUMP
0011   STORE       1001   JUMPNEGATIVE
0100   ADD         1010   HALT
0101   SUBTRACT
```

The addresses are integer numbers, so they can be represented in binary form. An instruction in the memory would then look like Figure 1.7, which represents the machine language instruction LOAD 25 in a 16-bit word.

FIGURE 1.7

LOAD 25

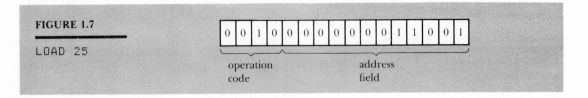

operation
code

address
field

EXAMPLE 1.1

A SIMPLE COMPUTATION

With this instruction set, let us now program the simple computation, in which a, b, and c are to be input data and x the result:

$$x = ab + c$$

First, we perform the input operations, storing the values in certain memory locations, which we will arbitrarily assign as 10 for a, 11 for b, 12 for c, and 13 for the result x. After the input is done, x is computed with one multiplication and one addition and the result is output. The machine language program for the complete computation is

```
0000000000001010
0000000000001011
0000000000001100
0010000000001010
0110000000001011
0100000000001100
0011000000001101
0001000000001101
1010000000000000
```

*assembly
language*

We rarely program in machine language because it would be extremely tedious and unpleasant; instead, we use a symbolic version of machine language called **assembly language.** In assembly language, both the binary operation codes and the memory addresses are replaced by descriptive names. Our program in assembly language is then:

```
INPUT a
INPUT b
INPUT c
LOAD a
MULTIPLY b
ADD c
STORE x
OUTPUT x
HALT
```

Assembly language is much easier to write and understand than machine language.

EXAMPLE 1.2

A COMPUTATION WITH ALTERNATIVES

The steps in Example 1.1 follow a strict sequence. We call this a *straightline program*. But suppose you were asked to program the following computation: input two numbers x and y; if x is greater than or equal to y, output the value of x, but otherwise output the value of y.

In this computation the final result is generated by one of two alternatives that are written into the program. To determine which alternative is to be used, the computer can subtract y from x. If the result is negative, it must output the value of y; if the result is zero or positive, it must output x. The JUMPNEGATIVE instruction can be used to test $x - y$ and provide an alternative path in the program. Note that the JUMPNEGATIVE instruction requires an address. If we assume that the program starts in memory location 100, we can write the following assembly language program:

```
memory location        instruction
          100      INPUT x
          101      INPUT y
          102      LOAD x
          103      SUBTRACT y
          104      JUMPNEGATIVE 107
          105      OUTPUT x
          106      JUMP 108
          107      OUTPUT y
          108      HALT
```

In Steps 100–103 the values of x and y are obtained as input and $x - y$ is computed. In Step 104, the value of $x - y$ (which is stored in the accumulator) is tested. If the value is negative, Step 107 is done and y is output. If in Step 104 the accumulator is nonnegative, then Step 105 is done and x is output. But now Step 107 must be skipped, so we insert the instruction JUMP 108 as Step 106.

higher level language

While assembly language is easier to use than machine language, most programming is done in even more convenient **higher level language.** *Pascal* is one such language. We will shortly study Pascal in detail and will see that in Pascal the computation in Example 1.1 is written as x := a*b + c, while the task in Example 1.2 can be specified by

```
if x>=y
  then write(x)
  else write (y)
```

compiler

Pascal is much easier to use than either assembly or machine language. A special program called a ***compiler*** then performs the task of translating the instructions into machine language.

computer classification by size

Computers are usually classified as *large* (main frame) *computers, minicomputers,* and *microcomputers.* Although these categories overlap, the distinctions are essentially based on speed, memory size, and associated secondary storage and peripheral devices. A large computer generally has a sizable memory (say, over 100,000 words), a variety of secondary storage devices, and many peripherals. Large computers usually serve many purposes and many users. Minicomputers have smaller memories, fewer secondary storage devices, and a limited number of peripherals, and are typically used for several related tasks. Microcomputers have small memories, limited secondary storage, and often only a single input/output device. Microcomputers are usually used for single specific tasks involving one or at most a few users.

EXERCISES 1.3

Consult with available experts to answer Exercises 1–4.

1. For your computer, find out
   a. the main memory size
   b. main memory access time
   c. approximate instruction execution times
2. Does your system have disk storage? If so, what is its capacity?
3. What types of peripheral devices are attached to your system?
4. Find out something about the machine language repertoire of your computer.
5. Using the machine and assembly language set given in this section, write a program for

   $$x = a^2 + b + c$$

6. Write machine and assembly language programs for

   $$x = a^2 + b^2 + c^2$$

7. Write an assembly language program for computing z by the rule

$z = x - y$ if x is greater than or equal to y

$z = y - x$ if y is greater than x

Assume that the first instruction of the program is in location 200.

1.4

system software

In theory, it is possible to solve problems using just the hardware, typing in programs in machine language, entering data, and initiating the computations by pressing special buttons on the computer. But this is such a cumbersome operation that it was used only in some very early computers. A set of programs, called the *system software*, is stored in the computer and used to make programming easier, more efficient, and less error prone.

the operating system

At the heart of the system software is the *operating system,* a program that essentially runs the computer. Users actually communicate with the operating system. The user issues requests to the operating system, which analyzes them and sees that they are carried out.

The operating system has complete control over the computer's resources and allocates them to the user when they are needed. For example, in a large system with many users, one normally provides an account number for billings and a password to demonstrate the right to use the account. The operating system uses its stored information to verify the account number/password sequence to protect against unauthorized access and to check which facilities the user is entitled to. When the program is typed in and run, the operating system keeps track of the task. If an error occurs or the program is finished, the operating system will take the appropriate action.

batch system

Roughly speaking, there are two types of operating systems. In a **batch system,** the user submits programs and data to a central facility, where they are collected in a batch and given to the computer. The programs are run in sequence; when one is completed the next one is started. Output is also collected in a batch, printed, and eventually distributed to the originators. The time from submission of the program to its return is called the *turnaround time.* In a typical batch system the turnaround time may be several hours.

interactive systems
time-sharing
systems

Interactive or **time-sharing** operating systems are a much newer approach. In a time-sharing system, many users are connected to the computer at the same time. Each user has a terminal on which the program and data are entered and on which results are received. To service many users simultaneously, the operating system generally uses a technique called *time slicing*. Each program is allowed a small time slice (perhaps a fraction of a second). When this time has elapsed, the program is temporarily suspended while others receive their slices. After a while, the system returns to the original program, repeating the cycle until the task is completed. The speed of the CPU is so much faster than human reaction time that the computer's response often seems instantaneous (or at least tolerably fast) to the user. The operating systems for most computers are now of the time-sharing variety.

other software programs

assembler

System software also includes a variety of other programs. An ***assembler*** program translates from assembly language into machine language (*See* Example 1.1). A compiler program translates from a given higher level language directly into machine language. Another important and useful software component is a ***text editor***. Data, programs, and other information are often stored in the computer for extended periods of time, during which changes may have to be made. A text editor can be used to insert, delete, or otherwise change stored information. System software may also include programs for statistical packages, for generating pictures and other graphic displays, for performing complicated scientific calculations, and so on.

text editor

EXERCISES 1.4

1. Does the operating system on your computer use time sharing? Does it allow batch processing?
2. Does your system have a text editor? If so, learn how to use its simpler features.

1.5

programming languages

Higher level languages are widely used for programming. We can give many more instructions to the computer in fewer words in a higher level language than in assembly language; in this way, higher level languages are more powerful than assembly language. Higher level languages also require much less attention to detail than assembly language, so that the programming process today is much simpler and more reliable than in the early days of computer application, when most of the programming was done in assembly language. Because compilers translate the program to machine language, we program as if the computer could understand the higher level languages directly.

Some of the many higher level languages were designed for very specific purposes, while others suit a variety of applications.

FORTRAN is one of the oldest and most widely used languages. It was designed primarily to simplify scientific computations, so that its appearance is close to mathematical notation (FORTRAN stands for "FORmula TRANslation"). Although the language is now considered to have severe shortcomings, its use has become so entrenched that its popularity will undoubtedly continue for some years.

COBOL ("COmmon Business Oriented Language") is of the same vintage as FORTRAN. It is used predominantly in business applications, where data manipulation (sorting and merging data, printing reports, and so on) is more important than lengthy mathematical computations. Like FORTRAN, it has shortcomings, but it is very popular in the business world.

ALGOL is a computation-oriented language whose design was based in part on rigorous mathematical formalism. Intended as a substitute for FORTRAN, it has never been widely used outside academic circles.

PL/I is a very powerful language that attempts to combine the best features of FORTRAN, ALGOL, and COBOL. In spite of initial high hopes, this language has not been widely accepted.

BASIC was originally intended for teaching. Its first version was very limited, but later additions made it more suitable for general purposes. A number of minicomputers and microcomputers use BASIC, making it a fairly popular language.

SNOBOL is an example of a language designed for quite specific purposes. Its aim is mainly to simplify the processing of character information, such as finding words or patterns in a length of text. In this it is very powerful, but it is not particularly well suited for numerical computations.

Pascal, one of the newer higher level languages, is an offshoot of ALGOL. Having the benefit of experience with older languages, Pascal's designer, Professor Niklaus Wirth, was able to construct a fairly simple, yet elegant and powerful language. Perhaps it is too early to speculate on its future, but many believe that it will eventually become as important as FORTRAN and COBOL.

EXERCISES 1.5

1. Which of the languages mentioned in this section are available on your system?

2. What languages not mentioned here are available? What are the principal uses of these languages?

---

further reading

Gear, C. W., *Introduction to Computer Science.* Chicago: SRA, 1976.

Graham, N., *The Mind Tool.* St. Paul, Minn.: West Publishing Co., 1976.

Rothman, S., and Mossman, C., *Computers and Society,* 2d. ed. Chicago: SRA, 1976.

Sanders, D. H., *Computers in Society,* 3d. ed. New York: McGraw-Hill, 1981.

programming and problem solving

As we learned in our introductory discussion of computer science, programming is writing a sequence of instructions in a language the computer can understand. On the surface, this may seem to be a matter of simply learning a new language. But because of the vast differences between the human mind and the computer, matters are much more complicated than they may seem to us at first. Statements and instructions we find quite simple are often much too complex for the computer. We must break such instructions into sequences of simpler steps, each of which can be carried out by the machine. Because the only processes that can be handled at the CPU level are arithmetic operations and comparisons of numbers and characters, we may have to do extensive reformulation.

Consider the simple task of adding all even numbers between two and 1000. The mathematically trained may discover a simple formula that gives the answer immediately, but most people would probably take the more pedestrian approach, adding $2 + 4 + 6 + \cdots + 1000$. However, by machine standards the statement "add all even numbers between 2 and 1000" is quite complicated, because it requires some five hundred additions and involves hidden assumptions (for example, the definition of an even number). To write a program for this problem, we must break our one-sentence instruction into a sequence of steps involving only simple, well-defined arithmetic operations. In general, such restatement can be one of the most challenging aspects of programming.

Your first task in learning to program will be to study some examples and general concepts. Briefly, to become programmers we must (1) learn a particular programming language, and (2) learn to analyze and rephrase our thoughts so that eventually we can express the solution of a problem in terms and operations that the computer can understand and perform. There is much more to programming than knowing one or more languages. The real challenge lies in the second point. We will study various problems and their solution to gain experience and develop skill; in the final analysis, ingenuity, insight, and experience are the keys to success.

Still, it is necessary to learn at least something about one language. Otherwise, we would have to discuss problem solving in the abstract, a rather unsatisfactory approach. In subsequent chapters we will study Pascal in enough depth that you will be able to program most of the problems you are likely to encounter. However, a few features of Pascal that are occasionally useful have been omitted. For a complete description of Pascal, you should consult a text devoted specifically to that language. Some references are given at the end of the chapter.

2.1

algorithms and their construction

Let us return to our first example, adding all the even numbers between two and 1000. How can it be broken into smaller pieces? On a calculator, we would do something like the following:

1. Enter 2 into register.
2. Push + button.
3. Enter 4 into register.
4. Push + button.
5. Enter 6 into register.

and so on.

The phrase "and so on" simply means that we have become tired of writing what seems an obvious continuation. However, computers cannot understand such a complicated phrase, because it really means "carry on using the established pattern," which has difficult implications. What then should we do? We could, of course, write down explicitly the 1000 or so steps required, but a little thought will show us that there is an alternative. In this example, we are just repeating a two-part pattern: (1) after every addition the sum appearing in the register is the sum of all even numbers added up to that point, and (2) the number added at each stage is obtained from the number from the previous stage by adding two.

Having detected the pattern, we are now ready to translate our observations into a concise set of instructions. But let us first adopt a convention to avoid getting lost in a mountain of words. Instead of saying "the sum of all even numbers added up to that point" we will use the shorthand SUM, while "the number to be added at each stage" will be called NUMBER. We can then write our solution as follows:

1. Set SUM to 2.
2. Set NUMBER to 4.
3. Add NUMBER to SUM. The result becomes the new value of SUM.
4. Increase NUMBER by 2.
5. If NUMBER ≤ 1000 go back to Step 3; otherwise, stop the computation.

Follow this set of instructions through a few times, using pencil and paper, to see that it works.

The main computational steps are 3 and 4; they are repeated many times. Steps 1 and 2 initialize the values of SUM and NUMBER, which is necessary to make the instructions complete. If we do not know the initial values of SUM and NUMBER, we cannot determine their final values. The process of adding 500 numbers is now expressed in only five instructions. The actual computation still requires 500 additions, but the set of instructions is quite short. We accomplished this by using the repetition in the steps to our advantage. The technique of repeating instructions many times makes it possible to specify thousands or even millions of operations with just a few instructions, and is one of the key elements of programming.

What we have just discussed is an example of an *algorithm*. An algorithm is a sequence of instructions for finding the solution of a problem. An algorithm must fulfill the following conditions:

1. The description of the algorithm must be complete, that is, all the necessary information must be contained in it. If we had left out Steps 1 or 2 in our example, the description would have been incomplete.
2. The description must be unambiguous; every step must allow one and only one interpretation.
3. The process must terminate after a finite number of operations.

In an algorithm, an individual step represents an operation that can be understood as a single unit and completed in a straightforward way. An algorithm for an intelligent human could contain some quite complicated steps, but our steps for computers will have to be extremely simple. In fact, for computers we use only four types of steps:

1. Computation. Carry out a simple numerical computation.
2. Decision. Compare numbers or characters; based on the outcome of the comparison, select one of several alternative successor steps.
3. Input. Accept data for computation.
4. Output. Return the computed results.

The names SUM and NUMBER were introduced as a convenient short-hand notation, but they actually serve another, subtler purpose than just convenience; they refer to quantities that have specific meaning in the computation, but their values are not fixed. SUM, for example, is originally set to two, but after the first addition its value becomes six, then twelve, and so on. We say that SUM is a *variable*. The value of a variable at any point is *variable* determined by the algorithm—that is, by what computations have been carried out. Variables generally represent the quantities that we want to compute or that are needed as intermediate results. We refer to variables *identifiers* by symbolic names, or *identifiers*. One way to visualize a variable is to think of it as a word in the memory of the computer. Changing the value of a variable involves changing the content of the memory word. But this is only a way to think of a variable, not a definition of one.

We tend to use descriptive names as reminders of what the variables stand for, but the name we choose for a variable has no effect on the algorithm. If in our example we were to substitute FRODO for SUM, we would not change the algorithm, and the computed results would be the same. Beginning students of programming sometimes assume that using names with some meaning will make the computer understand what is going on. Nothing could be further from the truth. The computer understands nothing. It will carry out properly written instructions, but that is all.

We will, however, have to use an appropriate language to write algorithms. In our example, we have used a somewhat restricted form of English. Because the description was meant entirely for our own use, this *pseudolanguage* *pseudolanguage* is adequate; as long as we are careful, the description will be understandable, if not unambiguous. But for programming a computer, it is unacceptable. Even a restricted subset of English is too rich to be easily translated into machine language. Furthermore, despite the greatest care, the programmer will miss occasional ambiguities. For example, in the sum-of-even-numbers algorithm, what is meant by "go back to Step 3"? Most people will interpret this as "start the new sequence of instructions at Step 3, using the latest values of SUM and NUMBER." But an occasional individualist may insist that it means "go back to Step 3 and restart the computations using values of SUM and NUMBER as they were when Step 3 was done last." In complicated problems, such ambiguities and imprecisions are hard to avoid.

flowchart language

Besides the various programming languages mentioned in Section 1.5, *flowchart language* is widely used in computer science. A *flowchart* describes an algorithm by showing the computations to be done and how they proceed, or "flow," from one step to the next. A flowchart is composed of four different "boxes," which correspond to the four types of operations described on p. 26. A rectangular computation box is shown in Figure 2.1. Inside the box, we write whatever computation we want performed, using notation slightly different from formal mathematical notation. For example, "replace the value of the variable B by the value of A+3," is written:

B:=A+3

The effect of this instruction is easily visualized if we think of A and B as the names of words in the computer memory. Figure 2.2 shows the result of B:=A+3 for some actual values of A and B.

assignment operator

The symbol := is called the **assignment operator.** It is one of a number of conventions used for designating assignment. Some languages use =, others ← , for example. We will stick to := because it is used in Pascal. Occasionally, for the sake of brevity, we will put several computations into one box; it is assumed that the instructions are carried out from the top down.

In flowcharting, a diamond-shaped decision box is used for defining alternatives. Inside this box is a test condition—a mathematical expression or other kind of statement that is either true or false. In Figure 2.3, the flow

FIGURE 2.1

Flowchart symbol for computation

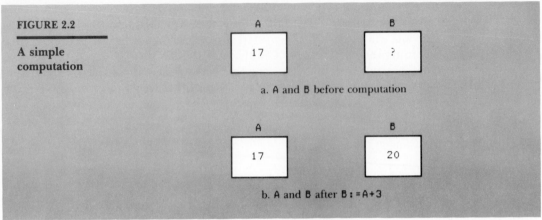

FIGURE 2.2

A simple computation

A

17

B

?

a. A and B before computation

A

17

B

20

b. A and B after B := A+3

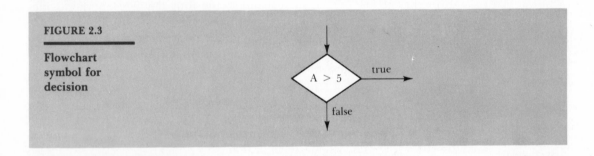

FIGURE 2.3

Flowchart symbol for decision

A > 5   true

false

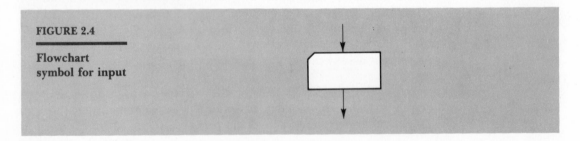

FIGURE 2.4

Flowchart symbol for input

will proceed in the direction marked "true" if A is greater than five; otherwise, the "false" exit will be taken.

An input box (Figure 2.4) looks a bit like a stylized picture of a punched card. It marks the place where data values are supplied to the algorithm. We write in this box something like:

Input A

which means that the data value supplied at that point is given to the variable A.

FIGURE 2.5

**Flowchart
symbol for
output**

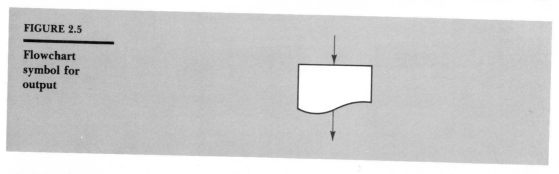

FIGURE 2.6

**Flowchart for
the sum-of-even-
numbers
problem**

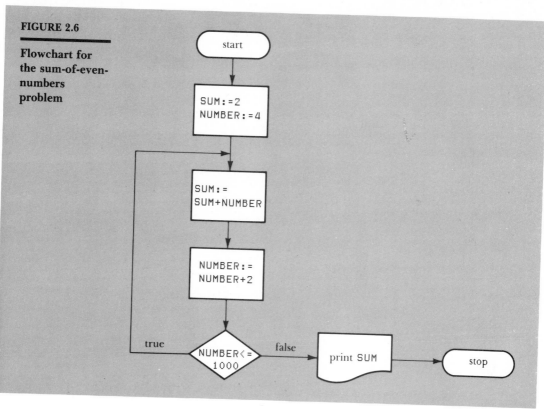

Results provided by the algorithm are shown by an output box (Figure 2.5). At the output points, the values of the variables in the box are returned in some convenient form, perhaps on a printout.

The flowchart's lines and arrows show the sequence in which the instructions are performed. Boxes with rounded sides, marked start and stop, mark the beginning and end of the computations.

We are now ready to represent the solution to the sum-of-even-numbers problem by a flowchart. We simply translate Steps 1–5 on p. 25 into flowchart language, giving Figure 2.6.

How useful is flowcharting? The answer to this question is somewhat controversial. Years ago, when much programming was done in assembly language, flowcharts were widely used. A flowchart was then a relatively compact representation of the algorithm, and a program was sometimes considered deficient unless accompanied by a flowchart. While this attitude persists in some places, the increased use of higher level languages has diminished the popularity of flowcharts. A well-designed program written in a higher level language is often easier to understand than the corresponding flowchart; consequently, flowcharts are gradually falling into disfavor.

Nevertheless, flowcharts may often be used to good advantage, especially by the beginning programmer. After you have become familiar with higher level languages, you may no longer need flowcharts, but to start with you should construct some just to learn about algorithms. First, sketch

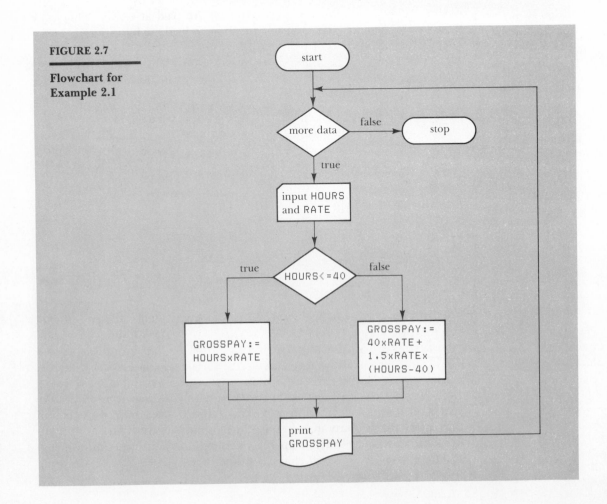

FIGURE 2.7

**Flowchart for
Example 2.1**

your solution using pseudolanguage, then make it precise by drawing a flowchart.

Flowcharts are also powerful descriptive devices. At times, they are much clearer than a verbal explanation. Throughout this text, we will occasionally give flow diagrams instead of or in addition to verbal explanations.

Let us now consider some simple examples of algorithm construction.

EXAMPLE 2.1

COMPUTATION OF WEEKLY PAY

Part of the payroll computations of a business firm involves the wages of hourly workers. This computation uses the hours worked, say in a week, and the hourly rate of the employee; in addition, let us assume that any hours worked over the standard 40 hours are paid at one and one-half times the hourly rate. The computations are to be done for as many sets of data as there are employees.

The basic computations are simple. Using the variable HOURS to denote the hours worked, RATE for the hourly rate, and GROSSPAY for the total earned pay, we have:

```
if HOURS<=40 then GROSSPAY is the product
                of HOURS and RATE
if HOURS>40 then GROSSPAY is the sum of
                40 times RATE
                plus 1.5 times RATE times (HOURS-40)
```

A pseudolanguage algorithm is

1. As long as there are data left repeat Steps 2–4.
2. Input HOURS and RATE.
3. If HOURS<=40 then GROSSPAY:= HOURS×RATE otherwise, GROSSPAY:= 40×RATE+1.5×RATE×(HOURS-40).
4. Print GROSSPAY.

The flowchart for this algorithm is just a restatement of Steps 1–4 in flowchart language (Figure 2.7). Note that in both Steps 1 and 3 a decision must be made.

The computations for this problem are quite simple, and it would be pointless to write a program if only a few cases were to be processed. However, once written, such a program could be used week after week to compute the payroll of hundreds of employees. The widespread use of computers, particularly in business, comes primarily from similar applications, in which relatively simple processing is done repeatedly on vast amounts of data.

EXAMPLE 2.2

COUNTING ITEMS

Surprisingly enough, writing algorithms for simple counting operations is one of the first things a programmer must learn. The need for counting items arises very frequently in all sorts of circumstances.

Assume that you are given a sequence of numbers such as

5 3 0 2 1 1 0 0 2 3 6 0 2

and want to count and print the number of zeros in the sequence. Thus, the algorithm should give the answer four for this example.

To find an algorithm, we need only to make precise what we see intuitively. Typically, we read the numbers from left to right while we count

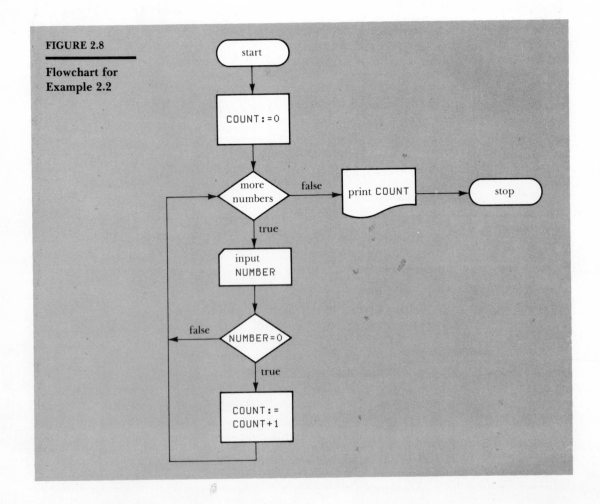

FIGURE 2.8

Flowchart for Example 2.2

the zeros. The algorithm therefore uses as variables the word NUMBER, for the number being examined, and COUNT, for the number of zeros encountered. The steps are as follows:

1. Set COUNT to zero.
2. Are there any numbers still to be examined?
3. If not, print the value of COUNT and stop.
4. If there are more numbers, perform Steps 5–8.
5. Input next number and give its value to NUMBER.
6. If NUMBER = 0, then increase COUNT by one.
7. If NUMBER ≠ 0, do not change COUNT.
8. Go back to Step 2.

The flowchart is given in Figure 2.8.

EXAMPLE 2.3

TESTING PAIRS OF NUMBERS

Given three numbers, determine if the sum of any pair is equal to the third. If so, print yes, otherwise print no. For example, if the numbers are

   3 7 4

then the answer is "yes" because $3 + 4 = 7$. On the other hand, for

   2 3 4

the result should be "no."

   To solve this problem, we can compare the sum of every pair to the other number. Because there are only three distinct pairs, this is easy to do.

   If we call the numbers A, B, and C, then the algorithm for the problem is

1. Input the values of A, B, and C.
2. If A+B = C, print yes and stop.
3. If A+C = B, print yes and stop.
4. If B+C = A, print yes and stop.
5. If you get to this step, there is no pair with sum equal to the other number. Print no and stop.

The flowchart is in Figure 2.9.

   In this problem, no single test can determine the answer. We have to perform a sequence of comparisons to reach the final result. These situations are common in programming, and solving them may be tricky. Many of the exercises at the end of this section are of this nature, and some of them will require hard thinking.

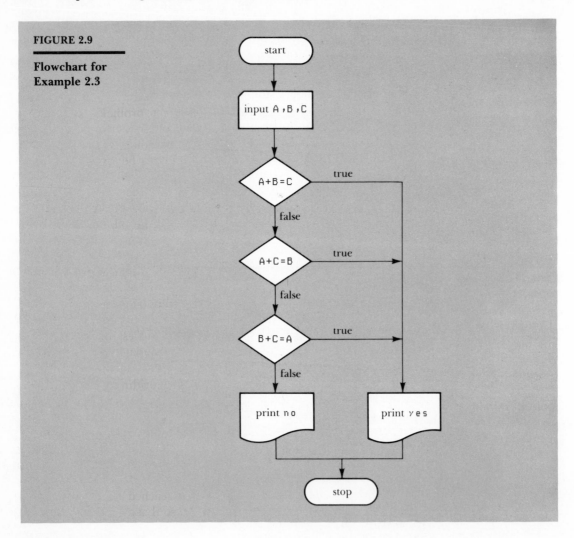

FIGURE 2.9

**Flowchart for
Example 2.3**

structured problem solving

Algorithms do not usually appear to us in a flash of insight, but are developed gradually, progressing from a general description to a more and more detailed one. To be successful in algorithm design, we must develop a formal method for constructing algorithms and, eventually, writing programs.

Perhaps the most powerful method for constructing algorithms is *structured problem solving*. Structured problem solving consists of three main phases:

1. Problem statement.
2. Algorithm design.
3. Implementation.

Each phase in turn can be broken into several steps.

The purpose of the *problem statement* phase is to help the programmer reach a clear understanding of the nature of the problem, to eliminate possible misunderstandings, and to answer all open questions. To define precisely what the problem is and what is to be done, we must (1) state exactly what the algorithm is to accomplish, (2) describe the input, and (3) describe the corresponding output.

In *algorithm design*, we must devise an algorithm to solve the problem. We first define the variables involved and give their relationships. The values of some of the variables will be input, while the values of others will have to be computed. The proper algorithm will tell how the computations are to be done.

stepwise refinement

An effective way to design algorithms is **stepwise refinement.** The algorithm is first described in pseudolanguage with fairly complicated steps. The first description should involve only a few steps (at most a dozen or so). Then, the first level steps are expanded into a more detailed description, in pseudolanguage, with more specific steps. The process of refinement is repeated until each step is explicit enough to be translated directly into the chosen programming language.

coding

In the *implementation* phase, the designed algorithm is translated into a programming language. This is also called **coding,** because the algorithm written in a particular programming language is called a "code."

Systematic adherence to this method greatly simplifies programming. The problem statement phase assures that the right problem is being solved. Stepwise refinement helps the programmer discover and develop the algorithm by breaking complicated problems into a sequence of simpler ones. By the time the implementation phase is reached, the way the problem is to be solved must be clearly understood so that all our attention can be focused on coding.

In examples to come, we will follow this pattern and distinguish between the three phases.

EXAMPLE 2.4

TEST SCORE ANALYSIS

As part of an examination, a student has taken two tests and obtained two numerical scores. The student passes the examination if either test score is 70 or higher. Design an algorithm that will accept the two test scores as input and print either Pass or Fail, depending on whether the test was passed or not. The input for this problem is just two numbers, the two test scores. The output will be either the word "Pass" or the word "Fail."

We will use the variables `SCORE1` and `SCORE2` to refer to the two test scores. The larger of the two will be found and called `MAXSCORE`, that is:

`MAXSCORE` = maximum of `SCORE1` and `SCORE2`

`MAXSCORE` must be at least 70 for a student to pass the examination.

The first level description of the algorithm has three relatively obvious steps.

1. Input `SCORE1` and `SCORE2`.
2. Find the larger of `SCORE1` and `SCORE2`, and call it `MAXSCORE`.
3. Print `Pass` if `MAXSCORE` is greater than or equal to 70; otherwise, print `Fail`.

Some of the steps of the algorithm will have to be refined before it is ready for implementation (say, in terms of flowchart language). In particular, Step 2 should be refined. To do so, we must find a way of assigning the larger of two numbers to a variable:

2.1. `if SCORE1>=SCORE2 then MAXSCORE:=SCORE1`
2.2. `if SCORE2>SCORE1 then MAXSCORE:=SCORE2`

The second level refinement of Step 2 is now sufficiently explicit and further refinement is unnecessary. Steps 1 and 3 are simple at the first level and need not be refined.

For the implementation phase, we need to know an actual programming language. In the next section we begin our study of Pascal, and then we will be able to write some real programs.

EXERCISES 2.1

For each of the following problems, design an algorithm, using the structured problem solving method and stepwise refinement. Draw a flowchart for each algorithm.

1. Determine how many successive positive integers can be added before the sum exceeds 10,000. More precisely, find the largest positive integer n such that $1 + 2 + 3 + \cdots + n \le 10{,}000$.
2. Given a positive integer n, determine whether there is another integer m such that $n = m^2$.
3. Find the largest of three numbers x, y, and z.
4. Find the largest of four numbers x, y, z, w.
5. For given numbers x, y, z, print out the largest first, the middle one next, and the smallest last.
6. Modify Example 2.1 so that any hours over 60 are paid at double the hourly rate.
7. Modify Example 2.2 to give a count of all numbers less than four.

8. Given a sequence of numbers, count the times two consecutive zeros occur. For instance, the answer for

2 0 0 3 1 0 2 0 0 4 6

should be two.

9. Given four numbers, design an algorithm that will give the answer y e s if the sum of any two numbers is equal to the sum of the other two. For the numbers

3 4 5 4

the answer is "yes," because 3 + 5 = 4 + 4.

10. Modify Example 2.4 so that the word P a s s is printed only if both scores were 70 or higher.

11. Modify Example 2.4 to handle three test scores, and so that passing requires a score of 70 or higher on at least two tests.

12. Modify Example 2.4 to handle three tests, and so that passing requires a score of 70 or higher on at least one test and an average score of at least 65 for all three tests.

2.2

statements, variables, and expressions

In programming we must always keep in mind the difference between an algorithm's design and its implementation in a particular language. Consequently, we must clearly distinguish between the concepts of programming and the way in which they are realized in a specific language. But once we understand the concepts of programming and know how to use them, learning a new language is relatively easy. In our discussion, we will distinguish between what is general and what is specific to Pascal by giving a description of the concept, then showing it in Pascal.

conventions for writing programs

syntax

Programming languages, as all other languages, have some basic elements that are used as building blocks, as well as rules by which the elements can be combined. These rules are called the *syntax* of the language. Only syntactically correct instructions can be translated by the compiler, and programs containing syntax errors are rejected by the computer.

In our study of Pascal, we will describe its various elements and syntactic rules. Often a new concept will be introduced in an example; later it may be necessary to show its general form. To avoid confusion let us adopt a special convention to describe instructions.

reserved words

A number of words in Pascal have special meanings. Some, ***reserved words,*** can be used only in a very limited way. Others, called ***standard***

standard
identifiers

identifiers, have a predefined meaning. In addition to these, the programmer can (within certain restrictions) choose identifiers such as variable
names.

When giving an example in this text, we will use lowercase letters to
show reserved words and standard identifiers. Identifiers chosen by the
programmer will appear in uppercase letters. (These will be printed in a
special typeface to remind you that they are actually as they might appear
in a program.) To illustrate this, consider the instruction

        var MYNAME:integer

For the moment, you need not be concerned with the meaning of this
instruction. What you should understand is that var is a reserved word,
integer is a standard identifier, and MYNAME is an identifier chosen by
the programmer. Appendix A lists Pascal's reserved words and standard
identifiers.

When we want to show general forms, we will use italic letters. For
example,

        var *name1, name2, . . . , namen:type*

indicates that *name1, name2, . . . , namen* and *type* are general terms, for
which actual names will have to be used in a program. The dots are meant
to show that any number of terms can be used. Some specific instances of
this general form are

        var MYNAME,YOURNAME,HERNAME:char

and

        var FIRST,SECOND,THIRD,FOURTH:integer

The meaning of these instructions will be explained shortly. Pascal uses
blanks and punctuation marks to distinguish one part of an instruction
from another. If an example shows blanks or punctuation marks, they are
generally necessary. Additional blanks can be inserted between parts of an
instruction, but not between groups of characters that belong together, for
example, in reserved words or other identifiers.

Later, when you know Pascal reasonably well, you may be interested
in getting precise information on what the language permits. For this purpose, you should refer to the Appendix. Appendix C shows how to use
syntax charts, which allow us to describe the syntax of a language precisely.

syntax charts

---

identifiers

Apart from reserved words, standard identifiers, and special characters
such as punctuation marks, a program will contain names chosen by the
programmer. For example, the programmer is free to choose variable
names and other identifiers. There are generally restrictions on the choice
of identifiers.

Pascal identifiers are composed of upper- and lowercase letters of the alphabet and digits, but no other characters or blanks. An identifier must start with a letter, not a number. MYTURN and AT130 are legal identifiers, but 2FORTEA and WHATSIT? are not. Reserved words and standard identifiers must not be used as programmer-chosen identifiers. (Actually, only reserved words cannot be used this way; the standard identifiers can be redefined. However, this is very poor practice.) In general, Pascal permits any length for identifiers, but in some computers only the first eight characters are used to distinguish one from another. To be on the safe side, never use identifiers in which the first eight characters are identical.

constants

A constant is a quantity whose value does not change during the computation. To express a constant, we explicitly write its value, for example, 1, −70, or 3.14159. Most languages allow several types of constants, the most common being integers, decimal numbers, characters, and boolean or logical constants.

integer constant

1. An *integer constant* is a number with an integer value, positive or negative, for example, 3, −4, 0.

real constant

2. A decimal or *real constant* is a number written with a decimal point. The numbers 1.2, −0.5, and 3.0 are decimal constants. Note that 3.0, while its value is a whole number, is considered a decimal constant.

character constant

3. A *character constant* is a single character from a set of available characters. Usually, the available characters are upper- and lowercase letters, digits, punctuation marks, and various other special symbols.

boolean constant

4. A *boolean constant* can have two possible values, true or false. Boolean values are useful in programming. For example, notice that in flowchart language, the decision box exits are marked true and false.

In Pascal, the following rules regulate the representation of constants.

1. Integer constants are written as numbers without decimal points, such as 5 and −23. For positive numbers, the sign is usually omitted.
2. Real constants can be written in decimal form or in exponent notation. In decimal form, the number is written with a decimal point, with digits before and after the decimal point. The numbers 25.5 and −30.1 are properly constructed, but .125 and 3. must be rewritten as 0.125 and 3.0. In exponent notation, we write a number as

decimal constant e ±n

where n is the power of ten by which the decimal constant is to be multiplied to give the correct value. For example, the decimal number 14.56 can also be written as

1.456e+01

or

```
145.6e-01
```

3. Character constants are written by enclosing the character in a single quotation mark as in `'A'` or `'*'`. In Pascal, a blank space, written as `' '`, is a character constant.

4. The boolean constants are written simply as `true` and `false`.

variables

Variables are quantities that change value during the computation. The results to be computed and those needed temporarily are both expressed as variables. We refer to variables by symbolic names or identifiers. Depending on the language, there are different types of variables, such as integer, real, character, and boolean variables.

A variable that is of a certain type can take on only values of that type. A character variable, for instance, can have as its value only a single character, while an integer variable can have only integer values. An attempt to assign a value of one type to a variable of another type is called a ***type error***.

type error

A question which has to be resolved is how to distinguish between the different variable types. One way is to make the type of variable dependent on the value assigned to the variable. Thus, if we write `A:=3`, A is considered an integer variable. A second way is to adopt some convention whereby certain names designate integer variables, others reals, and so on. The third way, used in Pascal, is to declare explicitly the type of each variable.

Pascal permits integer, real, character, and boolean variables. For each variable used in a program, we must declare a type. This is done in the `var` declaration. For example:

```
var MINE,YOURS:integer
```

declares the variables `MINE` and `YOURS` to be integer, while

```
var SUM,DIFFERENCE,PRODUCT:real;
    COUNTER:integer;
    REDFLAG,BLUEFLAG:boolean
```

establishes types for six different variables. The general form of the `var` declaration is

> `var` *variable1,variable2, . . . ,variablek:type;*
>
> *variablem, . . . ,variablen:type;*
>
> ⋮

where *type* can be `integer`, `real`, `char` (for character), or `boolean`. A semicolon is used to separate groups of variables of the same type.

expressions

Expressions are combinations of constants, variables, operation symbols, left and right parentheses, and special function names. The same ideas are used in traditional mathematical notation, for example:

$$a(b + 3) + \sqrt{c}$$

Here, parentheses indicate the order of computation, and $\sqrt{\ }$ denotes the square root function.

Every expression has a value, which is determined by taking the values of the variables and constants involved and carrying out the indicated operations. An expression must be well-formed. Without precisely defining what this means, we can recognize that expressions like a+b+ and (a−b+c are not well-formed.

arithmetic expressions in pascal

Pascal allows several types of expressions. *Arithmetic expressions* are analogous to mathematical formulas. The variables and constants are numerical (integer or real), and the operations are those of mathematics:

+ addition
− subtraction
* multiplication
/ division

These operators are used much in the same way as are their counterparts in mathematics. Thus, *AB* is written in Pascal as A*B, and $\frac{1}{4} \times C$ as C/4. As in mathematical notation, the minus sign plays a dual role, as subtraction in A−B and as negation in −A.

Parentheses are also used to group terms together and to assure that the operations are performed in the correct order. In the expression A*(B+3), the constant 3 is first added to the value of B, after which the whole is multiplied by A. On the other hand, in (A*B)+3, A and B are multiplied first, followed by the addition of 3. Occasionally, we may want to write just A*B+3. Any ambiguity is resolved by associating with each operator a ***priority*** or ***precedence*** and performing the operations with highest priority first. In Pascal, * and / have the same priority and + and − have the same priority, but * and / have higher priority than + and −. Consequently, A*B+3 is interpreted as (A*B)+3. Similarly, A+B/C+D is equivalent to A+(B/C)+D. In cases of equal priority, the left-most operation is performed first. This means that A+B/C+D is the same as (A+(B/C))+D, although in this case the order of the additions is essentially immaterial. (The results would be identical if all arithmetic operations were exact. However, roundoff error may cause small differences.) It is sometimes important to remember the left-to-right rule. The following

priority
precedence

example often leads beginning programmers astray: A*B/C*D is equivalent to ((A*B)/C)*D, not to (A*B)/(C*D).

The symbol / is used for regular division, but division can also be done as integer division, denoted by div, and used as in

    A div B

It can be used only if A and B are integer expressions and yield the integer part of A/B. Thus

    19 div 6

has the value 3. The remainder in integer division can be found using the mod operator:

    19 mod 6

has value 1.

If an expression contains only integer constants and variables and no / operator, its value will be an integer. If there are only real values involved in an expression, its value will be real. It is also possible to mix integer and real values, in which case the integers are treated as if they were real and the resulting expression is also real. Thus, 3*15.2 has the value 45.6 and 4/8 has the value 0.5. Integer division is not permitted on reals.

To obtain the integer part of a real number we can use the functions trunc or round. The first gives the integer part of a real number, while round first rounds the number, then takes the integer part. The value of

    trunc(14.6)

is 14, while

    round(14.6)

has the value 15.

Pascal also allows the use of such standard mathematical functions as square root. A list of these is:

$$\begin{array}{rl}
\text{abs}(X): & \text{the absolute value of } X \\
\text{sqr}(X): & \text{the square of } X \\
\text{sqrt}(X): & \text{the square root of } X \\
\text{sin}(X): & \text{the sine of } X \ (X \text{ in radians}) \\
\text{cos}(X): & \text{the cosine of } X \ (X \text{ in radians}) \\
\text{exp}(X): & e^X \\
\text{ln}(X): & \text{the natural logarithm of } X \\
\text{arctan}(X): & \text{the inverse tangent of } X
\end{array}$$

In each case, X can be any expression, real or integer, possibly involving other functions. For example, if Y has value 3.1, then:

    sqrt(sqr(Y)+4.2)=3.716

boolean expressions in pascal

A second type of expression is a *boolean expression*, the value of which is always either true or false. One way of generating boolean expressions is to combine boolean constants and boolean expressions by means of the boolean operators and, or, and not, defined as follows. If A and B are boolean expressions, then the expression A and B is true only if A and B are both true. Under all other circumstances A and B is false. The expression A or B is true if either A or B is true; A or B is false only if both A and B are false. Finally, the expression not A is true only if A is false. For example, if A is true and B is false, then

    not(A) or B = false

while

    not(A and B) = true

To be on the safe side, it is best to use parentheses to enclose subexpressions unless they are simple variables.

relational and comparison operators

We can also create boolean expressions by using the so-called *relational* or *comparison operators:*

=	equal
>	greater than
>=	greater than or equal to
<	less than
<=	less than or equal to
<>	not equal

Relational operators can be used to compare arithmetic expressions. The general form for such a comparison is

   expression1   *relational operator*   *expression2*

which is a boolean expression with the value either true or false. For example, if A = 4 and B = 3 then:

    A>B

is true, while:

    (A−2)<(B−4)

is false. Again, when using arithmetic and relational operators together, it is safest to use parentheses. Actually, the relational operators all have lower priority than the arithmetic operators, so that the expression we have just discussed could have been written without parentheses. A list of priorities for all operators is given in Appendix B.

Boolean operators can be applied only to boolean expressions. If A, B, and C are numerical variables, the condition that A be greater than B and that A also be greater than C is written as

```
(A > B) and (A > C)
```

and not as

```
A > (B and C)
```

The second form makes no sense because the and operation cannot be performed on the numerical variables B and C.

How are boolean expressions used? The diamond-shaped decision box in flowchart language gives us a clue, because it involves true and false conditions. Exactly how this is done in Pascal will be discussed a little later.

EXERCISES 2.2

1. Which of the following are not legal Pascal identifiers?

   ```
   NO WAY
   Thisisit
   Q59x
   m:9
   agent/007
   ```

2. Convert the following mathematical expressions to Pascal, using as few parentheses as possible.

   a. $\dfrac{a + b}{cd}$ b. $\dfrac{\sqrt{x} - \sqrt{y}}{x + y}$

   c. $\dfrac{1/x + 1/y}{x + y^2}$ d. $\dfrac{ab + cd}{e + fg}$

3. If A=3, B=4, C=2, D=2, and E=−3, determine the values of the following expressions:

   a. A/B/C   b. (A mod B) div C
   c. C/D*E   d. sqr(A+sqrt(abs(E−1)))

4. What are the values of the following expressions?

   a. sqrt(abs(trunc(−16.9)))
   b. round(15.6) div trunc(7.5)
   c. round(14.9)>trunc(15.1)

5. With values of A, B, C, D, and E as in Exercise 3, what are the values of the following expressions?

   a. (A*B)>C
   b. (D div B)=0
   c. (A>B) or (D>E)
   d. not(B>=C)

6. If A is true and B is false, what are the values of the following expressions?
   a. A and (not B)
   b. (not A) and A
   c. not((not A) and (not B))
7. Write a boolean expression that will be true if A is between two and five and B is negative.
8. When is ((I div 2) * 2) = I true?
9. Write Pascal expressions for the volume and surface area of a right circular cylinder of radius R and height H.
10. One Pascal function not discussed in the text is odd. This function when applied to an integer expression yields the result true if the value is an odd number, and false if it is not. What is the value of

    (not(odd(8 mod 3))) and ((5 div 4)>2)

11. Consult Appendix B to determine the order of evaluation in the expression

    not A and B or C and X=Y

12. The operators div and mod can be defined by

    A div B = trunc(A/B)
    A mod B = A-(A div B)*B

    for positive and negative integers. Use this definition to evaluate (-35) div 4, (-35) mod 4, and 35 mod (-4).

2.3

assignment statements

To carry out computations, we need statements that tell the computer what actions to perform. The basic tool for this is the *assignment statement*. Assignment statements are a central part of almost every programming language. In flowchart language, we have already encountered such statements as

    A:= B + 1

This is an instruction to perform the computation on the right side and to assign the value obtained to the variable on the left. The right side of the statement can be any legal expression; the left must be a variable name. In general, the expression on the right must have a value of the same type as the variable on the left. If several assignment statements are given, it is assumed that they are performed in the order in which they are written.

Note that we cannot have an expression on the left side. The assignment statement is not to be confused with a mathematical equation. Thus

```
A + 1:= B - 2
```

is not in correct form, although the mathematical equation

```
A + 1 = B - 2
```

makes sense. Conversely

```
I:= I + 1
```

is acceptable and simply· states that the value of the variable I is to be increased by one. While the form of the assignment statement varies from language to language, the basic idea remains the same.

In Pascal, the general form of the assignment statement is

variable **:** =*expression*

A program normally consists of a sequence of assignment statements and other instructions. To separate one instruction from the next, Pascal uses the semicolon. For example, in

```
A:=B+1;
C:=sqr(A)
```

A is computed first, followed by the evaluation of C as A^2. The semicolon is not part of the statement, but is used as a separator.

The assignment statement looks much like a mathematical formula. For example, the formulas for the area and circumference of a circle with radius R are

$$a = \pi R^2$$
$$c = 2\pi R$$

This is written in Pascal as

```
AREA:=3.1415926*RADIUS*RADIUS;
CIRCUMF:=6.283185*RADIUS
```

This example raises an important point. While in mathematics one tends to use one-letter symbols for variables, in programming it is much better to use longer, descriptive names. This makes the statements easier to understand and remember.

Assignment is not limited to numerical variables and expressions. If LETTER is a character variable, then

```
LETTER:='C'
```

assigns the alphabetical character C to the variable LETTER. Similarly, if REDFLAG is a boolean variable, then

```
REDFLAG:=true
```

is allowed.

To take a more complicated example: is the statement

```
A:=(B>C)
```

syntactically correct? The answer depends on the types of A, B, and C. If B and C are numerical, then B>C makes sense, generating a boolean expression. The value of the expression is assigned to A. Therefore, the statement is proper only if A is of type boolean.

EXERCISES 2.3

1. Write assignment statements that convert temperature from degrees Fahrenheit to centigrade and vice versa. (x degrees F = $5(x - 32)/9$ degrees C).
2. Write an assignment statement to compute the length of the hypotenuse of a right triangle with sides a and b.
3. What are the values of A, B, and C after execution of the following statements?

```
A:=3;
B:=4;
C:=A+2*B;
C:=C+B;
B:=C-A;
A:=B*C
```

4. What is the value of X after the following computations?

```
X:=2;
X:=sqr(X+X);
X:=sqrt(X+sqrt(X))
```

5. What must be the types of the variables for the statement

```
X:=(A<B) and C
```

to make sense?

6. Assume A, B, and C are boolean. What is wrong with the statement

```
not(A):=B and C ?
```

7. Why is it impossible for the statement

```
X:=(2*X=Y)
```

to be correct?

2.4

input and output

input

input file
sequential file

The purpose of the input statement is to take data from some peripheral device and store them in main memory. To understand exactly how this is done we must first discuss the concept of an *input file.* This file consists of the data with which we are working. It is called a *sequential file,* meaning that the information is in a special order. We visualize the input file as a sequence of data items. For example:

```
10  15  45  30
```

At any one time, only the left-most item of the file is available. When an operation such as

```
Input A
```

is performed, the front item is read and its value, in this case ten, is given to the variable A. This value essentially disappears from the file and the next item comes to the front. If the next instruction were

```
Input B
```

then B would be assigned the value 15.

Remember that the input file normally contains only data items (for example, numbers), but no identifiers. The values assigned to variables depend only on the order of the items in the file, the order in which the variable names occur in the input statements, and the order in which the input statements are executed. If in the example just discussed we had written first Input B, followed by Input A, the value ten would have been assigned to B, and the value 15 to A.

Note also that when an item is read, it disappears from the file, but this does not mean that the value is "gone" or irretrievable. When a data value is read from the input file, its value is assigned to a variable, that is, stored in the computer's memory. If it is needed later, we simply refer to that variable. The way in which the input file is created depends on the system, the language, and peripheral device used.

In Pascal, the simplest input statement has the form

```
read(A)
```

where A is any variable name. A slightly more complicated form is

```
read(A,B)
```

Here the first value in the input file is assigned to A, the second to B. The general form is read(*variable1, variable2, . . . , variablen*)

In Pascal, the input file is divided into lines. When we type data into the input file, a new line is created every time we hit the "return" key on the terminal. In the input file, the end of each line is marked so that it can be detected by the computer. Consecutive read statements take consecutive values from the input file without distinguishing between lines. Another form of the input command is

readln(A)

an abbreviation for "read line." The data item at the front of the input file is assigned to A, but the rest of the line is skipped. The next input statement will get its values from the next line. We can use readln without argument—that is, without any variable name. The command

readln

will skip over the rest of the current line.

To bring out the difference between read and readln, consider an input file consisting of six numbers on two lines:

```
1 2 3 4
5 6
```

If we write

```
read(A,B,C);
read(D,E)
```

we will get values A = 1, B = 2, C = 3, D = 4, and E = 5. On the other hand, with

```
readln(A,B,C);
read(D,E)
```

we get A = 1, B = 2, C = 3, D = 5, and E = 6.

Notice that numerical data items are separated by one or more blanks. Whenever a number is read, all blanks are skipped until the first digit is encountered; all contiguous digits are then taken to be part of one number. It is also possible to read character data, but no blanks are used as separators, simply because blanks are actual characters. For example, if the input file contains

15XY3

then read(A,B,C,D) will assign the values 15 to A and 3 to D, and the characters 'X' to B and 'Y' to C. (This assumes, of course, that the variables are all of the right type; A and D must be integer or real, while B and C must be of type char.)

It is possible in Pascal to detect the end of a line and the end of the input file. The standard identifiers eoln and eof both have boolean values, which are initially set to false. During input, the values of eoln and eof may change. To use eoln and eof properly, it is necessary to know exactly how the Pascal input file works. We can visualize the input file as in Figure 2.10a. The figure shows the initial state of the file for six numbers. The arrow in the picture points to the front of the file, that is, to the position currently being read. A read takes this value and advances the arrow to the next item. A readln, on the other hand, advances the arrow to the item beyond the end-of-line marker. For the purpose of a read, the end-of-line marker acts like a blank. If for the file in Figure 2.10a we start with

    read(A,B,C,D)

then eoln is true, while eof is false (Figure 2.10b). If we follow this with

    read(E,F)

then eoln will again be true. Note, however, that even though we have reached the end of the data, eof is still false, because the arrow points to the end-of-line marker (Figure 2.10c).

If instead of read(A,B,C,D) we begin with

    readln(A,B,C)

then eoln and eof will both be false. Following this with

    readln(D,E)

makes eoln false, but eof true. An attempt to read past the end-of-file marker is an error, and the computer will terminate the program.

output

The output statement provides the mechanism by which information is transmitted from the memory to an output device and presented in a suitable form, perhaps printed, displayed on a screen, or punched on cards. For the sake of discussion we will simply say "printed."

When we write a statement like

    Output A

the value of A is printed. This alone may not be enough; we may also want to print it in a certain form or in a particular place on the page. Essentially, there are two kinds of output commands. In *unformatted* or *free format* output, no form for the output is specified. The results are printed in a form determined by the system. In *formatted* output, we have complete control over the appearance of the results. Formatted output is obviously the more powerful. Unformatted output is a little simpler to use, and it can save some time during the early stages of programming. However, when a program is used for actual work, output will have to be neatly arranged, and because there is really very little effort involved in using formatted output, we do not recommend the use of unformatted output.

FIGURE 2.10

Several stages in reading an input file: ↑ marks current front of file, * is the end-of-line marker, and ✕ the end-of-file marker

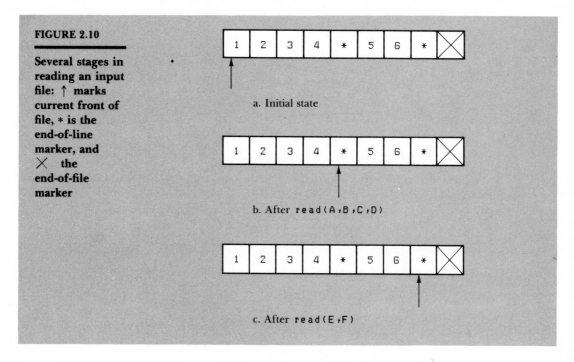

a. Initial state

b. After `read(A,B,C,D)`

c. After `read(E,F)`

format description

To produce formatted output, we must supply a ***format description***. For each item to be printed, we must specify a *field width*, that is, the number of character positions (columns) the item is to occupy. If not all columns are used, the value is usually "right justified" with blanks inserted on the left. By selecting correct field widths, we can align the output in any way we want. When printing decimal numbers, we also specify the number of decimal places to be given and whether decimals or exponents are to be used. This information has to be provided to the computer through a format description. The format descriptions vary with the language used.

Output statements must also allow for the printing of character strings. It is inadvisable to print just numbers, especially for complicated programs, because it is not always clear what the numbers mean. Results should instead be printed with headings or other descriptive messages for the sake of clarity.

In Pascal, the statement

`write(A)`

is an example of unformatted output. It will print the value of A in some way determined by the system. The general form of this statement is

`write`*(expression1, expression2, . . . , expressionk)*

The `write` statement allows not only variables, but also expressions. The expressions are evaluated and the result printed. When a `write` includes several expressions, their values will be printed on the same line until the line is filled. Subsequent values are then put on the next line. An alternative is the "write line" statement of the form

```
writeln(expression1, expression2, . . . , expressionk)
```

After the last expression is printed, the printer immediately goes to the next line. For example, suppose that A, B, C, D, and E are all integer variables with values A=1, B=2, C=3, D=4, and E=5. Then

```
write(A,B,C);
write(D,E)
```

will produce the following output (with horizontal spacing, depending on the system):

```
1 2 3 4 5
```

while

```
writeln(A,B,C);
writeln(D,E)
```

will give

```
1 2 3
4 5
```

It is possible to use writeln without argument to finish a line or to print a blank line, for example:

```
writeln;
writeln
```

will print two blank lines.

In Pascal, if A is an integer or character variable, then using

A:*field width*

in place of A will print the value of A in a field of specified width, right justified.

For real variables and expressions we have a choice. If we write

expression:w:f

where w and f are integer expressions, we specify that the number is to be printed in decimal format with f places after the decimal point in a field of width w. If instead we use

expression:w

then the value is printed in exponent notation in such a way that there are a total of w characters, with one space between numbers. The number of significant digits given depends on how much room there is in the field.

Character strings are printed by putting them in the output statement enclosed in single quotes, for example:

```
write('average=',AVE:10)
```

Review the following example carefully. The code contains a mixture of formatted and unformatted output.

```
var A,B,C:real;
    I,J:integer;
    L:char;

A:=3.4;
B:=0.45e+01;
C:=-3.1;
I:=3;
J:=-2;
L:='x';
writeln(A,B,I,L);
writeln(J:5,B:10:5,C:10);
write(A+B*J:15);
writeln('the value of A is',A:11:6)
```

When this code is run (with some additions to make it a complete program), it produces the output

```
3.40000000000000e+00   4.50000000000000e+00          3x
 -2   4.50000 -3.100e+00
-5.60000000e+00the value of A is   3.400000
```

Note that for positive numbers the + sign is suppressed and replaced by a blank.

Arranging the output is an important step in program design. It is essential that your results are neat, easy to read, and easy to understand. The following features can be used to produce essentially any layout you want:·

1. Horizontal spacing, controlled by field width.
2. Vertical arrangement, controlled by the use of write and writeln.
3. Labeling of items, done by the choice of suitable character strings.

Suppose that at some point in a program we want to print the values of the real variables A and B, as well as their sum. We decide to print A and B on one line and the sum on the next, all properly labeled. If we want to print each number with two digits after the decimal point, we can use the statements

```
writeln('A=',A:10:2,'B=',B:10:2);
writeln('The sum of A and B=',A+B:10:2)
```

When run on the computer with values A=3.4 and B=5.1, the result is

```
A=         3.40B=         5.10
The sum of A and B=         8.50
```

Notice that the space between the character strings and the numbers is quite wide. In this example, the specified field width is larger than necessary. If the value of A were longer, there would be fewer spaces between 'A= ' and the numerical value. In fact, if A were very large, it might not fit into the field at all. This would be a program error, and could be avoided by the use of exponent notation.

Perhaps you don't like what you have gotten, because on the first line the numerical value of A and the letter 'B' run together. To remove this slight flaw, all you need to do is insert some leading blanks into the second character string, perhaps by

```
writeln('A'=',A:10:2,'   B=',B:10:2);
writeln('The sum of A and B=',A+B:10:2)
```

which produces

```
A=         3.40  B=         5.10
The sum of A and B=         8.50
```

With the right field width and blanks in character strings, any horizontal spacing can be generated.

EXERCISES 2.4

1. Describe what is wrong with the following statements:
   a. Print(A)
   b. read(A:10)
   c. read(A+B)
   d. read(A) and write(B)
   e. writeln(the value of x is, x:10)
2. Give a sequence of output statements that will produce the pattern

   ```
   1xxxxx1
   2     2
   3xxxxx3
   ```

3. Assume that the input file contains

   ```
   1 2 3 4 5
   6 7 8
   9 10 11
   ```

   What will be printed by

   ```
   readln(A,B);
   read(C);
   ```

```
writeln(sqrt(C+1):10:2);
read(B,C);
writeln(A,B,C)
```

4. With the code in Exercise 3, what will be printed if the input file contains

```
1
2  3  4
5  6  7
8  9  10  11
```

5. In Exercise 3, what will be the values of `eoln` and `eof` after each input statement?

6. Boolean expressions can also be used in output statements. For each such expression either "true" or "false" will be printed. If the code in Exercise 3 were followed by

```
write(not(eof) and eoln);
```

what would be printed?

further reading

Graham, N. *Introduction to Computer Science*, Chapters 4 and 5. St. Paul, Minn.: West Publishing Co. 1979.

Koffman, E. B. *Problem Solving and Structured Programming in Pascal*, Chapter 1. Reading, Mass.: Addison-Wesley Publishing Co., 1981.

Tremblay, J. P., and Bunt, R. B. *An Introduction to Computer Science*, Chapter 2. New York: McGraw-Hill, 1979.

writing simple programs

Every language has certain conventions for structuring a program, governing, for example, the order in which instructions are given or what headings are necessary. Thus, our next step in this text is to consider the structure of Pascal programs. We must also learn how to instruct the computer to make decisions. In the flowcharts we had the decision box; now we must learn how this can be done in a programming language.

3.1

the structure of a simple program

statements

Most programming languages have several kinds of instructions, each playing a distinct role. **Statements** are instructions for operations to be carried out. Assignment, input, and output are all statements. The order in which statements are written is crucial; interchanging two statements may completely change the nature of the program.

declaration

Another kind of instruction is the **declaration**. Declarations do not directly result in computations, but instead communicate necessary information, for example, instructions for declaring the type of a variable. Usually there are conventions governing the use of declarations. Because, however, no computation is associated with declarations, there can sometimes be some variation in their forms.

comment

Finally, there is the surprisingly useful language construct called the **comment**. A comment is really not an instruction at all. Virtually anything can be written in a comment, but it has no effect on the computations. Its sole purpose is to allow the programmer to annotate a program, perhaps to describe its purpose, to guide the reader, or to clarify a point. The comment carries a message only to the human reader; it is completely ignored by the computer except that it appears in printed copies of the code.

We must remember that a program is written not just for the computer, but for the people who use it. It is not always easy to keep track of all a program's steps even when we are in the middle of constructing it. Later, when the program is used again or changed, it may require considerable effort to retrace the original train of thought. Quite simply, programming languages are precise and unambiguous, but they are not as explicit as English. Comments can explain the program in a form that human beings can understand. It is a good habit to use comments even in simple programs. Later, when programs become more complex, this good habit will pay off.

In Pascal, the rules for structuring a program include the following:

1. The first line of every program is a heading of the form

   ```
   program name (input,output)
   ```

   The word program is reserved and input and output are standard identifiers. The identifier *name* is the name of the program; it can be any legal identifier.

2. Declarations follow immediately after the program heading. The only declaration we have encountered so far is var, but there are others. There is some freedom in variable declaration; the order in which the variables are mentioned is immaterial. However, only one var declaration can appear in a simple program.

3. Statements follow the declarations. The set of statements must be preceded by the reserved word begin and terminated with the reserved word end, followed by a period. The words begin and end are common in Pascal, serving as delimiters to enclose groups of statements.

4. Everything enclosed between { and } is treated as comment. A comment may extend over several lines and can be inserted anywhere in a program.

In schematic form, the structure of a simple Pascal program is

```
program NAME(input,output);
var A,B,...,D: type;
    E,F,...,H: type;
    I,J,...,K: type;
  begin
  statement;
  statement;
    .
    .
    .
  statement
  end.
```

Note the position of the semicolons. In the var declaration, semicolons are used to separate groups of variables of the same type as well as to separate the whole declaration from the rest of the program. Each statement is separated from the next by a semicolon. However, begin and end are delimiters, so there is no semicolon after begin or before end.

Let us now consider a few examples of programs to review some of the concepts we have discussed. To emphasize the steps of structured problem solving described in Section 2.1, we will present examples in a special way. Like many puzzles, the solution of a programming problem becomes quite simple if the pieces are put together in the right order.

the puzzle solving approach in this text

The examples in this text are arranged in the progression that you will naturally use as you follow the steps of structured problem solving. To show exactly where the steps occur in the examples, they are marked in the text margin by puzzle piece symbols, as follows:

Problem statement. A formal statement of the problem that the program is intended to solve.

Algorithm. The process by which we intend to solve the programming problem.

Pascal code. The implementation of the algorithm in our chosen language, Pascal.

and finally,

Discussion. A discussion of the major noteworthy features of the code, with sample input and output to show what the program does.

EXAMPLE 3.1

INTEREST ON A SAVINGS ACCOUNT

Suppose that a bank has a number of savings accounts for which the interest is to be computed and added to the balance periodically. Let's consider the computation of a new balance from an old balance, using a yearly interest rate and the elapsed time in months. The formula for computing the new balance is

new balance = old balance + interest

where the interest is the product of the old balance, interest rate, and the elapsed time divided by 12.

The input data for this problem are the values of the old balance, the interest rate, and the elapsed time. The result will be the new balance. For input verification, we will also print the old balance and the interest. All output is to be given in decimal form, with two digits after the decimal place. All items are to be properly labeled.

The main variables involved here will be

OLDBAL	old balance
RATE	yearly interest rate
MONTHS	elapsed time in months
INTEREST	earned interest
NEWBAL	new balance

The relation between these variables is described in the problem statement.

The first level of the algorithm consists of three simple steps:

1. Read OLDBAL, RATE, MONTHS.
2. Compute INTEREST and NEWBAL.
3. Print OLDBAL, INTEREST, NEWBAL.

Step 2 can be refined to

```
2.1. INTEREST:=OLDBAL*RATE*MONTHS/12
2.2. NEWBAL:=OLDBAL+INTEREST
```

The description is now sufficiently simple, and we can proceed with its implementation.

```
Program ACCOUNT(input,output);
{this program computes interest and prints
new balance for a savings account}
var OLDBAL,NEWBAL,RATE,INTEREST:real;
    MONTHS:integer;
begin
  readln(OLDBAL,RATE,MONTHS);
  INTEREST:=OLDBAL*RATE*MONTHS/12;
  NEWBAL:=OLDBAL+INTEREST;
  writeln('Old balance',OLDBAL:10:2);
  writeln('Interest___',INTEREST:10:2);
  writeln('New balance',NEWBAL:10:2)
end.
```

Sample input

```
200 0.08 6
```

Output

```
Old balance    200.00
Interest         8.00
New balance    208.00
```

prologue   We have used only one comment, which describes the purpose of the program. Such a starting comment is sometimes called a *prologue.* Longer programs will need to be much more thoroughly commented, but a short explanation suffices here.

One way to make programs reasonably self-explanatory is to use descriptive variable names. In this program, we have used abbreviations of the names in the verbal description as identifiers. Formatted output makes the results explicit and gives them a pleasing appearance, and character string printout identifies the individual numbers. All of these are requirements of good programming.

EXAMPLE 3.2

COMPUTING THE ROOTS OF A QUADRATIC EQUATION

As a second exercise, let us write a program to compute the roots of the quadratic equation

$$ax^2 + bx + c = 0$$

As we know, such an equation generally has two roots given by

$$x_1 = \frac{-b + \sqrt{b^2 - 4ac}}{2a}$$

and

$$x_2 = \frac{-b - \sqrt{b^2 - 4ac}}{2a}$$

(For the purpose of this example, we will ignore the case in which $b^2 - 4ac \leq 0$.) The program is to accept as input the coefficients a, b, and c, and print them with the roots of the equation.

We will use the variable names A, B, C for the coefficients, and ROOT1 and ROOT2 for the solutions. The first level description of the algorithm is

1. Read A, B, C.
2. Compute ROOT1 and ROOT2.
3. Print A, B, C, ROOT1, ROOT2.

Step 2 is then refined to

2.1. Compute partial expression PART := B*B−4*A*C.
2.2. ROOT1:=(−B+PART)/(2*A).
2.3. ROOT2:=(−B−PART)/(2*A).

```
program QUADRATIC(input,output);
{ a program to compute the roots of the
  equation A*X*X+B*X+C=0 }
var A,B,C,PART,ROOT1,ROOT2:real;
begin
  readln(A,B,C);
  PART:=sqrt(B*B−4*A*C);
  ROOT1:=(−B+PART)/(2*A);
  ROOT2:=(−B−PART)/(2*A);
  writeln('A'=',A:10:5,' B=',B:10:5,' C=',C:10:5);
  writeln('First root =',ROOT1:15);
  writeln('Second root=',ROOT2:15)
end.
```

Sample input

```
4.1 3.2 −0.5
```

Output

```
A=   4.10000 B=   3.20000 C=  −0.50000
First root =  1.33436843e-01
Second root= −9.13924648e-01
```

Note that both roots contain the common expression B*B−4*A*C. In the program, this is called PART. Experienced programmers often use separate variable names for common subexpressions. Not only does it save typing, it tends to be more efficient, because the subexpression is evaluated only once. It does have a drawback, in that it introduces an extra variable and thereby makes the program a little less obvious.

For output we have printed not only the results produced by the program, but also the values of all the input. This "echoing" of the input is a good practice for several reasons. First, it shows clearly the input associated with the output, and second, it guards against errors in input, such as a dropped sign or a misplaced decimal point. Of course, there are times when echoing clutters up the output, so you may not want to use it in all programs.

EXAMPLE 3.3

CHANGE-MAKING PROGRAM

Given the amount of change, coin-dispensing machines automatically return the correct number of quarters, dimes, nickels, and pennies. Usually the change is returned so as to use the smallest number of coins, that is, as many quarters as possible are used, then as many dimes as possible, and so on. Let us write a program to control such a change maker.

We can immediately sketch the algorithm:

1. Read in amount of change in cents.
2. Compute the number of quarters and remaining amount.
3. From remaining amount, compute the number of dimes and new remainder.
4. From new remainder, compute the number of nickels; what is left is the number of pennies.
5. Print out the number of quarters, dimes, nickels, and pennies.

The only problem left is how to find the correct number of quarters and other coins. If you think about this for a minute, you will see the answer easily; divide the original amount by 25, using integer division. The quotient is the number of quarters. The remainder is used to determine the other change by an analogous process. Step 2 can then be expanded to

2.1. Compute number of quarters by integer division of original amount by 25.
2.2. Remaining change is remainder obtained in Step 2.1.

Refinement of Steps 3 and 4 is similar.

```
program CHANGE(input,output);
{ this program determines change returned using the
  smallest number of coins }
```

```
var AMOUNT,REMAINS,QUARTERS,DIMES,NICKELS,
    PENNIES:integer;
begin
  {read in amount of change }
  readln(AMOUNT);
  {compute number of quarters }
  QUARTERS:=AMOUNT div 25;
  REMAINS:=AMOUNT mod 25;
  {compute number of dimes }
  DIMES:=REMAINS div 10;
  REMAINS:=REMAINS mod 10;
  {compute number of nickels and pennies }
  NICKELS:=REMAINS div 5;
  PENNIES:=REMAINS mod 5;
  {print out original amount and coins returned}
  writeln('Original amount=',AMOUNT:5,' cents');
  writeln('Quarters:',QUARTERS:4);
  writeln('Dimes   :',DIMES:4);
  writeln('Nickels :',NICKELS:4);
  writeln('Pennies :',PENNIES:4)
end.
```

Sample input

```
   67
```

Output

```
   Original amount=   67 cents
   Quarters:   2
   Dimes   :   1
   Nickels :   1
   Pennies :   2
```

This program shows the usefulness of integer arithmetic. It is not advisable to make such variables as AMOUNT real, because the inaccuracies resulting from conversion and roundoff may produce incorrect results.

In using stepwise refinement, there arises invariably the question of how detailed a design to make at the pseudolanguage level before doing the code. Stepwise refinement is not a rigidly defined process. In the design of the algorithm for Example 3.3, we used a fairly informal pseudolanguage to define the overall process. More formally, we might have shown the variables to be used and the formulas for computing their values. We omitted this because the step from the pseudolanguage to the actual code is small.

A good guideline is to continue with the refinement until the transition to the code is trivial. At first, you may want to use many levels; when you gain more experience in programming, you will find that you can omit some of the finer steps.

EXERCISES 3.1

Write a program for each of the following problems. Use `read` *or* `readln` *to enter the data and label all output properly. Use comments liberally, but think first whether they will help in understanding the program.*

1. Given x, compute $\sqrt{x}$ and $1/\sqrt{x}$.
2. Compute the volume and surface area of a sphere of radius R.
3. Compute the volume and surface area of a right circular cylinder of height H and base radius R.
4. Compute the area and circumference of an equilateral triangle with side S.
5. Convert from degrees Fahrenheit to centigrade.
6. Convert from degrees centigrade to Fahrenheit.
7. Convert a distance given in miles, feet, and inches to its equivalent in kilometers and meters.
8. Make change for an amount given in dollars to dispense paper money as well as coins.

3.2

alternative computations

All the programs in Section 3.1 are rather simple, involving only the reading of data, evaluation of one or more mathematical formulas, and printing of results. This is typical of what we do on a pocket calculator. Writing a program does simplify such calculations; once the program is finished, we only enter the numbers and have no further need for pressing the operation buttons. But the kind of application for which computers are most useful is one that involves many thousands of operations, so that it would be cumbersome, if not impossible, to specify each step explicitly.

The limitations of what we have learned so far become apparent if we try to solve one of the problems introduced in Section 2.1—for example, the payroll problem. A glance at the flowchart reveals that we do not yet have a programming language equivalent of the decision box. What we have written so far are straightline programs, in which steps are executed in strict sequence and in which each computation requires just one statement. Obviously, if we want to write programs to perform thousands of individual operations, or programs in which several alternatives occur, we have to find a way to make decisions.

selection of one of two alternatives

If you look at the flowchart for the payroll problem, you see that the decision box is used to select between one of two alternatives for computing the gross pay. This situation is very common in programming; the basic construct involved is depicted in Figure 3.1. In words, we test a given condition; if it is satisfied, one sequence of operations is carried out, and if not, an alternative sequence is performed. Because of this interpretation, the two-way selection is commonly called the ***if-then-else construct.***

if-then-else-construct

The Pascal version of the `if-then-else` construct has the form

```
if condition
    then statement1
    else statement2
```

Here, *condition* is a boolean expression. If its value is true, then *statement1* is executed; if it is false, *statement2* is executed. For the payroll example, the code for computing the gross pay is

```
if HOURS<=40
    then GROSSPAY:=HOURS*RATE
    else GROSSPAY:=40*RATE+1.5*RATE*(HOURS-40)
```

A simplified version of the `if-then-else` construct is obtained by omitting the `else` clause. In

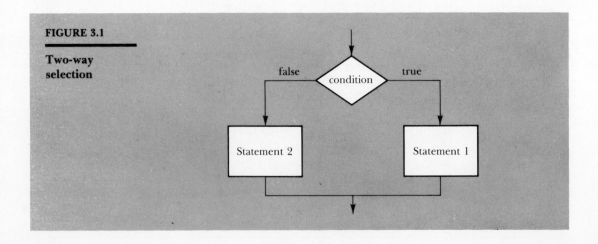

FIGURE 3.1

Two-way selection

```
if condition
   then statement
```

the statement is executed only if *condition* is true; otherwise, nothing is done on this step. This construct is called the `if-then` statement.

compound statement

Often, the alternatives require more than a single step. To allow for this, Pascal provides an elegant concept, the ***compound statement.*** A set of statements can be grouped together by enclosing them between `begin` and `end`, forming a compound statement. The general form of this is

```
begin
   statement1;
   statement2;
      .
      .
      .
   statementn
end
```

For the purpose of the `if-then-else` and other constructs, such a compound statement acts as if it were a single step. In fact, from now on, whenever we write "statement" we will include "compound statement" as an option. An example of an `if-then-else` with compound statements is

```
if A>=0
   then begin
           X:=0;
           Y:=1
        end
   else begin
           X:=1;
           Y:=0
        end
```

which assigns either zero or one to X and Y, depending on the value of A. Remember that `begin` and `end` are not statements, but markers. It is therefore incorrect to insert a semicolon between `end` and `else` or `else` and `begin`. It is also unnecessary, though possible, to put a semicolon between a statement and `end`—for example:

```
      .
      .
      .
   Y:=0;
end
```

This actually puts an "empty" statement before `end`. We will discuss a use for this a little later in the text.

Let us now return to the payroll problem. To make it more challenging and also closer to what an actual program might be, we will complicate it a little.

EXAMPLE 3.4

PAYROLL COMPUTATION

To the requirements of Example 2.1, we add the following:

1. An employee identification number will be used to identify the information.
2. A certain amount of money will be withheld, for income tax purposes, the amount of which depends on the employee's exemptions and marital status.
3. The output should be properly labeled and neatly arranged.

The input for this program will consist of (1) the employee number (a positive integer), (2) the hours worked, (3) hourly rate, (4) number of exemptions, and (5) marital status (a single character 'S' or 'M').

The computations to be performed will be (1) gross pay, to be computed as in Example 2.1, (2) taxable pay, obtained by subtracting 25 times the number of exemptions from gross pay, (3) tax rate, which will be 10% if the employee is married, 15% otherwise, (4) withholding tax, which is taxable pay times tax rate, and (5) net pay, which is gross pay minus withholding tax.

The algorithm for this problem is

1. Read data.
2. Compute gross pay.
3. Compute withholding tax.
4. Compute net pay.
5. Print gross pay, withholding tax, and net pay.

Step 3 needs to be refined.

3.1. Compute taxable pay.
3.2. Compute tax rate.
3.3. Withholding tax: = taxable pay times tax rate

Further refinement can be done by giving the formulas, for example

3.1.1. taxable pay: = gross pay minus 25 times number of exemptions

but this is already obvious from the problem statement.

```
program PAYROLL(input,output);
{ a simple payroll computation including tax
   withholding
```

```
      Input:IDNUMBER = employee id number
            HOURS    = hours worked
            RATE     = hourly rate
            EXEMPTS  = # of exemptions for tax
            STATUS   = marital status M(arried)
                                   or S(ingle) }
var HOURS,RATE,GROSSPAY,TAXPAY,TAXRATE,
    TAXKEPT,NETPAY:real;
    IDNUMBER,EXEMPTS:integer;
    STATUS:char;
begin
  { read data for employee }
  readln(IDNUMBER,HOURS,RATE, EXEMPTS,STATUS);
  { compute gross pay }
  if HOURS<=40
    then GROSSPAY:=HOURS*RATE
    else GROSSPAY:=40*RATE+(HOURS-40)*RATE*1.5;
  { compute taxable pay }
  TAXPAY:=GROSSPAY-25*EXEMPTS;
  { compute tax rate based on marital status }
  if STATUS='M'
    then TAXRATE:=0.10
    else TAXRATE:=0.15;
  { compute tax withheld and netpay }
  TAXKEPT:=TAXPAY*TAXRATE;
  NETPAY:=GROSSPAY-TAXKEPT;
  { print out pay information }
  writeln('Employee #','   Gross pay',
          '         Tax','   Net pay');
  writeln(IDNUMBER:10,GROSSPAY:12:2,TAXKEPT:10:2,
          NETPAY:10:2)
end.
```

Sample input

```
    99356 45.0 8.5 2M
```

Output

```
    Employee #   Gross pay     Tax   Net pay
       99356       403.75    35.38    368.38
```

A few of the features of this program deserve comment. First, this is not the only program that solves the problem. In fact, no two programmers are likely to come up with identical solutions even in the simplest programs. There are some features in our program that an expert may find objectionable (see Exercise 3 at the end of this section); we will devote a great deal of attention to what is good and bad in a program as we continue in this text.

Another point to consider is whether or not the program is correct. As programmers, we quickly learn that it is easy to make mistakes, not only those involving incorrect use of the language, but also in designing and coding the algorithm (logic errors). In complex situations, it is not easy to decide when a program is completely correct. We can usually get some confidence by running a few well-chosen examples. These examples should be such that the answers can be worked out independently and compared with the computed results. If we run enough test cases without detecting any errors, we tend to believe that the program is error-free.

Finally, a word on how the program was laid out. We have used comments liberally, including a prologue and comments to separate the different parts of the computation. In general, this is a good practice. We have also used indentation when writing statements. When a single statement extends over several lines, or when we have groups of statements that belong together, indentation should be used to emphasize visually what goes together. The specific conventions for indentation used in this book are summarized in Appendix D.

---

selection of many alternatives

The general form of two-way selection is shown in Figure 3.1. Each box contains some computations, meaning any sequence of statements. But in practice, a program must often distinguish between a number of alternatives.

For example, take a program that will read an integer number between zero and 40, and print out the word "large" if the number is between 30 and 40, "medium" if it is between ten and 29, and "small" otherwise. This is a three-way selection of alternative computations. If we replace one of the boxes in Figure 3.1 with an if-then-else statement, we get the picture shown in Figure 3.2, which represents a three-way selection. This process can be repeated to distinguish between as many cases as we like. But if we have, say, six alternatives, it is convenient to have a more direct way to express n-way selection. In Figure 3.3, c is a variable with possible values c1,c2,...,cn. Depending on the value of c, one or the other of the indicated statements is executed.

nesting
Three-way selection in Pascal can be done by compounding, or ***nesting,*** if statements. The computation for selection could be written as

```
if X>=30
   then writeln('large')
   else if X>=10
           then writeln('medium')
           else writeln('small')
```

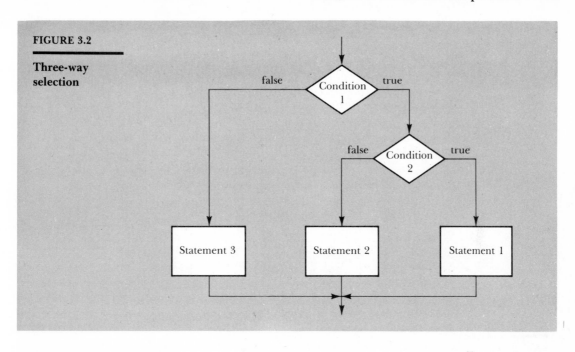

FIGURE 3.2

Three-way selection

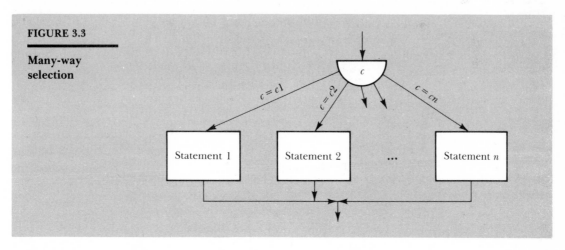

FIGURE 3.3

Many-way selection

Further nesting could achieve more selection, but it quickly becomes confusing.

One problem with nested `if` statements arises when we use the `if-then` construct. What does

```
if X=0 then if A=0 then B=1 else B=0
```

mean? It is not immediately clear whether the `else` clause is an alternative for the first or the second `if`. In other words, does the statement corre-

FIGURE 3.4

One possible interpretation of the `if-then-if-then-else` **construct**

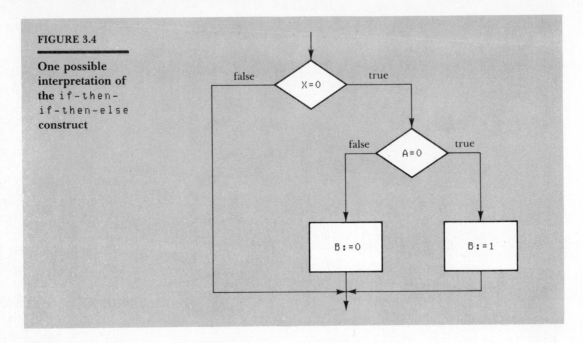

spond to Figure 3.4 or to Figure 3.5? The apparent ambiguity is called a
dangling else. It is resolved by associating the `else` with the last `if`, that is,
the statement represents Figure 3.4. However, such a construct can be quite
confusing to the programmer, and should be avoided.

dangling else

case statement

A more direct way for multiple selection is the ***case statement***. In
general, its form is

```
case c of
    c1: statement1;
    c2: statement2;
        .
        .
        .
    cn: statementn
end
```

which corresponds to Figure 3.3. When several values of the expression *c*
lead to the same alternative, we can combine them, as in

c2,c3, . . . , ck:statement

The *c* in the `case` statement can be any integer or character expression. It
cannot be of type `real`. The selectors *c1,c2, . . . , cn* must be constants of
the same type as *c*.

Using the `case` statement, we can write the selection problem as

FIGURE 3.5

Another possible
interpretation of
the `if-then-`
`if-then-else`
construct

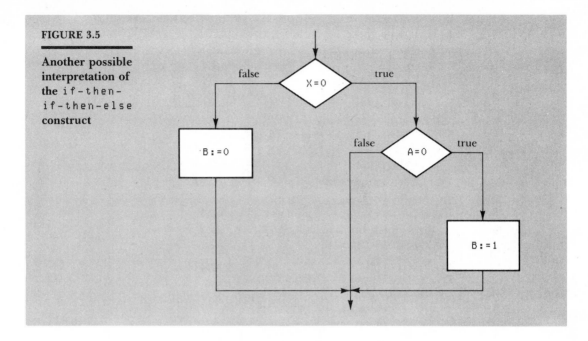

```
case (X div 10) of
  0: writeln('small');
  1,2 : writeln('medium');
  3,4 : writeln('large')
end
```

What would happen if we use this when X has the value 50? Then
X div 10 has value 5, an alternative not provided for in the statement.
The result of the statement is thus said to be *undefined,* which means we
cannot tell what, if anything, will be done. We cannot expect reasonable
results, because we have made a programming error by failing to consider
all possible values for X.

EXAMPLE 3.5

DATE CONVERSION

One of the two common ways of writing dates is to write out month, day,
and year:

July 4, 1976

The second is to use numerical values for the month and drop the first two
digits from the year, so that the example date is written as

7   4   76

Write a program that will convert from the second form to the first. The input will be three integers representing the month, day, and year. The output will be the character string for the date.

An algorithm for the problem is

1. Read month, day, year.
2. Determine alphabetical name of month and print it.
3. Print day, '19', year.

Step 2 involves selecting one of 12 possible character strings. It can be implemented immediately as a single case statement.

```
program DATE(input,output);
{this program converts a date in numeric form
 to the more explicit alphabetic version}
var MONTH,DAY,YEAR:integer;
begin
  {read date in numeric form}
  read(MONTH,DAY,YEAR);
  {select alphabetic name of month}
  case MONTH of
    1: write('January ');
    2: write('February ');
    3: write('March ');
    4: write('April ');
    5: write('May ');
    6: write('June ');
    7: write('July ');
    8: write('August ');
    9: write('September ');
    10:write('October ');
    11:write('November ');
    12:write('December ')
  end;
  writeln(DAY:3,' 19',YEAR:2)
end.
```

Sample input

    10 30 53

Output

    October 30 1953

To appreciate the usefulness of the case statement, try writing this program using only if-then-else statements. The program has a minor flaw; see if you can spot it. If you need help, look at Exercise 11 at the end of Section 3.2.

EXERCISES 3.2

1. Write a program that will accept three integer numbers and print the largest of them.
2. Rewrite the quadratic equations program in Example 3.2 so that it can handle the case when A = 0 and will print an appropriate message when B*B − 4*A*C < 0.
3. A program must give the right answer when presented with proper input, but we must also consider what will happen if the program is accidentally given incorrect data. Look at the programs in Section 3.2 to see what difficulties could arise from improper input.
4. Write a program that will convert from degrees Fahrenheit to centigrade and vice versa. The input should be the temperature and the letter F or C. The output should show the input and its converted equivalent; for example, for the input 95F the output should be

```
95F = 35C
```

5. How can three-way selection be done using if-then only? Try it on the small-medium-large selection problem.
6. To encourage energy conservation, many utility companies use sliding scales for electricity consumption. Write a program that will accept the amount of electricity used (in kilowatt-hours), and prepare a bill according to the following rates:

first 200 kilowatt-hours: four cents/kwh

next 400 kilowatt-hours: seven cents/kwh

over 600 kilowatt-hours: ten cents/kwh

7. Write a program that will determine whether a given positive integer represents a leap year. Remember that a year is a leap year if it is divisible by four, except if it is divisible by 100 but not 400.
8. Modify the selection example so that 'too large' will be printed if X is greater than 40, and 'too small' when X is negative.
9. Using the assembly language instructions described in Chapter 1, find a way of writing the equivalent of

```
if X>0
   then Y:=1/X
   else Y:=X
```

10. Why does the following statement not represent a dangling else?

```
if X=0 then begin if A=0 then B:=1 end
else B:=0
```

How does this statement differ from the example on p. 71?
11. What happens in program DATE when YEAR<10? Rewrite the program to handle this case correctly.

3.3

good programming habits

At this point, you may be wondering why we emphasize what may seem the fine points of programming, such as choosing good identifiers and using comments. Like a novice skier on top of a steep hill, you are perhaps more concerned with getting the job done, with the niceties of style a secondary consideration. Designing algorithms and learning a programming language are sufficiently challenging, so why worry about style?

The analogy with a sport still holds; if you concern yourself only with completing programs, but neglect to learn proper technique, you will find it difficult to improve—and incidentally, to enjoy the activity to the fullest. You may be able to muddle through simple programs with poor programming habits, but as your tasks become more complicated, proper technique will be indispensable.

Perhaps the most important habit in programming is to design programs carefully, following the basic steps of algorithm development given in Section 2.1:

1. Problem Statement. Specify the problem completely. Make sure you know exactly what input to expect, what process has to be carried out, and what the output should be. Do not begin the design of the algorithm before you understand what is to be done.
2. Algorithm Design. Identify the main variables and outline the way their values are to be computed. Find an algorithm for the computations. Write it out carefully and in detail, using pseudolanguage or a flowchart. Refine the algorithm, using as many levels as needed to make the solution method completely obvious. Go through a few examples on a piece of paper to convince yourself that it works. Do not begin coding until the algorithm design is complete.
3. Coding. Write the program carefully in the chosen language. Do not use constructs that you understand only vaguely. If in doubt, look it up. Use as your rule that unless you are absolutely sure of the code, it won't work. Go over your code several times until you are completely convinced that it is correct.

You should also produce programs that are easy and pleasant to read. In particular, keep the following points in mind:

1. Make your programs as uncomplicated as you can. Always ask yourself, "Can this be done in a more straightforward way?"
2. Use descriptive variable names.
3. Use indentation to give a visual picture of the structure of your program.
4. Use comments to guide the reader. Make sure your comments are helpful.

Don't be tempted to save time by ignoring these points. Sloppiness is counterproductive. If you find yourself spending a great deal of time on the computer correcting mistakes, you should reexamine your approach. With the structured problem solving method, you will avoid many difficulties and frustrations. But remember that algorithms may be difficult to discover, and several ways of coding may suggest themselves so that a choice has to be made. Even with the greatest care some mistakes will be made.

EXERCISES 3.3

1. Check all the programs you have written so far for examples of poor style. Are you following carefully the three basic steps of structured problem solving?
2. Exchange programs with friends. Evaluate their programs and get their criticisms of yours.

3.4

testing and debugging programs

There are two parts to checking a program's accuracy, *testing* and *debugging*. They are ordinarily done at the same time. Testing a program means running some examples to verify that the program performs according to specification. Debugging is the removal of the errors uncovered by testing. Ideally, a test example would be such that we can see from the results that the program is completely correct. Unfortunately, ideal examples do not exist. Testing can only detect the presence of errors, never conclusively prove their absence. To be confident that a program is correct, we usually require a number of test examples. All parts of a program should be tested, and as a minimal requirement each statement should be executed at least once. To limit the number of test cases, one needs to choose effective examples; a good test example is one that is likely to find as many potential errors as possible.

syntax errors
logic errors

In debugging, we distinguish between two kinds of errors: **syntax errors** and **logic errors.** Syntax errors are due to incorrect usage of the language. The compiler can detect almost all of these errors. Nonetheless, if you make many syntax errors, you are either a careless typist and proofreader or you do not know the language well enough.

More difficult to deal with are logic errors. When the program is run by the computer (once the syntax errors have been fixed), it may not give the correct answers, either because the algorithm is incorrect or because the implementation is faulty. To correct logic errors, you must first find them. If you cannot immediately see what the trouble is, divide your program into parts and try to find out where the error has occurred. The most effective way to localize errors is to put in temporarily, at selected points in the program, some output statements to print the values of certain variables or other identifying information. Select what is to be printed carefully to give useful information on the progress of the computation. Then check the actual output against a test case you have figured correctly by hand, and you will usually find the programming error. Not infrequently, fixing one error uncovers another, so that you may have to repeat the process several times.

We will say more about designing, testing, and debugging programs later. For the moment, just remember to be careful and systematic. Check and recheck every step. Limit the time you actually spend on the computer by going over your program carefully with several pencil and paper examples. Admit to yourself that you will make mistakes and plan ahead carefully so that you will be able to find and correct them quickly. If you make many mistakes and spend too much time on your programs, try to find the reason for it and correct your approach.

EXERCISES 3.4

1. Make a list of your most common syntax errors. Be especially alert for these errors in future programs.
2. Keep a count on how many tries you need before all the errors in your programs are corrected. If the average is much larger than two or three, try to reduce it by being more careful in algorithm design and coding.

---

further reading

Grogono, P. *Programming in Pascal,* Chapter 2. Reading, Mass.: Addison-Wesley Publishing·Co., 1978.

Jensen, K., and Wirth, N. *Pascal User Manual and Report,* 2d. ed., User Manual, Chapter 3. New York: Springer-Verlag, 1974.

Koffman, E. B. *Problem Solving and Structured Programming in Pascal,* Chapter 1. Reading, Mass.: Addison-Wesley Publishing Co., 1981.

Schneider, G. M., Weingart, S. W., and Perlman, D. M. *An Introduction to Programming and Problem Solving with Pascal,* Chapters 3 and 4. New York: John Wiley & Sons, 1978.

Welsh, J., and Elder, J. *Introduction to Pascal,* Chapter 2. Englewood Cliffs, N.J.: Prentice-Hall, 1979.

repetitive computations and control structure

The ideas introduced in the previous chapter allow us to write some simple, yet complete programs. But when we try to do more challenging exercises, we soon run into difficulty. Let us take another look at the cases discussed in Section 2.1: the sum-of-even-numbers problem and Examples 2.1 and 2.2. None of these can be done easily with our present knowledge. Even the payroll program, given in Example 3.4, is not quite complex enough to use for the problem in Example 2.1, because Example 3.4 handles only one case. Clearly, what we need is the abiiity to call for the repetition of a set of computations. The loop, which we introduce in this chapter, provides a natural way to do this.

4.1

loops

In programming, a sequence of instructions that is to be executed repeatedly is called a *loop,* a term descriptive of its appearance in a flowchart. A loop consists of a set of statements, called the *body* of the loop, and constructs that control the loop by describing how many times the body of the loop is traversed. Loops are so common in programming that it is rare to find a program without one.

Each traversal of the loop is called a *pass.* A loop may be traversed any number of times or not at all, but the number of passes must be finite, and eventually the loop must stop. If it does not, we have what is called an *infinite loop,* so that the program will not terminate. Programmers often construct infinite loops by mistake.

The body of a loop can contain any set of statements; in particular, it may include some other loops. When this happens, we say that loops are *nested.* Nesting of several levels of loops is not uncommon in complicated programs.

Depending on what happens in a loop and how it is terminated, we distinguish between two types of loops.

counted loops

A *counted loop* is controlled by a *loop variable.* This variable is initially set to some given value. With each traversal of the loop, it is increased by a value called the *increment.* When the loop variable reaches a final value, the loop is terminated. The number of times a loop is traversed depends only on the initial and final values of the loop variable and the increment. In Figure 4.1 (which is the flowchart for the sum-of-even-numbers problem described in Chapter 2), the main part of the computation is done in a loop, controlled by the loop variable NUMBER. Its initial value is four, the increment is two, and the final value is 1000.

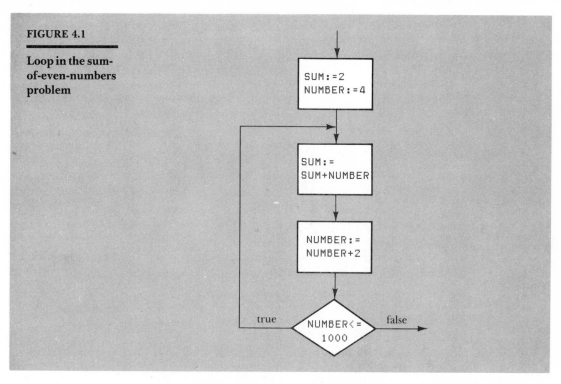

FIGURE 4.1

Loop in the sum-
of-even-numbers
problem

The Pascal version of the counted loop is provided by the f o r statement, whose form is

```
for variable:=expr1 to expr2 do
   statement
```

Here, *variable* is the loop variable, *expr1* is an expression giving the initial value, and *expr2* is the final value. The increment is not explicitly stated, but is implied to be one when *variable, expr1*, and *expr2* are of integer type. The body of the loop can be any simple or compound statement.

As a simple case consider

```
for I:=2 to 15 do
   write(I)
```

which will print the numbers 2, 3, . . . , 15. The loop for Figure 4.1 can be written as

```
for HALFNUMBER:=2 to 500 do
   SUM:=SUM+2*HALFNUMBER
```

Note that we have to employ a trick here. Our increment should be two, but because the f o r statement does not allow this, we use HALFNUMBER instead of NUMBER as the loop variable. HALFNUMBER takes on consecutive values 2, 3, . . . , 500. Because in each pass through the loop 2*HALFNUMBER is added to SUM, we effectively add $4 + 6 + \cdots + 1000$, as desired. Also, note that HALFNUMBER, being the loop variable, is automatically increased by one in each pass through the loop. It is incorrect to increase it additionally with an assignment statement. A general rule is that the loop variable, the initial value, and the final value must not be changed explicity in the loop.

Pascal allows loop control by character variables. The statement

```
for LETTER:='A' to 'K' do
    write(LETTER)
```

will print the string 'ABCDEFGHIJK'. This is possible because the letters are considered ordered in the usual alphabetical sequence. Real variables and expressions are not allowed for counted loops.

It is also possible to have a negative increment. To get this, replace the word to with downto. Thus

```
for I:=15 downto 11 do
    write(I)
```

will give output 15 14 13 12 11.

If the initial value is greater than the final value (or the other way around, with downto), the statements in the loop are not executed at all. For example, in

```
A:=3;
B:=4;
for I:= A+2 to B do
    write(I)
```

the loop is traversed zero times and no output is produced.

This type of loop is called a counted loop, because we know how many times the loop is to be traversed, and because we use the loop variable as a counter. There are other situations in which the number of traversals is less predictable, and for which we can use conditional loops.

conditional loops

A *conditional loop* is one that is performed until some recognizable event occurs. In the payroll algorithm, Figure 2.7, the condition looked for is end of data; if it occurs, the loop is terminated. It would not be easy to use a counted loop in this situation, because we do not know beforehand the number of data items.

initial-test
final-test

It has become fairly standard practice to allow two types of conditional loops, an ***initial-test*** loop and a ***final-test*** loop. The flow diagrams for them

FIGURE 4.2

Initial-test loop

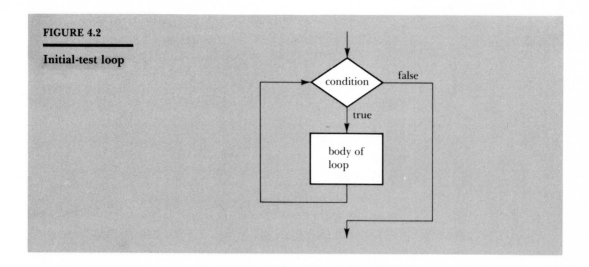

FIGURE 4.3

Final-test loop

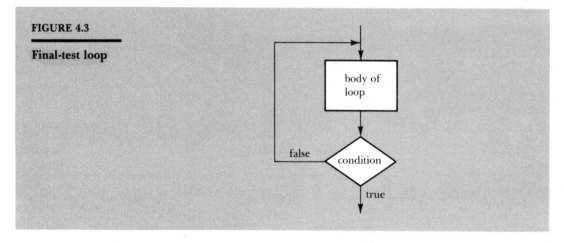

are given in Figure 4.2 and Figure 4.3. Note that an initial-test loop may conceivably never be traversed. A final-test loop, on the other hand, is traversed at least once.

In a conditional loop, the condition that terminates the loop has to be established in the loop, either explicitly through computation or less obviously through an event such as the end of data. While a counted loop always terminates, this is not necessarily the case with conditional loops. It is possible to construct infinite conditional loops, so we must take care.

while statement

The initial-test loop is provided in Pascal by the ***while statement***, the general form of which is

```
while condition do
    statement
```

Here, *condition* is a boolean expression. The body of the loop, represented by *statement*, is executed repeatedly as long as *condition* is true.

The end-test loop is provided by the **repeat statement** of the form

repeat statement

```
repeat
    statement1;
    statement2;
    •
    •
    •
    statementn
until condition
```

The given statements are repeated until *condition* becomes true.

The codes for the sum-of-even-numbers problem in Section 2.1, written in these two forms, are

```
SUM:=2;
NUMBER:=4;
while (NUMBER<=1000) do
    begin
        SUM:=SUM+NUMBER;
        NUMBER:=NUMBER+2
    end
```

and

```
SUM:=2;
NUMBER:=4;
repeat
    SUM:=SUM+NUMBER;
    NUMBER:=NUMBER+2
until NUMBER>1000
```

In these two versions, the variable NUMBER has to be initialized and incremented by the programmer. If we had failed to increment NUMBER, we would have generated an infinite loop. The condition for exit from the loop has to be considered carefully; if in the second version we had written

```
until NUMBER>=1000
```

we would of course get a wrong answer. The problem of being "off by one" often plagues programmers. It is an easy mistake to make and can be hard to detect. In this instance, it is not easy to spot the error by just looking at the answer. To see that

```
until NUMBER>1000
```

is correct, one must make a careful argument about what happens in the loop. By looking at the computations, we see that when the test is made with NUMBER=1000, the last addition was done with NUMBER=998. Therefore, the loop should not be terminated with NUMBER=1000.

When one nests loops, regardless of their form, the variables and conditions that control the loops have to be distinct. The doubly nested loop

```
for I:=1 to 5 do
   for J:=3 downto 1 do
      write (I*J:3)
```

is correctly written and produces output

```
3 2 1 6 4 2 9 6 3 12 8 4 15 10 5
```

However,

```
for I:= 1 to 5 do
   for I:=3 downto 1 do
      X:=X+1
```

cannot possibly be correct. The same loop variable cannot be used for loops that are nested. It is, of course, possible to use the same variables for separate loops.

EXAMPLE 4.1

COURSE GRADE ASSIGNMENT

Instructors often use computers to help them in various bookkeeping chores connected with their courses. One such task is the determination of a course grade from the scores on tests and homework. To write a program for this example, we take the input for each student to consist of

```
student#, test1, test2, final
```

where test1 and test2 are the percent scores on two midterm tests and final is the percent score on the final examination. First, an overall percent score is computed by

```
% score=(test1 + test2)/4 + final/2
```

then a letter grade is assigned as follows

```
if % score is >=90 then letter grade is A
if % score >=80 but <90 then letter grade is B
if % score >=70 but <80 then letter grade is C
if % score >=60 but <70 then letter grade is D
if % score <60 then letter grade is F
```

The first level of the algorithm is

1. Repeat steps 2–5 until all data are processed.
2. Read (student#, test1, test2, final).
3. Compute % score.
4. Determine letter grade.
5. Write (student#, % score, letter grade).

Only Step 4 presents any challenge. The most direct way of determining the letter grade is to use a sequence of if statements. Alternatively, we might notice that the letter grade is determined by the group of ten percentage points into which the score falls. If we find the right category, we can then use a case statement. We use this second approach and refine Step 4 to

4.1. Category 0, 1, . . . , 9, 10 is determined by taking the integer part of the percentage score divided by ten.

```
program GRADE(input,output);
{ program to prepare course grades for course XXX
  using scores on two midterms and final }
var IDNO,TEST1,TEST2,FINAL,CATEGORY: integer;
    PERCENT:real;
    LETTERGRADE:char;
begin
  {print title for grade sheet}
  writeln('Course grades for XXX');
  { read in successive student records
  and find grade}
  while not eof do
    begin
      readln(IDNO,TEST1,TEST2,FINAL);
      {compute % score}
      PERCENT:=0.25*(TEST1+TEST2)+0.5*FINAL;
      {determine letter grade}
      CATEGORY:=trunc(PERCENT) div 10;
      case CATEGORY of
        9,10:LETTERGRADE:='A';
        8:LETTERGRADE:='B';
        7:LETTERGRADE:='C';
        6:LETTERGRADE:='D';
        0,1,2,3,4,5:LETTERGRADE:='F'
      end;
      writeln(IDNO:10,PERCENT:7:2,
              LETTERGRADE:5)
    end
end.
```

Sample input

```
75361    50    80    80
76621    70    90    90
77001    99    90    95
77200     5    15    15
78100    60    50    67
78225    70    90    80
78345   100   100   100
79001    60    80    70
79019    60    60    60
```

Output

```
Course grades for XXX
    75361   72.50    C
    76621   85.00    B
    77001   94.75    A
    77200   12.50    F
    78100   61.00    D
    78225   80.00    B
    78345  100.00    A
    79001   70.00    C
    79019   60.00    D
```

To terminate the program, we test for the end-of-file condition. Remember that eof becomes true after the last item in the input file has been read. This will work only if there are no other data in the input file.

We have used the case statement effectively. It does, however, require a simple computation to convert from the percent score to the right category. In fact, this way of determining the letter grade has some objectionable features. First, it does not correspond to the verbal description given; a sequence of if statements would be clearer. The use of the case statement here is an example of "tricky" coding—it looks elegant, but would be better solved by a more direct approach. It also has another flaw that will be discussed in Section 7.6.

The test examples given were not chosen at random, but were selected to test the program thoroughly. Each letter grade is represented at least once to assure that each part of the case statement is executed. There is one case with a score of 100% and several with scores at the boundary between two letter grades. You can see that even a simple example may require many test cases.

EXERCISES 4.1

1. Rewrite GRADE using repeat instead of while.
2. Would it be possible to write GRADE using counted loops?
3. Modify program GRADE so that the letter grade A+ is given to students with a score of 99% or higher.
4. Rewrite program GRADE so that the percent score is computed by

    % score=0.25*highest midterm score + 0.75*final

5. Design a complete set of test cases for the modifications of GRADE in Exercises 3 and 4.
6. Write a program that will print a table of sales tax for amounts from $.10 to $2.00 in increments of $.10 and sales tax rate of four percent, five percent, six percent, and seven percent. Arrange and label the table neatly.
7. The so-called *Fibonacci numbers* are defined by the sequence

    1, 1, 2, 3, 5, 8, . . .

    To get the next entry we always add the previous two. Thus 13, which is the sum of 5 and 8, would be the next element. Write a program that will print the first 30 Fibonacci numbers.
8. A string of left and right parentheses is said to be well formed if it is one that could occur in a proper arithmetic expression. For example, (( )) is well formed, but ( )) (is not. Specifically, the requirements are that
    a. There must be an equal number of left and right parentheses.
    b. Scanning from the left, the number of right parentheses must never exceed the number of left parentheses.

    Write a program that decides whether a given string of parentheses is well formed.
9. Given a line of text composed of uppercase letters and terminated by a period, write a program that will count the number of vowels. For example, if the input is

    THIS IS A LINE OF TEXT.

    the output should be

    Number of Vowels=7

10. Given an integer number between one and 100, write a program that will print the corresponding roman numeral.
11. Translate the statement

    ```
    for I:=1 to 10 do
      write(I)
    ```

    into the assembly language of Chapter 1.

12. Write a program that will print a chessboard large enough to play on.
13. Consider the following code:

```
X:=0;
repeat
  X:=X+0.1;
  writeln(X:4:1)
until X=1.0
```

One might expect that this would print the numbers 0.1, 0.2, . . . , 1.0. However, when it was actually run on the computer, it produced an infinite loop. Why? What can one conclude from this problem?

4.2

the goto statement

We have learned how to use if-then-else and the loop constructs to create alternate paths for computation. On occasion, it is also convenient to use an idea with a long and controversial history, the *goto statement.*

   In a program without if statements or loops, statements are executed in sequence, and we say that control proceeds normally. At times, we break this normal flow by *transferring* or *branching* to a statement not in line, as for example in a loop, or by transferring control directly to some specified statement. To express the latter, we need: (1) a statement to accomplish the transfer of control, and (2) a way of referring to particular statements in the program. The second requirement can be satisfied by allowing statements
labeled statement   to be numbered or **labeled,** while the first is accomplished by the use of the goto statement, written basically as

```
goto label
```

This causes a transfer to the statement whose label is given. Normal flow of control resumes at that point.

   The goto is much like the JUMP instruction in machine language. Some of the problems that occur with the goto come from the fact that it reflects the properties of the machine rather than the way in which people think.

   In some of the earlier languages, such as FORTRAN, the goto was the common way of controlling the flow of the computations. More recently, though, it has been recognized that the extensive use of goto is not conducive to good programming.

   In Pascal, statements may be labeled with an unsigned integer. This number is put before the statement and separated from it by a colon, as in

```
1:A:=B+2.5
```

label declaration   Numbers used as labels have to be defined in the ***label declaration*** of the form

> `label` *number1, number2,..., numbern*

where *number1, number2,..., numbern* are labels used in the program. The `label` declaration must precede all other declarations—that is, it must come immediately after the `program` heading.

All labels used in a program must be mentioned in a `label` declaration. Note, however, that numerical values occurring in a `case` statement are not labels and must not be declared as such.

The transfer is specified by a statement of the form

> `goto` *n*

where *n* is the label of the statement to which we want to transfer. Notice that `goto` is a single, reserved word.

The use of labels and `goto` is restricted. To prevent ambiguity, no two statements of a simple program can have the same label. Also, while `goto` can be used to transfer control within a loop or compound statement, or to transfer from inside one to outside, it cannot be used to transfer into a loop or compound statement.

When is `goto` useful? First, we can see that the `goto` statement, together with an `if` statement, can be used to construct loops. For example, the loop

> `while` *condition* `do`
>   *statement*

can be replaced by the equivalent

> `1:` `if` `not` *condition* `then` `goto 2;`
>   *statement;*
>   `goto 1;`
> `2:` ... *next statement* ...

But this roundabout programming is not natural to our thinking, and should be avoided.

In fact, if you are a careful programmer, you will need to use `goto` only rarely. Some even say that `goto` should not be used at all, but this idea seems extreme. Take for example a lengthy computation, the execution of which is to be terminated by some condition that can arise in several parts of the program. We can write

> `if` *condition*
>   `then` `goto 1;`
>   ·
>   ·
>   *statements;*
>   ·
>   ·

```
if condition
   then goto 1
      ⋅
      ⋅
1:end⋅
```

or we could dispense with the goto by writing

```
if not condition
   then
      ⋅
      ⋅
   statements;
      ⋅
      ⋅
if not condition
   then
      ⋅
      ⋅
```

but the goto seems a little more direct.

There is one apparent inconsistency in the first version. It seems that we have labeled end, which is not a statement. Actually, what is labeled is an empty statement inserted just before end. This implies that the statement immediately preceding the label has to be terminated by a semicolon.

The point remains that in a good program, labels and goto are rare. At most there should be one or two. If you find yourself writing a program with many labels, you are not attacking the problem correctly; you should go back and reconsider your approach.

EXERCISES 4.2   3¸4

1. How can an if-then-else statement be rewritten using if-then and goto? Is there any conceivable advantage in this?
2. Use goto and if-then to replace the repeat construct.
3. Suppose we are given input consisting of a number of lines, each containing several integer numbers. We would like to read the input and print it using the same arrangement by lines. Consider the following code:

```
repeat
1:read(A);
   write(A);
   until eoln;
   writeln;
   if not eof
   then goto 1
```

What is wrong with this? Write a proper and readable code for the problem.

4. Rewrite the following without `goto`:

```
if A=0
  then goto 1;
if A=1
  then goto 2;
1:A:=A+1;
goto 3;
2:A:A+3;
goto 1;
3: write(A)
```

4.3

programming with complicated decisions

flow of control In programming, ***flow of control*** refers to the sequence in which instructions are executed. In a straightline program, control proceeds from one statement to the next. The statements that break this normal flow are called *control* or *decision* constructs. In Pascal these are the `if`, `case`, `for`, `while`, `repeat` and `goto` statements.

Programs that implement complicated decisions generally have complicated control structures. Such programs can be difficult to write, test, and debug. Careful algorithm design with several levels of refinement is essential to prevent errors and confusion.

EXAMPLE 4.2

DATA VALIDATION

input validation Programs are usually written with the assumption that the data have certain properties. Input should always be checked to see that it satisfies these assumptions. But ***input validation*** is not necessarily a simple matter, as this example shows.

Assume that the data consist of strings of characters, with each string on a separate line and terminated by one or more blanks. A string is to be considered valid only if it has the form

leading part · trailing part

The leading and trailing parts must each be a bit string of length at least one. Thus, `0.1` and `1.01` are valid, but `1.`, `1..01`, and `.11` are not.

The output from this program should be a sequence of printed messages of the form

```
error in data on line xxx
```

where *xxx* is the line number of an invalid data item.

Before you read on, design your own algorithm for this problem. Then, compare it with the one we will give.

An informal description of the method for solving the problem is something like the following:

1. Read consecutive characters (called CH) until the first blank is encountered.
2. If any of these is a character other than '0', '1', '.', or ' ', the string is invalid.
3. We flag it by setting a variable VALID to false.
4. The number of leading and trailing bits must be one or more. These will be counted with variables LEAD and TRAIL.
5. There must be exactly one period; we will count that with POINT.

To identify lines we will use LINECOUNT. More formally, we have: Algorithm: first level:

1. LINECOUNT:=1.
2. Repeat Steps 3–10 until end of file.
3. Initialize VALID:=true, POINT:=0, LEAD:=0, and TRAIL:=0.
4. Repeat Steps 5–8 until CH=' '.
5. read(CH)
6. If CH is not '0', '1', '.', or ' ',
   then
7. VALID:=false.
   else
8. Process CH.
9. If string is not valid, print error indication.
10. Prepare for processing next line.

All steps except 8, and possibly 9 and 10, are sufficiently simple for use.

Second level refinement of Step 8:

8.1 If CH<>' ', use CH to update LEAD, TRAIL, and POINT.

Second level refinement of Step 9:

9.1 If VALID=false, LEAD=0, TRAIL=0, or POINT<>1, then print LINECOUNT with error message.

Second level refinement of Step 10:

10.1 LINECOUNT:=LINECOUNT+1.
10.2 Skip rest of line.

Step 8.1 is still not obvious enough, so we proceed to the next level. We have to express exactly how the current character (known to be '0', '1', or '.') affects the variables LEAD, TRAIL, and POINT. What is done will depend on the values of CH and POINT. A concise way of describing the

TABLE 4.1

**Decision table
for testing of
valid bit string**

	CH=0 or 1	CH=,
POINT=0	LEAD:=LEAD+1	POINT:=POINT+1
POINT=1	TRAIL:=TRAIL+1	POINT:=POINT+1

decision table

actions is by a table that shows what is to be done in all cases (Table 4.1). This is an example of a ***decision table.*** Decision tables are very effective for describing complicated control structure.

```
Program DATAVALID(input,output);
 var CH:char;
     LINECOUNT,LEAD,TRAIL,POINT:integer;
     VALID:boolean;
 begin
   LINECOUNT:=1;
   {outer loop for processing one line}
  repeat
    {initialize for each line}
    VALID:=true;
    POINT:=0;
    LEAD:=0;
    TRAIL:=0;
    {inner loop, process each character}
    repeat
      read(CH);
      if (CH<>'0') and (CH<>'1')
         and (CH<>',') and (CH<>' ')
        then VALID:=false
        else if CH<>' '
                then begin
                       if CH=','
                         then POINT:=POINT+1
                         else if POINT=0
                                then LEAD:=LEAD+1
                                else TRAIL:=
                                       TRAIL+1
                     end
    until CH=' ';
    if not(VALID) or (LEAD=0) or (TRAIL=0) or (POINT<>1)
      then writeln('error in data on line',LINECOUNT:4);
    LINECOUNT:=LINECOUNT+1;
    readln
  until eof
 end.
```

Sample input

```
1.0
1.
a.1
100.11
11.1.
1.0011
```

Output

```
error in data on line 2
error in data on line 3
error in data on line 5
```

Programs with complicated decision structures are difficult both to write and to read, because there are usually a number of nested control structures and it is not always clear which statements go with what condition. Proper indenting is essential. By drawing lines around groups of statements, we can get a clearer picture of what goes together. In this way, we can see at a glance the extent of loops, the various clauses of if statements, and so on. One way of doing this kind of *blocking* is shown in the program we've just discussed.

blocking

When the program becomes complicated, it is often difficult to see whether the code is completely correct. Before putting such a program on the computer, check your logic by working through a few cases using a pencil and paper. Identify the main variables and compute their values, simulating the action of the computer. This will let you discover some of the most obvious errors quickly. A typical check case for input 11.0 is given in Table 4.2.

After several more paper-and-pencil examples like this have convinced you that there are no errors in the program, you are ready to put it into the computer.

It is important that you check several examples by hand for all but the simplest programs. In the long run, it will save you much time.

TABLE 4.2

Check example for DATAVALID

CH	initial	1	1	.	0
VALID	true	true	true	true	true
POINT	0	0	0	1	1
LEAD	0	1	2	2	2
TRAIL	0	0	0	0	1

EXERCISES 4.3

1. Modify program DATAVALID using case statements instead of if-then-else to implement the decision table.
2. Modify the program DATAVALID to also accept as valid bit strings without period. That is, in addition to the previous cases, strings like 10011 should be considered valid.
3. Write a program that examines bit strings and flags as invalid all except those that consist of one or more copies of 001. Thus, your program should consider 001, 001001001, and 001001001001 valid, but 00100, and 0010010001 as invalid.
4. Write a program similar to that in Exercise 3, except that valid strings must consist of an odd number of repetitions of 001.
5. Do you think that the test cases given in Example 4.2 are sufficient to test the program fully? If not, what other test cases should be run?

further reading

Grogono, P. *Programming in Pascal,* Chapter 3. Reading, Mass.: Addison-Wesley Publishing Co., 1978.

Jensen, K., and Wirth, N. *Pascal User Manual and Report,* 2d. ed. User Manual, Chapter 4. New York: Springer-Verlag, 1974.

Koffman, E. B. *Problem Solving and Structured Programming in Pascal,* Chapter 2. Reading, Mass.: Addison-Wesley Publishing Co., 1981.

Schneider, G. M., Weingart, S. W., and Perlman, D. M. *An Introduction to Programming and Problem Solving with Pascal,* Chapter 5. New York: John Wiley & Sons, 1978.

Welsh, J., and Elder, J. *Introduction to Pascal,* Chapter 6. Englewood Cliffs, N. J.: Prentice-Hall, 1979.

data structure

A complex program often involves a large number of separate, but related data items. We express this by saying that the information is structured. The concept of a ***data structure*** is of extreme importance in all of computer science. This topic will run through most of the later chapters of this book. In this chapter, we will get our first look at some simple data structures.

5.1

unstructured data types

The data types we have encountered so far are integer, real, boolean, and character. In Pascal, these are called *primitive* types, because they are used to construct more complicated types. The power and usefulness of a language are very strongly influenced by the primitive data types it allows, and most languages have some provision for the types just mentioned. In this section, we will discuss some additional data types, with emphasis on those available in Pascal.

constants

We have already encountered constants and expressed them by simply writing their values. But often it is convenient to use symbolic names to represent constants. For example, if we need the value of π = 3.141596 in several places in a program, we can write PI wherever the value is needed. This gives us the further advantage that if at some time it becomes necessary to increase the number of significant digits, we need only replace the definition of PI instead of changing every statement where its value occurs. The use of symbolic constants can also improve the readability of a program. Using the identifier SQUAREROOT2 instead of 1.4142 allows us to see more clearly what a particular statement may mean.

The use of symbolic names for constants can, however, be carried too far. Using TWO instead of the more explicit 2 would probably detract from a program. Perhaps a good rule of thumb is to use symbolic names for constants whose value may have to be redefined at some stage or whose meaning is not obvious from the values.

Is there any difference between symbolic constants and variables? At first sight you may not think so, because one can assign a value to a variable, then use it in place of the constant. If a symbolic constant is to have any meaning, it must be treated differently from a variable. In particular, the value should in fact be constant and therefore not subject to change by the program.

In Pascal, symbolic constants are assigned values by the *const declaration,* the form of which is

```
const constname1 = value1;
      constname2 = value2;
          .
          .
          .
```

where *constname1, constname2, . . .* are the identifiers, and *value1, value2, . . .* the corresponding values, for example:

```
const PI=3.14159265;
      E=2.71828;
      PERIOD='.'
```

Because the value of a constant cannot be changed, its name must not appear on the left side of an assignment or in an input statement.

The const declaration must precede all other declarations except label.

Strictly speaking, symbolic constants are not a Pascal data type and cannot be used as data types are. For instance, an identifier cannot be declared to be of type const in a var declaration. The only thing that can be done is to use the const declaration to associate a fixed value with an identifier.

type declarations

To work with variables of some type other than primitive, we must first define a new type. Once we associate a name with the new type and describe its structure, we can declare variables to be of this type. The *type declaration* in Pascal is:

type *typename* = *typedescription*

Here, *typename* is an identifier referring to the type, while *typedescription* shows the structure. Variables are declared to have this type by

var *variable identifier* : *typename*

It is also possible to put the type declaration directly into the var declaration. The form for this is

var *variable identifier* : *typedescription*

The type declarations must be put before var, but after const.

variables with restricted ranges

When we declare the type of a variable to be, say, integer, we imply that the variable can take on any integer value (within the limits of the word size of the computer). At times it is convenient to have a mechanism for restricting values to a subset of the original type. Consider the grading program, Example 4.1, assuming that all student numbers are to be exactly five digits. No check was made in the program for this, an omission that could be considered an error. If a digit were to be dropped by mistake, we would not catch it. To save a test in the program it would be convenient to state directly that the number should be a five-digit positive number. One way to achieve this is to define a new type consisting of all integers with values within the range 10000–99999.

In Pascal we define such types, called *subrange types,* with the declaration

```
type FIVEDIGITS=10000..99999
```

The two dots indicate that we are talking about a range of consecutive integers. The declaration defines a type called FIVEDIGITS. We can then declare

```
var IDNO:FIVEDIGITS
```

which indicates that IDNO can take only values between 10000 and 99999. If an attempt is made to assign to IDNO, or any other variable of this type, a value outside the range, the computer will recognize the error and terminate the program. A better way to safeguard against such mistakes might be a check by the program, with appropriate action such as printing an error message and proceeding to the next case. Nonetheless, the subrange does provide some protection against input errors. Another advantage of a subrange type is that it gives the reader of the program a clear picture of what values certain variables can have.

We cannot define subrange types for reals, but it can be done for character variables. By writing

```
type UPPERCASE='A'..'Z'
```

we define a new type consisting of all uppercase letters. This is possible because Pascal associates the usual alphabetical order with the letters.

A subrange can consist of consecutive elements of type integer or char. Subrange types can also be defined for the following data type.

---

enumerated data type

This data type, also called *scalar,* allows variable names to be associated with certain identifiers chosen by the programmer. The type is defined with a declaration of the form

```
type typename=(identifier1, identifier2, . . . , identifiern)
```

Variables of such a type can take on as values any of the mentioned identifiers. For example, for

```
type QUALITY=(GOOD,FAIR,BAD,HOPELESS)
```

and

```
var SAMPLE:QUALITY
```

the statement

```
SAMPLE:=GOOD
```

is correct syntactically and assigns the identifier `GOOD` to the variable `SAMPLE`. Here, the identifiers are not variable names; one cannot, for instance, assign a value to `GOOD` or print it.

The identifiers in an enumerated type are considered ordered in the sequence given in the definition. The relational operators are defined for this data type; in our example, the expression

```
GOOD<BAD
```

is true, because `GOOD` comes before `BAD` in the enumeration of the identifiers associated with type `QUALITY`.

A function `ord` is also defined; it gives the place of the identifier in the enumeration (starting with 0). Thus, in the example, `ord(GOOD)` has value 0 and `ord(HOPELESS)` has the value 3.

The elements of an enumerated type can be used as selectors in `case` statements and as control variables in counted loops. In Pascal, the enumerated data type helps in writing some programs in a more explicit and readable form. Unfortunately, Pascal does not allow input and output for variables of such types, so that their usefulness is somewhat limited.

All types discussed so far are *unstructured;* that is, at the level of the programming language, the elements making up the type cannot be broken into smaller pieces. (Of course, it is true that, at the machine level, even a simple type like `integer` is represented by a number of bits and therefore has some structure. However, in the higher level language an integer is a single unit that cannot be divided.) Unstructured data types are necessary for any programming, but to be really useful a language must allow for the combination of simple types. The major structured types will be discussed in the next four sections.

EXERCISES 5.1

1. Rewrite program `GRADE` to use symbolic constants and subrange types where appropriate.
2. Determine which expressions or statements are legal for the following:

```
type COLOR=(RED,WHITE,BLUE,GREEN,PINK,YELLOW);
var PAINT:COLOR
```

```
a. ord(PINK)-ord(WHITE)
b. BLUE<GREEN
c. RED:=WHITE
d. COLOR=WHITE
e. PAINT:=BLUE
```

3. In Exercise 2, what identifiers are included in the subrange WHITE..PINK?

4. In Exercise 2, what is printed by

```
for I:=BLUE to YELLOW do
  write(ord(I))
```

5.2

sets

A *set* is a mathematical concept defined as a collection of elements. In mathematics, sets are represented by writing the elements in braces, as in {*a,b,c*}. The idea is very general, and its usefulness lies in the operations defined on sets.

1. Set union. Set *S* is the union of two sets *A* and *B* if it contains all elements either in *A* or in *B*.
2. Set intersection. Set *S* is the intersection of two sets *A* and *B* if it consists of all elements both in *A* and in *B*.
3. Set difference. The set difference between set *A* and set *B* is the set of all elements in *A* but not in *B*.

Take the case *A* = {*a,b,c,d*} and *B* = {*a,c,d,e*}. Then the union of *A* and *B* is {*a,b,c,d,e*}, the intersection of *A* and *B* is {*a,c,d*}, and the difference between *A* and *B* is {*b*}.

Two sets are said to be equal if they have the same elements. Set *A* is said to be included in a set *B* if all elements in *A* are also in *B*, but not necessarily vice versa.

Pascal provides a type set. Set types are established by

type *typename* = set of *setelement*

The *typename* is whatever identifier we choose for this new type, and *setelement* is the type of the elements that make up such sets. (Elements that can be used in a set are usually restricted to limited subranges of integer, char, or enumerated types.) All elements in a set must be of the same type. To assign values to sets we use various *set expressions*, starting with set constants. A set constant is given by writing the elements in square brackets. For example:

```
['A','B','C']
```

is the set consisting of the letters A, B, and C, while

```
[1..3,6]
```

is the set of integer numbers 1, 2, 3, and 6. The expression `[ ]` denotes the *empty set*, that is, the set with no elements. In the same fashion, using expressions instead of constants, we can define simple set expressions such as

```
Z:=3;
X:=[Z+1,Z+2]
```

The set X will consist of the integers 4 and 5.

Set operations are specified by expressions of the form

S *setoperator* T

where S and T are sets, and *setoperator* is one of the following operations symbols:

+	set union
−	set difference
*	set intersection
=	set equality
< >	set inequality
< =	set inclusion (*S* is a subset of *T*)
> =	set inclusion (*T* is a subset of *S*)

The first three of these operations yield other sets, while the last four give boolean expressions. In addition, we also have the operator `in`, which has two operands. The left one is an element and the right one is a set. The result is a boolean expression that is true if the element is in the set. We write this, for example, as

```
'A' in ['A','B','C']
```

or

```
'X' in ['R','S','T']
```

The first expression is true, the second, false. As a slightly more complicated case, consider

```
program SETTEST(input,output);
type CHARSET=set of char;
var SET1,SET2,SET3,SET4:CHARSET;
    S,X,Y,Z,W:boolean;
    LETTER1,LETTER2:char;
begin
  LETTER1:='A';
  LETTER2:='C';
  SET1:=[LETTER1..LETTER2];
```

```
SET2:=['B','E','F'];
SET3:=SET1+SET2;        A,B,C,E,F
SET4:=SET1*SET2;          B
X:='F' in SET3;         TRUE
Y:='F' in SET4;         FALSE
Z:=SET3<=SET4;          FALSE
W:=SET1>=SET4;          FALSE TRUE
S:='B' in SET1;         TRUE
writeln(S,X,Y,Z,W)
end.
```

The output produced by this program is

```
  S    X    Y    Z      W
true true false false true
```

The concept of a set is not only of mathematical interest, but very useful to the programmer. Consider the simple case where we read a character and want to determine (perhaps for input validation) whether it is an uppercase letter. Specifically, if CH is an uppercase letter, set boolean OK to true. Obviously, the code

```
if CH='A' then OK:=true;
if CH='B' then OK:=true;
if CH='C' then OK:=true;
     .
     .
     .
```

will work, but as a programmer you will get little praise for thinking of it. A better solution is

```
for CHECK:='A' to 'Z' do
  if CH=CHECK
    then OK:=true
```

But the shortest and most elegant solution is

```
if CH in ['A'..'Z']
  then OK:=true
```

We will have many occasions to use sets in such situations.

EXAMPLE 5.1

TEST CLASSIFICATION

In a certain experiment subjects are asked to take three tests. On each their performance is rated as 'A', 'B', or 'C'. An overall classification is then made as follows.

1. If the subject received at least one 'A' and no 'C', performance is rated 'good'.

2. If the subject received no 'A' and at least one 'C', performance is rated 'unacceptable'.
3. If neither 1. nor 2. apply, performance is rated 'fair'.

The input to this program will be several lines, each containing

```
ID SCORE1 SCORE2 SCORE3
```

where ID is a five-digit positive integer, and SCORE1, SCORE2, and SCORE3 will be characters 'A', 'B', or 'C'.

For each line of input, the output is to be

```
ID SCORE1 SCORE2 SCORE3 RATING
```

where RATING is 'good', 'fair', or 'unacceptable'.

Algorithm: Level 1

1. Repeat Steps 2–4 until end of file.
2. Read (ID,SCORE1,SCORE2,SCORE3).
3. Find RATING.
4. Write (ID,SCORE1,SCORE2,SCORE3,RATING).

Level 2 refinement of Step 3:

3.1. SCORESET:=[SCORE1,SCORE2,SCORE3]
3.2. If 'A' is in SCORESET and 'C' is not, RATING:= 'good'
3.3. If 'A' is not in SCORESET, but 'C' is, RATING:= 'unacceptable'
3.4. If neither 3.2 nor 3.3 hold, RATING:='FAIR'

```
program TESTRATING(input,output);
{program to rate overall performance
of subjects on three tests}
var ID:10000..99999;
    SCORE1,SCORE2,SCORE3:'A'..'C';
    RATING:(GOOD,FAIR,UNACC);
    SCORESET:set of char;
begin
  repeat
    {read data for each subject}
    readln(ID,SCORE1,SCORE2,SCORE3);
    SCORESET:=[SCORE1,SCORE2,SCORE3];
    {find rating}
    if ('A' in SCORESET) and (not('C' in SCORESET))
      then RATING:=GOOD
      else if (not('A' in SCORESET))
              and ('C' in SCORESET)
            then RATING:=UNACC
            else RATING:=FAIR;
    {output test scores and rating}
    write(ID:5,SCORE1:2,SCORE2:2,SCORE3:2);
```

```
        case RATING of
          GOOD:writeln('  good');
          FAIR:writeln('  fair');
          UNACC:writeln('  unacceptable')
        end
      until eof
    end.
```

Sample input

```
    88293ABC
    99002BBA
    75045BAC
    23456CCB
    34321AAB
    34527ACC
```

Output

```
    88293 A B C  fair
    99002 B B A  good
    75045 B A C  fair
    23456 C C B  unacceptable
    34321 A A B  good
    34527 A C C  fair
```

In this program, no explicit input validation is done, but the use of subrange types will cause a program termination for some illegal data. This is a quick way to assure that invalid data are detected, but it is not always usable. A single bad data item will terminate the whole job even though the rest of the data are acceptable. More explicit input validation can overcome the problem, but requires more work.

The use of an enumerated data type for RATING makes the program a little easier to understand.

EXERCISES 5.2

1. If

```
    S1:=['A',,'C','D'];
    S2:=['A','C','D','E']
```

what are the values of

a. S1*S2
b. S1-S2
c. S1<>S2
d. (S1=S2) or (not ('A' in (S1-S2)))
e. S1=['D','A','C','B']

2. What is wrong with the following expression?

   ```
   'A' not (in S1)
   ```

3. If T is boolean and S is a set of integers, which of the following statements are legal?

   a. `S:=S+1`
   b. `S:=S+[1]`
   c. `T:=S in [1]`
   d. `T:=S = [1]+[2]`

4. Let S be a set of uppercase letters. Write a program that will print all elements in S.
5. Reexamine the program in Example 4.2 to see if sets can be used to simplify the code.
6. Rewrite program TESTRATING without enumerated data types.
7. Rewrite program TESTRATING without using sets.
8. Modify program TESTRATING to print 'excellent' if the subject has received at least two 'A's and no 'C'.

5.3

arrays

The way in which data are organized in the computer reflects to a large extent how we think of their relationship. One of the simplest structures consists of a sequence of elements of the same type, related to each other by the order in which they are given. Mathematicians and scientists generally use the elegant *index* or *subscript* notation to represent such structures. Thus,

$$x_1, x_2, \ldots, x_{100}$$

stands for 100 elements. The x is the general name by which an element is known, while the subscript gives its position in the sequence. In programming the analogous structure is called an *array*.

one-dimensional arrays

A *one-dimensional array* is an ordered set of elements, all of which are of any defined type, but must all be the same type. Each element is referred to by the name of the array and an index. In programming languages, the index is usually written after the array name and enclosed in parentheses or brackets. The set of permissible index values is generally restricted and has to be specified by the programmer.

FIGURE 5.1

A one-dimensional array named ROW

ROW [1] [2] [3] [4] [5] [6] [7] [8] [9] [10] [11] [12]

Pascal names for arrays follow the usual rules for identifiers. The index is enclosed in brackets following the name, as in

```
A[5]
```

and

```
EMPLOYEE[17]
```

For our examples, the indices will generally be integer expressions, although Pascal also permits indexing with character expressions or variables of enumerated type.

When arrays are used, their type must be declared. In addition to stating what the element type is, we must also define the range of permissible indices. When integer indices are used, this range will be a subrange of the integers. To make ROW an array of real numbers, with indices ranging from 1 to 12, we can write

```
type ONEDIM=array[1..12] of real;
var ROW:ONEDIM
```

or in the abbreviated form as

```
var ROW:array[1..12] of real
```

We visualize arrays as a contiguous set of boxes, each of which can hold one element. For ROW as defined, we get Figure 5.1.

The subrange defined by 1..12 implies that indices between 1 and 12 are allowed, but anything outside this range is not. If in the program we refer to ROW[13] we would be in error. An *invalid index* message would be given by the computer and the program terminated.

invalid index

EXAMPLE 5.2

DETECTION OF DUPLICATES

Let us write a program that will take a sequence of integer numbers and determine whether or not it contains any duplicates. We will assume that each number is on a separate line and that the end of the data is the end of the file. Our program is to print yes if a duplicate is found and no otherwise.

Because each number has to be compared with every other number, all of them must be available at the same time. One way to do this is to store the items in an array, say, NUMBER.

Algorithm: Level 1

1. Read all numbers into array NUMBER and set COUNT to total number of items.
2. For I:=1 to COUNT−1, compare NUMBER[I] with all successive entries in array.
3. If no equality is found in Step 2, print 'no'.

Step 2 involves a separate loop, so it can be expanded to

2.1. For J:=I+1 to COUNT, if NUMBER[I]=NUMBER[J], print 'yes' and stop.

```
program DUPLICATE(input,output);
{program to detect duplicates in a
 sequence of integers}
label 1;
var I,J,COUNT:integer;
    NUMBER:array[1..1000] of integer;
begin
  {read in all data and count # of items}
  COUNT:=0;
  while not eof do
    begin
      COUNT:=COUNT+1;
      readln(NUMBER[COUNT])
    end;
  {nested loop for detecting duplicates}
  for I:=1 to COUNT−1 do
    for J:=I+1 to COUNT do
      if NUMBER[I]=NUMBER[J]
        then begin
               writeln('yes');
               goto 1
             end;
  {if there are no duplicates the
  above loops will
  not cause early termination—
  so we get to here}
  writeln('no');
1:end.
```

The limited use of the goto in this program is not objectionable; in fact, it is a natural way of terminating the computation as soon as a duplicate has been found. To find a duplicate, we compare the Ith number with the

Jth number, J going from I+1 to COUNT. The whole process is done for I from one to COUNT−1. This is most easily expressed with the doubly nested loop used in the program. To control these loops, we use the variables named I and J. Since they have no particular meaning other than as counters for the loops, it is acceptable to use such short names without mnemonic content. Because of the limit on the index range of the array NUMBER, this program cannot be used for more than 1000 numbers.

Let us now take a slightly different approach that uses sets. Instead of an array, we will use a set SEEN to save the successive numbers. At each step, we check to see if a new number is already in SEEN. If it is not, we put it in; if it is, we have found a duplicate.

```
program DUPLISET(input,output);
type SOMEINTEGER=1..9999;
var NUMBER:SOMEINTEGER;
    SEEN:set of SOMEINTEGER;
    DUPFOUND:boolean;
begin
  {start with an empty set }
  SEEN:=[];
  DUPFOUND:=false;
  while (not eof) and (not DUPFOUND) do
    begin
      readln(NUMBER);
      {check if number is already in set }
      if NUMBER in SEEN
        then DUPFOUND:=true
        {if not, put number in set }
        else SEEN:=SEEN+[NUMBER]
    end;
  if DUPFOUND
    then writeln('yes')
    else writeln('no')
end.
```

EXAMPLE 5.3

SORTING NUMBERS

Given a list of integer numbers x_1, x_2,..., x_N we want to sort the numbers in order of increasing values. Sorting of numerical or alphabetical information is of great importance in computer applications, and there are many efficient methods. Here, we will discuss a fairly simple algorithm; more will be said on this subject later.

If we were given the data, we would probably have no difficulty in finding a way to sort them, although not all of us would use the same approach. If the number of items is small, we might use a fairly un-systematic approach, but for a large amount of data and for designing an algorithm, we must use a well-defined process. One way is the following:

1. Store the items in an array.
2. Look through this array to find the smallest and move it to the first place of the array.
3. Repeat the process with the rest of the array, to get the second smallest item into second place.
4. Continue until the whole array is sorted.

This algorithm is easily programmed.

A slightly different algorithm is based on the following process:

1. Look at two adjacent entries of the array.
2. If they are not in order, interchange them.
3. Make a complete pass through the array, starting from the bottom.

This has the same effect as first finding the smallest value, then moving it to the top. Because in this method the smallest items "rise" to the top, the algorithm is usually called a ***bubblesort***.

bubblesort

To carry out the indicated interchanges we again utilize a double loop. We work through the array, doing the necessary interchanges, at the end of which the smallest element is on top. We repeat from the bottom to the second from top, then to the third from top, and so on. After N-1 passes, the list will be completely sorted. Schematically, we have:

Algorithm: Level 1

1. Read all items into array NUMBERS and set COUNT to total number of items.
2. For I:=1 to COUNT−1 do Step 3.
3. For J:=COUNT−1 down to I, compare NUMBERS[J] with NUMBERS[J+1]. If they are not in correct order, interchange them.
4. Print out sorted array NUMBERS.

Step 3, the interchange of two elements of an array, needs some elaboration. If NUMBERS[J] and NUMBERS[J+1] are to be interchanged, we cannot just write

```
NUMBERS[J]:=NUMBERS[J+1];
NUMBERS[J+1]:=NUMBERS[J]
```

because the first operation will destroy the original value of NUMBERS[J]. To get around this, we first copy NUMBERS[J+1] to some temporary location. Thus, the interchange in Step 3 is expanded to

```
3.1. TEMP:=NUMBERS[J+1]
3.2. NUMBERS[J+1]:=NUMBERS[J]
3.3. NUMBERS[J]:=TEMP
```

```
program BUBBLESORT(input,output);
{ program to sort an array of numbers by the
  bubblesort method— no more than ITEMLIMIT numbers
  can be sorted }
const ITEMLIMIT=100;
var I,J,TEMP,COUNT:integer;
    NUMBERS:array[1..ITEMLIMIT] of integer;
begin
  {input numbers, count, but do not accept more
  than ITEMLIMIT items }
  COUNT:=0;
  while (not eof) and (COUNT< ITEMLIMIT) do
    begin
      COUNT:=COUNT+1;
      read(NUMBERS[COUNT]);
      if eoln
        then readln
    end;
  {check that all data were read in }
  if(not eof)
    {not all items read }
    then begin
        writeln('error in BUBBLESORT');
        writeln('there are too many items')
      end
    else begin
        {all items read, sort array
        using successive interchanges }
        for I:=1 to COUNT-1 do
          for J:=COUNT-1 downto I do
            if NUMBERS[J+1]<NUMBERS[J]
              then begin
                    TEMP:=NUMBERS[J+1];
                    NUMBERS[J+1]:=NUMBERS[J];
                    NUMBERS[J]:=TEMP
                  end;
        {array sorted—print with title }
        writeln('Sorted Numbers');
        for I:=1 to COUNT do
          writeln(NUMBERS[I]:10)
      end
end.
```

There is a good deal of similarity between this program and the first version of Example 5.2. We have, however, been a little more careful in monitoring the input. A check is made, and if the list contains more than 100 items an error message is printed and the program terminated.

This program allows for input in which there are several numbers on a line. But care must be taken during input, because when the last numerical value has been read, the file marker will point to the end of line, but not to end of file. We cannot detect the end of file until another read is executed, which would give an incorrect value of COUNT. To get around the difficulty, we insert the statement

```
if eoln then readln
```

which will take us either to the next line or to the end of file whenever eoln is true. This implies, however, that the program will not work correctly if the last number on the last line is followed by one or more blanks.

multidimensional arrays

An array with a single index is said to be one-dimensional. *Multidimensional* arrays are arrays with two or more indices. The number of indices necessary to specify an element of an array is said to be its *dimension.*

The most useful are the *two-dimensional* arrays, which we can think of as a rectangular array of *rows* (first index) and *columns* (second index), illustrated in Figure 5.2. In mathematics, two-dimensional arrays are called *matrices*; in everyday language, the term *table* is more common. Arrays with three or more indices do occur in some scientific computations, but are relatively rare in other applications.

In Pascal, the elements of a two-dimensional array are referenced by two expressions separated by a comma and enclosed in square brackets. Thus

```
A[I,J]
```

FIGURE 5.2

A two-dimensional array A

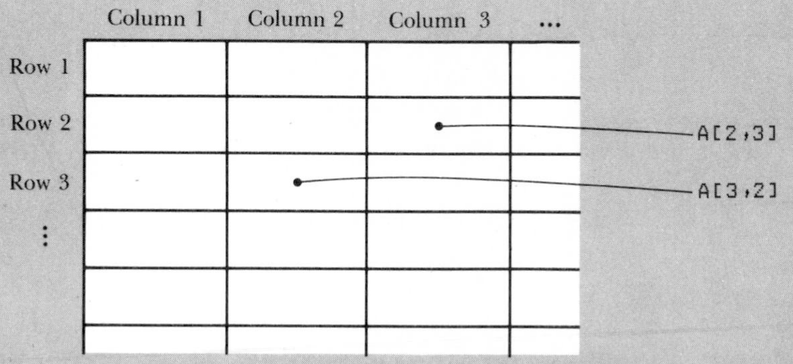

refers to the element in the I th row and the J th column of table A. The specification of the array type and its index ranges can be done in a t y p e declaration or, as in a one-dimensional array, directly in the v ar declaration. For example:

```
var A:array[1..20,2..40] of real
```

declares that A has 20 rows, numbered 1 to 20, and 39 columns, numbered 2 to 40. The elements of A are all real numbers.

When processing tabular data, the need often arises to find the location of certain entries. To search a table we may have to look at each element, a process accomplished easily by using a doubly nested loop. For example, suppose that we are given an array TABLE of type array[1..10,1..20] of real, and want to find the row and column (MAXROW and MAXCOL) where the largest value is located. For this, we can use the code

```
MAX:=TABLE[1,1];
MAXROW:=1;
MAXCOL:=1;
for I:=1 to 10 do
   for J:=1 to 20 do
      if TABLE[I,J]>MAX
         then begin
               MAX:=TABLE[I,J];
               MAXROW:=I;
               MAXCOL:=J
            end
```

Because tables occur in many practical problems, this algorithm is used often in various forms.

EXAMPLE 5.4

BUSINESS SALES FIGURES

A firm has collected figures on its income from sales during 1976 through 1980, with the amount given in units of ten thousand dollars for each month. We want to write a program to give a summary of the sales. The input for the program will be 5 lines, each with 12 decimal numbers. Line One represents 1976, Line Two, 1977, and so on. On each line, successive figures represent successive months of the year. The output should show

1. Yearly income for each year.
2. Average monthly income for each month.
3. The month and year for which the income was highest.

The computations are quite straightforward if we arrange the data in a table in which rows represent the years and columns represent months.

1. Read in all data.
2. Compute and print yearly sales.
3. Compute and print monthly averages.
4. Search rows and columns for maximum entry.
5. Print month, year, and income for best month.

Each of the steps is reasonably straightforward, although all involve a number of operations. A programmer with a little experience could implement them without further refinement. (However, try refining them for practice before reading on.)

```
Program SALES(input,output);
{ summary of sales figures for XYZ Co
  years 1976-1980 }
const FIRST=1976;
      LAST=1980;
var YEAR,MONTH,BESTYEAR,BESTMONTH:integer;
    SUM,MAX:real;
    SALES:array[FIRST..LAST,1..12] of real;
    YEARSALES:array[FIRST..LAST] of real;
    MONTHAV:array[1..12] of real;
begin
  {read in sales figures for years 1976-1980 }
  for YEAR:=FIRST to LAST do
    for MONTH:=1 to 12 do
      read (SALES[YEAR,MONTH]);
  {compute yearly sales }
  for YEAR:=FIRST to LAST do
    begin
      SUM:=0;
      for MONTH:=1 to 12 do
        SUM:=SUM+SALES[YEAR,MONTH];
      YEARSALES[YEAR]:=SUM
    end;
  {compute monthly averages }
  for MONTH:=1 to 12 do
    begin
      SUM:=0;
      for YEAR:=FIRST to LAST do
        SUM:=SUM+SALES[YEAR,MONTH];
      MONTHAV[MONTH]:=SUM/(LAST-FIRST+1)
    end;
  {search table for maximum entry }
  MAX:=0;
  for YEAR:=FIRST to LAST do
    for MONTH:=1 to 12 do
      if SALES[YEAR,MONTH]>MAX
```

```
                then begin
                        MAX:=SALES[YEAR,MONTH];
                        BESTYEAR:=YEAR;
                        BESTMONTH:=MONTH
                    end;
        {do all output}
        writeln(' Yearly sales');
        for YEAR:=FIRST to LAST do
            writeln(YEAR:6,YEARSALES[YEAR]:10:1);
        writeln(' Monthly averages');
        for MONTH:=1 to 12 do
            writeln(MONTH:3,MONTHAV[MONTH]:10:2);
        writeln(' Best sales');
        writeln(' YEAR',BESTYEAR:5,' MONTH',BESTMONTH:3,
                SALES[BESTYEAR,BESTMONTH]:10:1)
    end.
```

Sample input

```
15.1 16.0 10.3  9.4 10.0 11.2 13.5 14.6 13.5 12.6 11.2 13.1
14.3 13.5 13.5 14.2 14.6 12.6 11.3  9.4  9.3 10.3 11.4 12.3
15.0 14.6 12.8 12.5 12.5 14.6 16.8 16.9 15.8 14.7 14.0 13.7
12.1 13.2 12.5 12.4 14.6 14.6 13.7 12.4 12.2 11.1 10.4  9.3
13.1 12.6 13.2 13.3 13.2 12.5 12.5 12.2 13.1 14.2 15.5 15.6
```

Output

```
    Yearly sales
      1976     150.5
      1977     146.7
      1978     173.9
      1979     148.5
      1980     161.0
    Monthly averages
      1      13.92
      2      13.98
      3      12.46
      4      12.36
      5      12.98
      6      13.10
      7      13.56
      8      13.10
      9      12.78
     10      12.58
     11      12.50
     12      12.80
    Best sales
    YEAR 1978 MONTH  8     16.9
```

This example demonstrates the use of two-dimensional arrays. Most of the computations are performed in doubly nested loops, as one would expect when two-dimensional arrays are involved.

Notice that we have used the symbolic constants FIRST and LAST instead of 1976 and 1980. Symbolic constants make the program much more flexible. If we had used literal constants, the program would have worked just as well, but if we had wanted to use the program for another time period later on, we would have had to make extensive revisions.

EXERCISES 5.3

1. Design a method for sorting four integer numbers without using arrays. Is there any practical way to sort 100 integers without arrays?
2. Rewrite program DUPLICATE without goto.
3. Write a program for sorting using the algorithm suggested in the first paragraph of Example 5.3.
4. Another way of sorting is the *insertion* sort. The first element is inserted an empty array. The second element is inserted either before or after the first. We then find the proper place for successive elements in the array and insert them by moving the other elements. Write a program to sort numbers by this method.
5. Let A and B be two-dimensional arrays of integers, each containing N elements. From these, construct a merged and sorted array C. Array C should contain all elements in either A or B, but no duplicates. It should be sorted in order of increasing values.
6. An instructor in a computer science class is using the computer to score multiple choice tests. The input for each student in the class is

   student# q_1 q_2 ... q_n

   where q_1, q_2, ... , q_n are the student's answers to Questions 1 to n, each a number 1, 2, 3, 4, or 5. Also given is a key, which gives the correct answer for the questions. Write a program that will accept these data and print a table showing the number of questions right and wrong for each student.
7. The instructor in Exercise 6 also used the computer to detect possible cheating. Modify the program so that whenever two or more students have identical answers, their numbers are to be printed for further investigation.
8. What would happen in program DUPLICATE if it were used on data consisting of a single number?
9. Modify program SALES to give the following additional results:
   (a) All months in which sales were less than 10.0.
   (b) All four-month periods in which cumulative sales were less than 45.0.

10. In Example 5.3, explain why the program BUBBLESORT will not work correctly if the last item is followed by a blank. Find a way to correct this deficiency.
11. Modify program SALES so that output will print the actual names of the months instead of numerical values.
12. In program SALES, use an enumerated data type

```
MONTH:(JANUARY,FEBRUARY,MARCH,
       APRIL,MAY,JUNE,
       JULY,AUGUST,SEPTEMBER,
       OCTOBER,NOVEMBER,DECEMBER)
```

instead of

```
MONTH:integer
```

Rewrite the program with this. Does the new version have any advantages over the old one?
13. Examine the two programs DUPLICATE and DUPLISET in Example 5.2. In what way, other than implementation, do they differ? For example, does one work for some data for which the other does not?

5.4

processing character strings

Computers are used not only to do numerical computations, but also to process character data. In business applications, for example, the generation and updating of mailing lists, stock inventories, and others, alphabetical information is the rule rather than the exception.

A *character string* is a sequence of symbols including letters of the alphabet, digits, and special characters. Exactly what characters are available differs from language to language and system to system, but the set found on most terminal keyboards is usually included.

The manipulation of character data involves operations different from the usual numerical computations. The most common operations are

1. Comparing strings for equality, or establishing an order.
2. Combining strings.
3. Breaking up strings.
4. Finding patterns in strings.

Most of the popular programming languages do not have facilities for doing all of these directly, so that we must work character by character. One simple way, which is used in Pascal, is to store the string as a one-dimensional array, each element being a single character.

To define a character string, say WORD, in Pascal, we can use

```
var WORD:array[1..50] of char
```

This allows up to 50 characters in WORD. When this form is used, each character is stored in a separate word in memory. Now, as we know from our discussion in Chapter 1, a word in main memory can generally hold more than a single character, so that this method is a little wasteful in memory. If memory space is a problem, we can use the *"packed array"* structure, declared by

```
var WORD:packed array[1..50] of char
```

This will put as many characters as possible into each memory word.

With the array representation for character strings, the processing is conceptually simple, because the only operations we can perform are to compare single characters and to move them around within the string. However, there are a few practical problems.

When we manipulate names or words in English, the strings involved are of variable length. When we define a string, such as WORD, we reserve a certain amount of space, and thereby limit the length of the string. But this does not mean that the string will always have the maximum length; when words are combined or broken up, the length will change. Here the length of the string is itself a variable, so we will need to keep track of it explicitly in the program.

What order do we associate with alphabetical characters? Here we must adopt a convention: we think of all the characters as being arranged in a *collating sequence*. The collating sequence generally must preserve the normal alphabetical order—for example, A must come before B. Where digits and special characters fit into the collating sequence depends on the individual system.

If the collating sequence is needed for some problem, you will have to find what it is for your system. Pascal helps us in this by providing the functions ord and chr, which relate the collating sequence with the actual characters. The expression

```
ord(arg)
```

where arg is a single character, has an integer value that is the position of arg in the collating sequence. Because alphabetical order is preserved in the collating sequence, the expression

```
ord('C')-ord('A')
```

has the value 2, as expected.

The inverse of ord is chr. The expression

```
chr(i)
```

where i is an integer expression, gives the character in the ith position in the collating sequence.

Actually, Pascal provides some additional power for string processing. When strings are stored as packed arrays of the form

```
packed array[1..N] of char
```

they can, for the purpose of some operations, be considered as units. These operations are assignment, comparison, including order, and output. For comparison, the symbol = denotes equality, while < and > relate to the so-called *lexicographic* order. In this dictionary-like ordering,

```
'ABC'<'ABD'
```

and

```
'CD'<'CDE'   can't do this must be 'CD_'
```

are both true.

A short example will demonstrate some simple Pascal string operations.

```
program STRINGTEST(input,output);
type STRING=packed array[1..3] of char;
var X,Y,Z:STRING;
    TEST1,TEST2,TEST3:boolean;
begin
  X:='ABC';
  Y:='ABD';
  Z:='ABE';
  TEST1:=(X=Y);
  TEST2:=(X>Y);
  TEST3:=(X<Z);
  writeln(TEST1,TEST2,TEST3);
  writeln(X:4,Y:4,Z:4)
end.
```

The output produced by this program is

```
    false     false     true
ABC ABD ABE
```

Pascal string operations are quite useful in some circumstances. While they do not give us anything that could not be achieved with character-by-character processing, they do allow us to express certain operations more concisely and with less effort.

EXAMPLE 5.5

TRANSLATING FROM ENGLISH INTO PIG LATIN

Pig latin is a popular secret language of children. If a word starts with a vowel (A, E, I, O, or U), "ay" is added to the end of the word. If the word begins with a consonant, the consonant (or consonants) is moved to the end of the word and "ay" is appended. Let us write a program to translate into pig latin. We will assume that we have a sentence of words composed of uppercase letters separated by single blanks. The sentence will be contained on a single line and terminated by a period.

An algorithm in pseudolanguage is

1. Read in word plus extra character (blank or period) and check for valid characters.
2. Find leading consonants.
3. Print part of word after leading consonants.
4. Print leading part, followed by 'AY'.
5. Print extra character.
6. If extra character is '.' then stop; otherwise repeat from Step 1.

```
program PIGLATIN(input,output);
{ program to translate from English
  into Piglatin }
label 1;
const MAXLEN=20;
type CHARSET=set of char;
var I,LENGTH,LEAD:integer;
    LETTER:char;
    WORD:array[1..MAXLEN] of char;
    UPPERCASE,VOWEL:CHARSET;
begin
  {define permissible characters and vowels}
  UPPERCASE:=['A'..'Z'];
  VOWEL:=['A','E','I','O','U'];
  repeat
    {read word until blank or
     period is found- check that characters
     are upper case letters}
    LENGTH:=0;
    repeat
      LENGTH:=LENGTH+1;
      read(LETTER);
      if not(LETTER in (UPPERCASE+[' ','.']))
        then begin
                writeln('incorrect input');
                goto 1
             end;
      WORD[LENGTH]:=LETTER
    until ((LETTER=' ') or (LETTER='.'));
    {count number of leading consonants}
    LEAD:=1;
    while not(WORD[LEAD] in VOWEL) do
      LEAD:=LEAD+1;
```

```
    {print second part of word }
    for I:=LEAD to LENGTH-1 do
      write(WORD[I]);
    {followed by consonant part}
    for I:= 1 to LEAD-1 do
      write(WORD[I]);
    {followed by 'AY' }
    write('AY');
    {followed by extra character}
    write(WORD[LENGTH]);
    {until we reach the end of the sentence}
  until (WORD[LENGTH]=',');
  writeln;
1:end.
```

Sample input

```
    THIS IS A TEST OF PIGLATIN.
```

Output

```
    ISTHAY ISAY AAY ESTTAY OFAY IGLATINPAY.
```

This program does one thing that all good programs should—it checks the input. In particular, it checks that the input words contain only uppercase letters. For this, as well as for finding vowels, sets can be used effectively. The program cannot accommodate words longer than 20 letters, but the restriction is easily removed by changing the constant MAXLENGTH.

EXERCISES 5.4

1. Write a program to combine two strings. That is, for the two strings S1 and S2, the new string should consist of the characters of S1 followed by those of S2.
2. Write a program to detect whether one string is contained in another.
3. A palindrome is a word that is the same when read forward or backward. "Madam" and "radar" are palindromes. Write a program to check whether or not a given string is a palindrome.
4. A "stutter word" is a word made up entirely of two or more copies of a single pattern. 'ABCABC' and 'ABABAB' are stutter words; 'ABABA' is not. Write a program to determine whether a given string is a stutter word.
5. A sentence is a set of words separated by blanks and terminated by a period. Write a program that will accept a sentence and determine a

word length frequency count. For example, for the sentence

`This is a sample input to test the program.`

the output should be

```
Wordlength  Number
     1        1
     2        2
     3        1
     4        2
     5        1
     6        1
     7        1
```

6. Write a program to sort character strings in lexicographical order.
7. The letter 'Y' plays a dual role. If it occurs as the first letter, it is considered a consonant; otherwise, it is considered a vowel. Modify program PIGLATIN to handle the letter 'Y' properly.
8. What happens when PIGLATIN is applied to words without vowels?
9. What happens in PIGLATIN when words are separated by more than one blank?
10. Rewrite PIGLATIN without using sets.
11. Write a program to translate from pig latin into English.
12. Write a program to print all the stanzas of "The Twelve Days of Christmas."
13. Write a program that accepts sentences as in Exercise 5 and provides a table of frequency distribution for the letters of the alphabet.
14. Write a program that will accept your week's class schedule in a form such as the following:

```
MON  9 MU3A
MON 11 CS29B
```

and print a schedule in the usual timetable form. Give careful thought to what form the input should have and how to produce a timetable with a pleasing appearance. There are many options here. The quality of your answer will depend on how well you solve the input/output problem.
15. Find out the complete collating sequence for your system.

5.5

records

An array is the simplest type of data structure. Its elements are all of the same type, and they are related by a straightforward indexing scheme. In many applications, this is insufficient. Let us again go back to the data that a business firm might have for its employees. The data for an employee could consist of his or her name, which is a character string, the social security number, an integer, the home address, perhaps composed of several sections, and so on. We see here that the parts of the data are all of different types. Some adjustment could be made, for example, by using an employee number instead of the name. Unfortunately, to do so would complicate matters for the people who handle the information. What we really need is a data structure that can include elements of different types. Such a structure is called a *record.*

A record consists of several parts, generally called *fields,* having some relation to each other. To illustrate, our employee's record is depicted in Figure 5.3. This record consists of three parts: the name, the social security number, and the employee's address. Each part of the record has an assigned meaning and may also be subdivided. In this case, the name might be split into a first name, a middle initial, and a last name, while the employee's address has five parts (Figure 5.4). The resulting structure is usually called a *tree.* The end points are the *leaves.* Note that all the information is contained in the leaves, and that the rest of the structure gives meaning to the information in the leaves.

Pascal provides a special data type for records. To specify the structure of a record we define it in a `type` declaration. To represent the structure in Figure 5.3, we might define a type by

```
type EMPLOYEE=record
              NAME:array[1..50] of char;
              SOCSEC:integer;
              ADDRESS:array[1..100] of char
          end
```

We now have a new type, called `EMPLOYEE`. The descriptors `NAME`, `SOCSEC`, and `ADDRESS` are the names of the fields of such records. Variables of this type can take on values consisting of three different parts, as defined. Note that the description of the components of the record is *field list* bracketed by `record` and `end`. This is called the *field list.*

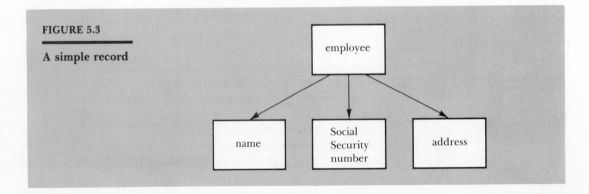

FIGURE 5.3

A simple record

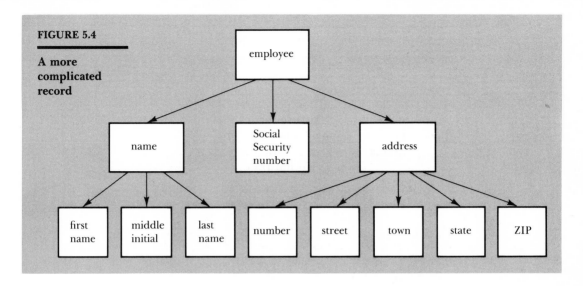

FIGURE 5.4

A more complicated record

Suppose that we now want to construct a more complicated situation, such as the one shown in Figure 5.4. In this case the name and the address are themselves records, expressed in Pascal by

```
type EMPLOYEE=
  record
    NAME:record
            FIRST:array[1..10] of char;
            MI:char;
            LAST:array[1..30] of char
         end;
    SOCSEC:integer;
    ADDRESS:record
            NO:integer;
            STREET:array[1..20] of char;
            TOWN:array[1..20] of char;
            STATE:array[1..2] of char;
            ZIP:integer
          end
  end
```

Take a close look at the syntax of this declaration, especially all the colons and semicolons. Essentially, a semicolon separates each part of the record declaration from the next, but there is no semicolon between the last part and `end`. When a declaration of a part is again a record, it must be separated from the others by a semicolon. That is why there is a semicolon between `end` and `SOCSEC`, but none between the second to last and last `end`.

Having declared this new type, we can now define variables and arrays with such elements, such as

```
var STAFF:array[1..100] of EMPLOYEE
```

establishing an array of records.

To refer to the components of a record we must give the name of the record (not the name of the type!), separated by a period from the field descriptor. For example, if we have the declarations

```
type AUTOMOBILE=record
                ENGINENO:integer;
                MODELNAME:array[1..20] of char;
                PRICE:real
              end;
var CHEVY,DATSUN,VW:AUTOMOBILE
```

then

```
DATSUN.PRICE
```

refers to the PRICE part of the record DATSUN, while

```
VW.MODELNAME[1]
```

is the first character in MODELNAME of VW.

When a component is itself a record, the field descriptor has a two-part form, consisting of the record identifier and the second level field descriptor. Every identifier, except the first-level one, is as it appears in the type declaration. The first-level identifier is the name of the record as given in the var declaration. In the company records example, the middle initial of the fifteenth record is referred to by

```
STAFF[15].NAME.MI
```

Suppose we now want to assign values to the various parts of a record, for example

```
STAFF[1].NAME.MI:='Q';
STAFF[1].SOCSEC:=131368654;
STAFF[1].ADDRESS.ZIP:=95616
```

with statement

This is quite wordy because the record identifier has to be repeated several times. A useful abbreviation is given by the *with statement,* which can be used to write

```
with STAFF[1] do
  begin
    NAME.MI:='Q';
    SOCSEC:=131368654;
    ADDRESS.ZIP:=95616
  end
```

The general form of the `with` statement is

```
with recordid do
    statement
```

Here *recordid* is the name of a record variable. Every reference to a field descriptor implies the record name given after `with`. For records with several levels, the record identifier may include higher level field descriptors; for example

```
with STAFF[1].NAME do
    MI:='Q'
```

This can also be written using two nested `with` statements:

```
with STAFF[1] do
    with NAME do
        MI:='Q'
```

EXAMPLE 5.6

INVENTORY UPDATING

A common business application of computers involves the automatic handling of a firm's inventory. This includes keeping track of the number of units of various items in stock and reordering when a particular item falls below a minimal level. In this example, the inventory consists of a number of records for various parts (of some unspecified machine) in stock. Each part is described by (1) a part number, (2) a verbal description, (3) minimal number to be stocked, and (4) the name of the supplier. We assume that the input will consist of N records, each describing the current stock for one part. We will simplify a little bit by assuming that N is known and fixed. This input we will call the *master input.* Following the master input we will have the *activity information,* giving the part number and the number used for parts for which there has been a change in inventory. The activity information will be used to bring the inventory up to date. The updated information is to be printed. Also, for each part for which the number in stock has fallen below the minimal level, we will print the part number and the number to be ordered to bring the stock up to minimal level. Each record in the master input will consist of

1. Part number: 0 to 9999.
2. Part description: character string of ten characters.
3. Number in stock: 0 to 9999.
4. Minimal number: 0 to 9999.
5. Supplier name: character string of ten characters.

The activity information will consist of

1. Part number: 0 to 9999.
2. Number used: 0 to 9999.

A sketch of the algorithm is straightforward.

1. Read master input consisting of N records.
2. For each item in activity list do Steps 3–6.
3. For I:=1 to N do 4–6.
4. Compare part number of Ith record with part number for item in activity list.
5. If they match, update number in stock for Ith part.
6. If number in stock is less than the minimal number for Ith item, write part number and number to be ordered.
7. Write updated master information.

```
program INVENTORY(input,output);
const N=4;
type FOURDIGITS=0..9999;
     PART=record
             NUMBER:FOURDIGITS;
             PARTNAME:packed array[1..10] of char;
             INSTOCK:FOURDIGITS;
             MINIMAL:FOURDIGITS;
             SUPPLIER:packed array[1..10] of char
          end;
var I,J,PARTNO,NOUSED:integer;
    STOCK:array[1..N] of PART;
begin
   { read in master list }
   for I:=1 to N do
     with STOCK[I] do
       begin
         read(NUMBER);
         for J:=1 to 10 do
           read(PARTNAME[J]);
         read(INSTOCK,MINIMAL);
         for J:=1 to 10 do
           read(SUPPLIER[J]);
       end;
{prepare order list and update master}
writeln;
writeln('Order List');
{ read in item from activity list
search master list for match
when match is found update master
if # of items in stock is less than
minimal, put in order list }
```

```
while not eof do
  begin
    {read item from activity list}
    readln(PARTNO,NOUSED);
    {search master list for matching part number}
    for I:=1 to N do
        with STOCK[I] do
          if NUMBER=PARTNO
            then begin
                   INSTOCK:=INSTOCK-NOUSED;
                   if INSTOCK<MINIMAL
                     then writeln(NUMBER:6,
                              MINIMAL-INSTOCK:6)
                 end
  end;
{print updated master list }
writeln;
writeln('updated master list');
for I:=1 to N do
  with STOCK[I] do
      writeln(NUMBER:6,PARTNAME:12,INSTOCK:6,
              MINIMAL:6,SUPPLIER:12);
end.
```

Sample input

```
7643      latch 700 600      whizco
9001       hose  20  15      whizco
9057      cable  35  30      conco
9090       bolt 150 120      conco
9001 10
9057  5
7643 300
```

Output

```
Order List
  9001      5
  7643    200

updated master list
  7643      latch     400   600      whizco
  9001       hose      10    15      whizco
  9057      cable      30    30      conco
  9090       bolt     150   120      conco
```

By using records, we have made the program quite self-explanatory, in the sense that we refer to data items in the program very much in the way we think. Several other points should be noted. We have made N a symbolic constant. As new parts are added or old ones removed, its value may change. We then simply change the declaration defining N. We have also defined a type FOURDIGITS. This will provide some monitoring of input; if the wrong part number were typed by mistake, the program might detect the error. In parts of the program we have used with statements to save some writing.

There are some potential dangers in writing the program, as we have done, for fixed N. If by mistake there were not exactly N records in the master input, the master information and the activity list would be confused, perhaps giving incorrect results. It would be much safer to mark in some way the end of the master input and then have the program check it. (We cannot, of course, use the end-of-file condition, because the activity information still follows.) One way of dealing with the difficulty is to include a fictitious and identifiable record at the end of the data—perhaps a record with a negative part number. This would clearly identify the end of the master file.

In the program we have used string operations to print PARTNAME and SUPPLIER. Unfortunately, Pascal does not allow string input, therefore PARTNAME and SUPPLIER have to be read character by character.

EXERCISES 5.5

1. The inventory for a used car lot consists of descriptions of the automobiles in the form

   MAKE   MODEL   YEAR   PRICE

   For example:

   ```
   FORD   MUSTANG  1976   2500
   VW     RABBIT   1980   4500
   FIAT   SPIDER   1972   1500
     .
     .
     .
   ```

   Write a program to read the whole inventory and print a list of the cars in order of increasing price.
2. What other checks should be added to INVENTORY to guard against bad input?
3. Modify Example 5.6 so that the computer will print a form letter ordering the required parts, say of the form

   ```
   Dear (supplier):
   Please send xxx of the following
   item:(item description)
                   Sincerely, (etc.)
   ```

   Do this for each part that requires an order.

4. If, in Exercise 3, several parts are to be ordered from the same supplier, modify your program so that only one letter, ordering all the required parts, is sent to each supplier.

further reading

Cherry, G. W. *Pascal Programming Structures,* Chapter 6. Reston, Va.: Reston Publishing Co., 1980.

Grogono, P. *Programming in Pascal,* Chapter 6. Reading, Mass.: Addison-Wesley Publishing Co., 1974.

Jensen, K., and Wirth, N. *Pascal User Manual and Report,* 2d. ed., User Manual, Chapters 6 and 7. New York: Springer-Verlag, 1974.

Koffman, E. B. *Problem Solving and Structured Programming in Pascal,* Chapters 6 and 7. Reading, Mass: Addison-Wesley Publishing Co., 1981.

Schneider, G. M., Weingart, S. W., and Perlman, D. M. *An Introduction to Programming and Problem Solving with Pascal,* Chapter 7. New York: John Wiley & Sons, 1978.

Welsh, J., and Elder, J. *Introduction to Pascal,* Chapters 9, 10, and 11. Englewood Cliffs, N.J.: Prentice-Hall, 1979.

Consider the following two situations:

1. In a certain program, several arrays of numbers are sorted—say, array A first, then array B, and finally array C. We already know algorithms for sorting, such as the bubblesort, so we first write the code for sorting A, then later repeat it with appropriate changes for sorting B and C. This is straightforward, but it requires that we use nearly identical codes for all three arrays. We could save effort if it were possible to write the code only once, then somehow apply it in turn to A, B, and C.

2. A manager of a large programming project wants to divide the work among several programmers. To avoid confusion, he or she must make each part as independent as possible from the others. How can a program, which is a single task, be divided into independent subproblems?

What we need to solve these two problems, as well as many others, is a way of splitting a program into parts that can be developed independently and eventually integrated into a unit. Such independent parts are called *subprograms*.

A subprogram can perform the same actions a program does: (1) accept data, (2) carry out some computations, and (3) return results. A subprogram, however, is used by the program for a specific purpose. The subprogram receives data from the program and returns results to it. We can think of the program as the boss who issues instructions to a subordinate; when the task is completed, the subordinate returns the results to the boss. We say that the program *calls* or *invokes* the subprogram. The subprogram performs a task, then *returns* control to the program. This may happen in several places in the program. Each time the subprogram is called, control returns to the place from which the call was made (Figure 6.1). A subprogram may also have its own subordinates (Figure 6.2). There are two major types of subprograms: *functions* and *procedures*.

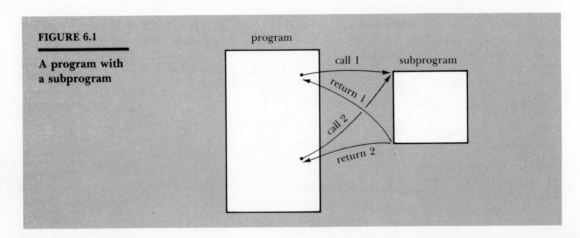

FIGURE 6.1

A program with a subprogram

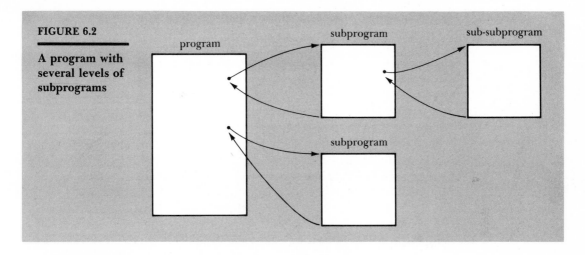

FIGURE 6.2

A program with several levels of subprograms

6.1

functions

In mathematics, a function is a rule which, when given one or more values, called *arguments,* produces a *result,* the value of the function for the given arguments. The rule defining the function can be given in many forms, for example:

$$f(x) = \frac{x}{1 + x^2}$$

formal parameter

Here, f is the name of the function and x is the argument. Note, however, that no specific value is associated with x; it is a **formal parameter** used in defining the recipe for computing the function. To evaluate f we must give an *actual value* to x; with this value we can then compute the result. With $x = 3$ we get the value 0.3, which we express by writing

$$f(3) = 0.3$$

A function may have several arguments. Thus

$$f(x, y) = \frac{x + y}{\sqrt{x} + \sqrt{y}}$$

is a function of two arguments. However, only a single, unique value is associated with the function for any given set of arguments. In mathematics, we have *standard* or predefined functions, as well as those which we define ourselves. In the example, the square root function is predefined.

Pascal has a number of *intrinsic* or "built-in" functions. A list of the more important ones was given in Section 2.2. These are predefined in the sense that the programs used to evaluate them are part of the system. We use these functions by writing their names, with the appropriate arguments, in expressions such as

```
sqrt(B+cos(X))
```

When the expression is evaluated, the value of X is first given to the cosine subprogram and `cos(X)` is computed. The value of `B+cos(X)` is then used as argument for the square root function, which evaluates the final result. Each function is invoked by using its name in an expression, with the actual arguments enclosed in parentheses.

To construct any function, we must give the sequence of steps that define it. In this we need to follow some conventions:

1. The first instruction of a function subprogram is of the form

   function *functionname(par1;par2; . . . ; parn):resulttype*

   with the following requirements. First, *functionname* is the name associated with the function. It must be a legal Pascal identifier. Second, *par1;par2; . . . ;parn* are the descriptions of the formal parameters, including their names and types. The general form of this description is

   parametername **:** *typeidentifier*

   where *parametername* and *typeidentifier* are Pascal identifiers. Finally, *resulttype* is the type of the value associated with the function. It must be an unstructured type.

2. The body of the function subprogram is arranged like that of a program. First come all the declarations in the proper order. All labels, constants, types, and variables used (except the formal parameters) must be declared in the function body. The body of the function is terminated by `end`.

3. To assign a value to the function, the body of the function must contain at least one statement of the form

   functionname **:** *= expression*

   The value of the expression on the right will be the value of the function.

For the example

$$f(x) = \frac{x}{1 + x^2}$$

the Pascal code is

```
function F(X:real):real;
begin
  F:=X/(1+X*X)
end
```

while for

$$f(x, y) = \frac{x + y}{\sqrt{x} + \sqrt{y}}$$

we could write

```
function F(X:real;Y:real):real;
begin
  F:=(X+Y)/(sqrt(X)+sqrt(Y))
end
```

Because neither of these examples involves any variables other than the formal parameters, no declarations are needed. In the second case, the definition of the function uses the intrinsic square root function. In general, a function can be defined in terms of other functions (with a few conditions, which will be discussed later).

EXAMPLE 6.1

A SIMPLE FUNCTION

For X and Y integers, a function GREATER is to have value true if X is greater than Y, and false otherwise. The function GREATER can take only boolean values, hence its type is boolean. The Pascal code for this function is

```
function GREATER(X,Y:integer):boolean;
begin
  if X>Y
    then GREATER:=true
    else GREATER:=false
end
```

We have used here a convenient shorthand notation, writing X,Y:integer instead of X:integer;Y:integer. Typical values for this function are

```
GREATER(5,4) = true
GREATER(3,5) = false
GREATER(4,15 div 3) = false
```

The arguments for a function need not be of a primitive type, but can be of any defined structured type, as is demonstrated in the next example.

EXAMPLE 6.2

THE MEAN OF A SET OF NUMBERS

Given a set of integer numbers $x_1, x_2, \ldots, x_N$, write a function subprogram to compute the mean

$$m = \frac{1}{N} (x_1 + x_2 + \cdots + x_N)$$

$$= \frac{1}{N} \sum_{i=1}^{N} x_i$$

We will assume that the numbers are stored in positions 1–N of a one-dimensional array. The function will then have two arguments, an integer N, and the name of the array in which the numbers are stored. The code for the function subprogram is

```
function MEAN(N:integer;X:DATAVALUES):real;
var I,SUM:integer;
begin
  SUM:=0;
  for I:=1 to N do
    SUM:=SUM+X[I];
  MEAN:=SUM/N
end
```

With this function definition, the data type DATAVALUES has to be defined, for example by

```
type DATAVALUES=array[1..100] of integer
```

The type specification in a subprogram header must be done with a type identifier, not a type description. It is incorrect to write

```
function MEAN(N:integer;
              X:array[1..100] of integer):real
```

The code for the function uses two variables, SUM and I, which are used entirely for bookeeping within the subprogram. Because they are not mentioned in the parameter list, they have to be declared inside the subprogram.

Functions can have many arguments, but only one result, the value of the function. This limits their use, although they are frequently encountered in scientific computations. A more powerful concept is provided by a procedure discussed in the next section.

EXERCISES 6.1

1. For the function

```
function F(X,Y:integer):boolean;
begin
   if (X mod Y)=0
      then F:=true
      else F:=false
end
```

give the values of F(3,2), F(18,6), and F(12,trunc (sqrt(4.1))). What is F(3.1,2.5)?

For each of the following, write the code for the function subprogram.

2. For three arguments x,y,z, let $f(x,y,z)$ be the ratio of the smallest to the largest of the three numbers.
3. For a given positive integer n, let

$$f(n) = 1 + \sum_{i=1}^{n} \frac{1}{i^2}$$

4. For a given positive integer n let $f(n)$ be a boolean function with value true if n is a prime number and false otherwise.
5. For positive real numbers x,y,z, let $f(x,y,z)$ be a boolean function whose value is true if and only if there is a triangle whose sides are x,y,z. (For a set of three numbers to represent the sides of a triangle, the sum of any pair of numbers must be larger than the third.)
6. Given a character string S of uppercase letters, let F(S) be an integer function whose value is the number of double consonants in S. For example:

F('MASSACHUSETTS')=2

7. Given a set S of uppercase letters, let F(S) be the number of elements in S.
8. In Example 6.2, if X[1]=3, X[2]=4, X[3]=5, X[4]=1, and X[5]=6, what are the values of MEAN(4,X) and MEAN(5,X)?

6.2

procedures

A procedure is a subprogram that will carry out a specified process. No value is associated with the name of the procedure, hence it cannot occur in an expression. A procedure is called by writing its name, say, SORT, to show that a procedure named SORT is to be used. When the procedure is invoked, the steps defining it are carried out and then control returned to the calling program.

To handle the communication between the procedure and the calling program, we use a parameter list, as in functions. But now we must specify not only the input to the subprogram, but also the results returned. A sorting procedure might be called by

    SORT(ARRAYIN,SORTED)

indicating that array ARRAYIN is to be sorted and the results are to be placed in another array called SORTED. Here is the main distinction between functions and procedures. A function gives only one result, the value associated with the function. Because the value is used in an expression, it must be of a simple type (it cannot be an array, for example). Procedures, on the other hand, can produce many results of different types.

The heading of a procedure in Pascal is of the form

    procedure *procedurename* (*par*1;*par*2; . . . ; *parn*)

where *procedurename* is the name of the procedure. The description of the formal parameters through *par*1;*par*2; . . . ; *parn* is the same as for functions—except that parameters representing results returned by the procedure are prefixed with var. For a sorting procedure, the heading might be

    procedure SORT(N:integer;ARRAYIN:NUMBERS;
                   var SORTED:NUMBERS)

where NUMBERS must be a defined data type, for example

    type NUMBERS=array[1..1000] of real

The distinction between the parameters preceded by var and parameters that are not is a little more complicated than just the difference between input to the procedure and results returned. We will come back to this point in Section 6.4.

All other rules for defining a procedure are the same as for functions, except that there is no statement of the form

    procedurename : = *expression*

because no value is associated with the name of the procedure.

EXAMPLE 6.3

A PROCEDURE FOR SOME STATISTICAL COMPUTATIONS

Let us assume that, as in Example 6.2, we have a set of integer numbers x_1, x_2, . . . , x_N stored in a one-dimensional array X[1..100]. For this example, we will assume that all the x_i are integers with values between 0 and 100.

We want to compute the mean

$$m = \frac{1}{N} \sum_{i=1}^{N} x_i$$

as well as the standard deviation

$$s = \sqrt{\frac{\sum\limits_{i=1}^{N} (x_i - m)^2}{N - 1}}$$

In addition, we also want to prepare a frequency count of the number of items in the ranges 0–24, 25–49, 50–74, and 75–100.

Algorithm: Level 1

1. SUM:= $x_1 + x_2 + \cdots + x_N$.
2. MEAN:=SUM/N.
3. SUM:= $(x_1 - MEAN)^2 + \cdots + (x_N - MEAN)^2$.
4. Standard deviation STANDEV:= $\sqrt{SUM/(N-1)}$.
5. Initialize frequency counts FREQ[1]..FREQ[4] to zero.
6. For I:=1 to N, determine frequency range for x_i and increase appropriate frequency count by one.

The algorithm consists mainly of a restatement of the formulas. In Step 6, to determine the correct frequency category, divide x_i by 25 and use the integer part as index to FREQ. The procedure SIMPLESTAT gives three results, the mean MEAN, the standard deviation STANDEV, and an array FREQ with four values.

```
procedure SIMPLESTAT(N:integer;X:VALUETAB;
                     var MEAN,STANDEV:real;
                     var FREQ:FREQTAB);
{procedure to compute mean, standard deviation
 and frequency distribution of a sequence of
 N integers stored in array X}
var I,SUM,RANGE:integer;
begin
  {compute mean }
  SUM:=0;
  for I:=1 to N do
    SUM:=SUM+X[I];
  MEAN:=SUM/N;
  {compute standard deviation }
  SUM:=0;
  for I:=1 to N do
    SUM:=SUM+sqr(X[I]-MEAN);
  STANDEV:=sqrt(SUM/(N-1));
  {compute frequency distribution }
```

```
for I:=1 to 4 do
   FREQ[I]:=0;
for I:= 1 to N do
   begin
      RANGE:=X[I] div 25 +1;
      FREQ[RANGE]:=FREQ[RANGE]+1
   end
end
```

To use this procedure, VALUETAB and FREQTAB must be properly defined types, possibly as

```
type VALUETAB=array[1..100] of integer;
     FREQTAB=array[1..4] of integer
```

Except that the computations are now expressed in terms of a procedure, we have encountered most of the concepts in this example before. However, the program has some flaws. It will not work if N = 1, or if the assumption that the x_i are between 0 and 100 is violated. The procedure should really include a check for this.

In addition, there is an outright error in the program. Can you spot it? We will give an improved and corrected version a little later, but before you look it up, see if you can find the problem.

EXERCISES 6.2

1. Write a procedure to sort an array of integers using the bubblesort algorithm.
2. Write a procedure to merge two sorted arrays to produce another sorted array.
3. Write a procedure to take a character string and replace all non-alphabetical and nonnumerical characters with blanks.
4. Write a subprogram that accepts a character string and checks whether it is a legal Pascal identifier. Write the subprogram both as a function and a procedure.
5. Write a procedure for computing the median of a set of numerical values $x_1, x_2, \ldots, x_N$. The median can be computed by first sorting the numbers, then taking the middle element if N is odd, or the average of the two middle items if N is even.
6. The range of integer numbers that can be represented in a particular computer depends on the word length. To handle larger integers one can, for example, use two words, one to store the lower order digits, the other the higher order digits, with each part having the same sign as the original number. A data type for such large integers might be

```
type LARGEINTEGER=record
                     UPPER,LOWER:integer
                  end
```

For this data type, write

a. An input procedure to convert a string of digits into type LARGEINTEGER.

b. An output procedure to print the values of variables of type LARGEINTEGER in the usual integer form.

c. A procedure for adding two numbers of type LARGEINTEGER.

7. Write a procedure for multiplying two numbers of type LARGEINTEGER.

8. Could the procedure in 7. be rewritten as a function, the value of which is the result of the multiplication?

9. The symmetric difference between two sets a and b is the set of all elements which are either in a or in b, but not in both. Write a procedure for computing the symmetric difference of two sets.

6.3

the structure of a program with subprograms

Sections 6.1 and 6.2 dealt primarily with the question of defining functions and procedures. We will now consider how these are to be integrated into a complete program. Because each programming language takes a somewhat different approach, what we say here is quite specific to Pascal.

Subprograms cannot stand alone, but must be used in the context of a *main* program. This main program calls the various subprograms, through which the relevant computations are carried out. How a subprogram is called depends on whether it is a function or a procedure. A function is called by writing its name as part of an expression. Thus, when we write

```
A:=1+F(X+2)
```

actual parameter

the function F is called. The value of the expression X+2 is transmitted to the subprogram, in which it is used in place of the formal parameter. The value X+2 is the **actual parameter.** Often a function is defined with several formal parameters; when we call such a function, there must be agreement in number and type between the formal parameters and the actual parameters. For example, if for

```
function F(X:real;Y:integer;Z:boolean):real
```

we write in the calling program

```
RESULT:=F(A,B,C)
```

then A must be real, B integer, and C boolean. The value of A will be used in place of the formal parameter X, B will be used for Y, and C for Z. RESULT must be of type real to match the function F.

A procedure is called with a statement giving the name of the procedure and the actual parameters, as in

```
PROCESS(A,B,C)
```

After the computations in procedure PROCESS are completed, control returns to the calling program, in which the next statement is executed. Again, there must be agreement in the number and type between the formal and actual parameters.

The idea of a *block* will help explain how the main program and various subprograms are put together. A Pascal block is a sequence of declarations and statements of the form

```
label...;
const...;
type ...;
var  ...;
```
function and procedure definitions;
```
begin
```
    statements
```
end
```

The label, const, type, and var declarations are optional, but they must be given in the order shown. Function and procedure definitions, if any, follow the var declaration. There can be any number of functions and procedures.

Function and procedure definitions have the form

function *functionname* (*parameter list*) : *resulttype* ;
block

and

procedure *procedurename* (*parameter list*) ;
block

To make this a little more explicit, consider the following example, which involves a program MAIN and two procedure subprograms A and B.

program MAIN(input,output);
declarations for MAIN;
procedure A(...);
  block for A;
procedure B(...);
  block for B;
begin
  statements for MAIN;
end.

The definition of a subprogram involves a block. Because any block can have subprograms, we can define subprograms within subprograms (Section 6.4 will explain this further).

It is possible for one subprogram to call another. When this is done we must follow the rule that a subprogram can be used only after it has been defined. In the preceding example, procedure B can use A, but A cannot use B.

EXAMPLE 6.4

MORE STATISTICAL COMPUTATIONS

For this example, let us assume that we have two sets of data, Sample A and Sample B. Each set consists of integer numbers between 0 and 100. For each we want to compute the statistics described in Example 6.3—the mean, the standard deviation, and the frequency distribution for the four categories. In addition, we also want to print a bar graph showing the frequency distribution of the data items. The desired appearance of the bar graph is shown in Figure 6.3, where each '*' represents one data item.

One problem we have to solve is how to handle the input. There are two samples involved and we have to be able to tell where one ends and the other begins. Clearly, we cannot use the end-of-file condition alone, as we have done in some of the previous examples. There are several ways around the difficulty; we will solve it by starting each line of input for Sample A with the letter A, and each line of Sample B with B. After each sample, we use an additional line containing only the single character E. This may seem a little artificial, but it is convenient for the program, and it also provides a visual separation for the input data.

To summarize, the input and output for this problem will be as follows:

Input: Several lines of the form

    A x x x...x

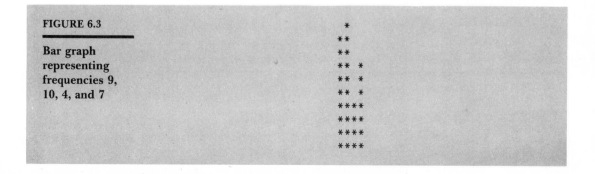

FIGURE 6.3

Bar graph representing frequencies 9, 10, 4, and 7

A line containing

E

Several lines of the form

B x x x . . . x

One line containing

E

Here, x stands for one data item, that is, an integer between 0 and 100.

Output: the mean, standard deviation, and bar graph for Samples A and B.

Algorithm: Level 1

1. Read data for Sample A.
2. Compute mean, standard deviation, and frequency distribution for A.
3. Print mean and standard deviation for A.
4. Print bar graph for A.
5. Read data for Sample B.
6. Compute mean, standard deviation, and frequency distribution for B.
7. Print mean and standard deviation for B.
8. Print bar graph for B.

The computations for the mean, standard deviation, and the frequency distribution have already been done in procedure SIMPLESTAT. We make only one modification to remove an error. The printing of a bar graph is not an entirely obvious process, and it is necessary to refine the step. To print anything, including a graph, we have to produce one line at a time from the top. If we look at the bar graph in Figure 6.4, we see that each line consists of a number of positions in which we print either '*' or a blank. The symbol '*' is printed only if the frequency for the category is at least as large as the height of the line at that point. The top line is printed at a

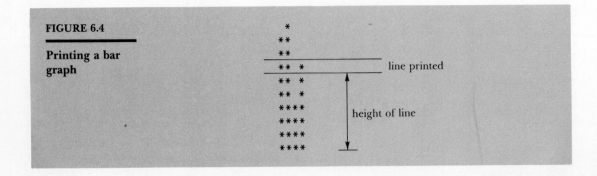

FIGURE 6.4

Printing a bar graph

height equal to the maximum frequency. The general considerations give us enough insight to provide details for the printing of the bar graph.

For Level 2 refinement of bar graph printing we use FREQ as defined in SIMPLESTAT. NOCAT will denote the total number of frequency categories handled by the bar graph printing algorithm.

1. MAX:= maximum of FREQ[1]..FREQ[NOCAT]
2. For HEIGHT:= MAX downto 1, print line. The Jth position (with J going from 1 to NOCAT) in the line is '*' if FREQ[J]>=HEIGHT, otherwise it is a blank.

The program will be written with three procedures: SIMPLESTAT to compute the mean, standard deviation, and frequency distribution, BARGRAPH to print the bar graph given the frequency distribution, and INDATA, which reads the data from the input file.

```
Program SAMPLES(input,output);
type OKDATA=0..100;
     VALUETAB=array[1..100] of OKDATA;
     FREQTAB=array[1..4] of integer;
var  COUNT:integer;
     MEANA,MEANB,STANDEVA,STANDEVB:real;
     VALUES:VALUETAB;
     FREQUENCY:FREQTAB;


Procedure SIMPLESTAT(N:integer;X:VALUETAB;
                     var MEAN,STANDEV:real;
                     var FREQ:FREQTAB);
{Procedure to compute mean, standard deviation
 and frequency distribution of X[1]..X[N] }
var I,RANGE:integer;
    SUM:real;
begin
  {compute mean }
  SUM:=0;
  for I:=1 to N do
    SUM:=SUM+X[I];
  MEAN:=SUM/N;
  {compute standard deviation }
  SUM:=0;
  for I:=1 to N do
    SUM:=SUM+sqr(X[I]-MEAN);
  STANDEV:=sqrt(SUM/(N-1));
  {compute frequency distribution }
  for I:=1 to 4 do
    FREQ[I]:=0;
```

```
            for I:= 1 to N do
              begin
                RANGE:=X[I] div 25 + 1;
                if X[I] =100
                  then RANGE:=4
                FREQ[RANGE]:= FREQ[RANGE]+1
              end
       end;

procedure BARGRAPH(NOCAT:integer;X:FREQTAB);
{procedure to print bargraph from frequency
distribution in X }
label 1;
const LINEWIDTH=50;
var I,J,MAX:integer;
begin
  if (2*NOCAT>LINEWIDTH)
    then begin
            writeln(' error in BARGRAPH);
            writeln(' graph will not fit');
            goto 1
          end;
  {find maximum height of graph }
  MAX:=0;
  for I:=1 to N do
    if X[I]>MAX
      then MAX:=X[I]
  {plot graph from top }
  for I:=MAX downto 1 do
    begin
      for J:=1 to NOCAT do
        if X[J]>=I
          then write('*':2)
          else write(' ':2);
      writeln
    end;
1:end;

procedure INDATA(var N:integer;var X:VALUETAB);
{input procedure, reads and count successive
values until terminator 'E' is found }
var CHECK:char;
begin
  N:=0;
  repeat
    read(CHECK);
```

```
      while not eoln do
        begin
          N:=N+1;
          read(X[N])
        end;
      readln
    until (CHECK='E')
end;

{body of main program }
begin
  {read sample A }
  INDATA(COUNT,VALUES);
  {statistics for sample A}
  SIMPLESTAT(COUNT,VALUES,MEANA,STANDEVA,
             FREQUENCY);
  writeln('    mean of A',MEANA:10:2);
  writeln('    standard deviation of A',
          STANDEVA:10:4);
  writeln('    frequency distribution for A');
  writeln;
  BARGRAPH(4,FREQUENCY);
  writeln;
  {input for sample B }
  INDATA(COUNT,VALUES);
  {statistics for B }
  SIMPLESTAT(COUNT,VALUES,MEANB,STANDEVB,
             FREQUENCY);
  writeln('    mean of B',MEANB:10:2);
  writeln('    standard deviation for B',
          STANDEVB:10:4);
  writeln('    frequency distribution for B');
  writeln;
  BARGRAPH(4,FREQUENCY)
end.
```

Sample input

```
A 10 25 71 65 31
A 21 70 36 41 52
A 75 80
E
B 16 18 21 31 32
B 15 28 29 36 34
B 46 34 90
E
```

Output

```
mean of A        48.08
standard deviation of A     23.8459
frequency distribution for A

    *  *
    *  *
 *  *  *  *
 *  *  *  *

mean of B        33.08
standard deviation for B     19.2720
frequency distribution for B

    *
    *
    *
    *
 *  *
 *  *
 *  *
 *  *     *
```

Compare the new version of SIMPLESTAT with the old one on page 141. In the original code, the case x = 100 was not handled correctly. This error has been removed in the new version.

The procedure BARGRAPH is more general than SIMPLESTAT. BARGRAPH can handle a variable number of frequency categories, while SIMPLESTAT always produces exactly four. Usually, procedures such as these, which may be used in a variety of circumstances, should be made as general as possible. For SIMPLESTAT, this would of course require a change in the algorithm by which the frequency distribution is computed.

scope of an identifier

Both SIMPLESTAT and BARGRAPH in Example 6.4 use the variable I, each procedure defining it in a var declaration. What, if any, relation exists between the identifier I in SIMPLESTAT and the I in BARGRAPH? Do they refer to the same variable? The answer is, emphatically, *no!* The meaning of a variable is confined to the procedure in which it is declared. When another subprogram uses the same name, a different variable is created, that is, the name refers to a different location in memory. We say that such variables are *local* to the subprogram in which they are declared. The part of the program in which an identifier is defined is said to be its *scope*.

Using local variables has many advantages. In particular, it makes the subprograms independent, with communication between the main program and the subprograms handled strictly through the parameter list. To use a procedure, we need only know what it does; we need not be concerned with how it has been programmed. It is this feature which makes it possible to split large projects into smaller independent pieces. When several programmers are involved, they can work essentially independently.

Despite the fact that it is important to keep subprograms independent and hence keep variables local, most programming languages provide some mechanism whereby strict locality can be circumvented.

An identifier that is local to one subprogram has no meaning as far as other subprograms are concerned. If a subprogram assigns a value to one of its local variables, this value is not accessible to other subprograms—that is, they cannot use this value. At times it is convenient to let an identifier have the same meaning for several subprograms by extending its scope. Identifiers whose scope is wider than one subprogram are called *nonlocal*. Identifiers defined for the whole program are said to be *global*. The argument in favor or nonlocal identifiers is that they make possible the sharing of information by several subprograms without a corresponding entry in the parameter list. This saves some writing, and when there are several dozen parameters involved, the argument is at least mildly convincing.

In Pascal, the scope of an identifier is the block in which it is declared and every subblock in which the identifier is not declared again. Thus, if we have

```
program A(...);
var X:integer;
procedure B(...);
 var Y:integer;

 .
 .
 .
 end; {of B}

 .
 .
 .
end. {of A}
```

where X does not occur in the var declaration in procedure B, then X is defined and can be used within B. The variable Y is defined in B, but not in A. If on the other hand we had

```
program A(...);
var X:integer;
procedure B(...);
 var X:integer;

 .
 .
 .
 end; {of B}

 .
 .
 .
end. {of A}
```

then the two variables named X are distinct and unrelated.

The use of nonlocal variables, by destroying the independence of the subprograms, can lead to obscure programming errors. Caution is advisable.

The rules for the scope of an identifier are not limited to variables. They also apply to type, const, and label declarations, and to function and procedure names. It is possible to nest subprograms within others, as shown in the following example. The brackets show the nesting of the subprograms.

```
┌─  program MAIN(...);
│ ┌─ procedure A(...);
│ │ ┌─ procedure B(...);
│ │ └  block of B;
│ │ ┌─ procedure C(...);
│ │ └  block of C;
│ └  end; {of A}
└─  end. {of MAIN}
```

In this case procedure B can be used by procedure C. This is because B and C are defined in the block of procedure A and hence known throughout it. Procedure B cannot use procedure C, but this is because of a general Pascal rule that before any identifier can be used it has to be defined. If we were to use the identifier C in procedure B, it would still be undefined. Neither procedure B nor procedure C can be used in MAIN, since the identifiers B and C are local to procedure A.

EXERCISES 6.3

1. Rewrite program SAMPLES to use completely global variables, so that all procedure calls are made with an empty parameter list.
2. Modify program SAMPLES so that the computations terminate when the graph is too wide.
3. What will happen in the data for Example 6.4 if the last item on a line is followed by one or more blanks?
4. Give an example in which it would be appropriate to nest one subprogram within another.

6.4
communication between subprograms

When a program calls a subprogram, information is communicated through the parameter list. We say that the actual parameters are "substituted" or "used in place of" the formal parameters. These terms are, however, quite vague; to understand them more completely we have to go to the machine language level to see what happens to the compiled code.

A subprogram, after compilation, is a piece of machine language code. When the calling program invokes the subprogram, a transfer to the first statement of the subprogram is made. At the same time, information on the parameters is transmitted to the called subprogram. There are several ways in which this transmission can be accomplished. For our discussion, let us assume that A is the actual parameter in the calling program, while X is the corresponding formal parameter in the subprogram. For the sake of simplicity, let us take A and X to be unstructured variables.

value parameter

1. The value of A is assigned to X. In this case the subprogram knows only the value of A, but not its memory address. Hence the value of A can be used, but not changed by the subprogram. Parameters of this type are called *value parameters.*

reference parameter

2. The memory address of the variable A is passed to the subprogram. The identifier X has no memory address associated with it; wherever it occurs, the compiled code will use the address of A. Now the subprogram does know where A is stored, so it can modify A. We call A a *reference parameter.*

There are good reasons for providing the two methods. The use of value parameters protects against the inadvertent destruction of information by a subprogram. Normally, this should not happen if the subprogram is coded and used correctly. But mistakes do occur, and safety features are useful. On the other hand, reference parameters are necessary so that procedures can return results to the calling program.

In Pascal, a formal parameter without the var prefix is treated as a value parameter. Such a parameter acts like a local variable whose value is initialized with the value of the actual parameter. Because only a value is needed, the actual parameter can be an expression. For example, for

```
procedure INVERT(X:real);
begin
   writeln(1/X)
end
```

the call

```
INVERT(5/2)
```

will print the reciprocal of 2.5.

When a parameter is defined with the var prefix, it is treated as a reference parameter. Because there is no memory address associated with an expression, the actual parameter cannot be an expression, but must be an identifier. If we had written

```
Procedure INVERT(var X:real);
begin
  writeln(1/X)
end
```

then the call

```
INVERT(5/2)
```

would be incorrect. To print the reciprocal of 5/2 it would be necessary to write something like

```
NUMBER:=5/2;
INVERT(NUMBER)
```

Our previous rule was that a parameter that is to be used but not changed should be made a value parameter, strictly for protection against mistakes. When the parameter is to be changed, then we have no choice but to make it a reference parameter. There is, however, one further point to consider. Suppose that we pass an array as a value parameter. Then the whole array has to be copied into the array used by the subprogram. If the array is large, this can be very time-consuming. Consequently, some programmers always pass arrays by reference.

Communication between subprograms can also be done through nonlocal variables, with the undesirable effect of destroying the independence of the subprograms. When only a few parameters are involved, you should avoid using nonlocal variables; but if many items have to be transmitted, using global variables will considerably shorten the parameter list and hence the program.

EXERCISES 6.4

1. What is the effect of

```
Z:=3;
PLUS(Z);
writeln(Z)
```

with the procedure PLUS defined by each of the following descriptions?

```
a. Procedure PLUS(X:integer);
   begin
     X:=X+1
   end
b. Procedure PLUS(var X:integer);
   begin
     X:=X+1
   end
```

2. For which of the two versions of PLUS in Exercise 1 is the statement PLUS(3) legal?

3. If a program contains the statement

   G:=F(3,F(2,4))

   can the function F be written with reference parameters only?

6.5

recursion

A subprogram can call any other subprogram known to it, to the depth of several levels. We might have

A calls B, B calls C, C calls D.

Eventually, when the task of the lowest level subprogram is done, control returns via

D returns to C, C returns to B, B returns to A.

What happens if two subprograms in this sequence are the same? At first sight

A calls A

or

A calls B, B calls A

seems incorrect. It appears that we have asked for the never-ending sequence

A calls A, A calls A, A calls A,...

Nevertheless, some programming languages do allow subprograms to call themselves. Such subprograms are said to be recursive. *Recursion* is a very powerful tool for some applications.

Of course, when using recursion, we have to avoid creating an infinite regression by making sure that we eventually break out of the recursive cycle. Take, for example, the factorial function, defined for nonnegative integers n by

$$n! = n \times (n-1) \times (n-2) \times \cdots \times 2 \times 1$$

This is the way $n!$ is usually defined, but it is also possible to define it by

$$n! = n \times (n-1)!$$
$$0! = 1$$

The first line of this definition defines $n!$ in terms of $(n-1)!$, that is, recursively. The second line provides the "escape" from the recursion.

Eventually, the argument reaches 0, and we return through the various levels of the recursion, as in

```
5! = 5×4!
   = 5×(4×3!)
   = 5×(4×(3×2!))
   = 5×(4×(3×(2×1!)))
   = 5×(4×(3×(2×(1×0!))))
   = 5×4×3×2×1×1
   = 120
```

Pascal allows recursion in functions and procedures. No additional features are needed: we simply write the subprogram as if the called function or procedure were already defined. A recursive Pascal program for the factorial function is

```
function FACT(N:integer):integer;
begin
  if N=0
    then FACT:=1
    else FACT:=N*FACT(N-1)
end
```

While this example serves to demonstrate the nature of recursion, it does not make a convincing case for its power. The nonrecursive definition of n! is easier to understand and simple to program. To see that recursion is indeed useful, we have to go to more complicated problems.

EXAMPLE 6.5

RECOGNIZING WELL-FORMED EXPRESSIONS

Although we have used expressions extensively, we have never fully defined what constitutes a well-formed expression. For our purposes, it was unnecessary to provide a rigorous mathematical definition; we are quite used to writing expressions and know by inspection when an expression is not well formed. However, to write a computer program to determine whether an expression is legal, we will have to put our intuitive understanding on a sounder basis.

To simplify considerably, let us take a subset of legal expressions. Only one variable, called a, will be allowed. The operators + and − will be allowed, but no others. Any number of parentheses can be used. We will also allow − as negation, but only in the context of (−a). Thus, the expressions

```
(-a)
a+a
(a+a+a)
```

will be considered legal, but

```
-(a+a)
a+-a
a-(a+)
```

are illegal.

While these cases give some idea of what expressions are legal, we must be more precise. The following rules define completely which expressions are valid.

1. a is a legal expression.
2. (-a) is a legal expression.
3. If x is a legal expression, then (x) is also legal.
4. If x and y are legal expressions, so are x+y and x-y.

Note that Rules 3 and 4 define legal expressions recursively, while Rules 1 and 2 provide the escape clauses.

The purpose of this exercise is to write a boolean function VALID. This function will operate on a character string stored in the global array EXPR, from EXPR[INIT] to EXPR[FINAL]. The value of VALID will be true if and only if the expression is valid according to the rules just given.

Because the statement of the problem is itself done recursively, it is quite natural to use recursion when writing the program. The algorithm for the solution, then, is simply a restatement of the definition of a valid expression.

1. If the string is 'a', then it is a valid expression.
2. If the string is '(-a)', then it is valid.
3. If the first character is '(' and the last is ')', then the expression is legal if the substring obtained by omitting the leading and trailing parentheses is legal.
4. If 1, 2, or 3 does not apply, scan the string to see if it can be broken into x+y or x-y, where x and y are both valid expressions.
5. If all tests fail, then the expression is not valid.

```
program TESTREC(input,output);
var EXPR: array [ 1..100] of char;
    I,N:integer;


function VALID(INIT,FINAL:integer):boolean;
{ checks a string consisting of a,+,-,(,)
  to determine if it is a valid expression}
label 1;
var I:integer;
begin
  {check that string is not empty}
  if INIT>FINAL
    then begin
```

```
                            VALID:=false;
                            goto 1
                        end;
            {check for string 'a'}
            if (INIT=FINAL)
               and (EXPR[INIT]='a')
              then begin
                            VALID:=true;
                            goto 1
                        end;
             {check for string '(-a)' }
             if (FINAL-INIT=3)
                and (EXPR[INIT]='(')
                and (EXPR[INIT+1]='-')
                and (EXPR[INIT+2]='a')
                and (EXPR[INIT+3]=')')
                 then begin
                            VALID:=true;
                            goto 1
                        end;
             {check for form (x) where x is valid}
             if (EXPR[INIT]='(')
                 and (EXPR[FINAL]=')')
                 and VALID(INIT+1,FINAL-1)
               then begin
                            VALID:=true;
                            goto 1
                        end;
             {if all fails, examine all substrings}
             VALID:=false;
             for I:=INIT+1 to FINAL-1 do
             {check for + or - separating expressions}
                if((EXPR[I]='+') or (EXPR[I]='-'))
                    and VALID(INIT,I-1)
                    and VALID(I+1,FINAL)
                    then VALID:=true;
          1:end;

          {main program to test VALID
             reads N, followed by a string of
             length N, terminated by eof}
          begin
             repeat
                read(N);
                for I:=1 to N do
```

```
       begin
          read(EXPR[I]);
          write(EXPR[I])
        end;
      readln;
      if VALID(1,N)
        then writeln(' valid')
        else writeln(' not valid')
    until eof
end.
```

Sample input

```
  2()
  4(a+a
  5(a+a)
  6(-a)+a
  6-a-a-a
  7(a+a+a)
  8(a++a+a)
  5a-a-a
  6a-(-a)
  9(a)+(a-a)
```

Output

```
  ( ) not valid
  (a+a not valid
  (a+a) valid
  (-a)+a valid
  -a-a-a not valid
  (a+a+a) valid
  (a++a+a) not valid
  a-a-a valid
  a-(-a) valid
  (a)+(a-a) valid
```

It is possible to write a nonrecursive version of this program, but it is more difficult and not as natural as the recursive approach, reflecting the fact that the definition of a legal expression is most easily made recursively.

A word of warning: the code was written in the simplest way to demonstrate recursion. It is extremely inefficient for long expressions. For an exploration of this point, see Section 7.7.

Example 6.5 shows that recursion is useful in some cases, particularly where the problem has some inherent recursive structure. Later we will encounter several more examples where recursion can be used very effectively. However, when a nonrecursive implementation is not overly difficult, recursion should be avoided. Recursive programs tend to be harder to understand, as well as harder to follow in printouts, than nonrecursive ones. When something goes wrong, debugging may be very difficult. As we get buried deeper and deeper in the recursion, the tracing of the flow by means of printouts can become quite difficult. Another disadvantage of recursion is inefficiency. On each entry to a recursive program it is necessary to save information, such as partially computed results. This bookkeeping is done automatically in recursion, but on the other hand it is time-consuming. Consider, for example, the factorial function. For $n = 10$, the nonrecursive version takes nine multiplications, while the recursive version requires nine entries to a function with the associated overhead. The recursive implementation would in this case be much slower.

EXERCISES 6.5

1. For nonnegative integers n and m, the binomial coefficient is defined by

$$\binom{n}{m} = \frac{n!}{m!(n-m)!}$$

Find a recursive definition for (n/m) without using factorials, then write a recursive function for it.

2. Write a recursive procedure to generate the first n Fibonacci numbers.

3. Write a recursive function POWER(X,N:integer):integer whose value is X to the power N.

4. Write a nonrecursive version of VALID.

5. Modify Example 6.5 to add the rule: If x is a legal expression, then (-(x)) is also legal. What new expressions, not previously allowed, does this provide?

6. Check function VALID for inefficiencies and make improvements which will save time for long expressions.

7. How could VALID be written without goto?

8. A string of parentheses and brackets is well formed if each pair of left and right parentheses (or brackets) is nested within another well-formed group. For example

```
[()]()
([([])])
```

are well formed, but

```
[()]
(([]])
```

are not. Make this notion precise, then write a recursive program to test whether a given string is well formed.

9. Write a nonrecursive program for 8.

further reading

Cherry, G. W. *Pascal Programming Structures,* Chapter 7. Reston, Va.: Reston Publishing Co., 1980.

Grogono, P. *Programming in Pascal,* Chapter 4. Reading, Mass.: Addison-Wesley Publishing Co., 1974.

Jensen, K., and Wirth, N. *Pascal User Manual and Report,* 2d. ed., User Manual, Chapter 4. New York: Springer-Verlag, 1974.

Koffman, E. B. *Problem Solving and Structured Programming in Pascal,* Chapters 5 and 7. Reading, Mass.: Addison-Wesley Publishing Co., 1981.

Schneider, G. M., Weingart, S. W., and Perlman, D. M. *An Introduction to Programming and Problem Solving with Pascal,* Chapter 8. New York: John Wiley & Sons, 1978.

Welsh, J., and Elder, J. *Introduction to Pascal,* Chapter 7. Englewood Cliffs, N.J.: Prentice-Hall, 1979.

Chapter Seven

effective program design and implementation

Let us return for a moment to our analogy of programming with sports. Like beginning skiers, we have learned the basics of how to handle our equipment, and like beginning skiers, we can now accomplish simpler tasks with a certain amount of confidence because of our grasp of basic skills. But also like beginners, our skills are not yet to be compared to those of professionals. As we go on to more complex tasks as programmers, we must sharpen our skills to become more effective in the design and coding of programs.

We have emphasized throughout previous chapters the importance of good programming habits and a systematic approach to programming. These are important because programming is an activity that seems to invite error. Sometimes, for example, we start a program with great confidence that we can complete it in a short time, but then discover that we have overlooked something. Other times we have to modify our approach repeatedly, and eventually end up with a program that leaves us with the feeling that it is not particularly good.

A perfect programmer would be able to produce an error-free and efficient code in a short time. The programs would be clear, simple, and easy to modify, and would use the resources of the system effectively. Good programming (like good skiing) depends to some extent on innate talent, but our abilities can be enhanced through the study of what makes a good program. While it is necessary to learn thoroughly the language we use, good programming does not depend on learning all the rules of one or more programming languages. Knowing all the rules of Pascal or any other language does not necessarily qualify us as expert programmers, any more than learning English grammar can alone make us novelists. We must also know how to use the language effectively. To write good programs, we must

structured also use effective program structure. Strictly speaking, the term ***structured***
programming ***programming*** has a technical meaning, but many people use it as a synonym

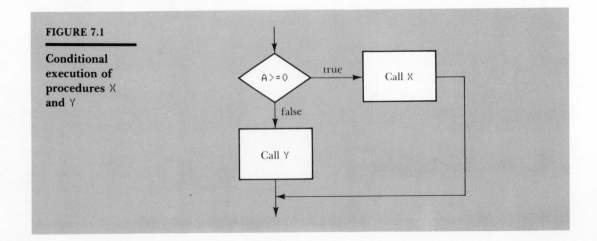

FIGURE 7.1

Conditional execution of procedures X **and** Y

for a way of writing programs that makes them easy to understand, debug, and modify.

The keys to success in programming are understanding of the program's purposes, organization, and the development of a systematic approach. We have stressed in our simple examples the importance of the three design steps: (1) problem description, (2) algorithm design with stepwise refinement, and (3) implementation, followed by careful debugging. The last step, testing and debugging, requires such an extensive discussion that we will devote the entire next chapter to it, but we will discuss the first two steps, design and implementation, in detail in this chapter. We will also discuss two important points to which we have so far paid little attention: efficiency and documentation.

7.1

programming style

Programming is in many ways like expository writing. Both programmer and writer start with an idea to be expressed and a language in which to write, and for both, there are many ways in which an idea may be communicated. Good style may seem less important to a programmer than to a writer, because a computer will run any program as long as it is syntactically and logically correct.

But a program must communicate with human readers, too. A programmer, in the course of writing the code, must develop a good understanding of what may be a very complex situation. Later, he or she may return to the program, having perhaps forgotten some of the reasons for the original implementation. Others who may have to understand and modify the code may have even more difficulty understanding the reasons for the implementation. That is why the program must not only be correct for the computer, but must also effectively communicate between people.

Just as in expository writing, there cannot be a complete set of rules for producing a perfect work, but there are still elements of good style that are necessary for success. In programming, the primary requirements of good style are simplicity and directness. The programmer should always be as straightforward as possible. This directive may seem confining to those who delight in finding new ways of expressing the obvious (even though efficiency or conciseness are the usual motives). But the careful programmer will avoid temptations to use obscure statements and clever tricks, realizing that tricky code may be hard to decipher later and may make the program vulnerable to minor changes.

One of the most effective ways to write a clear program is to follow as closely as possible the verbal description from which the program was written. The coding should always be a faithful reflection of the way we describe the algorithm in pseudolanguage. For example, if we state the algorithm so that a flowchart for a particular part looks like Figure 7.1, then the corresponding code should be

```
if A>=0
   then X
   else Y
```

rather than the functionally equivalent

```
if A<0
   then Y
   else X
```

Another way to ensure that a program is direct and straightforward is to see that statements are written to reflect their purposes as clearly as possible. For example, suppose that we have a boolean variable FLAG that is to be set to true if the integer variable NUMBER is divisible by three and set to false otherwise. One way of writing this is

```
FLAG:=((NUMBER mod 3)=0)
```

another way is

```
if (NUMBER mod 3)=0
   then FLAG:=true
   else FLAG:=false
```

The first version uses assignment of a boolean expression, a technique that has been used for demonstration in some previous examples. Nevertheless, it is less obvious than the second form. When we read a program containing the first version, we may have to pause to analyze the statement to see what is actually done. This diverts our attention from the main points and may cause us to lose track of what is happening. The second alternative is much closer to the verbal description and hence much easier to understand. (Note: this is not to say that assignment of boolean expressions should never be used. The real point of the example is that when several plausible alternatives exist, the alternative that gives the most readable code should be used.)

EXAMPLE 7.1

MAXIMUM OF THREE VALUES

Let A, B, and C be three numbers. Find the largest of them—that is

```
X=max(A,B,C)
```

This example was previously suggested as an exercise and you should compare your solution to the several versions we will give.

Perhaps the most direct way is to write

```
if (A>=B) and (A>=C)
   then X:=A;
```

```
if (B>=A) and (B>=C)
   then X:=B;
if (C>=A) and (C>=B)
   then X:=C
```

Most programmers would consider this inefficient and instead use

```
X:=A;
if B>=X
   then X:=B;
if C>=X
   then X:=C
```

which is more concise and elegant than the first version. It also tends to be more efficient, because only two comparisons have to be performed, rather than six. Finally, and perhaps most importantly, it generalizes easily to more than three numbers. It does, however, lose some transparency, because we have to grasp the underlying algorithm before the purpose of the code becomes clear.

Another version, produced by those who are enamored of if-then-else statements, is

```
if A>=B
   then if A>=C
           then X:=A
           else X:=C
   else if B>=C
           then X:=B
           else X:=C
```

This looks sophisticated, but is really quite awful. It does not read well, nor does it generalize easily to several numbers. In fact, it has no advantage other than being an example of nested if-then-else statements.

Finally, there is

```
if A>B then goto 1;
if B>C then X:=B
          else X:=C;
   goto 2;
1:if A>C then X:=A
          else X:=C;
2: ...
```

This is a total disaster. It requires a fair amount of effort to figure out what is happening, and it is not clear that the answer is always right. This sort of atrocity is relatively rare in Pascal because of its deemphasis of the goto. But in a FORTRAN or BASIC course, many a wayward student has produced the equivalent.

variable names

One essential element of good style is the use of well-chosen variable names. The name of a variable should show its meaning to help guide the reader through the program and make it easy to remember what each name stands for. Some programmers insist on using short identifiers because it saves typing. But if doing so causes confusion later, it is false economy. In a payroll example, the meaning of a variable named TOTALWAGES is easily understood. When we abbreviate it to TWAGES it loses something; if we call it TW, almost all possible identification with its purpose is gone. While excessively long variable names tend to clutter up a program and should be avoided, the consistent use of one- or two-character identifiers is also very poor practice. Some languages such as BASIC allow only short names, which is a serious flaw. Even FORTRAN, which normally allows up to six characters, is limiting.

There is, however, no inherent virtue in long names. The shortest name that clearly expresses the meaning and purpose of a variable is the one that should be used. In writing the code for a mathematical formula given in terms of x and y (assuming that these symbols have no special meaning), we should certainly use them in the program. As another example, take the coding of simple counted loops. We have generally written these in a form like the following:

```
for I:=INITIAL to FINAL do
   A[I]:=0
```

This seems quite clear; to rewrite it as

```
for LOOPCOUNTER:=INITIAL to FINAL do
   A[LOOPCOUNTER]:=0
```

is no improvement. The point here is that I has no special meaning; it is simply a bookkeeping device, so a fancy name does not help.

It is not a good idea to use names that are similar and easily confused, for example PART and PARTS or PARTI and PART1. Not only will this cause problems in reading the program, but a minor typing mistake may produce errors that are difficult to spot. It is also a poor idea to use zeros in identifiers because they are easily confused with capital O.

If the syntax of a language involves reserved words and standard identifiers, it is best not to use identifiers with names similar to any of these special words. In Pascal, using identifiers such as SETS, CASES, or THEM is pointless and just makes it hard to see at a glance what a statement does. Our practice here has been to provide a visual distinction between the words with special meaning and the programmer-defined identifiers by typing the former in lowercase letters. When lowercase and uppercase are available, it seems well worth the small extra effort. In fact, there is little extra work involved in choosing good names, so that there is no excuse for not doing so. In programming we should be as careful in choosing identifiers as we are in choosing words in English.

comments

Comments are not subject to any syntactic rules and carry no message to the computer. They are purely stylistic aids that allow us to insert additional information into the program where needed. When used properly, comments can be extremely valuable in guiding the reader through the code, explaining points that are unclear and generally helping our understanding. But unless they are written with as much care and thought as the rest of the program, they may add very little. When misused, comments may simply repeat what is already obvious from the code, and then make matters worse by increasing the length of the program.

A useful comment carries a message that is not immediately obvious from the code. For example, if the statement

```
if HOURS>100
   then ERROR
```

is "explained" by the comment

```
{ if HOURS is greater than 100
   transfer to procedure ERROR }
```

then the comment is completely useless; it does not say anything we cannot see just as easily from the code. On the other hand, if the comment were

```
{ if the hours worked are outside the plausible
  range, transfer to error handling procedure
  where the suspicious cases are printed }
```

then the reader is given some valuable information not explicit in the `if` statement.

A set of comments at the beginning of the code, called a *prologue,* can be very useful in identifying the purpose of the program or perhaps explaining the meaning of some of the variables. (All comments are really part of the documentation of a program, a subject we will treat in more detail in Section 7.8.)

How many comments there should be in a program is a controversial issue. Common sense is the best guide. For simple, more or less self-explanatory code, one needs only enough comments to remind the reader what is being done. When the algorithm or its implementation becomes difficult, extensive commenting may be necessary to clarify the code. When a program is well written, it is naturally easy to understand, so a few succinct comments may be all that is needed. For bad code, even extensive commenting will not help much. A very general guideline, though, is the following: if you were to remove all declarations and statements from the program, leaving only the comments, could you still see what the program does and get at least an idea of the algorithm being used? If not, consider adding more comments where the description is inadequate.

physical layout

The physical layout of the program makes an important contribution to its readability. If you accept the analogy that statements in programs play the role of sentences in writing, you will avoid using too many very short statements or extremely long and complex ones. Short statements tend to disconnect the ideas underlying the computations. To write

```
J:=I+1;
K:=I+2;
ATABLE[J]:=BTABLE[K]
```

instead of

```
ATABLE[I+1]:=BTABLE[I+2]
```

not only introduces the two meaningless variables J and K, but also splits one conceptual unit into three statements and thereby increases the burden on the reader.

On the other hand, exceedingly long statements should also be avoided. In Pascal, unless you insist on nesting several levels of if-then-else statements, there is little occasion for very long statements. One kind of exception is complex mathematical formulas, which for the purpose of coding should be broken into parts.

When dealing with constructs such as compound statements or loops that may extend over several lines, we use indentation to provide a visual grouping for conceptual units. With the layout

```
for I:= 1 to 100 do
    begin
        RADIUS:=RHO[I];
        for J:= 1 to 50 do
            begin
                ENTRY[I,J]:=J*RADIUS;
                EXIT[I,J]:=RADIUS/J
            end
    end
```

we see at a glance that we are dealing with a doubly nested loop, and we can easily identify the statements that belong to each loop. As far as the computer is concerned, we could just as well have written

```
for I:= 1 to 100 do begin RADIUS:=RHO[I]; for
J:=1 to 50 do begin ENTRY[I,J]:=J*RADIUS;
EXIT[I,J]:=RADIUS/J end end
```

but pity the poor reader.

As there are no generally accepted conventions for indentation, you are free to invent your own rules. What is important is that you use good judgment and apply the rules consistently. If you feel that the convention we have followed so far is good, use it. Otherwise, you can try to improve by adopting a convention more to your liking. The indentation conventions used here are summarized in Appendix D.

A few other practices are helpful in laying out programs in an easily understandable form. Insertion of blank lines between subprograms or even different parts of the same program may clarify the structure. In programs with a complicated flow of control, we can use blocking by drawing lines around groups of statements. A way of blocking was shown in Example 4.2. If you have trouble understanding the structure of a program, try blocking. It should help greatly.

EXERCISES 7.1

1. Reexamine all the programs you have written so far to evaluate your programming style.
2. Consult various programming texts for examples of good and bad style, for obscure code, and for useless comments.
3. Examine the programs in this book for examples of poor style.
4. Precedence rules for operators are generally used in all programming languages. What would happen to the readability of programs if all precedence rules were eliminated—that is, if all operators were given equal priority?
5. Pascal allows identifiers of arbitrary length, but in some systems only the first eight characters are used to distinguish between names. What reason could there be for such a restriction? What dangers are involved in this approach and what precautions should be taken? How limiting is such a feature to the programmer?
6. Decide on a set of indentation rules. Use them consistently in all your future programs.
7. Let CH be a character variable and FLAG a boolean variable. Write code to set FLAG to true if CH is an uppercase letter and to false otherwise. Write the code in as many different ways as you can, then compare the versions in terms of simplicity and directness.

7.2

program structure

Structure refers to the way in which individual pieces of information are put together. The power of a programming language depends very much on what data structures it allows. We should know how to exploit this power effectively. We have already discussed several kinds of data structures in connection with data types. In later chapters, we will study the question of data structure selection in some detail. Choosing the proper data structures for a program is important. We think of the data as organized in a certain way; when writing a program, we should keep as much of this conceptual structure as possible. When dealing with tabular data, we use two-dimensional arrays; if the information is more easily understood in terms of records, we use records as our data types. Using an "unnatural" data structure will complicate both the algorithm and its implementation.

When we write a program, we also set its structure. This structure should be as simple and explicit as possible to make the program intelligible. One school of thought takes the term "structured programming" to mean a set of techniques for producing well-organized and understandable code; another regards structured programming as programming with certain constructs, such as `while` and `repeat`, and without others, specifically `goto`. But the goal of both is the same—to write programs that are simple and easy to follow. Good structure is essentially synonymous with conceptual simplicity and logical coherence.

What makes the structure of a program simple? Certainly the most easily understood programs involve straightline code, in which statements are executed in the order in which they are written, without any branches. Furthermore, a good program proceeds in an orderly fashion. We do not start one computation, break if off in the middle to start another, to return later to complete the first part. A good program has a continuous train of thought. In a complex problem, of course, loops and alternate computations are indispensable. In these, we strive to approximate straightline code as much as possible.

Loops present few problems. The loop constructs bracket the body of the loop, so that the statements in a loop are easily assimilated as a unit and do not force us to divert our attention.

`If-then-else` statements may be a little more troublesome. Simple cases such as

```
if X<0
   then F:=X+1
   else F:=X-1
```

present no difficulty. The statement is simple enough to be read as a unit and its meaning is completeiy explicit. Even when compound statements are involved, we can still proceed essentially in a straight line. However, the nesting of `if-then-else` statements can cause significant deviations from the straightline structure. Consider the third version of the code for finding the maximum of three numbers, Example 7.1 on page 167. This is only a double nesting, but even so, to understand it we may have to back up several times to check the various conditions. When three or more levels of nesting are involved, the result may be very difficult to decipher. The first two versions in Example 7.1 are much easier to follow because the statements can be understood independently and read in sequence from top to bottom.

Really severe deviations from straightline code can be generated by the indiscriminate use of goto. With a goto, one can jump from any part of the program to any other, perhaps many lines or pages removed. Continuity can be completely destroyed, generating what has been dubbed "rat's nest code" or "logical spaghetti." Anyone who ever had the misfortune of having to deal with this type of program will realize the difficulty in understanding it. Often it is simpler to discard the program and start from the beginning than it is to modify a poorly structured program.

Older languages such as FORTRAN rely heavily on the goto statement for flow of control. Consequently, some years ago logical spaghetti was more the rule than the exception. It was the realization that the misuse of the goto was responsible for this situation that spawned the so-called structured programming revolution. At first it was thought that a complete ban on goto was needed, but it was quickly realized that it is possible to write bad code even without goto. In fact, the complete elimination of goto makes the nesting of if-then-else statements unavoidable. A more balanced viewpoint permits the use of goto in limited circumstances. In some of our examples, we have used them to terminate a program or a loop under exceptional circumstances. Because the purpose of the goto is strictly terminal, the resulting code can still be read in a straightline fashion. The branch does not lead to any alternate computation, so its path need not be followed. Once we understand the situation, we simply proceed to the next statement.

Good programming does not depend on the use or avoidance of any particular constructs. It is entirely governed by the judgment and common sense employed in using what is available. Well-structured code is code that can be read like a good essay. Sentences follow each other in an orderly fashion and are connected by a logical thread. A book in which consecutive paragraphs are printed on different pages or in which sentences are strung together randomly would be so difficult to read that it would be useless, and so is a poorly constructed program.

For small problems, such as the ones we have encountered so far, it is not difficult to achieve a good and clear structure. For larger problems, though, the sheer amount of detail becomes an important factor. Fortunately, there is a way in which even very large problems can be reduced to manageable proportions.

EXERCISES 7.2

1. Find examples where a goto is not only acceptable, but where its absence would be quite inconvenient. Can you find examples where a

`goto` is actually necessary? If not, does this suggest a way to prove that `goto` is unnecessary?

2. Why is the `case` statement preferable to nested `if-then-else` statements for multiple branching?

3. If the claim in Exercise 2 is correct, and `case` is better than nested `if-then-else` statements, why is a case statement not always used for multiple branching?

7.3

modular structure and top-down design

Large programs are difficult mainly because of their complexity; there are usually many parts with complicated relationships and considerable detail.

Of course, not only programs are complex. We are accustomed to dealing with complex objects and issues of many kinds. Often, we obtain an understanding of a complex phenomenon by considering it at various levels. At the highest level, that is, at the level of least detail, we may simply deal with a very rough description of its overall nature or purpose. Going somewhat deeper, we can then explain it in terms of its constituent parts and their interconnection. If these parts are still too complicated to be completely grasped, we can repeat the breakdown and explain each part in terms of its subparts, and so on.

Take for example our understanding of an airplane. On the first level we may simply think of it as a machine capable of flying through the air at a certain speed. While this description may be adequate for someone interested only in traveling, it explains little. We reach a deeper understanding of an airplane by noting that it is constructed of a jet engine, wings and fuselage, a navigation system, and so on. If we understand the basic functions of these parts and know how they are related, we begin to understand how an airplane works. To go further, we might study the physics and engineering behind the engine or explain the lift of the wings in terms of aerodynamics. Each level adds to our understanding, but also increases the amount of information we have to deal with.

We can follow the same pattern in studying complex programs. First, we consider a program as a whole to understand its purpose and expected performance. Next, we explain its structure in terms of a collection of subprograms. If these are too complicated, we break them down again. We continue until we are dealing with quite simple processes. The whole problem can then be perceived in a hierarchical fashion (Figure 7.2). This approach is called *top-down design*. It is, of course, just an application of stepwise refinement to complicated problems. At each stage, we ignore how the subprograms are to be implemented and concern ourselves only with understanding the structure at that level. Once we are satisfied that it is correct, we go down to the next level. Eventually we will reach the stage

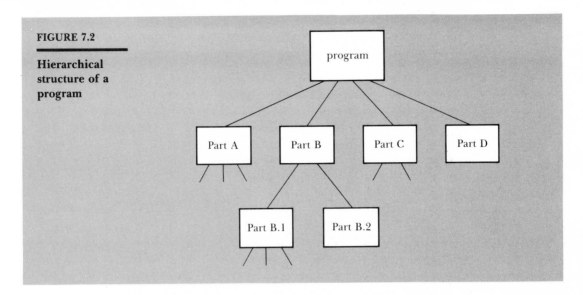

FIGURE 7.2

Hierarchical structure of a program

modular programming

where all subprograms are so simple that they can be implemented easily. The subprograms are sometimes called *modules;* hence its name, **modular programming.**

The advantage of top-down design is that each stage deals with a relatively simple problem, because each level ignores the details of the lower levels. In this way, a complex process is broken into a sequence of relatively easy steps. The end result is a number of simple modules. The idea seems obvious—too simple to be very useful. But try it on some difficult problems. In Section 7.4, we will present some relatively simple, yet by no means trivial examples to illustrate the approach.

In top-down design, we should strive to produce modules with the following features.

1. A module should implement a single, logically self-contained, and easily understood process.
2. Modules should be independent. How a particular module is written should not depend on the implementation of other modules.
3. Modules should be relatively short. In terms of their implementation, it is sometimes recommended that the code for a module be no longer than one page, but this is a guideline rather than a rigid requirement.

The requirements for writing a good module are much like those for writing functions and procedures.

EXERCISES 7.3

1. Is the top-down design method used in fields outside computer programming?

2. Why is one page a good upper limit for the length of a module? Why not make this limit smaller, say, ten lines?

7.4

program design

The design of a large program must be done carefully and systematically; the basic steps of problem solving will themselves become complicated subproblems requiring a good deal of work and attention.

problem specification

In problem specification, we describe the purpose and requirements of the program. For the student in an introductory course, the specifications for a program are usually given as part of an assignment. In real life, though, we do not often have this advantage, so we must start by drawing up a set of complete and detailed specifications. The importance of this step cannot be overemphasized. A mistake at this stage has serious consequences for all later work, because no amount of good programming can overcome errors in the problem statement.

Clarifying the program's purpose may itself be a major task. While the original description of the aims of the program may come from someone else, we are often called on to review, clarify, and expand on it. It is imperative that the programmer first pin down what is really needed, which may require considerable effort and cooperation between the programmer and the originator of the problem. The programmer must establish exactly what the program is supposed to do, what form and range the input will have, and how the output is to be returned. In the process, we often discover misunderstandings and difficulties that must be addressed. It is an unfortunate fact that, in the real world, the original specifications are often incomplete and ambiguous.

The programmer must also consider exceptions to the program's usual cases. Unusual cases, although of importance, are often overlooked initially. People used to dealing with problems on a more personal basis usually do not think about exceptional cases until they arise, at which time they deal with the situation on an ad hoc basis. But in a program, we have to plan ahead for all possible circumstances, and must get instructions on what is to be done in all cases from those who will be using the program. The goal of the specification phase should be a *specification document,* giving precise answers to these questions without loopholes or unanswered questions.

algorithm design

Except for the very simplest problems, algorithm design should be done top down. We break the problem into a few major parts, and in turn subdivide these where necessary until the lowest level modules are simple enough to pose no difficulty. We specify what each module does and how the various modules are interrelated. Any convenient pseudolanguage may be used. We must also decide what data structures are most appropriate for the problem at hand.

The algorithm design phase is completed when we have a full description of the method by which the problem is to be solved. At this point, we should review the specifications to make sure that all points have been covered. When this review uncovers no problems, we are ready to proceed with the coding.

coding

In coding, we translate the design into an actual programming language. Most of the difficulties should have been overcome at the previous stages, leaving us free to devote our full attention to style and effectiveness in using the language. Using a modular design allows the coding of each part separately. Once this is done the modules are integrated to produce the final program.

First, a programming language must be chosen that is suitable for the problem at hand. Every language, no matter how well designed, has some tricky features—for example, the dangling else in Pascal, discussed on page 72. We should have a thorough understanding of the language we use. We should be aware of the problem areas and treat them with care or avoid them altogether.

Code cleanly and simply. While minor modifications of a code are inevitable, beware of major changes. If significant changes are necessary, discard the old code and restart. Modules are supposed to be short and independent, so redoing one from the beginning should not be a major undertaking.

Let us now do two examples to show how these general concepts work in practice. The first one we will do in full detail; the second, which is actually a fair-sized problem, will be treated much more superficially.

EXAMPLE 7.2

PLOTTING A BAR GRAPH

The program in Example 6.4 includes a procedure for plotting a bar graph. This procedure, BARGRAPH, is quite minimal. A more sophisticated procedure should not only print bars, but should also provide axes with labels and scale the values so that the graph fits into a specified size. Our new program BETTERBAR will do this.

The input to the program will be

1. HEIGHT, an integer giving the number of vertical positions in the graph.
2. A number of records, each consisting of (a) a two-character category identifier CATEGORYID, and (b) the corresponding frequency count FREQ, which can be any nonnegative integer.

The number of records will be variable, the end being the end of the input file. The input will then look like

```
HEIGHT
CATEGORYID FREQ
CATEGORYID FREQ
  .
  .
  .
CATEGORYID FREQ
end of file
```

For output, the program will use symbols '*'to print bars. Each '*' will represent a number of units, chosen so that the graph does not exceed the specified height. The left axis will be printed with dots, except every fifth dot will be replaced with '−', preceded by a number giving the axis value at that point. The bottom axis will be a line of '−'s, below which the category identifiers will be printed vertically.

As far as exceptional conditions are concerned, we will check that FREQ is nonnegative. If FREQ is negative, an error message will be printed and the program terminated. In addition, if there are more categories than will fit into the width of the graph, an error message will be printed and the program terminated. The maximum allowable width will be specified by a constant LINEWIDTH.

There are four major parts to this program:

1. INDATA. Read and check data.
2. SCALEGRAPH. Determine the scale factor SCALE for the graph.
3. DRAWLINE. Print a complete horizontal line for the graph.
4. DRAWBOTTOM. Print the three lines at bottom, that is, the bottom axis and the category identifiers.

With these four parts, the program can be written as

```
INDATA;
SCALEGRAPH;
for I:=HEIGHT downto 1 do
   DRAWLINE(I);
DRAWBOTTOM
```

We next consider each part in more detail.

1. INDATA. Read HEIGHT, then successive values of CATEGORYID and FREQ until the end of the file is reached. Let CATEG be the total number of categories. Check that CATEG is not too large and that FREQ is nonnegative. If an error is found, set ERRORFLAG to true.

2. SCALEGRAPH. Find MAX, the maximum of all FREQ values. Compute scale factor SCALE by

   SCALE= (MAX div HEIGHT)+1

3. DRAWLINE(I). This prints the Ith line. When I is a multiple of five, the line will have the appearance

   S— x x ... x

   where x is either a '*' or a blank, and S=SCALE*I. When I is not a multiple of five, the line drawn is

   , x x ... x

4. DRAWBOTTOM. The three lines for the bottom are

   - - - - - - - - - - - - - -
   X X X X X X X
   Y Y Y Y Y Y Y

   where X and Y represent the first and second characters of CATEGORYID, respectively.

The pseudolanguage used here to describe the algorithm is rather mixed and informal, but it is convenient for this particular case. At this point, the description of each part is sufficiently detailed that coding should be relatively easy.

We will implement each part as a procedure. The main program will call these procedures as shown. The data structures have to be defined and one addition is made to the main program given before. The variable ERRORFLAG, set in INDATA, will be tested and the graph plotted only if ERRORFLAG is false.

```
Program BETTERBAR(input,output);
{ prints bar graph, scaled to size,
  with labelled axes }
const LINEWIDTH=50;
type DATA=record
            ID:array[1..2] of char;
            FREQ:integer
          end;
var HEIGHT,CATEG,I,SCALE:integer;
    SAMPLE:array[1..50] of DATA;
    ERRORFLAG:boolean;

procedure INDATA;
{ input procedure, reads data
```

```
      checks for negative frequencies
      and too many categories
      if error is found ERRORFLAG is set to true }
begin
   ERRORFLAG:=false;
   {read all data, count # of categories }
   readln(HEIGHT);
   CATEG:=0;
   repeat
     CATEG:=CATEG+1;
     readln(SAMPLE[CATEG].ID[1],
            SAMPLE[CATEG].ID[2],
            SAMPLE[CATEG].FREQ);
    if (SAMPLE[CATEG].FREQ<0)
       or (2*CATEG>LINEWIDTH)
      then ERRORFLAG:=true
   until eof or ERRORFLAG;
   {bad data recognized if some frequency is
    negative or there are too many categories}
   if ERRORFLAG
     then begin
             writeln('error in INDATA');
             writeln('bad data')
          end
end;


procedure SCALEGRAPH;
{ determines a scale factor for graph
  SCALE is smallest value so that
  graph will fit into HEIGHT }
var I,MAX:integer;
begin
   MAX:=0;
   for I:=1 to CATEG do
     if SAMPLE[I].FREQ>MAX
       then MAX:=SAMPLE[I].FREQ;
   SCALE:=MAX div HEIGHT+1
end;


procedure DRAWLINE(J:integer);
{ prints a complete horizontal line }
var I:integer;
begin
   if (J mod 5=0)
     then write(J*SCALE:4,'-')
     else write('    ,');
```

```
    for I:=1 to CATEG do
      if SAMPLE[I].FREQ>=J*SCALE
        then write(' *')
        else write('  ');
    writeln
end;

procedure DRAWBOTTOM;
{ prints three bottom lines }
var I:integer;
begin
  write('      ');
  for I:=1 to CATEG do
    write('--');
  writeln;
  write('      ');
  for I:=1 to CATEG do
    write(' ',SAMPLE[I].ID[1]);
  writeln;
  write('      ');
  for I:=1 to CATEG do
    write(' ',SAMPLE[I].ID[2]);
  writeln
end;

{ main program, integrating four
  procedures into bar graph printing
  algorithm }
begin
  INDATA;
  if not ERRORFLAG
    then begin
           SCALEGRAPH;
           for I:=HEIGHT downto 1 do
             DRAWLINE(I);
           DRAWBOTTOM
         end
end.
```

Sample input

```
    20
    FR 50
    SO 64
    JR 45
    SR 31
    GR 21
```

Output

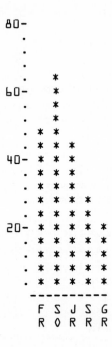

```
80-
  .
  .
  .
  .        *
60-        *
  .        *
  .        *
  .    *   *
  .    *   *   *
40-    *   *   *
  .    *   *   *
  .    *   *   *
  .    *   *   *   *
  .    *   *   *   *
20-    *   *   *   *   *
  .    *   *   *   *   *
  .    *   *   *   *   *
  .    *   *   *   *   *
  .    *   *   *   *   *
   ----------------------
       F   S   J   S   G
       R   O   R   R   R
```

One noteworthy feature of this program is its almost exclusive use of global variables. This is not ideal, because it makes the modules somewhat dependent. While logically separate, the modules are coupled through the use of common data. But the alternative of using all local variables, unfortunately, would require lengthy parameter lists and thereby complicate what is still a rather simple exercise.

Note the method of terminating the program when an error in input is found. When INDATA detects an error, it sets ERRORFLAG to true and prints a suitable message. The main program uses ERRORFLAG to determine if the graph can be drawn. An alternative would be to use a global label for the last statement of the main program. A goto statement could then be used to terminate the computations when an error is found. The use of global labels is generally not a good practice, since they make it difficult to use a subprogram in some instances. For example, a programmer who wants to use such a procedure must be aware of what labels are used and has to provide them in the main program. The programmer therefore has to know not only what the procedure does, but also how it is coded.

Top-down design can be effective even in short problems such as this. By breaking the problem into four parts, we have made each part simple enough to have an easy algorithm and straightforward implementation.

EXAMPLE 7.3

A GAME-PLAYING PROGRAM

Programming a computer to play various games is a popular pastime with computer enthusiasts. These programs range from ticktacktoe to chess. Such a program can be very lengthy even for the simpler games. It would lead us too far afield to do such a program in as much detail as the previous example, so we will limit ourselves to showing the overall structure and a framework that you can use for further expansion.

For the sake of argument, think of checkers. Actually, we will not go to the level where a complete stragegy has to be found (not a simple task), so the exact rules of the game are immaterial. We will assume that we are dealing with some sort of board game in which the human player and the computer alternate moves. The game ends after a finite number of moves in a win, a loss, or a draw.

First, we need to consider the specifications. Let us assume that we have a visual display terminal available that we use to communicate with the computer. We will assume that the communication is interactive, that is, that the computer takes as input what is typed on the terminal and displays the output on a video screen. Input and output alternate, simulating a conversation between the user and the computer. We also assume that the computer always yields the first move to its opponent, then alternately makes its move and accepts its adversary's response. When the game is finished, the computer is to print an appropriate message, then terminate the session. The specifications as given are quite rough and not particularly precise, but are sufficient to explain generally what is required. If we were actually to complete the program, we would need to draw up a much more detailed set of specifications.

Let us begin the algorithm design by understanding the various parts of our program called GAME. The human user must be able to initiate play by giving a certain message. Explanation of the rules or protocol for communication may have to be given by the computer at this time. Next, the computer will need to obtain input from the user describing the user's move. The computer also needs an algorithm for making its own move. It will need to be programmed to display the board. Finally, it will need to detect the end of the game and carry out termination action. In a real situation, there may be further requirements, but we will stop at this point.

Having defined the major parts that make up GAME, we can draw the first level in our top-down design. Figure 7.3 shows the different subprograms that are needed to implement GAME.

Omitting details of the underlying data structures, we can now sketch the program.

```
program GAME(input,output);
var FINISHED:boolean;
```

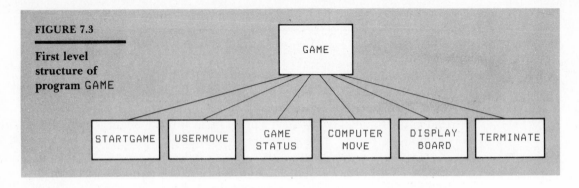

FIGURE 7.3

**First level
structure of
program** GAME

```
begin
  STARTGAME;
  repeat
    USERMOVE;
    GAMESTATUS(FINISHED);
    if not FINISHED
      then begin
              COMPUTERMOVE;
              GAMESTATUS(FINISHED)
           end;
    DISPLAYBOARD;
  until FINISHED;
  TERMINATE
end.
```

This is not a complete program, because we have not declared the data
structures to be used. Otherwise, though, it gives a full implementation of
GAME in terms of a number of procedures yet to be written. To continue,
we need to implement these procedures, so we go to the next level.

Take for example the module USERMOVE. What is required here is
that the computer ask the user for the next move (by printing some appropriate prompting message), check and accept valid moves, and update the
stored information to remember the move. This gives us the structure for
USERMOVE shown in Figure 7.4. The code for USERMOVE is

```
procedure USERMOVE;
var VALID:boolean;
begin
  repeat
    USERINPUT;
    VALIDITYCHECK(VALID);
    if VALID
      then ACCEPT
```

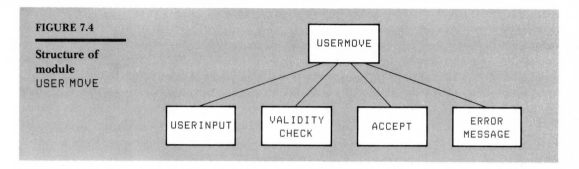

FIGURE 7.4

**Structure of
module
USER MOVE**

```
         else ERRORMESSAGE
      until VALID
   end
```

In this procedure, the modules used are quite simple and it should be possible to code them without further subdivision. For the other parts of GAME, such as COMPUTERMOVE for a complicated game, it may be necessary to have several more levels before the stage is reached where the modules are simple enough.

This example, although only sketched, gives insight into the power of top-down design. Even in a fairly difficult problem, every step of the way is logically simple, easy to understand, and simple to implement. In this way we avoid getting entangled in details or becoming overwhelmed by the task. Top-down design is effective in reducing the complexity of even the lengthiest programs.

EXERCISES 7.4

1. Rewrite BETTERBAR using only local variables.
2. What will happen in BETTERBAR if HEIGHT<5? What, if anything, should be done to improve the program in this case?
3. Modify program GAME (and the relevant modules) so that the computer will give special instructions to the user after five consecutive illegal moves have been made.
4. For each of the following problems, complete the specifications and carry out the design and implementation.
   a. A bar graph printing program that can handle both positive and negative counts in the same data set.
   b. A program to print out a calendar for any given year of the twentieth century.

    c. A program for constructing from a piece of text a list of all words in the text, together with a count of their frequency of occurrence.

    d. A program to play ticktacktoe.

    e. A program that simulates the machine language described in Chapter 1. This program should accept machine language statements and carry out the specified steps. Effectively, this means that the simulation program should accept the same input and produce the same output as any machine language code.

7.5

input-output handling

Many programs are written to be used by nonexperts, in some instances by people with little or no technical training. In such cases, it is essential that communication between the user and the computer be as safe and easy as possible. Proper handling of input and output is an important component of good programming and deserves special attention.

Output must be presented in readable form. Just printing long strings of numbers and leaving it to the reader to determine what each item means is unacceptable. Results must be properly identified with meaningful labels. When several pages are produced, each page should have a number and a title. It must be possible to understand the output without knowing anything about the program. When appropriate, output should be arranged in tabular form or given in some other visually concise way, such as a graph.

Safety and convenience should be primary in the choice of input format. The format should make it easy to check the input visually. In Example 6.4, each line of input was prefixed with a sample identification letter, and individual samples were separated by a special line. It is much easier this way to see where one sample ends and the next begins than it would be if we just ran all input items together.

In an interactive environment in which user input is needed, a cue should be given. Rather than rely on the user to give the right value at the right time, a prompting message such as

```
Number of parts of type X ?
```

will alert the user to what is needed. Make it a rule to design the input part to make it easy for people, not to save work or cut down on computer time.

We must also take into account that people are often careless. We frequently hear about spectacular "computer mistakes," such as a computer's issuing a paycheck for a million dollars. Most of the time, such disasters are the result of input errors. Although data are generally double-checked, errors can slip through. It is a good practice to check the input for validity and plausibility.

How far a program should go in checking input is a delicate question. Extensive validation may be so expensive that it seriously affects the performance of the program. Consider, for example, the program BETTERBAR. Some input checking is done to catch the most obvious errors, but the validation is certainly not complete. We have not, for instance, checked that all category identifiers are different, as one would expect, or that the frequencies are in some plausible range (what is plausible would, of course, depend on the source of the data). We could provide for all of this by making the program longer. The extent of input validation must be decided for each individual case, by considering the likelihood of certain types of errors and weighing the effort required for their detection against the consequences of missing them. To be avoided at all costs is the situation in which the program accepts invalid input and produces plausible but incorrect results without any indication of trouble. One widely used practice is to *echo* the input, that is, print the input values together with the output. This allows an easy check to ascertain whether the input was correct.

The input design should not place any unnecessary demands on the user. As a case in point, suppose that a programmer is writing a program to process a variable number of items. Suppose that, for one reason or another, it is not possible to use the end-of-file condition to detect the end of the data (perhaps there are several sets of data in the input file). A thoughtless programmer might solve the problem by writing

```
readln(N);
for I:=1 to N do
   read(ITEM[I])
```

asking that the user include a header item N, giving the number of data items to be expected. This not only makes much additional work for the user, but it is also extremely susceptible to error. A wrong count may play havoc with the rest of the run. There is little excuse for such a practice. A better solution is to add a fictitious but clearly identifiable item at the end of the input, say, the number −999999. If such a number cannot be a regular data item, then the test

```
if ITEM[I]=-999999
```

will detect the end of the data. Another reasonable solution is the one suggested in Example 6.4.

EXERCISES 7.5

1. Is input echoing ever inconvenient or undesirable?
2. Redesign the input part of SAMPLES in Example 6.4 for interactive input.
3. Redesign procedure INDATA in program BETTERBAR to do more complete input validation.

4. Redesign INDATA for interactive input.
5. Is there anything objectionable in the input design for program RATING in Example 5.1? If so, can you improve on it?
6. Improve the input design for program INVENTORY in Example 5.6.

7.6

program modification

A good program, as we know, should be easy to modify. Although programmers tend to think of their work as a completely finished product that will never have to be changed, this is rarely the case. First, there may be undetected errors. No matter how careful the check of a complex code, some errors may remain. These errors usually occur in connection with exceptional data, and it may be months or years before they are discovered. Second, the requirements of a program may change. The results produced by the initial version often suggest alternate approaches or raise unanticipated questions. Many times a program written by one person will be adapted by another to a somewhat different purpose. All of these reasons make the need for program modification common; in fact, programs that are never modified are the exception rather than the rule. The task of making changes in existing programs is called *program maintenance*. Many computer installations devote a significant part of their available resources to such maintenance activity.

We should always try, within practical limits, to make our programs as readily modifiable as possible. Some elementary techniques for achieving this have already been mentioned. Use symbolic constants wherever a change is conceivable. Keep the modules independent. Make sure that your modules are written so that a change in one will not affect the others. A major reason why programs are sensitive to modification is that a change in one module causes a "ripple effect" that spreads to others. For example, take a case in which one module requires that some variable be initialized to zero, and assume that the module used immediately before does indeed leave the variable in question with value zero. The clever programmer, to save time, may omit initialization in the latter module, because it appears to be redundant. However, when later changes are made, what might be only an incidental feature of the first module could be altered, causing the second module to malfunction and putting the whole program in danger of collapse. The programmer made the mistake of using a feature of one module when writing another. Keeping modules independent is the easiest way of writing modifiable programs.

One factor that strongly affects the modifiability of a program is the choice of the algorithm. Within practical limits, the algorithm should be general, independent of accidental properties of the data. If the algorithm is too closely tied to specific requirements, a change in these requirements may make lengthy reprogramming necessary.

Take as a simple case the program GRADE in Example 4.1. The algorithm to determine the letter grade category from the percent score uses the statement

```
CATEGORY:=trunc(PERCENT) div 10
```

This is short and efficient, but depends very much on the fact that each category extends exactly over 10%. For some modifications, say a change in the range of As to 88%–100%, the computation of CATEGORY will have to be done in a completely different way. The program GRADE could be made much more general by using another algorithm for computing LETTERGRADE. For example, we could define

```
const ALIMIT=90;
      BLIMIT=80;
      CLIMIT=70;
         .
         .
         .
```

and then write

```
if PERCENT>=ALIMIT
   then LETTERGRADE:='A';
if (PERCENT>=BLIMIT) and (PERCENT<ALIMIT)
   then LETTERGRADE:='B';
      .
      .
      .
```

The use of symbolic constants, together with a more flexible algorithm, makes a change in the grade ranges a trivial matter.

As another example, consider program BETTERBAR in Example 6.2. The extensive use of global variables reduces the independence of the modules and makes the program vulnerable to changes. Actually, the situation is not particularly complicated, and the modular dependence through the data is not as serious as it might be in less obvious situations. Some features of the code help. The use of the symbolic constant LINEWIDTH makes it easy to narrow or widen the graph. On the other hand, to change the spacing between the bars (not an unreasonable potential modification) is a more difficult matter and will require some reprogramming. Other features, such as limiting the number of categories to 50, are unnecessarily restrictive.

Certainly neither GRADE nor BETTERBAR are very general and flexible. An excuse, if not a justification, is that to make a program general usually requires much additional work. It also requires that we anticipate likely changes. In most actual applications, the effort to do this is worthwhile, but in our examples, it might have obscured the points we were trying to bring out. (Try to make GRADE and BETTERBAR more modifiable as an exercise.)

EXERCISES 7.6

1. What other changes can you foresee in GRADE? Rewrite the program to make it more suitable for such changes.
2. Rewrite BETTERBAR to make it as general as you can.
3. Evaluate all the programs in this book to find features that make plausible modifications difficult.

7.7
writing efficient programs

The term "efficiency" permits several interpretations. Efficiency is defined with respect to available resources; these include both computer hardware and manpower. Twenty-five years ago, computers were slow and expensive, and problems that are considered trivial today were complicated enough to tax the power of computers. Consequently, it was imperative to utilize the hardware as efficiently as possible. In the intervening years, computers have grown phenomenally in capacity and speed, and the cost of hardware has dropped significantly. At the same time, costs of program preparation and maintenance have risen, so that these are the major concerns nowadays.

The various types of efficiency are often in conflict. A program that is well structured and readable may be much slower than one written specifically with execution speed in mind. Extensive input validation may make the program safer, but may increase its size and slow it down. Consequently, priorities must be established when the program is designed that take into account the nature and ultimate use of the program. If a program is to be used in a limited environment or used only a few times, it is clearly more important to save time in writing and debugging. The style of coding should be chosen accordingly. Conversely, in a program that will be used again and again (for example, a sorting procedure), speed of execution ought to be a major concern, because even a small saving will pay large dividends over a long period of time. There are certain applications, called *real-time* problems, where the computer must process and respond to signals within a limited and often very short time. For example, a computer used to guide a missile must process data and initiate proper actions within as little as a fraction of a second. If the necessary computations are not completed in that time, they are useless. In such a situation, execution speed may be an overriding factor.

We have already discussed some ways to make the actual writing of a program more time efficient; the techniques of producing good code also reduce programming time by eliminating errors and reducing the need for reprogramming. Methods for efficient testing and debugging will be discussed in Chapter 8. In this section, we will discuss some ways to utilize hardware efficiently.

The best way to design a fast and efficient program is to use the best available algorithm. Different algorithms can have widely varying efficiencies. It is in the selection of the algorithm that the programmer can most profitably exercise creativity and ingenuity. We will discuss the challenge of discovering algorithms in Chapters 12 and 13. After an algorithm has been selected, the two major factors for efficiency are execution (CPU) time and storage space. Let us consider first the somewhat more easily treated execution time.

execution time

To predict how much CPU time a program will take, the programmer must know what will happen at the machine language level. We need to know not only the characteristics of the machine language instructions, but also how the compiler translates code in a higher level language into machine language. Few application programmers have this kind of information, and it is difficult to obtain. Nevertheless, by anticipating the likely action of a compiler and by knowing some general characteristics of hardware, we can establish some rules of thumb. Let us consider a few cases to illustrate this point.

The statement `A:=B+B` is likely to be more efficient than `A:=2*B`, because addition is usually faster than multiplication. Similarly, because multiplication is usually faster than division, `A:=0.1*B` is better than `A:=B/10`. (However, this is only a generalization. Some computers have instructions that can manipulate the bits in a word. Shifting bits left or right allows a fast multiplication by powers of two. When a smart compiler takes advantage of this, `2*B` may actually be faster than `B+B`.)

Sometimes, unnecessary computations can be eliminated by extracting common subexpressions. In

```
SOLUTION1:=X+B*sqrt(Y);
SOLUTION2:=X-B*sqrt(Y)
```

we can improve efficiency by using

```
TEMP:=B*sqrt(Y);
SOLUTION1:=X+TEMP;
SOLUTION2:=X-TEMP
```

Note, however, that the introduction of the extra variable `TEMP` decreases the directness of the code. Here, execution efficiency conflicts with good style.

In a loop, we should remove computations that are the same during each traversal. Thus, in

```
for I:= 1 to N do
   X[I]:=0.5*sin(A)*Y[I]
```

we can substitute

```
C:=0.5*sin(A);
for I:= 1 to N do
  X[I]:=C*Y[I]
```

saving a considerable amount of computation.

Look for other unnecessary computations. For example

```
if  X=0
   then  Y:=1;
if  X<>0
   then  Y:=0
```

is improved by

```
if  X=0
   then  Y:=1
   else  Y:=0
```

because the second version needs only one test.

As a more complicated example, take the following. X is a one-dimensional array of N elements. FLAG is a boolean variable that is to be set to true if X contains any zero entry, and to false otherwise. We can write this as

```
FLAG:=false;
for I:=1 to N do
   if X[I]=0
      then FLAG:=true
```

On occasion, this code will do much more work than necessary. If X[1] is zero the rest of the array is still checked, although the answer is known after the first comparison. We can therefore try

```
FLAG:=false;
I:=0;
repeat
   I:=I+1;
   if X[I]=0
      then FLAG:=true
until (FLAG=true) or (I=N)
```

Here, the loop terminates as soon as a zero is found. But is the second version better? The answer is not clear. The loop in the second version probably takes more time than the first one. If there are no zeros in X, the first version is undoubtedly better. For cases where there are zeros near the beginning of X, one might prefer the second code.

A similar situation occurred in the function VALID in Example 6.5. The loop

```
for I:=INIT+1 to FINAL-1 do
   if (EXPR[I]='+') or (EXPR[I]='-')
      and VALID(INIT,I-1)
      and VALID(I+1,FINAL)
   then VALID:=true
```

tests whether the expression can be split into two subexpressions, and continues even after a valid split has been found. Because of the recursion, the computations in the loop can be extensive for long expressions. In this case, it is much more effective to assure that the loop terminates as soon as possible. The given code can be replaced with

```
I:=INIT;
OK:=false;
while (I<FINAL-1) and (not(OK)) do
   begin
      I:=I+1;
      if (EXPR[I]='+') or (EXPR[I]='-')
         and VALID(INIT,I-1)
         and VALID(I+1,FINAL)
      then OK:=true
   end
VALID:=OK
```

In addition, the program can benefit from other modifications (we will leave these as exercises). One can improve the program considerably this way. The original version, although conceptually simple, is extremely inefficient for long expressions.

Indexing of arrays generates a certain amount of overhead, because computations have to be performed to map the index notation into an actual address in the computer memory. This overhead can be quite high for multidimensional arrays. A very common process in scientific computations is matrix multiplication, for which a simple form is

```
for I:=1 to N do
   for J:=1 to N do
      begin
         C[I,J]:=0;
         for K:=1 to N do
            C[I,J]:=C[I,J]+A[I,K]*B[K,J]
      end
```

This is considerably improved by

```
for I:=1 to N do
  for J:=1 to N do
    begin
      SUM:=0;
      for K:=1 to N do
        SUM:=SUM+A[I,K]*B[K,J];
      C[I,J]:=SUM
    end
```

By reducing the use of double subscripts in the innermost loop, we can increase speed significantly.

Another source of overhead in indexing is checking of the index for range. Although not all languages have this feature, Pascal does. Whenever an index is computed, it must be checked against the allowable limits, so that an extra few operations are done. For efficiency, arrays should be used only when necessary.

Loop control involves some overhead for testing and incrementing the loop variables. If possible, loops should be combined. Thus

```
for I:=1 to N do
  A[I]:=0;
for I:=1 to N do
  B[I]:=0
```

can be rewritten as a single loop

```
for I:=1 to N do
  begin
    A[I]:=0;
    B[I]:=0
  end
```

Function and procedure calls also generate some extra work, because each call requires passing parameters from the calling program to the subprogram. The use of procedures is desirable from a structural viewpoint, but overdoing it may lead to a degeneration of performance.

With a little thought, you will discover additional plausible optimization rules. But remember, what is important is not the specifics, but the realization that code can be improved. To develop rules that are useful in a particular situation, you must know something more about the compiler than we have discussed. The guidelines given here are based on the assumption that the translation from the higher level language to machine language is done simply, with expressions translated essentially as they are written. This is not always the case. Many compilers have facilities for code optimization, and some of the suggested improvements may be done automatically. When working with an optimizing compiler, it is best to leave at least the most obvious improvements to the compiler. In any case, it is sometimes difficult to predict the actions of a compiler. It is therefore essential to investigate the various versions by actual measurement of CPU time. Don't assume that some trick will work just because it seems plausible.

Finally, remember that most programs contain some crucial segments, perhaps one or two inner loops, where most of the CPU time is used. These segments should be identified and carefully optimized. It is a waste of time to optimize parts of the program that are executed only a few times.

storage space

Storage optimization involves writing the program so that its demand for main memory (perhaps also secondary storage) is minimized. The most crucial element here is the choice of the data structures and their representation in memory. We will discuss this topic in more detail in Chapters 9 and 10. But apart from a careful choice of the data structures, we have very few ways to decrease storage requirements when using a higher level language. This is particularly true for Pascal.

Storage optimization is complicated (or perhaps made unnecessary) by the increasing tendency in modern operating systems to remove storage assignment completely from the programmer's consideration. In a time-sharing system, only those parts of a program that are immediately needed may be kept in main memory. Other parts are kept in secondary storage. When needed information is not in main memory, the operating system will recognize this and bring the information into main memory, at the same time removing parts of the program that are no longer needed. In such an environment, the total size of a program is much less important than the frequency with which information is transported to and from secondary storage. Optimizing under such circumstances requires a great deal of insight into the operating system.

EXERCISES 7.7

1. Find out whether, in your system, the improvements suggested in this section actually work.
2. Does your compiler do code optimization? If so, find out what sorts of improvements it can and cannot make.
3. Make a rough estimate of the CPU time saved by the optimization of the matrix multiplication code on page 193.
4. Give all the reasons why

```
R:=Z+1;
if Z>Y+3
   then X:=R
   else X:=R+1
```

can be expected to be more efficient than

```
R:=Z+1;
if  Z-1>Y+2
   then  X:=Z+1
   else  X:=Z+2
```

5. Optimize the code

```
for  I:=1 to  N  do
   for  J:=1 to  N  do
      C[I,J]:=A[I+1]*B[J-1]-sqrt(abs(A[I+1]))
```

6. Improve the following code:

```
for  I:=1 to  N  do
   for  J:=1 to  N  do
      if  I>J
         then  writeln(A[I],A[J])
```

7. For the example on page 192, we can also write

```
I:=0;
repeat
   I:=I+1;
until  (X[I]=0)  or  (I=N)
FLAG:=(X[I]=0)
```

How does this compare in efficiency and readability to the previous versions?

8. The code

```
S:=0;
for  I:=1 to  10  do
   S:=S+A[I]
```

can be improved by

```
S:=A[1];
for  I:=2 to  10  do
   S:=S+A[I]
```

Give a rough estimate of the percentage of time saved by the improvement.

9. Complete the suggested improvement for VALID. Then carry out an actual computer test to compare the efficiency of the original version and the modification.

10. Look for other inefficiencies in VALID. Write a new function that is as efficient as you can make it. Then run some computer tests to compare it with the original.

7.8

documentation

No program can ever be so well constructed that its meaning is completely explicit. *Documentation* is additional information and description that help us to understand a given code. Its purpose is to provide guidance and explanation to the user.

We can distinguish here between *internal* and *external* documentation. Internal documentation is actually part of the code—essentially, just an explanation of the various aspects through comments. External documentation exists separately and may involve descriptions in various forms. Internal and external documentation must be consistent with each other and with the code. A great deal of care is needed to assure that this is so.

It is sometimes said that a properly constructed program with good internal documentation is adequate, and that such self-documenting programs largely eliminate the need for external documentation. It is certainly true that internal documentation is important, but external documentation provides a great deal more flexibility. For example, external documentation allows the use of graphs, charts, and mathematical symbols that are not easily expressed as comments. Thus, external documentation is usually a necessary complement to internal documentation.

Proper documentation is important for all programs; it is crucial for programs receiving wide use. Poor documentation detracts from the best program, even to the point of making it useless. Programmers will generally not release their programs while they contain known errors; it should also be (but unfortunately is not) a universal practice not to release a program without adequate documentation.

Because documentation is essentially for the program's users, its form should depend on its prospective audience. There are a variety of users, hence various forms of documentation are needed. At the simplest level, a user may be interested only in what the program can do to determine whether it is suitable for a given purpose. If someone decides to use a program, he or she will need more detailed information on how to use it. If modifications are to be made, even more details are needed. These different needs call for several levels of documentation.

Documentation should mirror the design of the program. The most satisfactory way is to develop a program and its documentation simultaneously, rather than adding the documentation to the finished code. Because program development is a hierarchical process, documentation will have the same structure. The various parts necessary to describe a particular project are shown in Figure 7.5. Each part of the documentation can be essentially self-contained, referring to lower levels for details and to

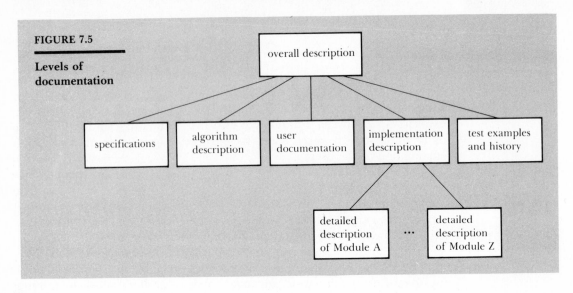

FIGURE 7.5

Levels of documentation

higher levels for an overview of organization. The parts shown in Figure 7.5 are quite standard. The specifications tell the purpose of the program and the circumstances under which it will work. The description of the algorithm and user documentation are valuable to potential users. The user documentation is especially important. It should give the details of usage, requirements of the input, what to expect, estimates of running time, exceptional cases, and so on. The implementation description, with its several levels, describes the actual code and should be closely related to the corresponding top-down design and stepwise refinement.

The language used for the documentation will depend on what we are describing. The overall specifications and the user documentation are usually in the form of a verbal discussion. Structure diagrams and flowcharts are usually used to describe the implementation. In general, it is best to use the language most easily understood by those most likely to be interested in the program.

The extent of the required documentation depends on the projected use of the program. A program that will be used frequently and is expected to have a long life will certainly need extensive documentation, in contrast to programs that are used only a few times. Overdocumentation is rare, however. Most programs are poorly and insufficiently documented. It is best to be cautious and document every program thoroughly.

Documentation must also be maintained along with the program. As the program is changed, the various parts of the documentation will have to be revised to reflect the modifications.

7.9

summary

Some have proposed that specific rules and standards be established for programming: limiting the length of modules, requiring a minimum ratio of comments to executable statements, or prohibiting the use of `goto` statements. There are good reasons for introducing standards into a field characterized by individualism. But there are no magic formulas for writing effective programs; when rules are made rigid and followed blindly, the results are likely to be disappointing. In short, success in programming depends primarily on discipline and good judgment.

To become a good programmer, you must be able to think clearly and to resist the temptation to be clever for no particular purpose. You must be willing to admit that you will make mistakes and plan for them in advance. You must have sufficient perspective to put yourself in the place of the future reader to anticipate difficulties. You should be considerate in trying to help those who will later have to deal with the results of your efforts. There is nothing very sophisticated in this, only common sense. The major obstacle to good programming is not a lack of some arcane techniques, but the steadfast and perverse refusal of some to adopt these simple and obvious practices.

Our discussion of effective programming has by no means been exhaustive. But the topic is important; good programming habits can greatly improve both the programmer's efficiency and the quality of the final program. A number of quite enjoyable books have been written on good programming techniques, and some of the more helpful ones are listed at the end of this chapter. We encourage you to refer to them for more information.

further reading

Kernighan, B. W., and Plauger, P. J. *The Elements of Programming Style*, 2d. ed. New York: McGraw-Hill, 1978.

Schneider, G. M., Weingart, S. W., and Perlman, D. M. *An Introduction to Programming and Problem Solving with Pascal*, Chapter 9. New York: John Wiley & Sons, 1978.

Van Tassel, D. *Programming Style, Design, Efficiency, Debugging, and Testing*, Chapters 1, 2, and 3. Englewood Cliffs, N. J.: Prentice-Hall, 1978.

Yourdon, E. *Techniques for Program Structure and Design*. Englewood Cliffs, N. J.: Prentice-Hall, 1975.

testing and debugging programs

No matter how sincere our intentions as programmers, errors somehow slip into our work. Sometimes they are caused by the sheer difficulty and magnitude of the project; more often they are the result of haste and carelessness. In any case, when coding is completed, any but the simplest programs must be expected to contain errors. To detect and correct errors can be a major undertaking, often requiring as much or more time than the design and coding (especially if these are done sloppily). It is therefore very important to learn how to test and debug programs well, both to reduce the effort required for this phase and to improve the program's reliability.

In practice, testing and debugging tend to overlap. In testing, we examine the program until we are satisfied that it is free of errors. Program testing relies heavily on running the program under various conditions or with inputs for which the results can be predicted. We usually run a good many different test examples to be reasonably sure that no errors remain. Unfortunately, testing cannot absolutely assure us that a program is correct. If the test cases do not reveal errors, it may simply mean that the tests were not sufficiently thorough. It is not uncommon for long programs to contain undiscovered errors even after extensive testing. Test examples have to be selected carefully if we can hope to have reasonable confidence in a program.

In debugging, we fix the errors that have been detected. Debugging involves locating the part of the code responsible for the error and correcting it. Often, locating the error is the most difficult part. When a program is well structured, the task is much simpler.

It pays to be skeptical and to employ what is sometimes called *defensive programming*. We have to admit that we will make mistakes and plan for them when we design the program—that is, we should write code so that detecting and removing errors are as simple as possible. This is a subtle business that deserves more attention than is given it by most programmers.

8.1

error types

specification errors

Errors of varying degrees of seriousness can and do arise in all phases of programming. Good arguments can be made that the specification phase is the most critical, and that misunderstanding of the problem is the most common source of error. It is certainly true that these **specification errors** are the most serious. A program written to incorrect specifications may be completely useless. The programmer must avoid any misunderstanding by carrying out a thorough review and discussing the specifications with the originator of the problem. Errors in the algorithm or the design are also quite serious. If undiscovered until the coding is well advanced, extensive recoding may be required. Again, a careful analysis of the algorithm and of all the stages of the design is essential.

syntax errors

At the coding stage, **syntax errors** are quite common. They can arise from typing errors or from misunderstanding of the language used. Most of the time, syntax errors are detected by the compiler and corrected easily. (Nevertheless, too many syntax errors will waste much of your time.) There are rare occasions when, due to an error in the compiler, a syntax error will go undetected. When this happens, the compiler may assign some more or less unpredictable meaning to the offending statement, which, needless to say, can cause very obscure errors.

execution errors

Once a program runs, we may encounter **execution errors,** for example, a division by zero or an invalid index condition. Most execution errors arise because the programmer did not foresee and make provision in the program for some situation. Another source of execution errors is improper data—data not of the form assumed by the program and for which input validation did not detect any errors. Identifying the data item or erroneous statement is usually enough to allow us to correct the problem. Operating systems provide at least limited help for detecting execution errors. For example, for a division by zero, an error message is usually printed and the program terminated. Other execution errors may go unnoticed. Some systems and languages do not check for an invalid index. When an index is out of range, the computation may proceed. The incorrect results may be difficult to trace. In this respect, Pascal is very safe; checking for invalid indices is part of the language.

implementation errors

Much of debugging involves the correction of errors due to an incorrect implementation of the intended algorithm. There is virtually no limit to the kinds of **implementation errors** programmers make, but we can single out some of the most common.

1. Mistyped variable names. In Pascal, where the type of every variable has to be declared, most of these are easy to spot. If an undeclared identifier is used, a syntax error is detected when the program is compiled. If, however, we mistakenly generate the name of another, declared variable, then the code makes sense syntactically. The error created by this may be quite hard to find. This is one reason (but certainly not the only one) for avoiding variables with very similar names.
2. Improperly initialized variables. Variables used for running sums, counters in conditional loops, and so on, often have to be initialized. When initialization is omitted or made incorrectly, the wrong initial values will cause erroneous results.
3. Incorrect loop control. The most common problems are infinite loops or loops that are "off by one"—that is, executed once too few or once too many times.
4. Misunderstood language constructs. Even if you know the language very well, there are always some parts of a language that tend to be confusing. The dangling else in Pascal is an example. Another difficulty that sometimes plagues inexperienced Pascal programmers is incorrect handling of end-of-line and end-of-file conditions.

5. Incorrect interfacing of modules. When subprograms are used, there must be an exact correspondence between the formal and actual parameter lists. Confusion between local and global identifiers may also occur when modules are not strictly independent.

Finally, there are errors due to *incompleteness* A program may work correctly in most, but not all, cases. It is this kind of error that most frequently escapes detection. Usually, the exceptional cases occur on the *boundary* of the program's range of inputs. For example, a sorting procedure may not work for an array with only one element. We encountered an error of this type in the original version of SIMPLESTAT in Example 6.3. This example shows why such boundary errors are difficult to detect with random testing. Unless we actually had a test case with frequency 100, we would not have known that it was not handled correctly. In testing, special attention should be given to possible exceptional cases.

EXERCISES 8.1

1. Keep a record over a period of several months of all the syntax errors you make. In future programs, check carefully for those errors. Do the same for implementation errors.
2. Write programs to generate various kinds of execution errors. How helpful is the information given by your system?
3. Generate a list of Pascal features that are prone to syntax errors.
4. Make a list of Pascal features that lead to frequent implementation errors.
5. Find examples of off-by-one errors that are easy to make.

8.2

program testing

Many good programmers, otherwise proud of their skill and competence, are casual about program testing. They run a few more or less random test cases until no more errors appear; then, they pronounce the program correct and release it to the public. Few realize that proper testing can be as challenging intellectually as programming.

Program testing can only reveal the presence of errors; it can never assure complete correctness. Our hope is that by running a sufficient number of test cases we can become confident that no undetected errors remain. Because testing is time-consuming, we want to cover as many situations in as few test cases as possible. Complete testing—running the program with all possible inputs—is clearly impractical for all but the simplest problems.

Consequently, choosing test examples can be a real challenge. We need to select each sample input in such a way that, if the program works for it, we can with reasonable assurance claim that it will work for all similar inputs. If we can select one representative of each class of possible inputs, we have done well. Take for example the program PIGLATIN in Chapter 5. There are several classes of inputs: words may start with a vowel, a single consonant, or several consonants; they may consist of a single vowel or of a single vowel and a single consonant. Our test set should include at least one case from each of these categories. Because of the way in which the program was written, it is reasonably clear that if it works for one of the representative examples it will work for others that are similar. Consequently, it is possible to pick a small test set for PIGLATIN that gives us a high degree of confidence that the program works correctly. Unfortunately, it is not always as easy to choose representative test cases.

The selection of test cases should be neither random nor totally predetermined. An intelligent selection will take the structure of the program and the algorithm into account. Only by using our knowledge of a program's structure can we determine what kinds of test examples will be most effective.

However, there are a few rules of thumb for testing. A minimal requirement is to run enough test cases so that every statement in the program is executed at least once. We cannot do less, because, obviously, all we can tell about statements that are never executed is whether they are syntactically correct. Another approach is to test until every possible path has been traversed at least once. (A path here is to be interpreted as a possible way to go from START to STOP in a flowchart for the program.) But on the one hand, for a complicated program this may involve an impractically large amount of testing, because there may be many possible paths. On the other hand, it cannot take into account the effect of data values on the results. Still, traversing every path is a fairly thorough test. If the program structure is simple, as it is in modular programming, this approach may be feasible if the number of paths for each module is small.

We should keep test cases general, because special patterns in the data may hide errors. For example, if our program has input variables M and N, we should not take M=N for all examples, as a mixup in the program between M and N will not affect the results. Similarly, when working with arrays or character strings, one should not use examples with only even or odd lengths, because there may be something in the program that does not work for the untested case. Many times, however, it is the special cases that need to be considered. In particular, the boundary cases mentioned before can be troublesome.

To be more specific, let us develop a set of good test examples for the program BETTERBAR in Example 7.2. First, consider the test case given in the discussion of the program. The data for this case are reasonably general; there are several categories, the scale factor is not unity, and the categories have different frequencies. Because these data produce correct output, we can be reasonably confident that at least the usual cases will be handled correctly. We can run several more or less randomly chosen examples of this type for confirmation.

For more rigorous testing, more unusual data should be used. Certainly one test should involve some frequencies with value zero. In fact, because some scaling is involved, we should try some frequencies smaller than the scale factor. For this reason the test case

```
13
AA    0
BB    2
CC   40
DD   17
```

was chosen. It produced the output

```
    .
    .
    .
40-         *
    .       *
    .       *
    .       *
    .       *
20-         *
    .       *  *
    .       *  *
    .       *  *
    .       *  *
    ---------
        A B C D
        A B C D
```

While the zero frequency is handled correctly, we see that a frequency of two also shows up as zero.

Another possible boundary case is a very short graph. The data

```
3
AA 20
BB 30
CC 35
```

produced the result

```
    .
    .     *  *
    .  *  *  *
    ------
       A B C
       A B C
```

Although correct, it is not a very satisfying product; for one thing, it gives no reference scale at all.

One feature to investigate is the scaling method used. A boundary case here is when MAX is an exact multiple of HEIGHT. (This is where the scale changes by one unit.) The data set

```
10
AA 15
BB 20
CC  6
```

gave the result

```
30-
  .
  .
  .
  .    *
15- *  *
  . *  *
  . *  *
  . *  *  *
  . *  *  *
  ------
    A B C
    A B C
```

A scale factor of two would be better than three, which was used. Apparently the scaling algorithm does not work as well as it could.

Finally, we should run some test cases to check the error conditions, that is, cases with negative frequencies and graphs that are too wide.

The test results, although they did not reveal any outright errors, do indicate some flaws in the program. Not all graphs will have labels on the vertical axis and at times there will be some loss of information due to scaling. In some cases, the scaling method leaves something to be desired. The reason for these shortcomings is that the original specifications did not address these unusual situations. Tests often reveal omissions in the specifications; if so, it may be necessary to return to the specifications, decide what to do, then modify the program accordingly. Considerable effort can be saved by drawing up better specifications at the beginning.

In testing, be pessimistic. Assume that there will be errors in the program, then devise test cases that will locate them as quickly as possible. Unfortunately, having written a program, we tend to be reluctant to find errors. Thus, we tend to design less exacting tests than we should. One way around this is to ask someone else to do some final testing (after you have concluded that the code is completely correct). Specifically, you should ask him or her to "break" the program—that is, find its errors and flaws. A disinterested person will probably construct tougher tests than the original programmer.

A good test strategy is difficult to produce; it should not be discarded when testing is stopped. When later modifications have to be made, the program will have to be retested. Much time will be saved if the test examples are still available. This is why we indicated in the discussion of documentation that test examples should become part of the external documentation of the program.

For complicated problems, testing generally has to be done in stages. There are two strategies for testing modular programs. In *bottom-up testing*, we complete all coding for the lowest level modules, then test them. When they are correct, they are integrated to the next level and tested again. Bottom-up testing requires some *driver* programs, which call the modules and supply the data—a significant increase in the programming. For example, the main program TESTREC in Example 6.5 is a driver program for testing the function VALID. The driver program is of no interest by itself; it is constructed solely for testing VALID.

The second way is *top-down testing*, which tests the highest level of the hierarchical design first. This will involve modules not yet tested or perhaps not even coded. Instead of these modules we can use *stubs*, simple subprograms that either do nothing or else return the results that the corresponding subprogram is to give for some specific input. To test GAME in Example 7.3, one could write a stub for COMPUTERMOVE that simply makes a random move. The program GAME could be tested with this and other stubs like it. Eventually, one would want to use a procedure COMPUTERMOVE with a better strategy. Top-down testing checks the overall logic and the interface of the higher modules before checking the lower level modules.

Arguments can be made for or against either of these two approaches. Bottom-up testing requires much extra work to write the drivers. Much of the testing may be done when there still is some doubt about the overall organization. In top-down testing, we have to provide the stubs, which may have to be changed for every test case. The design is tested at a high level even before it is clear that the lower level modules can be implemented as specified. Neither top-down nor bottom-up testing is always satisfactory. Perhaps the best approach is to keep an open mind and use a judicious mix of the two alternatives. As a general rule it is best to test those modules first in which an error will have the most significant effect on other parts. It is inefficient as well as discouraging to spend a great deal of time finding all the minor errors, only to discover a snag later which requires extensive rethinking and reprogramming.

No matter how careful we are, we must stop testing sometime. The question is when to stop. Overoptimistic programmers stop testing too soon, leaving errors that could have been detected with a little more effort. On the other hand, we must learn to recognize the point of diminishing returns in testing.

EXERCISES 8.2

1. Reexamine all programs you have written. For each establish an effective set of test cases.
2. For all the programs in this and the preceding chapters, determine what the boundary cases are.
3. Look at VALID in Example 6.5. Are the test cases given there sufficient to test the procedure thoroughly?
4. Outline a set of stubs to test the program GAME in Example 7.3.
5. Outline a set of stubs to test the procedure USERMOVE in Example 7.3.
6. Are there any programs in this book simple enough to make it practical to test all possible inputs?
7. Write a new program that remedies the shortcomings of BETTERBAR. Start with a complete set of specifications.

8.3

debugging

Debugging is removing the errors uncovered by testing. It can be very time-consuming, particularly for those who, after being careless in design and coding, approach debugging in the same way. By following a few simple rules, we can usually speed up the process considerably.

The first rule is to program in a way that minimizes errors. Error-free programming is rarely achievable, but we can cut down on mistakes. The design and coding should be done carefully and without haste. Every step should be double-checked. If you are in doubt on some language construct, check it in the description or look at the syntax chart. Go through your code several times, using different paper-and-pencil examples. Be critical; assume that the program is incorrect until your analysis has convinced you otherwise.

Do not put doubtful code on the computer. Check and double-check your typing. Some programmers do this very superficially on the assumption that typing mistakes will create syntax errors that can be detected by the compiler. Unfortunately, this is not always the case, as has been pointed out (page 203). Another source of frustration is the "quick fix." A programmer, glancing at the output, discovers an error. Making a superficial analysis, he decides what went wrong and fixes it, only to discover later that his analysis of the error was incorrect. Take your time in correcting errors; make sure that the change removes the error and does not introduce any new ones. Above all, never make "experimental" fixes. This is quite common in beginning programming classes. A student, unable to understand completely the cause of an error, will often change one or two doubtful statements in the hope that this will correct the error. Needless to say, the "quick fix" is a complete waste of time. Analyze each situation carefully. Form a hypothesis as to the cause of the error, then use all available information to see if it supports the hypothesis. Only when you are confident that your evaluation is correct should you make the change and rerun the program. Also, try to find several errors at once. Don't stop when the first incorrect statement is found, but carry on until all discrepancies in your test run have been resolved.

Plan for debugging as you design and code. Try to predict where the errors are most likely to occur by studying the parts that are most difficult to understand and code. Consider what information will be needed to pinpoint errors that may occur. Incorporate output statements in the appropriate places. If the code is so complicated that you cannot see what information will be useful for debugging, you are on the wrong track altogether. Rethink the algorithm and produce simpler code.

The major difficulty in debugging is to localize the errors, that is, find the statements or part of the program where the errors occur. Once we know where the error is, a careful reading of the defective part will usually reveal the source of the difficulty. A systematic approach to error localization can save much time. The most popular technique is to insert into the program a number of temporary output statements to print selected variables at various points in the program. Careful consideration should be given to what information will be most useful in uncovering the source of error. The programmer who takes extra time to make everything explicit and easy to read will in the long run do much better than one who tries to save time and typing. When the check output looks like

```
Program execution at end of module 7
I=100   J=10   AVERAGE=3.45
```

an analysis of the run can proceed much faster than if we had just printed numbers

```
7   100   10   3.45
```

The printout should be arranged so that it is easy to follow the flow of the program as well as to check the state of the computations at various points. When this is done, errors can usually be located quickly.

Special care should be taken in debugging recursive programs. Just printing a message that tells us where in the program we are may be insufficient, because we cannot tell the level of the recursion. What distinguishes one entry from another is the values of the parameters. These should be printed on entry. For example, in debugging the function VALID in Chapter 6, we inserted at the beginning the statements

```
writeln('INIT',INIT,'FINAL',FINAL);
writeln('expression at entry');
for I:=INIT to FINAL do
   write(EXPR[I])
```

This gave a clear picture of how the recursion was progressing. When a recursive procedure calls itself from several places, information on the origin of the call will also be helpful. Recursive programs can be very difficult to debug even when complete information is available.

Occasionally, situations arise where the error can be localized but its nature still cannot be determined. This happens often to beginners who have a poor understanding of the language. But it can also happen to the more experienced programmers when using language features that are counter-intuitive or easy to misinterpret. For example, the Pascal statement

```
X:=A/B*C
```

looks like the equivalent of $X = \dfrac{A}{BC}$ but, as we know, is really $X = \dfrac{A}{B}C$. Some errors that are hard to see arise from a kind of optical illusion. For example, in

```
for I:=1 to N do
   X:=X+Z[I];
   Y:=Y*Y
```

the indentation makes it appear as if the body of the loop contains two statements. Of course, once this is pointed out, we see easily that only the statement X:=X+Z[I] belongs to the loop. But if such a sequence is embedded in a longer program, it is easy to be led astray. With a little experience, we learn how to spot this sort of problem, but every language has some features that can give even an expert trouble.

Computer error is only a rare source of incorrect results, and hardware or software failure should be considered only after all other explanations have been ruled out. When a hardware error has occurred, rerunning the program at a later date should clear up the matter. Software errors, such as an incorrect translation by a compiler, can be quite troublesome. When a compiler error is suspected in a particular statement, we can try to substantiate our conjecture by writing another, simpler program that uses the suspected construct. The help of a compiler expert will invariably be needed in cases of possible compiler error.

Many systems have special aids for debugging. These include procedures for printing certain values when specified conditions arise, establishing points in the program where the computations will be stopped temporarily so that the programmer can set or examine selected variables, or counting the number of times a statement is executed. The nature and the availability of debugging aids depend on the language and the system used, and there is little uniformity. They are often useful tools. You should familiarize yourself with what is available on your system.

EXERCISES 8.3

1. Write a program with deliberately obscure errors. Trade programs with a friend to see who can debug most quickly.
2. Try to break some of the programs in this book.
3. Find out what debugging aids are available on your system.

8.4

proving program correctness

Because program testing can never conclusively rule out the possibility of undetected errors, computer scientists have looked for more powerful techniques for the construction of correct programs. The idea that one could use rigorous mathematical arguments to prove that a program is correct has attracted much attention. Unfortunately, this subject is still of more theoretical than practical interest.

Despite its often obscure mathematical formalism, the idea behind correctness proving is quite simple. At the beginning of each part of a program, we assume that the state of the computation, that is, the form and values of the variables, satisfies certain conditions. This is called the *entry assertion*. We next argue, by a detailed consideration of the individual steps, that at the end of the part the state of the computation satisfies other conditions, the *exit assertion*. In addition, it must also be shown that the computations can be carried out, and that they will eventually terminate. We do this for successive pieces of code, progressively splitting into smaller pieces until the arguments needed to connect the entry assertions with the exit assertions become simple enough to be logically obvious. In effect, correctness proving is simply a detailed and precise reasoning on the state of the computation at each step.

In spite of the conceptual simplicity, the difficulties with a very rigorous approach to correctness proving are severe. The process is tedious, and the length of a proof may be greater by an order of magnitude than the code itself. Because it relies heavily on mathematical precision, it is probably not within the abilities of most programmers; it seems unlikely that someone who has difficulty writing the program will be able to produce rigorous arguments demonstrating its correctness. The complexity of correctness proofs far exceeds the complexity of the programming. This raises another point. What confidence can we have that the proofs themselves have no errors? The literature of mathematics abounds with false proofs. Someone who makes errors in coding can hardly be expected to be immune to errors in precise mathematical reasoning.

Proponents of correctness proving argue that eventually it will be possible to automate the task and point to the success in theorem proving by computer to substantiate their claim. While there have been some successes with automated correctness proving in limited experimental environments, its future seems uncertain. It is certainly not yet available for routine programming.

Even so, if we approach the idea in the right spirit, it can be very helpful. First, the programmer who thinks in terms of precise proofs will have an incentive to use a simple structure for the program, because any kind of complication will make precise arguments too arduous. This will result in better code. Second, the attempt to prove correctness, even if it cannot be carried out completely and rigorously, is of value. It involves taking a detailed look at the code from another angle and can therefore uncover errors that have escaped detection by testing. Let us illustrate this with two examples.

EXAMPLE 8.1

ERROR IN SIMPLESTAT

The first version of SIMPLESTAT in Example 6.3 contains an error in the computation of the frequency count for the value 100. Let us see if an attempt at correctness proving can uncover this error.

The piece of code in which the error occurs is

```
for I:=1 to N do
  begin
    RANGE:=X[I] div 25+1;
    FREQ[RANGE]:=FREQ[RANGE]+1
  end
```

Our entry assertion is that X[I] for I:=1 to N is between 0 and 100. Also, FREQ[1] = FREQ[2] = FREQ[3] = FREQ[4] = 0. The second of these assumptions can be seen to be true by checking the code leading to the part in question. That the X[I] are between 0 and 100 is an assumption of the program. Incorrect results may be produced if this assumption is violated.

Our exit assertions are that FREQ[1] is the count of items with value in the range 0–24, FREQ[2] is the count of items in the range 25–49, FREQ[3] is the count of items in the range 50–74, and FREQ[4] is the count of items in the range 75–100.

To prove that the exit assertions follow from the entry assertions, we must show that

1. The loop terminates.
2. All computations in the loop can be done.
3. The computation of the frequency count is done correctly.

We know the loop will terminate, because in Pascal all counted loops are traversed a finite number of times. Next, we consider whether all the computations can be done. X[I] is assumed to be nonnegative; therefore, RANGE is always greater than or equal to one. Because FREQ is of type array[1..4] of integer, the statement

```
FREQ[RANGE]:=FREQ[RANGE]+1
```

can be carried out only if RANGE<=4. This means that

```
X[I] div 25<=3
```

or

```
X[I]<=99
```

Because the assumption is that X[I]<=100, we have found an inconsistency and thereby located the error.

The next example is in some ways not really incorrect. Nevertheless, a careful analysis reveals some unexpected features.

EXAMPLE 8.2

ROOTS OF A QUADRATIC EQUATION

In Example 3.2 we wrote a program to compute the roots of the equation

```
A*X*X+B*X+C = 0
```

There were, however, some omissions in that program. To rewrite it, we begin, as we always should, with detailed specifications.

The exercise is to write a procedure QUADRATIC, which will compute for all representable floating point numbers A,B,C the roots of the preceding equation to an accuracy determined by the precision of the floating point arithmetic. In cases where there are no real roots, we will set the answers to some very large positive number and print an error message.

In writing down the specification, we have already recognized some problems. We restrict the program to values of A,B,C, which can be represented as single floating point words. It would be unreasonable to require that the program work for all real numbers. To allow for roundoff error, we also qualify the output by saying that the results need not be exact, but only accurate within a limit. Because we want only real roots, B*B−4*A*C must be nonnegative. With all these requirements in mind, we can come up with the following algorithm and code:

1. Compute the discriminant $B*B-4*A*C$.
2. If the discriminant is negative, or A and B are zero, no real roots exist. Set answers to 10^{10} and terminate the program.
3. If the discriminant is nonnegative, compute roots by the standard formula. The case $A=0$, $B \neq 0$ has solution $-C/B$; both roots will be set to this value.

```
procedure QUADRATIC(A,B,C:real;
                        var ROOT1,ROOT2:real);
label 1;
var DISCRIM:real;
begin
  DISCRIM:=B*B-4*A*C;
  {real roots do not exist}
  if (DISCRIM<0) or ((A=0) and (B=0))
  then begin
          ROOT1:=1.0e+10;
          ROOT2:=1.0e+10;
          writeln(' error in QUADRATIC');
          goto 1
       end;
  {real roots exist, the case when A=0
   and the case A<>0, require different
   formulas }
  if A=0
    then begin
            ROOT1:=-C/B;
            ROOT2:=ROOT1
         end
    else begin
            ROOT1:=(-B+sqrt(DISCRIM))/(2*A);
            ROOT2:=(-B-sqrt(DISCRIM))/(2*A)
         end;
  1:end;
```

The program looks correct; it is, after all, a simple problem. We have recognized several exceptional conditions, such as $A=0$ and $B=0$, that could cause trouble. But did we think of everything, and is the code exactly as required by the specifications? Let us now try to prove that we did.

Our entry assertion is that A,B,C are any floating point numbers. As exit assertion we claim that ROOT1 and ROOT2 are the roots of the quadratic equation within a certain accuracy, provided the equation has real roots. If not, ROOT1 and ROOT2 are set to 10^{10} and an error message is printed.

It should be fairly self-evident that if the computations can be carried out, ROOT1 and ROOT2 will be correct, assuming that the function sqrt performs properly. If you have any doubts about this, you should trace explicitly through the code, showing that it accurately represents the mathematical formula for the various values of A, B, and C. If we find that they are indeed correct, we still have to show that all computations can be carried out. When we try to do this, we immediately spot a problem in the first statement. The first instruction

```
DISCRIM:=B*B-4*A*C
```

cannot be carried out for all values of A,B,C. For example, if B is very large, then B*B may be too large to be representable in floating point, and B*B will give an exponent overflow. For very large values of B (or by a similar argument, for very small A) the program may fail. We have discovered an error.

If such cases are of no importance, we can change the specifications (say, by restricting the values of A,B,C to certain ranges) and leave the program as it is. If the exceptional cases need to be treated properly, then we have to change the algorithm and the program (no easy matter).

Note that the program fails only under very special conditions, which probably would not have been uncovered by even extensive random testing. It is not uncommon for the informal proof method to reveal errors in the boundary cases more easily than testing.

Certainly, to be precise, the arguments we have made do not in any sense constitute a proof. An informal approach to correctness proving is just another way of thinking carefully about the program. It is, however, useful, because it provides methods complementary to program testing.

EXERCISES 8.4

1. Use the informal proof method to investigate the correctness of the programs DUPLICATE and DUPLISET in Example 5.2.
2. Improve the execution efficiency of QUADRATIC.
3. Suppose it were important that QUADRATIC perform properly with very small values for A. How could the program be modified to allow this?
4. The nonrecursive definition of $n!$ for nonnegative integer n is

```
0! = 1
n! =n×(n−1)×(n−2)×...2×1
```

Consider the following code:

```
function FACT(N:integer):integer;
var I,PRODUCT:integer;
begin
   I:=0;
   PRODUCT:=1;
   repeat
      I:=I+1;
      PRODUCT:=PRODUCT*I
   until I=N;
   FACT:=PRODUCT
end
```

Is this correct? If you cannot see any errors, try to prove that the program is correct.

5. Apply the arguments used in Example 8.1 to the corrected version of SIMPLESTAT in Example 6.4.

further reading

Kernighan, B. W., and Plauger, P. J. *The Elements of Programming Style*, 2d. ed. New York: McGraw-Hill, 1978.

Schneider, G. M., Weingart, S. W., and Perlman, D. M. *An Introduction to Programming and Problem Solving with Pascal*, Chapter 6. New York: John Wiley & Sons, 1978.

Van Tassel, D. *Programming Style, Design, Efficiency, Debugging, and Testing*, Chapters 4 and 5. Englewood Cliffs, N.J.: Prentice-Hall, 1978.

Yourdon, E. *Techniques for Program Structure and Design*. Englewood Cliffs, N.J.: Prentice-Hall, 1975.

Chapter Nine

data structures and their implementation

The purpose of a computer is to store, process, and transmit data. The data generally come from some external source and are encoded as numbers or character strings, which the computer, through its programs, transforms into useful information. In most applications, the data consist of a large number of items which, fortunately, are related in some way reflecting the original problem. Even the simple examples we have seen so far exhibit a common feature: the data are usually not an amorphous collection of elements, but have some underlying structure. In writing programs, one must take into account (and take advantage of) the relationship between the various data items. A data structure is a construct by which we can represent and manipulate such relationships. The concept of a data structure is of fundamental importance in computer science. For the programmer, choosing the right data structure is one of the most crucial design decisions.

9.1

structure and relation in data

We have encountered a number of different data types and structures. The primitive types such as `integer`, `real`, and `char` are used to construct more complicated types like arrays and records, called *composite* or *aggregate* data structures. They have a structure because the elements are related. Composite structures, such as arrays, are provided by most programming languages because they are needed in almost all applications. We have already seen in a number of examples how useful arrays and other Pascal data types can be. There are, however, many problems for which we need structures not provided by Pascal and other higher level languages.

At a conceptual level, we have some picture in mind of how the data are organized in a particular problem. The character string

`THIS IS A SENTENCE`

consists of a set of letters and blanks, and the order in which the characters appear is significant. Here the relationship between the elements is a simple linear order. In a table, the relationship between the items is exhibited by arranging them in rows and columns. Record-like structures represent an even more complicated relationship.

To make programming easier and less susceptible to error, the code should reflect as closely as possible our conceptual view of the data's organization. Every higher level language has means for representing directly some of the more common structures. In other words, the language allows us to specify and work with the structures in a manner closely related to our visualization. A good example is the use of two-dimensional arrays for tables. Almost all higher level languages provide arrays with one or more dimensions. Pascal also has records and sets, but these are less common in other languages.

The convenience and power of a language are closely related to the data structures it provides. Programming complicated algorithms may become quite cumbersome in a language with restricted data structures. For example, programming in a language like Pascal, but without arrays, may be reasonable for some very simple problems, but it would be quite unsuitable for general purposes.

When a particular application calls for a data structure that the language does not provide directly, it becomes necessary to use what is available to represent it. We say that we need to *implement* the data structure. This, of course, means more work for the programmer. Furthermore, if the implementation is not done properly, programming may be difficult and time-consuming. For example, suppose we have a language like Pascal, but which allows one-dimensional arrays of `real` and `integer`, but no multidimensional arrays or arrays with more complex elements. To implement a table with five rows and ten columns, we can use

```
type ROW=array[1..10] of real;
var ROW1,ROW2,ROW3,ROW4,ROW5:ROW
```

Reference to the entry in the third row and sixth column would then be made by

```
ROW3[6]
```

Although this is feasible for a small number of rows, programming with such an implementation becomes unwieldy when large tables are involved.

A very efficient way of handling programmer-implemented data structures is to write a set of functions and procedures that carry out the common operations that are to be performed on the structures. These subprograms are then used for all manipulations, and the structures can be processed without continual attention to the details of the implementation. Effectively, this approach extends the language to include the new data structure. For example, if Pascal did not allow sets, we could perhaps use arrays to implement them, then write procedures for set union, intersection, and so on. Sets would then be processed with these procedures. If the collection of subprograms is chosen well, working with programmer-defined data structures is almost as easy as working with the structures provided by the language.

Arrays and records are called *static* data structures. Operations on an array, for example, can change the values of one or more of its elements, but not the array itself. No matter what is done, the number of elements and their relationship is preserved. A data structure that can undergo structural changes during the execution of a program is said to be *dynamic*. For example, when we form the union of two sets, we generate a new set with a different and generally unpredictable number of elements. Thus, the structure of a set is not fixed, and a set can be considered a dynamic data type.

The major static data types are arrays and records, which have already been discussed in detail. However, many applications call for dynamic data structures. Consequently, the emphasis of our discussion in this and the next chapter will be on the efficient implementation and processing of some of the more important dynamic data structures.

EXERCISES 9.1

1. In a language like Pascal, but without arrays, how difficult is it to do each of the following?
   a. Find the largest of 100 integer numbers.
   b. Sort a sequence of 100 integer numbers.
   c. Translate from English into pig latin.
2. Consider the program SALES in Example 5.4. Rewrite it using one-dimensional arrays only.
3. Rewrite the program INVENTORY in Example 5.6 without using record structures.

9.2

stacks and queues

A multitude of applications have elements in a linearly ordered sequence. One-dimensional arrays are static structures of this type. The structures become dynamic when the elements can be inserted or deleted. We distinguish between several such dynamic structures by the ways in which insertions and deletions can be made. Two of these dynamic structures are stacks and queues.

stacks

A *stack* is an ordered sequence of elements of the same type. Insertions in and deletions from a stack can be made only in one place, called the *top* of the stack. While a stack may contain any number of elements, only the top is accessible at any time. When a new element is to be added to the stack, it is put on the top and the other elements are *pushed* down. The top element can be accessed for processing by removing it from the top of the stack, *popping* up the rest of the stack. To visualize a stack, think of a stack of trays in a cafeteria. When you need a tray, you take the top one and the rest pop up. When you want to return a tray, you can only place it on top of the stack.

What is in a stack at a particular time depends on the order in which insertions and deletions have been made. Suppose that we start with an empty stack. If we first insert A, then B, the stack will look like

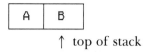

↑ top of stack

If we now add C to the stack, we have

| A | B | C |

↑ top of stack

If next the top element (which is the only one accessible) is retrieved, we get again

| A | B |

↑ top of stack

Because of the way in which items are inserted in and removed from a stack, the terms *pushdown list* or *pushdown store* are sometimes used. Also, because the latest item to be put into the stack is the one immediately accessible, a stack is often called a *last-in-first-out store*.

Most programming languages do not have stacks as a data type. If stacks are needed, they have to be implemented with existing structures. One easy, although at times restrictive, implementation involves arrays. A one-dimensional array of some fixed size, say 1..MAXLENGTH, is used to hold the stack. Also associated with the stack is an integer, say TOP, that points to the top of the stack, that is, gives the position of the top of the stack in the array. Figure 9.1 shows a typical example. Originally, when the stack is empty, TOP is set to zero. To push an element onto the stack, increase TOP by one and insert the element into position TOP. To pop the stack, decrease TOP by one (after using the top element).

In manipulating stacks, some checks have to be made. An empty stack cannot be popped. Also, when a stack is implemented with an array of fixed size, it may become full. When TOP equals MAXLENGTH, there is no more room for insertions, and an attempt to push an element onto the stack will cause a *stack overflow*. Ideally, a stack can contain an unlimited number of

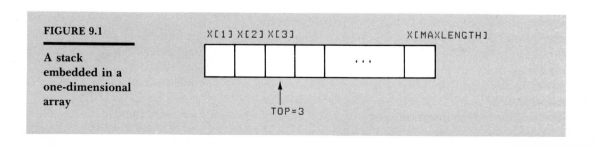

FIGURE 9.1

A stack embedded in a one-dimensional array

elements and can never overflow. In practice, however, the total storage available is finite. Therefore, no matter how a stack is implemented, overflow can occur.

In this implementation, the coding of the stack operations is straightforward, but the embedding of the stack (a dynamic data structure) in a static array lacks flexibility. If MAXLENGTH is made too large, memory space is wasted, whereas a small value for MAXLENGTH may cause frequent overflows.

To make it easy to work with stacks, we write the basic stack operations of pushing and popping as procedures PUSH and POP. It is also often necessary to check whether a stack is empty; for this purpose, we can use a boolean function EMPTY, the value of which will be true when the stack is empty and false otherwise.

EXAMPLE 9.1

PASCAL IMPLEMENTATION OF STACKS AND STACK OPERATIONS

Assume that we have a single stack, stored in a global array STACK defined by

```
var STACK:array[1..MAXLENGTH] of integer
```

with a global variable TOP pointing to the top of the stack. The stack function EMPTY and the procedures PUSH and POP are then quite elementary. We use here stack elements of type integer, because this will be needed for several later applications. But there is nothing special about this. The code for other element types will be quite similar to what is given here.

```
function EMPTY:boolean;
{ boolean function which has value
   true if the stack is empty}
begin
   if TOP=0
     then EMPTY:=true
     else EMPTY:=false
end;

procedure PUSH(NEWTOP:integer);
{ this procedure pushes NEWTOP
   onto the stack. An overflow
   will give an error message }
begin
   if TOP>=MAXLENGTH
     then begin
```

```
                 writeln('error in PUSH');
                 writeln('stack overflow')
            end
      else begin
            TOP:=TOP+1;
            STACK[TOP]:=NEWTOP
         end
 end;


procedure POP(var TOPVALUE:integer);
{ this procedure puts the value at the
  top of the stack into TOPVALUE and
  pops the stack. An empty stack will
  give an error message }
begin
   if EMPTY
      then begin
             writeln('error in POP');
             writeln('stack is empty')
          end
      else begin
             TOPVALUE:=STACK[TOP];
             TOP:=TOP-1
          end
 end
```

These subprograms will be useful in subsequent programs involving stacks.

Stacks are often used in programs in which information has to be saved for later use and in which the amount of information to be saved is unpredictable. Because a stack is a dynamic structure, it can grow as the situation demands. Suppose that we are reading character information and want to separate the characters into letters, digits, and other characters, perhaps to be used later in the program for some other purpose. Three separate stacks can be used to hold the different kinds of characters, and the distribution can be made by the following algorithm:

1. Repeat Steps 2–5 for all characters.
2. Read character.
3. If character is a letter, push it onto LETTERSTACK.
4. If character is a digit, push it onto DIGITSTACK.
5. If character is neither letter nor digit, push it onto OTHERSTACK.

After this initial separation, the information can be retrieved from the stack by popping off successive elements until the stack is empty. No explicit count of the number of elements need be kept; we are done when the stack is empty.

This is a rather trivial example of the use of stacks, and many other data structures (e.g., sets) would have been just as effective. A real need for stacks arises in situations in which information must not only be saved, but must be retrieved later in the reverse order in which the data were originally saved. This is the "last-in-first-out" property of the stack. There are a number of important problems in computer application where this is exactly what is needed.

Stacks are used extensively in connection with recursive programs. Whenever a program calls a subprogram, some information, including partially computed results and the location from which the call was made, has to be saved. In a recursive situation, the number of calls, and hence the amount of information to be saved, is unpredictable. Suppose we have the sequence of calls.

A_1 calls A_2, A_2 calls A_3, A_3 calls A_4

where A_1 stands for the first call to procedure A, A_2 for the second (recursive) call of A to itself, and so on. When A_1 calls A_2, the information to be saved, denoted by S_1, is put on a stack. When A_2 calls A_3, the information S_2 will be put on the stack, and so on. After the given sequence of calls, the stack will contain

S_1	S_2	S_3

↑ top of stack

When A_4 returns to A_3, the saved information S_3 is popped off the stack and used by A_3. This brings S_2 to the top, and it is then available when A_2 regains control. In this instance, the stack mechanism is ideal, because the saved information is needed in reverse order in which it was saved.

Another use of stacks arises in connection with the evaluation of arithmetic and other expressions. To see how this comes about, consider some problems connected with the usual way of writing expressions. For simplicity, let us restrict the discussion to arithmetic expressions involving only addition and multiplication, with operands restricted to single-digit positive integers.

In evaluating an expression such as

5 * (2 * 3 + 1)

we first compute 2 * 3, then add one, and finally multiply by five. We are so used to seeing expressions in this form that we have little difficulty in determining the order in which the computations are to be done. But when we try to write an algorithm for evaluating such expressions, we quickly see that it is not an easy matter. Because of the parentheses and the differing operator priorities, it is a lengthy job to find a systematic way of determining the order of the operations. There are other notational conventions for writing expressions that are much better in this respect; the one we will

postfix notation discuss here is the so-called ***postfix notation.*** In postfix, a simple expression consisting of one operator and two operands is written with the two operands first, followed by the operator. Thus, 2 * 3 becomes 2 3 * . More complex expressions are generated by repeating this pattern with subexpressions; 2 * 3 + 1 is written as 2 3 * 1 +, and finally

    5 * (2 * 3 + 1)

has the postfix equivalent

    5 2 3 * 1 + *

To evaluate an expression in postfix notation, the expression is scanned for two operands followed by an operator. This partial expression is evaluated and the result substituted back in the expression. This is repeated until a single number, the value of the expression, remains. For our example

    5 2 3 * 1 + *

we first find 2 3 * , evaluate it, and substitute back. This gives

    5 6 1 + *

Again we scan, finding now 6 1 +, which reduces the expression to

    5 7 *

so that the final result is 35. Postfix notation does not require any parentheses or any priority rules. The notation is unambiguous without them.

To construct an algorithm for evaluating postfix expressions, we still need a systematic way of finding sequences of two operands followed by an operator. To remove the need for repeated scanning, the following elegant way can be used. We read the expression from left to right. Whenever an operand is encountered, it is saved in a stack. When an operator is encountered, it is applied to the two preceding operands, which, because of the way they were saved, are in the top two positions of the stack. They are used to evaluate the subexpression, and the result put back into the stack. The complete algorithm for evaluating postfix expressions is

1. Start with an empty stack.
2. For all symbols in the postfix expression, scanning from left to right, repeat Steps 3 and 4.

3. If symbol is an operand, push it onto stack.
4. If symbol is an operator, pop the two top elements from stack, apply the operator to them, and push result back onto stack.
5. At the end, stack contains a single number, the result of the expression.

Run through a few examples to see that this does in fact work. Of course, not every sequence of operands and operators represents a valid expression. At Step 5, if the stack does not contain exactly one number, the expression is not valid.

EXAMPLE 9.2

EVALUATION OF POSTFIX EXPRESSIONS

We will write a Pascal program for evaluating postfix expressions of the type just discussed. The input to the program is to be a character string consisting of digits '0'..'9', and '+' and '*', representing an arithmetic expression in postfix notation. The output from the program will be the numerical value of the expression if it is valid, or an error message if it is not valid.

The pseudolanguage description has already been given for the main steps in the algorithm. We still need to address the question of invalid expressions. For example

```
3 + 42 *
```

is not a valid postfix expression. When '+' is encountered, Step 4 cannot be performed because the stack contains only one element. The expression

```
3 4 2 *
```

is also invalid; in this case the stack will end up with more than one element. It is not hard to see that these are the only error conditions possible.

A minor point is that the operands are given in character form. To perform arithmetic operations, it is convenient to convert the operands to integer values. For this, the Pascal function ord is useful. For example, the expression

```
ord('6')-ord('0')
```

has the integer value six.

The program will implement the stack with an array and use the stack operation subprograms given in Example 9.1.

```
program POSTVALUE(input,output);
{ this program evaluates arithmetic
  expressions given in postfix form}
const MAXLENGTH=20;
```

```
var SYMBOL:char;
    OPVALUE,FIRSTOP,SECONDOP,RESULT,TOP:integer;
    STACK:array[1..MAXLENGTH] of integer;

function EMPTY:boolean;
{ boolean function which has value
  true if the stack is empty}
begin
  if TOP=0
    then EMPTY:=true
    else EMPTY:=false
end;

procedure PUSH(NEWTOP:integer);
{ this procedure pushes NEWTOP
  onto the stack. An overflow
  will give an error message}
begin
  if TOP>=MAXLENGTH
    then begin
           writeln(' error in PUSH');
           writeln(' stack overflow')
         end
    else begin
           TOP:=TOP+1;
           STACK[TOP]:=NEWTOP
         end
end;

procedure POP(var TOPVALUE:integer);
{ this procedure puts the value at the
  top of the stack into TOPVALUE and
  pops the stack. An empty stack will
  give an error message }
begin
  if EMPTY
    then begin
           writeln(' error in POP');
           writeln(' stack is empty')
         end
    else begin
           TOPVALUE:=STACK[TOP];
           TOP:=TOP-1
         end
end;
```

```
begin
  VALID:=true;
  TOP:=0;
  write (' postfix expression ');
  repeat
    { read and echo input symbols }
    read(SYMBOL);
    write(SYMBOL);
    { if SYMBOL is a digit, convert it
      to integer and push it onto stack }
    if SYMBOL in ['0'..'9']
      then begin
              OPVALUE:=ord(SYMBOL)-ord('0');
              PUSH(OPVALUE)
           end
    { if SYMBOL is an operator, perform
      operation on top 2 elements of stack
      and push result back onto stack. If
      the stack does not have two elements
      in it the expression is not valid }
      else begin
              if EMPTY
                then VALID:=false
                else POP(FIRSTOP);
              if EMPTY
                then VALID:=false
                else POP(SECONDOP);
              case SYMBOL of
                '+':RESULT:=FIRSTOP+SECONDOP;
                '*':RESULT:=FIRSTOP*SECONDOP
              end;
              PUSH(RESULT)
           end
  until eoln;
  writeln;
  { if stack has a single element and VALID
    is true, then result is on top of stack,
    otherwise expression is invalid }
  POP(RESULT);
  if VALID and EMPTY
    then writeln(' has the value',RESULT:5)
    else writeln(' is invalid')
end.
```

The input

        523*1+*

produced the result

        postfix expression 523*1+*
        has the value   35

while

        6231****

gave output

        postfix expression 6231****
        is invalid

Expressions in a higher level language eventually have to be translated into machine language by the compiler. If expressions were given in postfix notation, this translation would be greatly simplified; the compiler could use a version of the algorithm in the preceding example. Unfortunately, most of us are not very familiar with this notation. A language that used postfix notation would place a heavy burden on the programmer. For this reason, higher level languages still use standard notation (also called *infix*), but often the compiler will first make a translation from infix to postfix before the final conversion to machine language. The translation from infix to postfix uses techniques similar to those in evaluating postfix expressions.

EXAMPLE 9.3

TRANSLATION FROM INFIX TO POSTFIX NOTATION

To discover an algorithm, it sometimes helps to do a few simple examples. Look at

        A+B*C

which in postfix is

        ABC*+

Let us try to do the conversion by scanning the infix expression left to right while building the postfix expression left to right. First note that the order of the operands is the same in both expressions. A few more examples will convince you that this is always the case. However, the order of the operators can change because of their differing priorities. When a ' + ' is encountered, it may have to wait. A waiting operation can be put into the postfix expression only when another operator of equal or lower priority is encountered. Parentheses change this rule; the infix expression

    (A+B)*C

has the postfix form

    AB+C*

Any part enclosed in parentheses acts as a unit, with the parentheses marking the beginning and end of a subexpression. When a right parenthesis is encountered, all waiting operations of the subexpression closed by that parenthesis can be put into the postfix string.

Working along these lines with a few more examples, you will eventually see that the following algorithm will accomplish the translation.

1. For all characters in the infix string, scanning from left to right, repeat Steps 2–7.
2. Read symbol.
3. If symbol is an operand, add it to the right of the postfix string.
4. If symbol is ' (', push it onto stack.
5. If symbol is ' + ', pop successive operators from stack and add them to

infix to post-fix

FIGURE 9.2

Translation of (A*B+C)*D into postfix notation

symbol read	stack	postfix string
(	(	
A	(	A
*	(*	A
B	(*	AB
+	(+	AB*
C	(+	AB*C
)		AB*C+
*	*	AB*C+
D	*	AB*C+D
		AB*C+D*

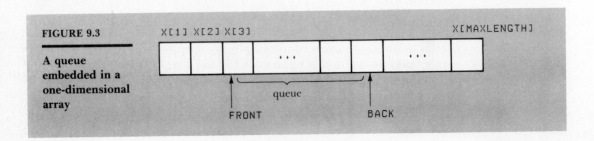

FIGURE 9.3

A queue embedded in a one-dimensional array

X[1] X[2] X[3]   X[MAXLENGTH]

FRONT   queue   BACK

postfix string. Repeat until ' (' is on top of stack or stack is empty. Then push symbol onto stack.

6. If symbol is ' * ', pop successive operators from stack and add them to postfix string. Repeat until top of stack is either ' (' or ' + ', or stack is empty. Then push symbol onto stack.

7. If symbol is ') ', pop successive operators from stack and add them to postfix string. Repeat until top of stack is ' ('. Pop stack once more to remove ' ('.

8. Pop all remaining operations from stack and add them to postfix string.

Figure 9.2 shows the state of the stack and the postfix expression during the translation of the infix string (A*B+C)*D.

This is not a simple algorithm, and its discovery is not a routine matter. Work through a few more examples to convince yourself that it does work. In doing so, you will also discover that the use of a stack automatically enforces the rule that, in cases of equal operator priority, the evaluation is always from left to right.

The translation from the pseudolanguage to Pascal is not difficult and will be left as an exercise.

queues

A *queue* is an ordered sequence of elements of the same type in which deletions are made on one end (front), while insertions are made at the other (back). In a queue, items that have been present the longest are removed first. Hence, a queue is also a *first-in-first-out store.*

The implementation of a queue by means of an array is similar to that of a stack, but now one marker is needed for the front and another for the back (Figure 9.3). To delete an item, the marker FRONT is increased by one; for an insertion, BACK is increased. This, however, creates a problem. Because deletions are made in front and insertions in back, the queue will continually shift toward the higher-indexed locations of the array. Eventually, BACK will reach the maximum allowable index and we will not be able to continue with any insertions, even though there may be plenty of room available. We could at this point shift every item in the queue so that the front of the queue is in the first element of the array, but a somewhat more efficient solution is to consider the array as circular, that is, as if the last location were followed by the first. Then, when the back of the queue reaches the end of the array, new elements will be inserted starting at the beginning of the array. Similarly, when FRONT reaches the end of the array, it can be reset to point to the beginning (Figure 9.4). The basic queue operations of adding and deleting elements are implemented in the next example.

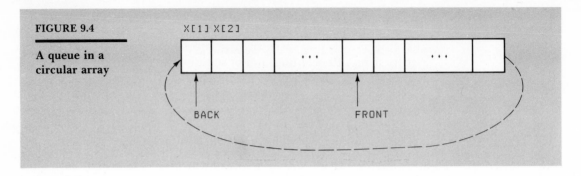

FIGURE 9.4

A queue in a circular array

X[1] X[2]

BACK

FRONT

EXAMPLE 9.4

IMPLEMENTATION OF QUEUE OPERATIONS

The queue will be implemented with the global array

```
QUEUE:array[1..MAXLENGTH] of integer
```

With global variables FRONT and BACK, procedures for adding and removing items from the queue are

```
procedure ADD(NEWVALUE:integer);
begin
  BACK:=BACK+1;
  if BACK=MAXLENGTH+1
    then BACK:=1;
  QUEUE[BACK]:=NEWVALUE
end

procedure REMOVE(var FRONTVALUE:integer)
begin
  FRONTVALUE:=QUEUE[FRONT];
  FRONT:=FRONT+1;
  if FRONT=MAXLENGTH+1
    then FRONT:=1
end
```

Actually, these procedures are not complete, because they do not check for error conditions. An error should be recognized if an attempt is made to remove something from an empty queue. There is also the possibility of queue overflow if the number of elements becomes larger than MAXLENGTH. We leave the required modifications as an exercise.

Queues occur frequently in everyday situations, for example, the waiting lines at the bank or in a grocery store. Cars stopped at a traffic light form a queue. In a computer system the jobs waiting to be processed are normally put into a queue.

Simulation is often used to investigate complex phenomena of the real world with computers. In computer simulation, we build a conceptual model of the actual situation, then write a program to represent the model. The model is often considerably simpler than the real situation, but if it contains its essential features it can give valuable information. The simulation program can then be run under a variety of assumptions and its output used to predict the behavior of the actual situation. For example, a bank may need to decide how many teller windows to open. Too many tellers will be quite expensive; on the other hand, if there are too few there will be long lines and irate customers. The bank management will therefore be interested in knowing the smallest number of tellers that can be used and still keep the customers happy. A simple model of this situation is depicted in Figure 9.5. It is assumed that the customers will stand in a single line and that newly arrived customers will go to the end of the line. When a teller has finished serving a customer, he or she will serve next the one at the front of the line. Obviously, the waiting line is a queue.

A computer program modeling this simple situation is easily written. A queue will be the prominent data structure. The program can be run with various parameters, such as the number of tellers and the frequency of arrival of customers. This is a quick, inexpensive way to get the pertinent information, including the average length of the line, the average amount of idle time for tellers, and a variety of other results.

EXERCISES 9.2

For Exercises 1–3, manipulate the stack using only the stack operations PUSH, POP, *and* EMPTY. *You may use other stacks for the temporary storage of values. If more*

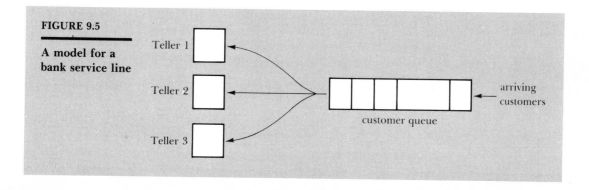

FIGURE 9.5

A model for a bank service line

Teller 1

Teller 2

Teller 3

customer queue

arriving customers

than one stack is needed, rewrite the stack operation subprograms so that the stack names are part of the parameter list. Do not use any data structures other than stacks.

1. Write a procedure to copy a stack, leaving the original stack unchanged.
2. Write a procedure to count the number of elements in a stack. Again, the stack should not be changed.
3. Write a procedure to reverse the elements in a stack in place. That is, the elements should end up in the original stack in reverse order.
4. Rewrite procedures PUSH and POP in Example 9.1 for a stack whose elements are of type array[1..100] of integer.
5. Evaluate the following postfix expressions
   a. 3 4 + 5 6 * + 7 +.
   b. 3 4 5 6 7 + + * *.
   c. 3 4 5 * 6 7 * + +.
6. Convert the following infix expressions to postfix
   a. A*(B+C)/(D+E).
   b. A*B*C/(D+E+F*G).
   c. A+B/C/D.
7. Design a complete set of test examples for program POSTVALUE.
8. Are there invalid expressions in POSTVALUE that will not result in an error message? What will happen in these cases?
9. Write a program for the algorithm in Example 9.3.
10. Modify the algorithm in Example 9.3 so that it can handle expressions involving subtraction and division.
11. What will happen in the algorithm in Example 9.3 for various kinds of invalid infix expressions?
12. Modify the algorithm in Example 9.3 so that it can detect illegal expressions.
13. Find an algorithm and write a program for converting from postfix to infix notation.
14. Write a program that will convert from postfix notation to the assembly language of Chapter 1.
15. Another notation in which parentheses and priority rules are unnecessary is *prefix* notation. Here, a simple expression consists of the operator followed by the two operands. Thus + 3 4 is the same as the infix expression 3 + 4. More complicated expressions are constructed by combining subexpressions. The prefix expression + * 3 4 5 has the value 17, because it is equivalent to 3 * 4 + 5.

    Evaluate the following prefix expressions:
    a. + * * * 3 4 5 6 7.
    b. + * * 3 * 4 5 6 7.
    c. + * * 3 4 * 5 6 7.
16. Write a program similar to POSTVALUE in Example 9.2 to evaluate prefix expressions.
17. Find an algorithm and write a program to translate from infix to prefix notation.

18. In Example 9.4, modify procedures ADD and REMOVE to check for overflow and for an empty queue.
19. Figure 9.5 represents a model with a single queue and several servers (that is, stations where the tasks waiting in the queue are processed). Find some everyday situations where there are several queues and a single server and several queues and several servers.
20. A double-ended queue (deque) is a linearly ordered sequence of elements in which additions and deletions can be made at both ends. For a deque implemented with an array, write procedures for adding and removing elements.
21. Extend Example 9.2 so that the algorithm can handle positive and negative integers with more than one digit. Assume that here the operands and operators are separated by one or more blanks.

9.3

lists

Much of the information processed by computers is in character form, arranged in words, lines, or paragraphs. A collection of such character strings is often called a *text*. Usually text processing involves frequent insertions into a string or deletion of part of it. The completely static implementation of character strings by means of arrays, discussed in Section 5.4, is inadequate for such purposes. To accommodate strings that can grow and shrink, we need a dynamic data structure, one that represents a linearly ordered sequence in which changes can be made anywhere. Such a structure is called a *list*.

Our previous method for implementing stacks and queues, namely to embed each in a static array of fixed size, is unsuitable for most applications involving lists, because these applications usually involve many lists of widely varying and unpredictable lengths. If each were implemented as an array of fixed size, the arrays would have to be made very large in order to allow for the longest possible list. Much memory space would be wasted by this arrangement. One way around the difficulty is to allow all lists to share a single large array, which we will call the *workspace*. We then have to worry about how to store the lists in workspace and how to keep track of where they are.

For the sake of simplicity we will assume for most of this section that all lists are character lists, that is, each item is a single character. Actually, elements can be other, perhaps quite complicated data structures. In those cases, the code will change, but the basic ideas remain the same.

sequential allocation

One of the simplest ways of putting lists into the workspace is to store the elements of each list in consecutive positions of the array, with one list following another. This is called **sequential allocation.** Because the lists are of unpredictable lengths, some convention will have to be chosen to determine where one list ends and the next one starts. We will use here the method of using a *tag*. A tag is a special symbol that can be distinguished from the other allowable characters. We will use the character ' * ' as tag, placing it at the end of each list. Thus

THIS IS A PIECE*OF TEXT*IN WORKSPACE*

represents three lists stored sequentially in workspace.

Sequential allocation has the advantage of simplicity. Also, the processing of sequentially stored lists is easy to visualize. Elements are stored in successive positions in the workspace, and standard array manipulation techniques can be used to work on lists. Each list, in addition to its elements, also contains a tag. This tag is redundant information (which could be omitted if the programmer were able to keep track of the length of each list) and is therefore wasted overhead space. This overhead, however, is small, just one character per list. From the point of view of effective memory utilization, sequential allocation is highly efficient.

But sequential allocation has some serious disadvantages. A very common operation in applications in which lists are used (such as editing of alphabetical text) is insertion of one or more new elements. This is very cumbersome with sequential allocation. If in the previous example we wanted to insert the word NEW between A and PIECE, the information in the workspace would have to be shifted from

THIS IS A PIECE*OF TEXT*IN WORKSPACE*
↑
beginning of workspace

to

THIS IS A NEW PIECE*OF TEXT*IN WORKSPACE*
↑
beginning of workspace

Every letter following the inserted part has to be moved. Because the workspace may contain many thousands of characters, an insertion (or a deletion) may be prohibitively time-consuming. This shortcoming provides the motivation to investigate alternative data structures that are more efficient for insertion and deletion.

linked list To avoid having to move information around in the workspace, we might try to put new information into some unused part of the workspace, then somehow link it to the rest of the list. This intuitive notion is formalized by the concept of a **linked list.** In a linked list, each element consists of two parts: the actual value of the element and a link connecting one element to the next (Figure 9.6). In Figure 9.6, the links are represented by arrows. The last element of a list has a special *null* link, represented in the diagram by a dot marking the end of the list.

FIGURE 9.6

**A linked list
with three
letters T, H, E**

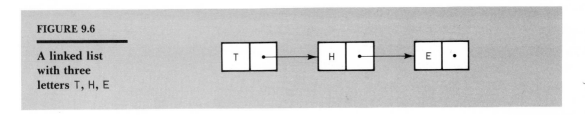

FIGURE 9.7

**A sequence of
insertions and
deletions in a
linked list**

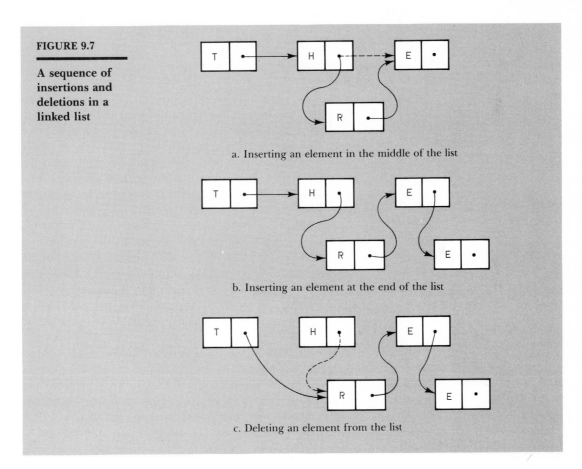

a. Inserting an element in the middle of the list

b. Inserting an element at the end of the list

c. Deleting an element from the list

With linked lists, it is not necessary that list elements be stored in consecutive locations in workspace, because the link shows where the next element is to be found. Therefore insertion and deletion do not require moving elements around; only a manipulation of the links has to be done. A simple insertion and deletion sequence is depicted in Figure 9.7.

When there are several lists in workspace, the name of each list can be considered a link to the first element of the list. In this simple case, the name of a list is actually an integer variable whose value is the position of the start

FIGURE 9.8

Several linked
lists in
workspace

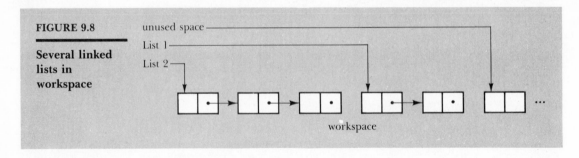

of the list in workspace. The unused part of the workspace can also be kept track of with an integer variable (Figure 9.8).

*workspace
management*

In a program that uses many lists, it is important that the workspace be used efficiently. This introduces the need for *workspace management.* When a new element is to be inserted into a list, the space for it must be obtained from the unused part of the workspace. Because we know where the unused part of workspace starts, this is easy. When an element is deleted, its space must be released; that is, made available for later use. Otherwise, the available workspace will gradually shrink, and the program may eventually have to be terminated because the workspace is exhausted. One of the simplest methods for workspace management is to collect all unused space into a separate list. When space is needed for a new element, it is taken from this unused space list. Freed space is returned by adding it to the unused space list. Figure 9.9 depicts the same sequence of insertion and deletion as Figure 9.7, with the addition of the unused space list. Note that elements are taken from and returned to the unused space list only at one end. The unused space list is in fact a stack, implemented as a linked list.

This description of linked lists is quite intuitive and idealized. Most higher level languages do not have linked lists as a data type, so they must be suitably implemented and the procedures for insertion, deletion, and workspace management written. Let us now look at a Pascal implementation of linked lists and some code for their manipulation.

Because, in general, the value of a list element and the link are of different types, a list element is conveniently defined as a record, in this case as

```
type ELEMENT=record
              VALUE:char;
              LINK:integer
           end
```

Workspace can then be made an array of such elements by

```
var WORKSPACE:array[1..WORKMAX] of ELEMENT
```

FIGURE 9.9

Insertion and deletion in a linked list with workspace management

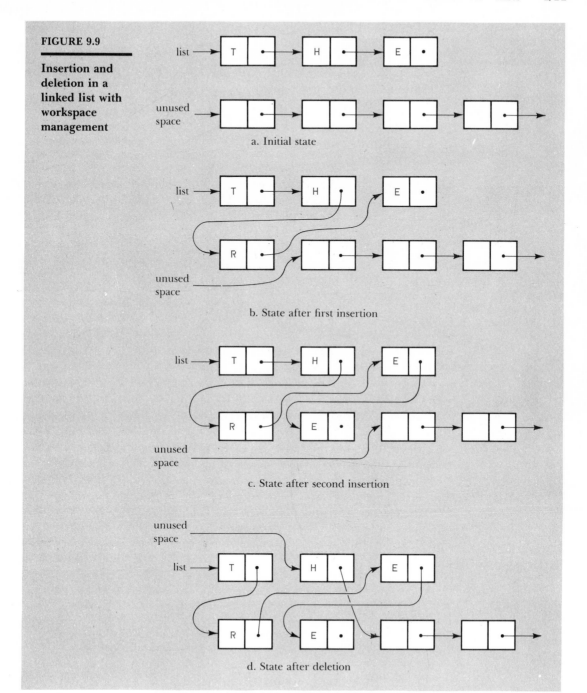

a. Initial state

b. State after first insertion

c. State after second insertion

d. State after deletion

All list names will be of type `integer`. The value of a list name is the position of its first element in `WORKSPACE`. The unused workspace is a list with name `UNUSED`. Null links will be represented by zero.

First, we need to initialize the workspace, creating the linked list `UNUSED`. This can be done with

```
for I:=1 to WORKMAX-1 do
   WORKSPACE[I].LINK:=I+1;
WORKSPACE[WORKMAX].LINK:=0;
UNUSED:=1
```

This sets up the links for the workspace and defines all workspace as unused. The value fields of the unused workspace need not be set because they are never used. The actual values in `WORKSPACE` are shown in Figure 9.10(a).

To create a new list with a single element, say, `NEWLIST` with element value `FIRST`, space is obtained from `UNUSED` and `NEWLIST` set up. The value of `UNUSED` has to be changed so that it now points to the next element in the unused space.

```
{assign first element of unused space to NEWLIST}
NEWLIST:=UNUSED;
{change start of unused space}
UNUSED:=WORKSPACE[UNUSED].LINK;
{set up value and link for new element}
WORKSPACE[NEWLIST].VALUE:=FIRST;
WORKSPACE[NEWLIST].LINK:=0
```

Figure 9.10(b) shows the values on `WORKSPACE` after creation of the first element of the first list. Insertion in existing lists is done along similar lines.

To delete an item from a list, the item has to be found first. Then the links are changed to remove the item from the list and return the element to unused space. To find an item in `LIST`, the value of which is `SYMBOL`, the list is scanned from the beginning until the value is found. Actually, for updating the links it is a little more convenient to stop at the element immediately preceding the one to be deleted. Let `POS` be the position in `WORKSPACE` of this preceding element; then `WORKSPACE[POS].LINK` is the location of the item to be deleted. The value of `POS` can be found by

```
POS:=LIST;
NEXTPOS:=WORKSPACE[POS].LINK;
while WORKSPACE[NEXTPOS].VALUE<>SYMBOL do
   begin
     POS:=NEXTPOS;
     NEXTPOS:=WORKSPACE[POS].LINK
   end
```

Once `POS` has been found, the changing of the links can be done with

FIGURE 9.10

Implementation of workspace as an array of records

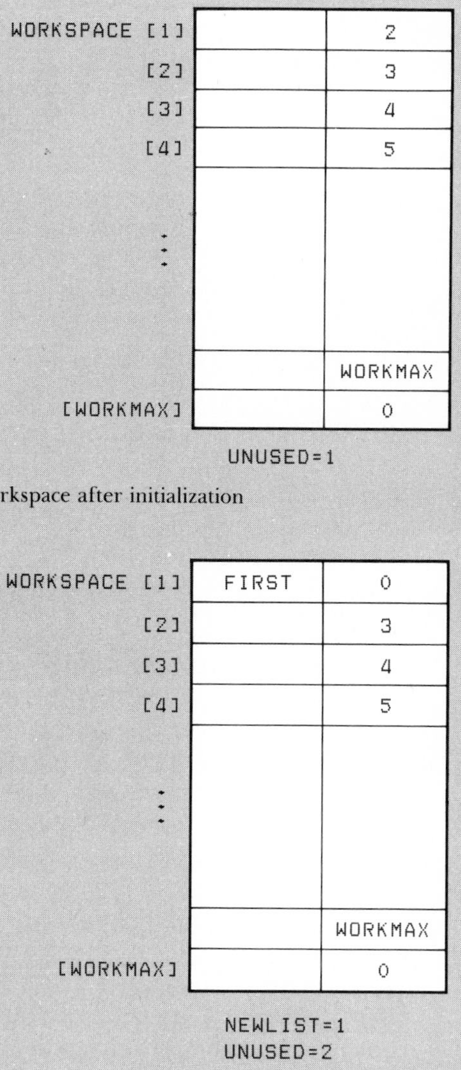

WORKSPACE [1]		2
[2]		3
[3]		4
[4]		5
		WORKMAX
[WORKMAX]		0

UNUSED=1

a. Workspace after initialization

WORKSPACE [1]	FIRST	0
[2]		3
[3]		4
[4]		5
		WORKMAX
[WORKMAX]		0

NEWLIST=1
UNUSED=2

b. Workspace after creation of a list with one element

```
{ remove element from list }
WORKSPACE[POS].LINK:=WORKSPACE[NEXTPOS].LINK;
{ return space to UNUSED }
WORKSPACE[NEXTPOS].LINK:=UNUSED;
UNUSED:=NEXTPOS
```

FIGURE 9.11

A doubly linked
list

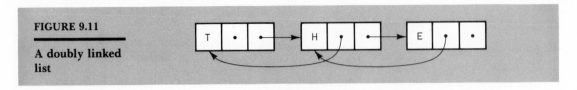

FIGURE 9.12

A list of lists

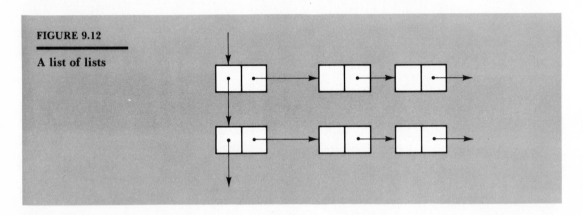

The code given is just a sketch giving the main ideas of linked list manipulation. To write a complete set of procedures for insertion and deletion, we must deal with various details such as correct handling of the beginning and the end of the list, what to do when the looked-for value is not in the list, and others. (Try the details as exercises.)

The linked lists described so far are of a particularly uncomplicated type called *simply linked lists*. Many applications call for more complex linked structures. What kind of linking is used will depend on the operations that are to be performed.

The linking in a simply linked structure allows traversal of the list in only one direction, the direction of the links. When it is necessary to traverse the list in the opposite direction, we can include backward links to get a *doubly linked list*. A picture of a doubly linked list is given in Figure 9.11. Each element of a doubly linked list has a forward and a backward link as indicated by the arrows.

The value field of a linked list need not be primitive data types, but can be more complicated structures. In particular, each value may itself be another linked list, giving the situation shown in Figure 9.12. Some applications of such complex list structures will be described in the next section.

EXERCISES 9.3

1. In Figure 9.9, draw the new picture if after d. the character 'S' is appended to the end of the list.

Do Exercises 2–7 for simply linked lists, implemented as described in this section. You may limit the list values to single characters. In writing the programs, consider carefully any possible exceptional conditions, such as lists that are empty or that become empty after deletion. Include storage management in your algorithms.

2. Write a procedure for creating a linked list from input values.
3. Write a procedure for printing the values in a linked list.
4. Write a procedure for deleting the first (left-most) occurrence of a given character.
5. Write a procedure for inserting a new character immediately after the first occurrence of a given character.
6. Write a procedure for deleting an entire list.
7. Write a procedure for combining or *concatenating* two lists. For example, if the first list is 'ABC' and the second is 'DE', their concatenation is 'ABCDE'.
8. Show how stacks can be implemented as linked lists. Write procedures PUSH and POP for this implementation, using the procedures developed in Exercises 2–7.
9. What kind of linking is needed for a linked list implementation of queues?
10. Compare the storage efficiency of the linked list implementation described in this section with that of sequential allocation.
11. Give an implementation for doubly linked lists. Repeat Exercises 2–7 for this implementation.
12. Write a procedure for printing the elements of a list of integers in reverse order (that is, last number first). Do this for simply and doubly linked lists. Which structure is more suitable?
13. Suppose LIST1 and LIST2 are two existing lists and that we want to assign the values in LIST1 to LIST2. We could simply write LIST2:=LIST1, because the list names are just integers—but is this an efficient way of copying a list? Are there some undesirable side effects?

9.4

some applications of linked lists

Linked lists are used in many applications. Depending on the nature of the problem and the operations that need to be performed, a variety of linking schemes are employed. In this section, we will outline several programs that use linked structures effectively.

EXAMPLE 9.5

MANIPULATION OF POLYNOMIALS

A polynomial is a simple mathematical function consisting of sums of powers of a variable. A general form is

$$P(x) = a_n x^n + a_{n-1} x^{n-1} + \cdots + a_1 x + a_0$$

Here, n is the *degree* of the polynomial and the a_i are its *coefficients*. The x is called the independent variable; it is in fact just a formal parameter. If the coefficients of the polynomial are given, then for any x, the value $P(x)$ of the polynomial is easily computed.

Polynomials occur in a wide variety of computations and there exist a number of software programs for the manipulation of polynomials. One of the simplest processes in this manipulation is the addition of two polynomials. This yields another polynomial in an obvious way. If $P(x)$ and $Q(x)$ are two polynomials, and

$$P(x) = a_n x^n + a_{n-1} x^{n-1} + \cdots + a_0$$
$$Q(x) = b_m x^m + b_{m-1} x^{m-1} + \cdots + b_0$$

then their sum $R(x)$ is given by (assuming $n \geq m$)

$$R(x) = c_n x^n + c_{n-1} x^{n-1} + \cdots + c_0$$

where

$$c_i = a_i + b_i \quad \text{if } i \leq m$$
$$= a_i \quad\quad\ \text{if } m < i \leq n$$

Similarly, the product of two polynomials can be found by writing out their terms, multiplying out, and collecting terms. Other common processes to be performed on polynomials are factoring, division of one polynomial by another, and integration and differentiation. Our interest here is not in these processes, but rather in the most suitable way for representing polynomials.

A polynomial is completely specified by its coefficients, because the variable x is a formal parameter. The simplest way to represent a polynomial is to store all its coefficients in a one-dimensional array, say `COEFF`, of type `array[0..N] of real`, such that a_0 is stored in `COEFF[0]`, a_1 in `COEFF[1]`, and so on. For any missing powers, or where $n \leq N$, a zero is stored in the corresponding place of `COEFF`. Clearly, addition (and similarly multiplication) is a very simple matter in this representation.

This is a completely static implementation and, like many static structures, it has disadvantages. How large should N be? If it is made too large, a lot of space will be wasted for polynomials with small n. Also, the algorithms may become inefficient, because the zero coefficients have to be processed along with the nonzero ones. On the other hand, if we make N small, the program will not be able to handle polynomials of high degree. We know that the difficulty can be overcome by using a dynamic data structure. A simply linked list is suitable here. Each entry will have a value field with two parts: the coefficient of the term, and the power to which the formal parameter is raised. The latter is necessary because some of the powers may be missing so that it is impossible to infer the power from the position in the list. For example, the polynomial

$$P(x) = 7x^5 - 4x^3 + 3x^2 + 1$$

is represented by the linked list shown in Figure 9.13. The addition and multiplication of polynomials in this implementation is an easy matter left as an exercise.

EXAMPLE 9.6

TEXT EDITING

A text editor is a program for creating and modifying character data stored in the computer. Text editors are part of the software of most computer systems. The data are generally organized in some way, typically by being divided into consecutively numbered lines. Text editors are usually capable of performing a wide variety of operations, of which some of the simpler ones are:

1. Delete a given line.
2. Insert a new line in a certain place.
3. Replace the first occurrence of a given character in a specified line with another character.

If these processes are to be done efficiently, the data must be structured properly.

Because insertions and deletions in one form or another are the major function of a text editor, sequential allocation is obviously unsuitable, and some form of a linked structure must be considered. However, arranging all data as a simply linked list may not be the best solution. Consider the deletion of a line. First, the line has to be found. In a simply linked list,

FIGURE 9.13

A linked list for $7x^5 - 4x^3 + 3x^2 + 1$

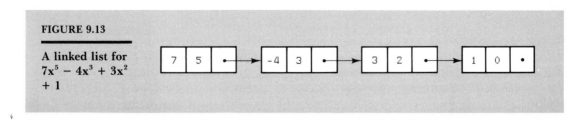

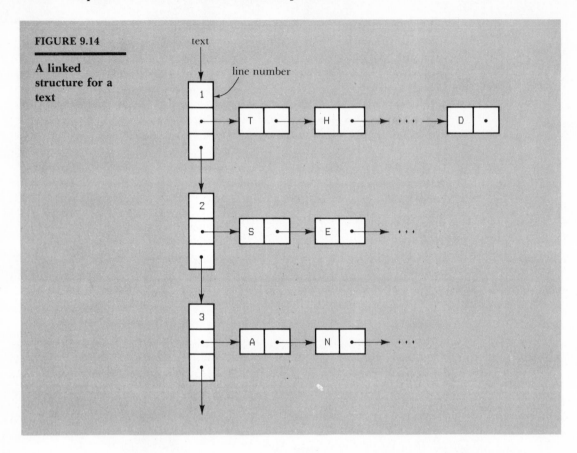

FIGURE 9.14

A linked structure for a text

because no information on lines is available directly, all of the data have to be examined starting from the beginning until the right line is reached. In a long piece of text, this can be very time-consuming. Perhaps a more suitable structure is the one shown in Figure 9.14.

This structure is a linked list of lines, where the value of each element of the line list is a linked list of characters. Locating a line with a given number can be done quickly. We simply follow the line links until we get to the right line. Editing a particular line is then done by following the links connecting the individual characters. This rather complicated structure looks quite efficient for processing, but whether one would actually use it in practice depends on other factors. We will return to this question in Section 10.3.

EXAMPLE 9.7

SPARSE TABLES AND MATRICES

Many applications involve tables or, in scientific computations, matrices. In some of these, the matrices contain relatively few nonzero entries and are called *sparse* matrices. Figure 9.15 shows a four by four matrix that is fairly sparse. Especially for large tables and matrices it is essential, for both processing and storage efficiency, to take advantage of any significant sparseness. The zero elements, which generally carry no information, should not be stored or processed.

To implement a sparse matrix, we can create a list of all the nonzero elements. Each element in such a list carries, in addition to any links, three pieces of information: the row number, the column number, and the value of the entry. Such a list would contain all the pertinent information, but unless it is given more organization, it probably cannot be processed very efficiently. It would make little sense just to put all elements in a simply linked list in some random fashion. This may be efficient for storage, but any processing would require repeated searches of the entire list. To determine what structure is acceptable, we need to know what processes are to be done.

A much more amenable structure uses a separate list for each row, with entries in each row ordered by the column number. The matrix in

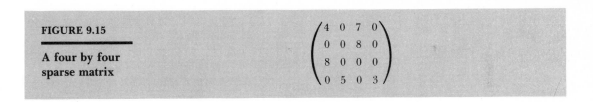

FIGURE 9.15

A four by four sparse matrix

$$\begin{pmatrix} 4 & 0 & 7 & 0 \\ 0 & 0 & 8 & 0 \\ 8 & 0 & 0 & 0 \\ 0 & 5 & 0 & 3 \end{pmatrix}$$

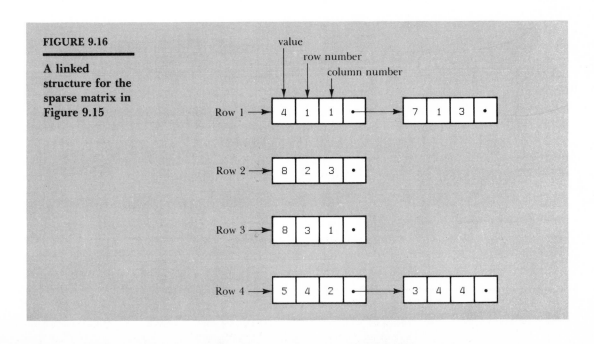

FIGURE 9.16

A linked structure for the sparse matrix in Figure 9.15

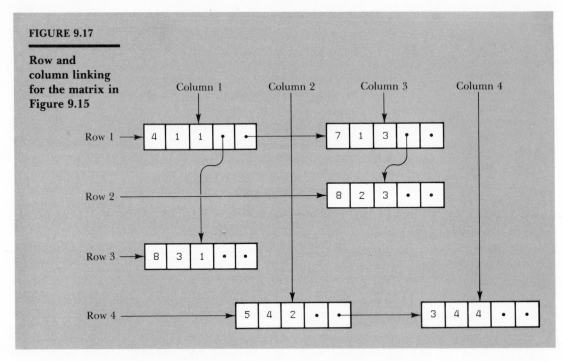

FIGURE 9.17

Row and column linking for the matrix in Figure 9.15

Figure 9.15 will then be represented by the scheme in Figure 9.16. This is still a very storage-efficient way. It is also quite acceptable for some processing, such as changing the entry in a given row and column. If the entry is in row I and column J, we start at the beginning of row I. This is easy, because there is a link to the beginning of each row. We then follow the row links to the entry in the Jth column. At most, all of the entries in row I will have to be examined.

But there are other processes for which the structure in Figure 9.16 is not very good. If we are asked, for instance, to find the largest entry in some given row, there is no difficulty. We can check consecutive elements of the row by following the links until the end (indicated by a null link) is reached. But if instead we wanted to find the largest element in a given column, we would run into considerable difficulty. There is no way of examining the entries in one column without looking at entries in other columns. To find a column maximum in such a structure would be much less efficient than finding a row maximum.

Sparse matrices and tables often have to be processed by columns as well as rows. If it is necessary to provide for efficient processing in both directions, a better structure involves linking both rows and columns. The example in Figure 9.15 might then be represented by the fairly complicated linked structure in Figure 9.17.

Linked structures are useful in many applications in diverse fields. The examples given here by no means exhaust the useful linked structures, and many other types of linking are widely used. As our examples indicate, the decision on what sort of linking to use must depend on the kinds of operations that are commonly applied. A structure that may be very effective in one situation may be completely useless in another.

EXERCISES 9.4

For Exercises 1–4, use the linked list representation described in Example 9.5.

1. Design an algorithm and write a program to evaluate a polynomial; that is, given x, compute $P(x)$.
2. Write a program to add two polynomials.
3. Write a program to multiply two polynomials.
4. Write a program to print a polynomial in a readable form.

For Exercises 5–8, use the linked structure described in Example 9.6. Begin by choosing an implementation. Note that there are two types of list elements involved; one consists of an integer and two links, the other of one character and one link. Your programs should also include workspace management. You may want to divide the workspace into two arrays with different elements.

5. Write a procedure for deleting the Ith line.
6. Write a procedure for inserting a new line after the Ith line. The characters for the new line should come from the input file.
7. Write a procedure for appending a new line at the end of the text.
8. Write a procedure for deleting the first occurrence of a given character in the Ith line.
9. Comment of the storage efficiency of the structure in Example 9.6. What is an approximate ratio of overhead to useful information?
10. For the matrix

    ```
    3  0  0  1
    0  0  2  0
    1  0  0  2
    3  1  2  0
    ```

    draw the linked structures corresponding to Figures 9.16 and 9.17.
11. Give an implementation for the structure in Figure 9.17. Use this to write procedures for finding row and column maxima.
12. In Figure 9.17, each element contains the row and column number. This is redundant information, because the linking makes it possible to deduce these numbers. Give a reason why such redundant information is useful.

further reading

Horowitz, E., and Sahni, S. *Fundamentals of Data Structures,* Chapters 3 and 4. Potomac, Md.: Computer Science Press, 1976.

Knuth, D. E. *The Art of Computer Programming. Vol. 1, Fundamental Algorithms,* 2d. ed., Chapter 2. Reading, Mass.: Addison-Wesley Publishing Co., 1973.

Maly, K., and Hanson, A. R. *Fundamentals of Computing Science,* Chapter 9. Englewood Cliffs, N.J.: Prentice-Hall, 1978.

Tenenbaum, A. M., and Augenstein, M. J. *Data Structures Using Pascal,* Chapters 2 and 4. Englewood Cliffs, N.J.: Prentice-Hall, 1981.

Tremblay, J., and Bunt, R. B. *An Introduction to Computer Science,* Chapter 10. New York: McGraw-Hill, 1979.

Chapter Ten

more on data structures

List structures embody a particularly simple relationship, linear order. Although fairly complicated linking is possible, each element is still part of an ordered linear sequence (at least with respect to each mode of linking). There are other data types, such as records, that cannot be described by a linear ordering. To express relationships more complicated than linear order, other structures are needed. Tree structures, which we will describe briefly in this chapter, represent the next level of complexity in data organization and are encountered in many applications. The record structures shown in Figures 5.1 and 5.2 are examples of trees. Control structures such as nested if-then-else and case statements can also be thought of as trees. These are just a few simple examples pointing to the fact that trees are important data structures in computer science.

10.1

trees

A *tree* is a structure composed of *nodes*, which carry information, and *branches*, which connect the nodes and thereby show the relationship between them. The information in the node is said to be the *label* of the node. Figure 10.1 shows an example of a tree. In our convention, the nodes are shown as circles containing the labels, while branches are given as lines with arrows.

The descriptive terminology for trees mixes terms for natural trees with some that come from genealogical charts ("family trees"). If there is a branch from one node to another, the first is said to be the *parent* of the second, and the second node the *child* of the first. In Figure 10.1, the nodes labeled D and E are the children of B, while C is the parent of F and G. In every tree, there is one and only one node without a parent; this is the *root* of the tree. Nodes with no children are the *leaves* of the tree. In Figure 10.1,

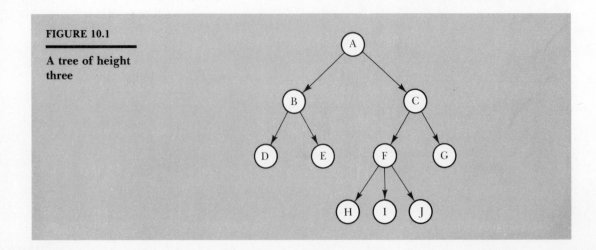

FIGURE 10.1

A tree of height three

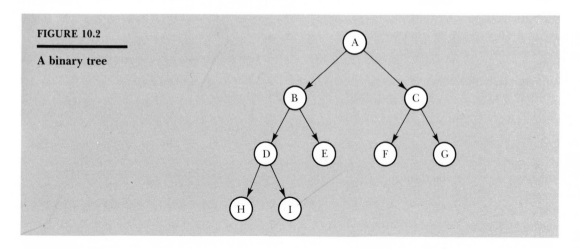

FIGURE 10.2

A binary tree

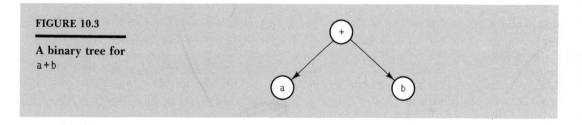

FIGURE 10.3

A binary tree for
a+b

binary trees

the node labelled A is the root of the tree and the nodes D, E, G, H, I, and J are its leaves. The *height* of a tree is the maximum number of branches in a path from the root to any leaf. The tree in Figure 10.1 has height three.

Particularly useful are **binary trees.** A binary tree is a tree in which each node has at most two children, referred to as *left* and *right* children. The tree in Figure 10.1 is not a binary tree, but the one in Figure 10.2 is. Restricting the number of children makes the structure simple enough that its implementation and processing are relatively easy. Practically, of course, not every tree structure is of binary form. But binary trees are very common and there are ways in which general trees can be redrawn as binary trees. Consequently, our discussion will be almost entirely restricted to binary trees.

As an example of an application of binary trees, take the representation of arithmetic expressions. In Chapter 9, we discussed the relation between the standard infix notation and the less well-known prefix and postfix forms. Arithmetic expressions can also be represented by binary trees. In this form, the operators and operands become the labels of the tree, and the branches show how they are combined. The simple expression

a+b

is represented by the tree in Figure 10.3. Because more complicated expres-

FIGURE 10.4

Tree
representation
of the
expression
a+b*(c+d)/e

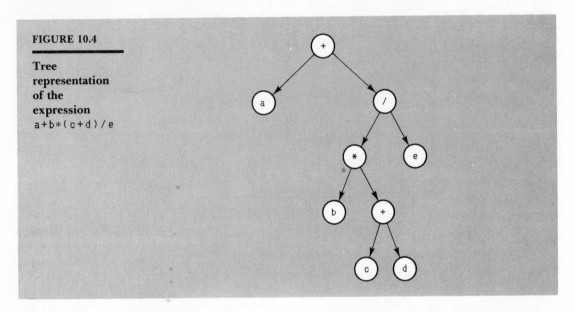

sions are built by combining subexpressions, the expression trees are also combined. Thus the expression

    a+b*(c+d)/e

has the binary tree form shown in Figure 10.4. This representation requires no parentheses or priority rules. All operands are in the leaves of the tree, with the operators restricted to the interior nodes (nodes that are not leaves).

A less technical example of a binary tree is the chart for an elimination tennis tournament (Figure 10.5). In the leaves are the names of the starting players. The names of the winners of each round are the labels of the nodes for the next round. The name of the winner is in the root.

There are many ways in which binary trees can be implemented. (As a rule, the more complex the structure, the more options there are for its implementation.) A generalization of the linked list concept to binary trees is immediate. With each node are associated three parts: the information stored in the node, that is, the label value, a left link pointing to the left child (and its associated subtree), and a right link, pointing to the right child (Figure 10.6). The data types needed for the actual implementation are also quite similar to those used for linked lists. For example, if the node labels are single characters, we can define a node type by

```
type NODE=record
          VALUE:char;
          LEFTLINK,RIGHTLINK:integer
     end
```

FIGURE 10.5

**A tennis
tournament tree**

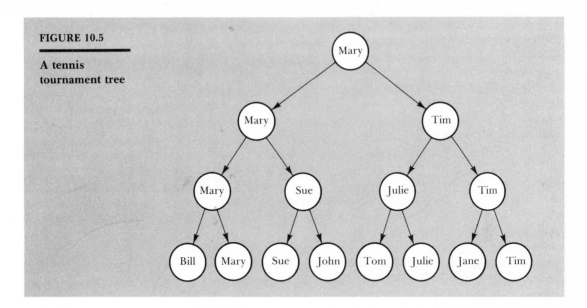

To store trees, we use

```
TREE:array[1..MAXNODES] of NODE
```

The links are integer values giving the index in the array TREE in which the child node is stored. We can use our previous convention and take zero as the null link. In this scheme, TREE is actually the workspace in which different trees can be stored. The name of an individual tree will be an integer variable, the value of which is the location of its root in the workspace TREE.

There are many different operations that must be performed on binary trees in various applications. These include input (that is, construction of the internal representation from some convenient input form), output (printing a tree in some visually explicit way), eliminating nodes or parts of a tree, and combining trees. Basic to all these operations is the need to locate a node with some specified label, just as in processing a list we first have to find the place where the change has to be made. In a linked list, we simply followed the links to the right element. But a tree structure is not linear, and searching is a little harder. A systematic approach assures that all nodes are considered.

---

preorder traversal

There are several search strategies for binary trees. One is *preorder traversal.* Starting with the root, each node is examined or processed. If the left branch has not yet been explored, go down to the left and continue with the left child. If the left branch has been done but not the right, go down to the right child. If at a node both the right and left sides have been processed, back up one level to the parent node and repeat the process. When you back into the root from the right, the whole tree has been traversed. The preorder traversal of the tree in Figure 10.2 checks the nodes in the order

```
A B D H I E C F G
```

while in Figure 10.4, the order is

```
+ a / * b + c d e
```

The method looks simple enough, but the algorithm for it is not.

EXAMPLE 10.1

PRINTING LABELS OF A BINARY TREE IN PREORDER

In this example, we write a procedure for printing the labels of a binary tree when traversal is made in preorder. The labels will be limited to single characters. The procedure will assume that the tree is stored in a global array TREE, structured as described on page 256. The procedure PREPRINT will have one parameter ROOT, which is an integer giving the position of the root in TREE.

The description of preorder traversal needs some elaboration before the algorithm is obvious. The main trouble lies in the meaning of the phrase "back up." This is easy to visualize, but a little harder to code. The tree branches from parent to child, but not from child to parent, so the links cannot be used directly for backing up. The point of backing up is to process any nodes not yet done. Rather than devise some method for going from child to parent, let us simply save all nodes until we are ready to print their labels. The information to be saved varies with the tree so we should use some dynamic structure. When the algorithm backs up, it must take the node most recently saved; this suggests that a stack is appropriate. Every time a node is encountered, its right and left children are put on the stack. To process a node, we pop the top one from the stack. A pseudolanguage algorithm is

1. Push ROOT onto stack.
2. Repeat Steps 3–5 until stack is empty.
3. Pop integer THISNODE from stack and print value of TREE[THISNODE].
4. If right link of TREE[THISNODE] is not null, push it onto stack.
5. If left link of TREE[THISNODE] is not null, push it onto stack.

Before proceeding, trace this algorithm with a few simple examples.

The code will be written as a procedure using the global array TREE. It uses the stack structure and the subprograms PUSH, POP, and EMPTY, which are described in Example 9.1. The main program PRETEST is a driver for testing PREPRINT.

```
program PRETEST(input,output);
const MAXLENGTH=20;
type NODE=record
             VALUE:char;
             LEFTLINK,RIGHTLINK:integer
          end;
var TREE:array[1..MAXLENGTH] of NODE;
    STACK:array[1..MAXLENGTH] of integer;
    TOP,I:integer;

function EMPTY:boolean;
{ boolean function which has value
  true if the stack is empty}
begin
  if TOP=0
    then EMPTY:=true
    else EMPTY:=false
end;

procedure PUSH(NEWTOP:integer);
{ this procedure pushes NEWTOP
  onto the stack. An overflow
  will give an error message}
begin
  if TOP>=MAXLENGTH
    then begin
           writeln(' error in PUSH');
           writeln(' stack overflow')
         end
    else begin
           TOP:=TOP+1;
           STACK[TOP]:=NEWTOP
         end
end;

procedure POP(var TOPVALUE:integer);
{ this procedure puts the value at the
  top of the stack into TOPVALUE and
  pops the stack. An empty stack will
  give an error message }
```

```
begin
  if EMPTY
    then begin
            writeln(' error in POP');
            writeln(' stack is empty')
         end
    else begin
            TOPVALUE:=STACK[TOP];
            TOP:=TOP-1
         end
end;

procedure PREPRINT(ROOT:integer);
{ this procedure prints the labels
of a binary tree in preorder}
var THISNODE:integer;
begin
  {set stack to empty, start at root}
  TOP:=0;
  PUSH(ROOT);
  repeat
    {traverse tree in preorder, stacking
     right and left subtrees for later use}
    POP(THISNODE);
    writeln(TREE[THISNODE].VALUE);
    if TREE[THISNODE].RIGHTLINK<>0
      then PUSH(TREE[THISNODE].RIGHTLINK);
    if TREE[THISNODE].LEFTLINK<>0
      then PUSH(TREE[THISNODE].LEFTLINK)
    {terminate when stack is empty}
  until EMPTY
end;

{main program is driver to test PREPRINT}
begin
  I:=0;
  repeat
    I:=I+1;
    with TREE[I] do
      readln(VALUE,LEFTLINK,RIGHTLINK)
  until eof;
  PREPRINT(1)
end.
```

As test case, the program was run with data

```
A 2 3
B 4 5
C 6 7
D 8 9
E 0 0
F 0 0
G 0 0
H 0 0
I 0 0
```

The driver program reads these data and constructs the internal representation for TREE.

	VALUE	LEFTLINK	RIGHTLINK
TREE[1]	A	2	3
[2]	B	4	5
[3]	C	6	7
[4]	D	8	9
[5]	E	0	0
[6]	F	0	0
[7]	G	0	0
[8]	H	0	0
[9]	I	0	0

This set of data corresponds to the tree in Figure 10.2. When the procedure was applied to these data, the output was

```
A
B
D
H
I
E
C
F
G
```

as expected.

Although procedure PREPRINT is relatively short, it took some time and effort to discover the algorithm and to write the code. When working with binary trees, we can solve many problems quickly and elegantly if we

FIGURE 10.6

Forms of a binary tree

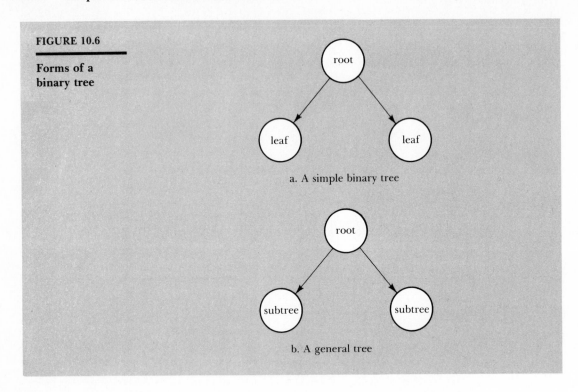

a. A simple binary tree

b. A general tree

recognize the inherent recursive nature of such a tree. A simple binary tree has a root and two leaves (Figure 10.6(a)). More extensive trees can be thought of in the same way if we replace the word "leaf" with "subtree" and take "subtree" to mean any other binary tree, including an empty tree or a leaf (Figure 10.6(b)). A preorder traversal of the tree in Figure 10.6 (a) is easily accomplished with

1. Process root.
2. Process left subtree.
3. Process right subtree.

Exactly the same algorithm can be used to process an arbitrary binary tree, provided the algorithm is applied recursively.

EXAMPLE 10.2

RECURSIVE PROCEDURE FOR PRINTING LABELS OF A BINARY TREE

The procedure PREPRINTREC will do exactly the same thing as PREPRINT in Example 10.1. It will utilize the same global variables and data structures. The same driver program can be used to test it. The only difference is that PREPRINTREC is recursive.

To write the program, it is necessary only to rewrite the algorithm just given in Pascal.

```
procedure PREPRINTREC(ROOT:integer);
begin
  writeln(TREE[ROOT].VALUE);
  if TREE[ROOT].LEFTLINK<>0
    then PREPRINTREC(TREE[ROOT].LEFTLINK);
  if TREE[ROOT].RIGHTLINK<>0
    then PREPRINTREC(TREE[ROOT].RIGHTLINK)
end
```

The brevity and elegance of this code demonstrates the power of recursion when used with tree structures.

postorder and inorder traversal

There are other common tree traversal methods. In *postorder traversal,* the same path is taken as in preorder, but a node is processed on the last visit rather than on the first. Formally, postorder is defined by

1. Process left subtree.
2. Process right subtree.
3. Process root.

A postorder printing of the labels in Figure 10.2 gives

```
H  I  D  E  B  F  G  C  A
```

Lastly, there is *inorder traversal,* defined by

1. Process left subtree.
2. Process root.
3. Process right subtree.

For the tree in Figure 10.2 inorder printing produces

```
H  D  I  B  E  A  F  C  G
```

EXERCISES 10.1

1. With the internal representation used in Example 10.1, draw the picture of the tree specified by

TREE[1]	A	2	0
[2]	B	3	4
[3]	C	0	0
[4]	D	5	0
[5]	E	6	7
[6]	F	0	0
[7]	G	0	0

2. For the tree in Exercise 1, show the output produced if the labels are printed in
   a. Preorder.
   b. Postorder.
   c. Inorder.

3. What is the relation between postorder traversal of a tree and postfix notation for algebraic expressions?

4. One way of storing a binary tree is to use a one-dimensional array, say TREE, the elements of which are of the same type as the labels. The root is stored in TREE[1], its left child in TREE[2], and its right child in TREE[3]. The left child of TREE[2] goes into TREE[4], and so on. Any missing nodes can be marked with a special symbol. Because every node is in a known location in TREE, no links are necessary in this implementation. Discuss the advantages and disadvantages of such an implementation. In particular, consider
   a. Ease of programming and readability of the code.
   b. Storage efficiency.
   c. Methods for traversal.
   d. Ease of insertion and deletion of nodes.

For Exercises 5–14, use the implementation of binary trees described in this section.

5. Write a function for determining the height of a binary tree.

6. Write recursive and nonrecursive procedures for printing labels of a binary tree in postorder.

7. Write recursive and nonrecursive procedures for printing labels of a binary tree in inorder.

8. Design a method for tree input. Remember that it is the responsibility of the programmer to design input procedures that make it easy for the user to communicate with the computer. The form in which the program will expect the input must be easy for the user to understand and work with.

9. Write a procedure for printing trees. Aim to produce a clear and explicit picture. For simplicity's sake, assume that the height of the tree is no larger than four.

10. Write a procedure to convert expressions in postfix notation to binary tree form.

11. Write a procedure to convert from infix notation to binary tree form.

12. Write a function to evaluate an arithmetic expression given in binary tree form. For simplicity, assume that only the operators +, −, *, and / are allowed and that all operands are single-digit, positive integers.

13. Another method of binary tree traversal is to process the root first, then all nodes at height one from left to right, then all nodes at height two from left to right, and so on. For the tree in Figure 10.2, the order in this traversal is

    A B C D E F G H I

    Write a program to print tree labels in this order. Is a stack the best choice for the data structure?

14. Study what is involved in workspace management for tree structures, using an approach similar to that described in Section 9.3. In particular, consider what happens when a tree or some part of it is deleted. How is the released space made available for later use?

15. A *ternary* tree is a tree in which each node can have at most three children (left, middle, and right). Establish an implementation for ternary trees.

16. Find an analogue of preorder traversal for ternary trees. With the data structure established in Exercise 15, write recursive and nonrecursive procedures for printing the labels of ternary trees in preorder.

17. Do Exercises 15 and 16 for general trees (that is, trees in which nodes can have any number of children).

10.2
dynamic memory allocation

Whenever dynamic data structures are used, the question of how to manage memory space arises. The most simpleminded approach, used in our implementation of stacks and queues, is to embed each dynamic structure in a static one. By manipulating information that relates the static to the dynamic structure (such as the position of the stack top in the array), we can, within some limits, simulate the behavior of the dynamic structure. This is relatively easy to do, but it utilizes memory very inefficiently. Considerably better is the method suggested in Section 9.3, where a number of dynamic structures share one single, large static array. We manage memory by taking space from and returning it to the workspace. Because the available space is shared by many dynamic structures, this tends to utilize memory more efficiently than assigning a fixed amount of space to each structure. But we must still decide the size of the workspace. Making it too large will be wasteful; on the other hand, some computations may exhaust available

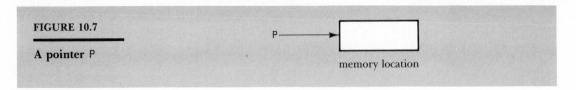

FIGURE 10.7

A pointer P

memory location

space if it is too small. The problem is compounded when, as in Example 9.6, the workspace has to accommodate several data types.

The difficulty arises because we are forced to decide how much space is needed at the coding stage. Because the amount of space required depends on the data, it would be much more appropriate to base the decision on the data, that is, assign the space during the execution of the program. This is called *dynamic memory allocation.* Not all programming languages have such a feature, but Pascal does.

pointer　　　　　Dynamic memory allocation in Pascal is done by means of **pointer** variables. A pointer variable "points" to some place in memory. We can visualize a pointer as an arrow pointing to a data element, similar to the way in which we depicted links in a linked structure (Figure 10.7). The value associated with the pointer P in Figure 10.7 is not the content of the memory location to which it points, but the location itself. This is a major difference between pointers and regular variables; the value associated with a regular variable is the content of one or more memory locations. When a pointer is changed, the new value associated with the pointer is a new memory location (visualized by redrawing the arrow for the pointer). Pointers are a little less straightforward than regular variables. A good way to keep track of what is happening is to draw simple diagrams showing where the pointers point and what the values in the corresponding locations are. We will do this for several subsequent examples.

Pointers can be created and destroyed during the execution of a program. When a pointer is created, memory space is made available by the operating system and the pointer is pointed to this space. By referring to the pointer, we have access to this space. Later, when the space is no longer needed, it can be released by destroying the pointer.

Every pointer variable used in a program must have a defined pointer type. To define a pointer type, we use a declaration such as

```
type REALPOINTER=↑real
```

which makes REALPOINTER an identifier for a pointer type. Any variables of this type are pointers, pointing to data items that are single real numbers. The general form of this declaration is

```
type pointertype = ↑ elementtype
```

where *pointertype* is any legal identifier and *elementtype* is a defined data type. A pointer variable that is declared to be of a certain type can only point to data items of the type given in the declaration.

Once a pointer type has been defined, we can use the v a r declaration to define pointer variables. For example,

```
var P,Q:REALPOINTER
```

defines P and Q to be pointer variables that can point to real numbers.

Data values are stored in the locations to which the pointer variables point. To refer to this information, the pointer variable name, followed by ↑, is used. Thus, if P and Q are of type REALPOINTER, then the statements

```
P↑:=3.4;
Q↑:=2.1
```

are syntactically correct and result in the assignment of numerical values to the locations to which P and Q point (Figure 10.8).

Pointer types can be associated with any data type. The declarations

```
type ROWPTR=↑array[1..100] of integer;
var DATA:ROWPTR
```

make DATA a pointer variable pointing to an array of 100 integer numbers. To initialize such an array to all zeros, we could write

```
for I:=1 to 100 do
  DATA↑[I]:=0
```

When P is any pointer, then P↑ acts like a regular variable identifier.

Although the elements to which pointer variables point can be treated like regular variables (for example, they can occur in expressions if they are of the right type), the operations that can be done on the pointers themselves are more limited. Pointers can appear in simple assignment statements such as

```
P:=Q
```

This assigns the value of the pointer Q to P, which means that P now points to the same location as Q, with Q unchanged. If we start with the situation in Figure 10.8, then after P:=Q we have the situation shown in Figure 10.9. Nothing points to the location containing the value 3.4, and therefore the location is no longer accessible to the program.

Assignment and reassignment of pointers has to be done with care. Some errors can be obscure. Consider

```
P↑ :=3;
Q:=P;
Q↑ :=2
```

What is the value of P↑ after the execution of these three statements? P does not appear on the left side in the last two statements, so one might expect that the value of P↑ is unchanged from the first statement. (This would certainly be the case if P were a regular variable.) But this is not so;

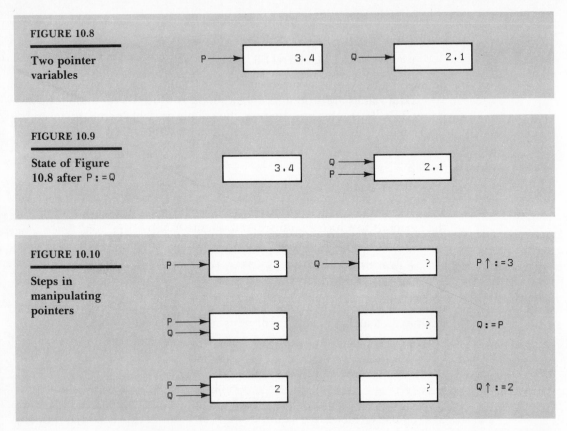

FIGURE 10.8

Two pointer variables

FIGURE 10.9

State of Figure 10.8 after P:=Q

FIGURE 10.10

Steps in manipulating pointers

to see why not, look at Figure 10.10. The value of P ↑ after the completion of the third statement is 2.

At times is is necessary to create a pointer but have it not point anywhere. This is a situation encountered with the null links in linked lists. For a pointer P, we assign such a null value by

    P:=nil

where nil is a reserved word.

The major purpose of pointers is to allow dynamic allocation and releasing (deallocation) of memory. The procedure new allocates space; if P is a pointer of a certain type, then

    new(P)

creates space for a variable of the type associated with P and points P to that space. Every time the procedure new is invoked, a different part of memory is allocated.

The release of memory is done with the procedure dispose. The statement

    dispose(P)

releases the memory space to which P points. The pointer P no longer points anywhere and its value is said to be undefined (its value is not nil). Any reference to P will give an execution error.

There is usually no need to use pointers for variables of primitive type. Pointer variables are most useful in connection with dynamic data structures such as stacks, lists, and trees. Let us redo the previous implementations using pointers.

EXAMPLE 10.3

IMPLEMENTATION OF A STACK WITH POINTERS

For this implementation, we will use a linked list version of a stack. We again assume, for the sake of simplicity, that the element values are integers; the stack element will then consist of a value field of type integer and a link field, which will be a pointer. In this case, the pointer points to another stack element. This can be expressed by the declaration

```
type STACKPOINTER= ↑ELEMENT;
     ELEMENT=record
                 VALUE:integer;
                 LINK:STACKPOINTER
             end
```

There is one peculiarity in this declaration. The definition of STACKPOINTER refers to type ELEMENT, while the definition of ELEMENT involves STACKPOINTER. This seemingly circular definition is unavoidable; each element does in fact contain a pointer to another element (that is, the structure has recursive aspects). This makes it necessary to allow the definition of a pointer in terms of a data type not yet defined. As a general rule, an undeclared identifier cannot be used in another declaration, but an exception has to be made here.

The top of the stack can be referred to by the pointer

```
var TOP:STACKPOINTER
```

To create an empty stack, we can write

```
TOP:=nil
```

which plays the same role as the statement TOP:=0 in the stack implementation of Example 9.1. The function EMPTY is now coded as

```
if TOP=nil
   then EMPTY:=true
   else EMPTY:=false
```

To push an element onto the stack, it is first necessary to obtain the space for it by creating a new pointer. The value to be pushed onto the stack is then stored in the newly created location, and this location is linked to the previous top of the stack. Assuming that TOP is global, the complete code is

```
Procedure PUSH(NEWTOP:integer);
var P:STACKPOINTER;
begin
   new(P);
   P↑.VALUE:=NEWTOP;
   P↑.LINK:=TOP;
   TOP:=P
end
```

Figure 10.11 shows the steps in this procedure as they can be visualized. To pop the stack and store the value in TOPVALUE, one can write

```
TOPVALUE:=TOP↑.VALUE;
TOP:=TOP↑.LINK
```

which pops the top of the stack by merely moving the pointer (Figure 10.12). This, however, is not the complete story, because the element removed from the stack has not been deallocated. If it is necessary to release the space, one could use

```
TOPVALUE:=TOP↑.VALUE;
TEMP:=TOP↑.LINK;
dispose(TOP);
TOP:=TEMP
```

FIGURE 10.11

**Pushing element
onto a stack
implemented
with pointers**

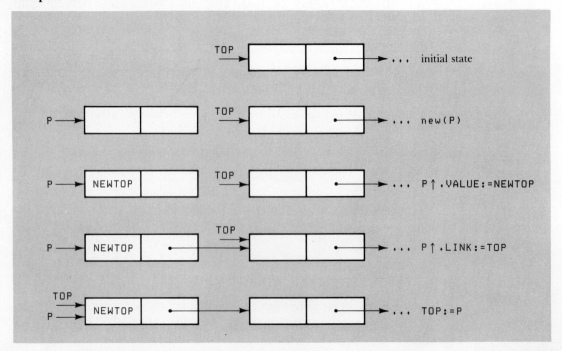

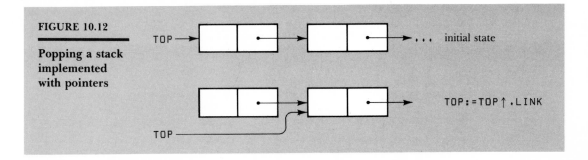

FIGURE 10.12

Popping a stack implemented with pointers

EXAMPLE 10.4

IMPLEMENTATION OF LINKED LISTS WITH POINTERS

The structure used in Example 10.3 is also suitable for linked lists. For this purpose we will use the definitions

```
type LISTPOINTER= ↑ELEMENT;
     ELEMENT=record
                  VALUE:integer;
                  LINK:LISTPOINTER
             end
```

We will use this implementation to write two simple list processing procedures. The first, PRINTLIST, is very elementary. It prints all the values in the list LIST. The second procedure, INSERT, will insert a new element in the list. It has three arguments: LIST, which is a pointer pointing to the list to be processed; and SCANVALUE and NEWVALUE, both integer parameters. The list is searched for the first occurrence of SCANVALUE; if it is found, NEWVALUE is inserted immediately after it.

The algorithm for PRINTLIST is obvious, because it requires only a traversal of the list following the links. The algorithm for INSERT involves first a search of the list until SCANVALUE is found. Once the matching element is found, a new pointer is created, NEWVALUE inserted in the corresponding location, and the links supplied. A check is also made to determine when the end of the list is reached without finding SCANVALUE.

```
procedure PRINTLIST(LIST:LISTPOINTER);
{ procedure for printing values in a linked list.
  If the list is empty, nothing will be printed}
var P:LISTPOINTER;
begin
  P:=LIST;
  while P<>nil do
    begin
      write(P↑.VALUE:5);
```

```
              P:=P↑.LINK
        end;
     writeln
  end;


  procedure INSERT(LIST:LISTPOINTER;
                   SCANVALUE,NEWVALUE:integer);
  { procedure to insert NEWVALUE immediately after
  SCANVALUE in linked list LIST. An error condition
  is recognized if SCANVALUE is not found }
  var P,Q:LISTPOINTER;
      FOUND:boolean;
  begin
    {initialize pointer P which is used to mark
     the current position during the search}
    P:=LIST;
    FOUND:=false;
    {look for SCANVALUE, if found, P will
     point to it and FOUND will be true.
     If SCANVALUE is not in LIST, loop will
     terminate with FOUND false}
    repeat
      if P↑.VALUE=SCANVALUE
        then FOUND:=true
        else P:=P↑.LINK
    until (P=nil) or FOUND;
    { if SCANVALUE was found insert
      NEWVALUE after it, otherwise print
      error message }
    if FOUND
      then begin
             new(Q);
             Q↑.VALUE:=NEWVALUE;
             Q↑.LINK:=P↑.LINK;
             P↑.LINK:=Q
           end
      else writeln('error in INSERT')
  end
```

If procedure INSERT is used with the steps

```
new(NUMBERLIST);
NUMBERLIST↑.VALUE:=10;
NUMBERLIST↑.LINK:=nil;
INSERT(NUMBERLIST,10,5);
INSERT(NUMBERLIST,10,7);
```

FIGURE 10.13

**List created by
successive
insertions**

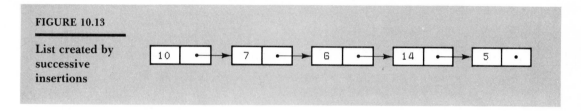

```
INSERT(NUMBERLIST,7,6);
INSERT(NUMBERLIST,6,14)
```

the list shown in Figure 10.13 is created.

EXAMPLE 10.5

IMPLEMENTATION OF BINARY TREES WITH POINTERS

The data structure for implementing binary trees with pointers is a simple extrapolation from what was discussed in the previous two examples. We can use, for instance

```
type TREEPOINTER=↑NODE;
     NODE=record
              VALUE:integer;
              LEFTLINK,RIGHTLINK:TREEPOINTER
          end
```

The pointers are then manipulated in much the same way as were the links in the previous implementations, and the algorithms will be in essence very close to the ones in Section 10.1. For example, the recursive procedure for printing a binary tree in preorder is

```
procedure PREPRINTREC(ROOT:TREEPOINTER);
begin
   writeln(ROOT↑.VALUE);
   if ROOT↑.LEFTLINK<>nil
     then PREPRINTREC(ROOT↑.LEFTLINK);
   if ROOT↑.RIGHTLINK<>nil
     then PREPRINTREC(ROOT↑.RIGHTLINK)
end
```

Compare this with the code in Section 10.1. The syntax has changed, but the algorithm is the same.

EXERCISES 10.2

1. If P and Q are pointers of type INTPTR, where

   ```
   type INTPTR=↑integer
   ```

   determine what is printed by the following piece of code:

   ```
   new(P);
   new(Q);
   P↑:=1;
   Q↑:=2;
   P:=Q;
   new(Q);
   Q↑:=3;
   writeln(P↑,Q↑)
   ```

   Draw pictures showing the state of the computation after each step.

2. Choose an implementation for queues using pointers. Write procedures for adding elements to a queue and removing elements from it.

3. In Example 10.3, why does the procedure PUSH not check for stack overflow?

4. In Example 10.3, to pop the stack and deallocate the element, why can we not just write

   ```
   TOPVALUE:=TOP↑.VALUE;
   TOP:=TOP↑.LINK;
   dispose(TOP)
   ```

   instead of the code given?

5. In Example 10.4, modify procedure INSERT so that NEWVALUE is inserted at the end of the list if SCANVALUE is not found.

6. In Example 10.4, what will happen if INSERT is applied to an empty list?

7. With the implementation in Example 10.4, write a procedure for deleting the first occurrence of SCANVALUE from a list.

8. Design a pointer implementation for doubly linked lists. With this, write a procedure analogous to INSERT in Example 10.4.

9. With the implementation of Example 10.5, write nonrecursive procedures for postorder and inorder traversal.

10. With the implementation of Example 10.5, write recursive procedures for postorder and inorder traversal.

11. How can ternary trees (see Exercise 15 in Section 10.1) be implemented with pointers?

12. Use the implementation in Exercise 11 to write a procedure for the traversal of ternary trees.

10.3

criteria for selecting data structures

When working with a programming language, we are provided with certain "built-in" data structures that are part of the language. These include at least the primitive types and arrays, although many languages have other data types. When an existing data structure naturally fits the problem at hand, it should be used. The available data structures are usually handled efficiently, and programming is as straightforward as it can be. But when we need a data structure not provided by the programming language, we must find an implementation for it in terms of the available data types. The right choice must take into account all the requirements of the program. There are several major criteria for selecting the best data structure and implementation.

access programs

The transparency of the algorithm and the code is a major consideration. The data structure should mirror our visualization so that the algorithms can be written as we think of them. To keep the code clear, it is often convenient to write a set of functions and procedures (sometimes called *access programs*), which perform the operations most frequently done on the structures. For example, for stacks the procedures PUSH and POP are written first; subsequent stack operations then use them. Several of our programs involved stacks, and using PUSH and POP instead of writing code for them each time saved us considerable effort. An added advantage of using access programs is that programs that use them are insensitive to the details of the data structure implementation. A change in the implementation may require a reprogramming of the access subprograms, but not the programs that use them. Furthermore, the modularization inherent in writing the access programs greatly benefits the structure and readability of the code.

Another consideration is the amount of memory used by the data structure. This may be affected significantly by the implementation. Clearly, a linked list with multiple links needs more space than the corresponding sequential list.

Third, we need to consider the efficiency of the algorithm and the code. While undue worry about small inefficiencies is usually a waste of time, the choice of a data structure can make a significant difference. The major reason for using linked lists rather than sequential lists is that the latter are extremely inefficient when frequent insertions and deletions are to be made.

The transparency of the algorithm and the code should always be a consideration in choosing a data structure implementation. Storage and processing efficiency must also be taken into account where one or the other becomes a significant limiting factor. Unfortunately, these requirements are at times incompatible. An implementation efficient in storage may result in a slow algorithm; an implementation selected for processing speed may require more space or make the algorithm harder. We must make a careful analysis of the relative importance of the various criteria when choosing an implementation. The next three examples illustrate this.

EXAMPLE 10.6

REPRESENTATION OF SETS

Sets, although very useful, are provided as data types by relatively few programming languages. But even in languages where they exist, the question of how sets are stored in the memory of the computer is of some interest to the programmer, because it can give insight into the efficiency and limitations of set operations.

An obvious way of implementing sets is by a dynamic data structure such as a list. With linked lists, the addition and deletion of single elements is a reasonably simple matter, but some of the standard set operations, such as union and intersection, become inefficient. To form the intersection of two sets, each element of one set has to be compared to every element of the second set. This requires repeated searches through one set.

A less obvious set representation is by way of the so-called *characteristic vector*. First, we define a *universal set U*, which contains all possible elements. We must also associate some order with the elements in U. Any set S is then represented by a set of zeros and ones, specifying whether any given element in U is in S. For example, if the universal set is defined by

$$U = \{\text{red, green, blue, pink, brown, yellow}\}$$

then the set

$$S = \{\text{green, blue, yellow}\}$$

is represented by the characteristic vector

    0 1 1 0 0 1

indicating that red is not in S, green is in S, blue is in S, and so on.

The characteristic vector can be stored in a one-dimensional array. This completely static implementation is very efficient for processing, because all set operations can be done with a few comparisons, or at most a simple loop. The characteristic vector representation can, however, be very inefficient in storage. At the machine language level, it is possible to use a single bit to store each zero and one, but even so, each set needs n bits of memory, where n is the size of U (that is, the number of elements in the set). If U is very large, this may be prohibitive. If, for instance, U is the set of all computer-representable integers, then on most computers n would be larger than the size of main memory.

Despite its limitations, characteristic vector representation is popular in set implementation because of its processing efficiency. It is commonly used in Pascal, which explains why sets are normally restricted to small subranges of `integer` and `char`.

EXAMPLE 10.7

SYMMETRIC TABLES

Often, the tables and matrices that occur in a particular application are *symmetric*. If T_{IJ} denotes the entry in the Ith row and Jth column of a table, then the table is said to be symmetric if

$$T_{IJ} = T_{JI}$$

for all I and J. A well-known example of a symmetric table is the table of distances between cities given on most road maps. Generally, such tables show only the distance from, say, point A to point B, but not the distance from B to A, simply because it is as far from A to B as from B to A.

The storage of a symmetric table in a two-dimensional array is wasteful because much redundant information is included. Both T_{IJ} and T_{JI} are put into the table even though it is known that $T_{IJ} = T_{JI}$. To take advantage of the symmetry, only one of these should be stored. A possible scheme is to store the table in a one-dimensional array, say `TABLE`. `TABLE[1]` holds T_{11}, `TABLE[2]` holds T_{21}, `TABLE[3]` holds T_{22}, `TABLE[4]` holds T_{31}, and so on (Figure 10.14). The values of $T_{12}, T_{13}, \ldots,$ are not stored because they are known to be the same as $T_{21}, T_{31}, \ldots,$ respectively.

Such a storage scheme is very compact and efficient. For example, if the original table has 100 rows and 100 columns, then the two-dimensional representation will take 10,000 elements. It is not hard to show that the one-dimensional array scheme has only 5050 elements, a saving of nearly 50%.

The disadvantage of the compact scheme is that it is harder to write the code for manipulating the elements in the table. If you look at a few

---

FIGURE 10.14

Storing a symmetric table in a one-dimensional array

TABLE	[1]	[2]	[3]	[4]	[5]
	T_{11}	T_{21}	T_{22}	T_{31}	T_{32}	

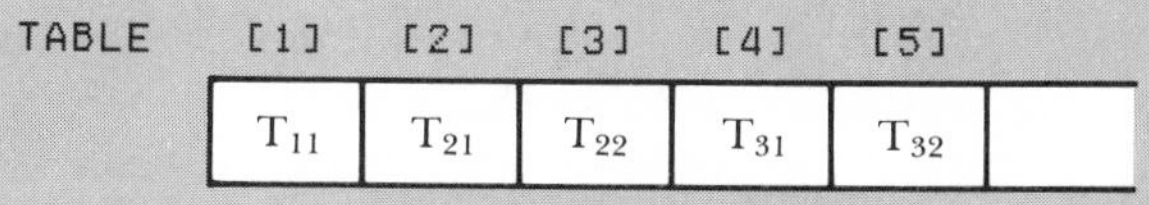

cases, you will see that in this implementation the element T_{IJ} (for $I \geq J$) is stored in

```
TABLE[((I-1)*I) div 2+J]
```

We can use this expression to get to the right element, but the code will be much less transparent than with the two-dimensional array, in which T_{IJ} is referred to by T[I,J].

To make coding easier, we can write an access function for the structure, perhaps as

```
function ENTRY(I,J:integer):integer;
begin
  if I>=J
    then ENTRY:=((I-1)*I) div 2+J
    else ENTRY:=((J-1)*J) div 2+I
end
```

Then, to refer to T_{IJ}, we write

```
TABLE[ENTRY(I,J)]
```

which is fairly explicit. The disadvantage with this approach is that every reference to a table entry involves a function call, which can be quite inefficient in execution time.

EXAMPLE 10.8

TEXT EDITING REVISITED

Let us take another look at the text editing problem in Example 9.6. The linked structure shown in Figure 9.14 is very efficient for processing, but comes with a high storage overhead. Each character is associated with a link. Because a character takes only one byte of memory and the link (being an integer) a full word, the ratio of overhead to useful information may be three or four to one. Most of the memory space will be taken up by the links. If this is unacceptable, a different organization must be used.

A scheme that is still effective is to retain the linking between lines, but to make each line a static array with a fixed number of characters. The storage within each line is sequential, with any unused space filled in with blanks (Figure 10.15). Insertion and deletion of lines is a simple matter involving link manipulation. To edit a line involves shifting characters within the line, but presumably with short lines, so it is not too time-consuming. If a line is too long, one might create an extra line, or perhaps allow linking of several fixed size blocks for a single line. This design decision must take into account the circumstances under which such an editing program will be used.

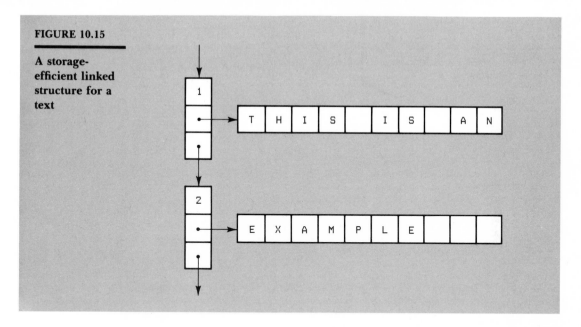

FIGURE 10.15

A storage-efficient linked structure for a text

EXERCISES 10.3

1. Write procedures for set union and intersection using both linked list and characteristic vector implementations.
2. If a computer has a word with 32 bits, what is the size of the universal set of all computer representable integers?
3. Let T be a table with N rows and N columns. Show that the compact scheme for storing symmetric tables described in Example 10.7 requires a one-dimensional array with $N \times (N + 1)/2$ elements.
4. Using the data structure described in Example 10.8, design algorithms for deleting and inserting lines, and for deleting and inserting characters within a line.
5. Investigate possible methods for storage management for the problem in Example 10.8. How efficiently do the organization and memory management utilize the workspace?

---

further reading

Horowitz, E., and Sahni, S. *Fundamentals of Data Structures,* Chapter 5. Potomac, Md.: Computer Science Press, 1976.

Knuth, D. E. *The Art of Computer Programming, Vol I. Fundamental Algorithms,* 2d. ed., Chapter 2. Reading, Mass: Addison-Wesley Publishing Co., 1973.

Standish, T. A., *Data Structure Techniques,* Chapter 3. Reading Mass.: Addison-Wesley Publishing Co., 1980.

Tenenbaum, A. M., and Augenstein, M. J. *Data Structures Using Pascal,* Chapter 6. Englewood Cliffs, N.J.: Prentice-Hall, 1981.

Wirth, N. *Algorithms + Data Structures = Programs,* Chapter 4. Englewood Cliffs, N.J.: Prentice-Hall, 1976.

The problems that arise in engineering and other scientific disciplines often involve very complex mathematical models and equations. The solution of these equations requires a large number of computations, for which computers are indispensable. In scientific programs a great many arithmetic operations are generally done on a small amount of data; a complex mathematical model may require many millions of additions and multiplications, but relatively few input/output operations. For these applications, computation speed is usually more important than easy access to particular data.

In contrast, problems arising in business and other nonscientific applications call for very simple operations on a large amount of data. For example, think of the records of the Internal Revenue Service, which include information on many millions of taxpayers. In such cases, computing speeds are less important than the ease with which data can be accessed.

So far we have paid little attention to data access; it was assumed that referring to a particular variable made it immediately available. This is a reasonable assumption if all data are stored in main memory. Access times for information in main memory are usually less than the times for arithmetic operations. But when there is so much information that the slower secondary storage has to be used, access times become important.

The storage and retrieval of information was a topic of concern long before the advent of computers. Over the centuries, dictionaries, encyclopedias, telephone directories, and card catalogues in libraries all helped organize information to give easier access to the stored information. In fact, most of the data organizations used in computers were simply taken over (or modified) from known methods. What is different in computer data base systems is the amount of data and the need for rapid retrieval. The methods for handling large amounts of data are called *file processing* or **data management.** Most higher level programming languages have few facilities for the manipulation of files, and it is necessary to use special system software for processing data in secondary storage. Consequently, most of our discussion of this subject will be on a conceptual level; the only specific language feature we will discuss is the Pascal method for handling sequential files. Our first task is to study the characteristics of the more common secondary storage devices.

data management

11.1

characteristics of secondary storage devices

The main memory of the computer is characterized by the fact that the information in it is easily and quickly retrieved. Each word in main memory is addressable; when its address is known, only one memory access is needed to get what is stored there. Access times for main memory are of the order of microseconds—generally shorter than the times for the other operations. In main memory, data access presents no problem. In estimating the efficiency of programs, we have so far counted only arithmetic operations (additions, multiplications, and comparisons), but not even considered the time required to get values from memory. But with secondary storage devices, data access times may be several orders of magnitude larger than CPU arithmetic speeds, and in these cases we ignore the arithmetic operations and count only the time needed to bring the information from secondary storage into main memory.

magnetic tapes

One widely used secondary storage device is magnetic tape. A magnetic tape is a long plastic ribbon coated with a magnetizable material. Information is recorded on the surface by means of magnetized spots. The tape winds from one reel to another, meanwhile passing a *read–write head* that senses and records information (Figure 11.1). Reading and writing can usually be done only when the tape travels forward. The tape can, of course, be rewound.

Each manufacturer's tape has different properties, and there is a wide range of characteristics. But very roughly, a typical tape is 4000 feet long, can record 2000 bits per inch, and travels at 50 inches per second. This

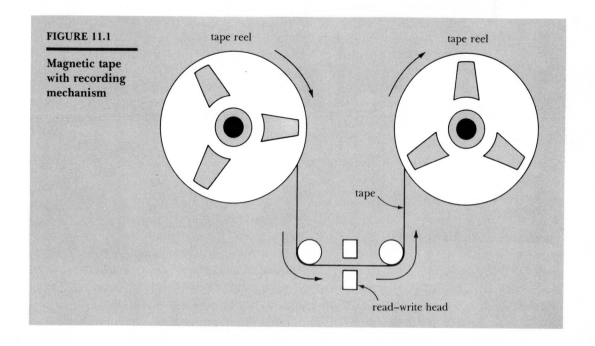

FIGURE 11.1

Magnetic tape with recording mechanism

tape reel

tape reel

tape

read–write head

means that the tape can store 12 million 8-bit characters and that it takes about 16 minutes to read all the information on it.

The retrieval of information from a tape is governed by the fact that what is contained on the tape is not addressable; that is, there is no way of referring to a specific part of the tape. To find a piece of data, it is necessary to read the tape from the beginning until the right information is found. The time required to retrieve a sequence of consecutive data items consists of (1) the time required to locate the start of the data, and (2) the time required to read the items wanted. The time required to locate the start of the data depends on where it is. On the average, it will be necessary to read half of the tape to reach the right place. The time for this is of the order of minutes, making it completely impractical to retrieve isolated data items randomly. The information on a tape must be processed in an essentially sequential manner; hence it is called a ***sequential storage device.***

sequential
storage device

A typical magnetic tape costs about $30. This makes it an inexpensive device for storing large amounts of information, but its sequential character limits its usefulness.

magnetic disks

Another common secondary storage device is the magnetic disk. The surface of a disk, which looks like a phonograph record, is magnetizable. Information is detected and recorded as the disk rotates past a read–write head (Figure 11.2). Unlike the magnetic tape, which is moved only when information is read from it or written onto it, the disk is in continual rotation. The surface of the disk is divided into concentric ***tracks***, which in turn are usually further subdivided into ***sectors*** (Figure 11.3). Each sector of the disk is addressable with a track and sector number.

tracks
sectors

One type of disk unit has a single read–write head for each surface. To read or write information on a given track, the read–write head moves radially on an access arm to the correct track. A more elaborate and expensive kind of disk has one read–write head for each track, in which case no movement of the heads is necessary.

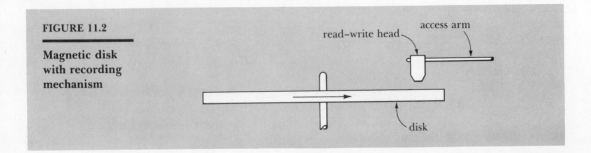

FIGURE 11.2

Magnetic disk with recording mechanism

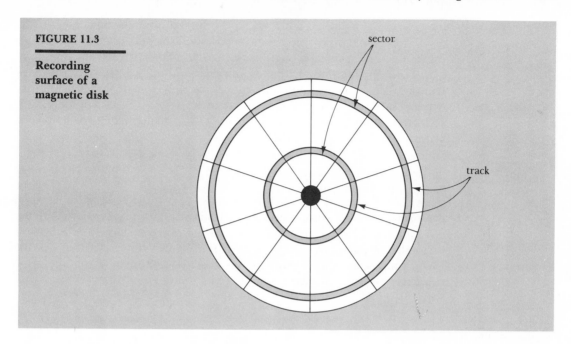

FIGURE 11.3

Recording surface of a magnetic disk

When a command is given to read or write on a certain track and sector, the command cannot be carried out until the right sector is under the read–write head. How long this takes depends on the position of the read–write head at the time the command is issued and the disk's speed of rotation. In a disk with a single head, the head has to be positioned on the right track. This is a mechanical movement and the time for it, called the *seek time*, is appreciable. For multiple-head disks the seek time is zero. Once the track is located, it is still necessary to wait until the right sector comes under the read–write head. This is called the *rotational delay*, and is on the average

$$t = \frac{1}{2r} \text{ seconds}$$

where the speed of revolution is r revolutions per second.

Typical disks can have 1000 tracks with 20 sectors per track and 100 bytes per sector; the average seek time may be 100 milliseconds, and the average rotational delay 20 milliseconds. A complete disk unit (disk drive) can accommodate around 20 individual disks. Such a unit would have an approximate capacity of 40 million bytes.

direct access or random access devices

Disks are often called ***direct access*** or ***random access devices***. The latter term is meant to indicate that information is just as easily retrieved randomly as sequentially. In a disk, each sector is as accessible as any other. This is different from a tape, where the information near the beginning of the tape is much more readily available than that near the end. What really distinguishes the disk from the tape is that all sectors are addressable and that to find one sector it is not necessary to examine all preceding ones first. It is, however, not quite true that information can be retrieved effectively from a disk in a purely random fashion. Skipping from one track to another will increase the seek time considerably. Rotational delay will increase if sectors are not read sequentially. Reading information from a disk must be orderly and well planned to be efficient.

magnetic drums

There are a number of other storage devices. *Magnetic drums* were used extensively in early computers, and are still part of some systems. A drum is a cylindrical body with a magnetic coating on its surface. The surface is divided into parallel tracks on which the information is written. As the drum rotates, the information passes a read–write head. Generally, each track has its own read–write head, so that in effect a drum acts like a disk with one head per track (Figure 11.4).

floppy disks

Small mini- and microcomputers often use "floppy" disks. A floppy disk is a small, flexible plastic disk that looks much like a 45-RPM record. Like a record, it is easily inserted in and removed from the recording mechanism. Floppy disks are very cheap and portable, making them suitable for storing small amounts of information. Many personal or home computers can use floppy disks. Some microcomputers also use cassette tapes. These are somewhat slower, but just as cheap and convenient as floppy disks.

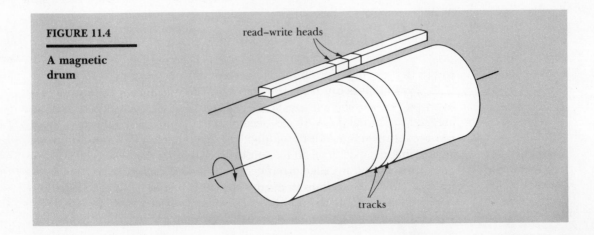

FIGURE 11.4

A magnetic drum

read–write heads

tracks

EXERCISES 11.1

1. If a magnetic tape is 3000 feet long, with a recording density of 1600 bits per inch, and travels at the rate of 40 inches per second, determine
   a. The tape capacity.
   b. Time needed to read the whole tape.
   c. Average time to read a group of 1000 characters.
   d. Average time to read a group of 10,000 characters.
   (Assume that the time needed to start the tape is negligible.)
2. Consider a disk that rotates at 3600 revolutions per minute. What is the average rotational delay?
3. A single-head disk has 500 tracks. The time required by the access arm to go from one track to the next is one millisecond. What is the average seek time?
4. Find out the performance characteristics of the tapes and disks used in your installation.

11.2

files and their structure

record

A *file* is defined as an ordered sequence of records. A *record* in turn consists of a number of parts called *fields,* which contain information. The term record as used here is not identical with the Pascal record type, although there is a close connection. Both can consist of a number of parts of different types.

key

For the purpose of retrieving and processing records, one field may be given special status, so that the record can be identified by its value. This is called the *key* of the record. For example, the savings account file of a bank might consist of a sequence of records of the form

```
account number, customer name, current balance,...
```

Because an account number is unique, it can be used as the key by which a record can be identified.

We usually think of files as being stored on secondary storage devices. Because retrieving information from secondary storage can be very time-consuming, the manner in which the files are constructed is critical. When records are arranged in order and accessed in strict sequence, the file is called *sequential.* When records are arranged so that they can be accessed in any order, we call it a *nonsequential, direct access,* or *random access* file. Clearly, the storage device dictates to a large extent what kind of files can be stored. A magnetic tape allows only sequential files, whereas a disk allows both sequential and nonsequential files.

The most familiar examples of sequential files are the standard input and output files (in Pascal, as well as other languages). The data items in these files are ordered. In the input file, one item after the other is read, while whatever is written in the output file appears in the order in which it is inserted. In general, the records in a sequential file are ordered in a linear sequence, but there is no mechanism by which individual records can be addressed. The end of the file is marked with an end-of-file marker (Figure 11.5). Once a record has been read from the file, we can check its key to see if it is the one we want, but first the record has to be retrieved (that is, brought from secondary storage to main memory). Basically, the only operations that can be done on a sequential file are

```
read the next record
```

and

```
write a record into the next position
```

The word "next" refers here to the current state of the file. To visualize this, think of a magnetic tape, where "next" means the part of the tape immediately after the current position of the read–write head. Whenever a read or a write is done, the tape moves, repositioning the read–write head. By repeating the instruction "read the next record," we can eventually read the whole tape.

A sequential file has to be processed starting from the beginning. To get the nth record, all previous records $1, 2, \ldots, n-1$ have to be read first. This makes retrieval of all but the first few records a slow process. For example, it would take nearly ten minutes for the tape described to get a record in the middle of the tape. This is completely unacceptable in a system where processing speeds are measured in microseconds. Sequential files are useful only when the records can be processed in the order in which they are in the file.

the records are addressable, no need to examine other parts of the file to get one specific record

In a nonsequential file, no order is associated with the records. (The physical order of the records on the device is irrelevant.) The records can be retrieved without necessarily going through the file in any particular sequence. This implies that individual records must be addressable, which in turn means that some random access device must be used for storage. We will use a disk as a model for the discussion.

The accessing of nonsequential files is done by instructions such as

```
read record ID
```

and

```
write record ID
```

where ID is either the symbolic name of the record or its actual address on the storage device. Because most higher level languages, including Pascal, do not provide a facility for processing nonsequential files, we cannot give more specific information here. The manipulation of nonsequential files is usually done with special software, and the syntax and usage vary widely from system to system. For our purposes here, such details are unnecessary; what is important is to understand that records in a nonsequential file are addressable and that it is unnecessary to examine other parts of the file to get to one specific record.

Actually, disk files are not completely nonsequential. When the records are short, several of them may be stored in a single sector. To find a particular record, the whole sector has to be loaded into main memory and searched for the information. The time needed for getting one record, then, is disk access time plus main memory search time. Disk access time involves seek time, rotational delay, and the time needed to read a sector. For a typical case, the disk access time may be around 50 milliseconds. Main memory search time is usually much shorter. If many records are to be found and processed, an access time of even a few milliseconds may be too much. It is important to limit the number of disk accesses for disk files. This imposes some limits on the sequence in which the records are processed. How to organize a file for effective retrieval of information will be discussed in Section 11.5.

EXERCISES 11.2

1. What are the similarities and the differences between a sequential file and a stack?
2. What would happen if a sequential storage device were used for a nonsequential file? What would typical access time for a single record be?
3. Investigate what facilities are provided by your system for the processing of nonsequential files.
4. Find some examples of sequential and nonsequential storage of information in everyday life.

11.3

sequential files in pascal

While standard Pascal does not support nonsequential files, it does have some facilities for defining and processing sequential files. These files are defined without reference to any kind of physical device, so you need not know what actual secondary storage is used. The only important feature is that the files are sequential.

In addition to the standard input and output files introduced in Chapter 2 and used in all programs, the programmer can define other files.

These can be used to store information independent of the program over a period of time. When a programming session is terminated, all data internal to the program stored in arrays, records, and so on disappear from main memory. However, all of the information stored in files will remain.

Pascal files are sequential, and consequently have the structure shown in Figure 11.5. But to understand completely what goes on in Pascal, we should visualize the file as in Figure 11.6. With each file is associated a *buffer*, which is a variable of the same type as the records of the file. All communication between the program and a file is done through the file's buffer. Information to be written on the file must first be placed in the buffer, while information read from the file is put in the buffer. The buffer points to a particular record in the file. What is passed between the file and the buffer either comes from or goes to the record to which the buffer points. The buffer can move from one record to another, advancing in one direction (but not in reverse) from one record to the next.

buffer

A program can involve any number of files, but each file must be defined. First, the name of each file must be a legal Pascal identifier. All file names must be mentioned in the program header. This includes the standard input and output files, which are denoted by the standard identifiers `input` and `output`. The header

        `program CONVERT(input,output,DATAFILE)`

states that, in addition to the standard input and output files, the program `CONVERT` also uses a programmer-defined file named `DATAFILE`.

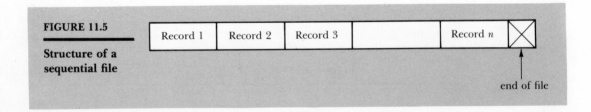

FIGURE 11.5

Structure of a sequential file

| Record 1 | Record 2 | Record 3 | | Record n | ✕ |

end of file

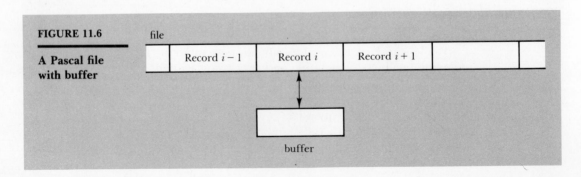

FIGURE 11.6

A Pascal file with buffer

file

| | Record $i-1$ | Record i | Record $i+1$ | | |

buffer

Except for the standard input and output files, the nature of all files—that is, the structure of the records in the file—must be defined. All records in a file must be of the same type. A file type can be defined with a declaration of the form

type *filetype*=file of *recordtype*

where *filetype* is the identifier for a type of file and *recordtype* can be any defined data type. This can then be used in a var declaration to associate a file type with a set of identifiers. As a specific example, take

```
type INTEGERFILE=file of integer;
     CHARFILE=file of char;
var DATAFILE,OLDFILE:INTEGERFILE;
    RESULTFILE:CHARFILE
```

which declares types for three files. DATAFILE and OLDFILE are files with records composed of single integers, while RESULTFILE is a file of characters.

With each file is associated a separate buffer that is referenced by

filename ↑

Thus,

DATAFILE↑:=0

will put the value zero in the buffer of DATAFILE (but does not by itself put anything in DATAFILE).

The use of the symbol ↑ is reminiscent of pointers. This is not accidental. A buffer acts somewhat like a pointer, pointing to different records in the file as the execution of the program progresses. However, a buffer is not a standard pointer and cannot be created and destroyed dynamically.

One can either read or write a Pascal file, but these operations cannot be done simultaneously. Before we can read from a file, it must first be prepared for reading. This is done with the procedure reset; the statement

reset (*filename*)

points the buffer *filename* ↑ to the first record of the file and places the value of the record in the buffer. Because *filename* ↑ is a variable, the contents of the record are now available to the program.

To advance the buffer to the next record, the procedure get is used. The statement

get (*filename*)

advances the buffer to the next record and places the value of that record into the buffer *filename* ↑.

A file on which information is to be written must be prepared with the procedure rewrite. The statement

[handwritten margin note: reset—prepares for reading]

[handwritten margin note: rewrite—prepares for writing]

rewrite(*filename*)

destroys all previous records in the file. After the execution of the rewrite instruction, the file will be empty except for an end-of-file marker. The buffer will point to this end-of-file marker. To write on the file, we use the procedure put. The instruction

put(*filename*)

inserts the contents of the buffer *filename* ↑ immediately before the end-of-file marker. The buffer remains pointed to the end of the file.

In addition to these four procedures, there is a function eof. The expression

eof(*filename*)

is true if the buffer for the mentioned file points to the end-of-file marker.

Before any information can be read or written on a file, either a reset or a rewrite has to be performed. An exception is made for the standard input and output files. These are prepared automatically, so reset and rewrite cannot be used on them.

EXAMPLE 11.1

SPLITTING A FILE

As a simple example of file processing, let us assume that DATAFILE contains uppercase letters, which are to be separated by putting all vowels into a file called VOWELS and all consonants into a file CONSONANTS.

The algorithm is simple enough to need no elaboration. The purpose of the following code is to demonstrate the syntax of the instructions for the processing of Pascal files.

```
program EXTRACT(input,output,DATAFILE,
                VOWELS,CONSONANTS);
{ this program reads DATAFILE and separates the
vowels and the consonants }
var DATAFILE,VOWELS,CONSONANTS:file of char;
begin
  {prepare all files }
  reset(DATAFILE);
  rewrite(VOWELS);
  rewrite(CONSONANTS);
  {read successive characters from DATAFILE,
   put consonants into CONSONANTS and
   vowels into VOWELS }
  while not eof(DATAFILE) do
```

```
        begin
          if DATAFILE↑ in ['A','E','I','O','U']
            then begin
                   VOWELS↑:=DATAFILE↑;
                   put(VOWELS)
                 end
            else begin
                   CONSONANTS↑:=DATAFILE↑;
                   put(CONSONANTS)
                 end;
          get(DATAFILE)
        end
end.
```

Note the placement of get(DATAFILE) at the end of the loop. It would be incorrect to write

```
while not eof(DATAFILE) do
  begin
    get(DATAFILE);
    if DATAFILE↑ in ['A','E','I','O','U']
      .
      .
      .
```

One reason is that reset(DATAFILE) puts the first record into the buffer. If we start with get(DATAFILE), we miss the first character in DATAFILE altogether. The second problem is with the end-of-file condition. After the last character has been processed, get(DATAFILE) advances the buffer to the end-of-file marker. The value of DATAFILE↑ in this case is undefined, possibly resulting in an execution error. The placement of the get at the end of the loop overcomes both difficulties.

Example 11.1 shows the syntax and usage of file manipulation procedures, but uses data with an oversimplified structure. The next example involves records of a more complicated and realistic nature.

EXAMPLE 11.2

EXTRACTING INFORMATION FROM A FILE

A bank has information on its savings accounts in the form

    account identifier, customer name, balance

where account identifier is a five-character alphanumeric string, customer name is a ten-character alphabetical string, and balance is a real number. This information is in the standard input file with each account record on a separate line. From this a new file LARGEACCOUNTS is to be created, containing the account identifiers and customer names for all accounts whose balance is over a certain limit, say $1000.

The algorithm is again quite simple: the information in each account is read, the balance checked, and the pertinent part of the account written onto LARGEACCOUNTS if the balance is sufficiently large.

```
Program GOODCUSTOMERS(input,output,LARGEACCOUNTS);
{ this program examines a file of accounts
  for accounts with a large balance }
const LARGE=1000;
var I:integer;
    ACCOUNT:record
               ID:packed array[1..5] of char;
               NAME:packed array[1..10] of char;
               BALANCE:real
            end;
    LARGEACCOUNTS:file of record
                           ID:packed
                              array[1..5] of char;
                           NAME:packed
                                array[1..10] of char
                        end;
begin
  rewrite(LARGEACCOUNTS);
  {process successive accounts stored
   in the standard input file}
  repeat
    { read customer record }
    with ACCOUNT do
      begin
        for I:=1 to 5 do
          read(ID[I]);
        for I:=1 to 10 do
          read(NAME[I]);
        readln(BALANCE)
      end;
    {check balance to see if part of record
     is to be copied to LARGEACCOUNTS file }
    if ACCOUNT.BALANCE>=LARGE
      then begin
             LARGEACCOUNTS↑.ID:=ACCOUNT.ID;
             LARGEACCOUNTS↑.NAME:=ACCOUNT.NAME;
```

```
                    put(LARGEACCOUNTS)
            end
    until eof
end.
```

A run with the input file containing

```
    10510    JONES   900.00
    10991    SMITH  1002.32
    20111    BROWN   500.19
    21863    GREEN  2000.56
    31439    SWIFT  1000.00
```

generates a file LARGEACCOUNTS with the structure

10991 SMITH	21863 GREEN	31439 SWIFT
Record 1	Record 2	Record 3

Many versions of Pascal have abbreviated and more explicit constructs for reading and writing. The statement

```
    read(THISFILE,ITEM)
```

reads the current record from THISFILE by copying the content of the buffer into ITEM and advancing the buffer. The statement is equivalent to

```
    ITEM:=THISFILE↑;
    get(THISFILE)
```

Similarly

```
    write(THISFILE,ITEM)
```

writes a record onto a file. It is equivalent to

```
    THISFILE↑:=ITEM;
    put(THISFILE)
```

Both read and write can specify more than one variable to be read or written, but there can be only one file name. When there are several variables, they are processed in order, as in the read and write for standard input and output. The read and write instructions have the advantage of being more explicit than put and get. On the other hand, with put and get, the buffer can be manipulated without copying its content.

text files

The standard input and output files are of type `char`. All files of type `char` have some special properties, and are called **text files.** The word `text` is a standard identifier denoting a file of `char`. Thus,

    `type CHARFILE=text`

is equivalent to

    `type CHARFILE=file of char`

The information in a text file can be arranged by lines; that is, end-of-line markers can be inserted into the file. This is done with a statement of the form

    `writeln(`*filename,var1,var2, . . . , varn*`)`

which places the end-of-line marker immediately after the record *varn*. For text files, as for the standard input file, `readln` can be used to read past the end-of-line marker. Thus

    `readln(`*filename*`)`

will skip part of a line in the text file *filename*. Also, the function `eoln` is defined for text files;

    `eoln(`*filename*`)`

is true if the buffer of *filename* points to an end-of-line marker.

For `get` and `put`, the buffer variable is of the same type as the file record. Normally, the variables and expressions for `read` and `write` must also be of that type. Text files are an exception. In a `read` and `write` with a text file, the variables can be not only of type `char`, but also `integer` and `real`. A translation from the character string to the internal representation of integers and reals, and vice versa, is performed automatically. For output, the variables may be replaced by expressions and a format description can be included, just as for the standard output file. The conversion from the character string to internal representation is automatic. This is an advantage to the programmer; it can also be a drawback. If a file containing numerical values that have to be used many times is made a text file, the conversion has to be done every time the file is read. In this case it might be better to make the file an integer or real file.

EXAMPLE 11.3

DATA EDITING

Assume that we are given a text file `DATAFILE`, consisting of a sequence of real numbers, either in Pascal decimal or exponent form, but separated by commas as well as blanks. The file has one single end-of-line marker following the last record. From this, we want to produce another text file

EDITEDFILE, containing the same numbers, but all given in decimal form with two digits after the decimal point, and arranged in columns, three numbers per line. For example, if DATAFILE contains

```
15,1  ,-3,62, 1,0e+01, 714,1,316,2, 7,5,9,3
```

then the generated EDITEDFILE, when printed, should give

```
    15,10    -3,62   10,00
   714,10   316,20    7,50
     9,30
```

If the original DATAFILE had used blanks instead of commas to separate numbers, this would be an easy problem. Items in DATAFILE could be read as real numbers and copied to EDITEDFILE properly formatted. The commas, however, make this impossible. An attempt to read DATAFILE using real variables will result in a data error.

One possibility is to read DATAFILE as characters, converting each digit string into a real number, then writing it onto EDITEDFILE. This would require a somewhat complicated conversion process, so let us look for an easier way. Considerable effort can be saved by generating an intermediate text file TEMPFILE, identical in all respects with DATAFILE except that the commas are replaced with blanks. This temporary file can then be read using real variables and is easily copied in the correct format. The algorithm for this process is

1. Copy DATAFILE onto TEMPFILE, replacing commas with blanks. All data are handled as characters.
2. Copy TEMPFILE onto EDITEDFILE, using real variables for reading and writing.

The second step is relatively straightforward, but requires a simple counting to arrange items in groups of three. Because the number of items in DATAFILE is not necessarily a multiple of three, the last line has to be considered specially.

```pascal
program EDITDATA(output,DATAFILE,
                 TEMPFILE,EDITEDFILE);
var DATAFILE,TEMPFILE,EDITEDFILE:text;
    CH:char;
    COUNT:integer;
    NUMBER:real;
begin
  reset(DATAFILE);
  rewrite(TEMPFILE);
  { read DATAFILE as characters, copy
    everything except the commas,
    replace comma with blank}
  while not eoln(DATAFILE) do
```

```
    begin
       read(DATAFILE,CH);
       if CH<>','
          then write(TEMPFILE,CH)
          else write(TEMPFILE,' ')
    end;
writeln(TEMPFILE);
{now read TEMPFILE as real numbers and
 copy to EDITEDFILE in proper format}
reset(TEMPFILE);
rewrite(EDITEDFILE);
COUNT:=0;
while not eoln(TEMPFILE) do
    begin
       COUNT:=COUNT+1;
       read(TEMPFILE,NUMBER);
       write(EDITEDFILE,NUMBER:8:2);
       if COUNT=3
          then begin
                  writeln(EDITEDFILE);
                  COUNT:=0
               end
    end;
if COUNT<>0
    then writeln(EDITEDFILE)
end.
```

Similar programs are common in data processing. Data generated with one set of assumptions may eventually be used under quite different circumstances. A file may have been prepared for one computer or language and used later on another system, so that the file must be suitably edited. The form used here, with items separated by commas, is used in languages such as BASIC.

The program EDITDATA does not use the standard input file; hence, the identifier input does not appear in the program heading. Actually, the standard output file was not used either, but because some systems require the presence of the standard output file, it was retained here.

EXERCISES 11.3

1. Assume that an integer file contains both positive and negative integers. Write a program to produce a new integer file containing only the positive integers.
2. For Exercise 1, write a program to print the contents of the created file.

3. Let `AFILE` and `BFILE` be two files of type

```
type ENTRY=record
            KEY:integer;
            INFO:array[1..20] of char
      end
```

with the records in both files sorted so that the values of `KEY` are in ascending order. Write a program to create a file `CFILE`, containing all records in `AFILE` and `BFILE`, but no duplicate keys. Assume that an error condition exists if identical `KEY` fields have different `INFO` parts.

4. Rewrite the programs in Examples 11.1 and 11.2 to use `read` and `write` instead of `get` and `put`.

5. Write a program to print out the file `LARGEACCOUNTS` generated in Example 11.2.

6. Rewrite program `EDITDATA` in Example 11.3 without the use of any intermediate files.

7. Let `DATAFILE` be a text file containing no end-of-line markers. Create a new text file which contains the same information, but with an end-of-line marker after every 40 characters.

For the next two exercises, write programs with effects identical to program `EDITDATA` *in Example 11.3, but which work under different assumptions on* `DATAFILE`.

8. `DATAFILE` contains the same kind of data as in Example 11.3, except that the data are arranged in lines with an arbitrary number of items and preceded by the string `'DATA'`; for example,

```
DATA 11.3,7.5,19.6,-3.4
DATA 14.1,16.2
```

9. `DATAFILE` contains the same kind of data as in Example 11.3, but may also contain decimal numbers without digits before or after the decimal point, for example

```
11.2, .6, 7., 9.31
```

11.4

information retrieval

As our examples show, the processing of files involves a number of possible steps: (1) searching a file for one or more records, (2) updating records, (3) inserting and deleting records, (4) extracting part of a file, and (5) combining files. What kind of file is appropriate and how it is to be organized depends very much on the frequency with which and order in which such operations are to be performed. This, in turn, depends on the requirements of the problem to be solved.

Let us contrast two applications with different requirements. For the first, take the simple situation in which a company keeps a file of information on its employees for the computation of the payroll. Normally, the computation for each employee is independent of the others, and processing can be done in whatever order is most convenient. The payroll file can therefore be processed completely sequentially. Furthermore, one can expect relatively infrequent additions and deletions in such a file, so it is reasonable to consider a magnetic tape as the appropriate secondary storage device.

For the second example, take the information stored by a bank on its accounts. The records are to be made available to the tellers whenever a transaction is made. In this case, the order in which the records have to be accessed is completely unpredictable. What is needed here is fast, random access. Clearly, magnetic tape storage is unsuitable, and a disk should be considered.

The second example is the more difficult (and hence the more interesting). Externally, the user will request a particular record by typing some identification, typically the account number. Internally, at the level of the storage device, the physical address (the sector and track numbers) are needed. How this physical address is determined from a given key depends on how the file is organized. Several possible ways will be discussed in Section 11.5.

A still more difficult situation arises when retrieval is not made by the key, but on some other properties of the record, called *secondary attributes* or secondary keys. In our second example, if the account number is the key and the file is organized accordingly, obtaining the account information given the account number is fairly straightforward. Occasionally, though, customers forget their account numbers, in which case it may be necessary to look for the record via a secondary attribute, say the customer's name. On other occasions, the bank may want to prepare a list of overdrawn accounts, so that the balance becomes the secondary attribute. Unless the file is organized properly, the retrieval of records by secondary attributes may be very inefficient.

data base   As files become larger and the search criteria become more general, severe practical difficulties arise. A collection of files, together with a set of programs for their processing, is called a ***data base***. Extensive data bases are becoming more and more common, and the need for getting information from a large data base arises often. A library, for instance, may decide to put all its books and articles on the computer to make information more easily accessible to a wider variety of users. Such a data base may contain many millions of words, and its management is not an easy matter, given the potential uses of the system. For example, a user may want to issue a command such as "find all papers on text editing written between 1970 and

1980," and have the computer print a list of all relevant information. Even aside from the question of what language is to be used, it is not easy to see how to organize the data base for such a request. Clearly, we cannot search the whole library to find all articles that contain the term "text editing." A typical library can contain several billion characters. Even at the rate of a million characters per second, it would take several hours to read all the data to service a single request. Moreover, this approach may miss some important material or mistakenly include irrelevant information. A better way is to associate with each book and article a set of key words as secondary attributes for a search. A typical paper of interest may contain the key words "text editing," "word processing," "linked lists," and so on. This would still leave the imposing task of checking the key words of every document to determine which satisfy the specified search criteria. Obviously, the data base must be organized suitably for information retrieval to be practical.

Information retrieval and data base management are important and challenging topics of computer science, and many problems remain unsolved.

EXERCISES 11.4

1. A library data base contains 200,000 books. A book has, on the average, one million characters. With each book is associated a set of key words consisting of 50 characters. Using the disk characteristics given in Section 11.1, how many sectors will be needed to store all the information?
2. If, for the data base in Exercise 1, information can be retrieved at the rate of 500,000 characters per second, how long will it take to do each of the following:
   a. Read the whole library.
   b. Read all the key words.

11.5

file organization

There are a great many ways in which the information in a data base can be organized for simple and efficient retrieval. Often very complex organizations are needed to answer questions posed by the user in an acceptable amount of time.

The emphasis of our brief discussion will be on the organization of nonsequential files, so for the purpose of discussion we assume that all the files are stored on disks.

directories

A *directory* is a table that associates the key of a record with its physical address. In Figure 11.7, each entry contains the key, say the account number of a bank account, and the corresponding track and sector numbers where the record is stored. An everyday example of a directory is your address book, where the names of your friends and acquaintances are recorded with their addresses.

To retrieve a record, we first search the directory for the key to find the physical address. This address is then used to obtain the record from the disk. When a new record is to be inserted, some unused sector is taken, the record written into it, and the key and address inserted into the directory. To delete a record from a file, we simply remove the corresponding entry from the directory. Unfortunately, this does not automatically make the disk space available for some other record. Storage must be managed so that the released space becomes available for later use. The technique for storage management discussed in Section 9.3 is one possibility, although in practice many other algorithms are used.

The directory approach is simple, but complications do arise. For example, if there are several records in one sector or if some records extend over more than one sector, some modifications have to be made.

When a file contains many records, the directory itself may become so large that searching for the key becomes very time-consuming. To overcome this, we may introduce several levels of directories. A typical case is in a time-sharing computer system, in which there may be thousands of users with several files each. A general directory gives the location of each user directory, which contains the addresses of the file directories. The file

FIGURE 11.7

A disk directory

key	track/sector
10234	03/15
23001	04/06
33189	17/11
⋮	⋮
44100	01/05
⋮	⋮

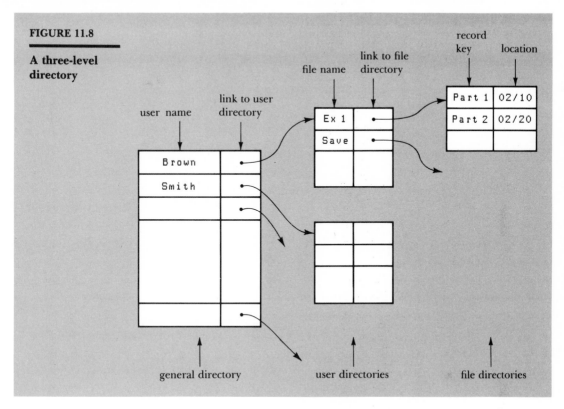

FIGURE 11.8

A three-level directory

directories give the addresses of the individual records (Figure 11.8). If the general directory is stored in main memory, but the user and file directories are on disk, three disk accesses will be needed to get one record. Because disk access is expensive, it is inefficient to have too many levels in the directory.

hashing functions

We can avoid having to build extensive directories if we can use the key to infer directly where on disk the record is stored. One way to do this is to construct some function, called a *hashing function,* whose argument is the key and whose value is the physical address; that is,

physical address : = HASH(key)

When a record is to be stored, we first compute the hashing function for its key, then use the physical address so obtained to insert the record into the file. Later, when we need the record, we again compute the hashing function and use the computed address to retrieve the record.

As a rather simple (and somewhat unrealistic) example, take the following situation. You have a disk with 1000 tracks numbered 0–999, each with 20 sectors numbered 0–19. The file to be stored has keys that are integers in the range 00000–99999. A possible hashing function assigns the track number by taking the three higher order digits of the key, while the sector is given by

two lower order digits mod 20

collision

The use of a hashing function can be very efficient, because potentially only one disk access is needed to get a record. Unfortunately, this assumes that different keys always generate different physical addresses. If two or more keys give the same address, a *collision* is said to occur. In our simple example, the keys 12301 and 12321 will cause a collision, because 21 mod 20 = 1 mod 20. It is very difficult to find a hashing function that avoids all collisions. If collisions occur, the problems arising in connection with their resolution make this organization less attractive. A more thorough discussion of hashing will be given in Section 13.2 in connection with general search algorithms.

indexed sequential organization

If the keys can be ordered in some way, the file can be constructed so that all records with keys in a certain range are stored in a block of contiguous sectors. The directory is then constructed so that a range of key values is associated with a single disk address (Figure 11.9). For a given key, we first find the range, obtain the address from the directory, and bring the whole block into main memory. The block is then searched until the right record is found. Because each entry in the directory now refers to a range of keys, the directory size is reduced. True, a whole block of information has to be read and searched; but searches in main memory are very quick. Indexed sequential organizations are widely used for this reason.

We see examples of indexed sequential organization occasionally in everyday life. Most large telephone directories will list at the top of each page a range such as

BRO–BYE

indicating that the page contains only names beginning with the letters BRO through BYE. A quick look through this index gives us the right page, which we search for the actual name.

However, indexed sequential organization is less effective when frequent insertions and deletions have to be made. For the sake of argument, assume that each key range in Figure 11.9 is assigned ten sectors. When some of the records are removed, certain sectors may be only partially filled or empty altogether. But the free space cannot be used for records with keys outside the range; this would destroy the whole scheme. Conversely, as records are added, all the records with keys in some range may require

FIGURE 11.9

Directory for indexed sequential organization

key range	track/sector
10000-19999	03/05
20000-29999	11/05
30000-39999	03/06

more than ten sectors, raising the question of what to do with the "overflow." Again, we see here the need for a flexible and efficient storage management. No one scheme is always best. We must work out a good solution in each case, taking into account the nature and requirements of the application.

inverted files

So far, we have discussed quick retrieval using the primary key. When retrieval is done using secondary attributes, some new problems arise.

In the bank account example, one may want to perform a retrieval according to the criterion "all accounts having a balance of more than $200." Examining all records in the file may take too long. One way to make the search more efficient is to use an *inverted file*. An inverted file is a directory-like table in which the secondary attributes (or ranges thereof) are associated with the primary keys or the actual address. For example, an inverted file for the bank accounts might look like Figure 11.10.

Libraries provide one example of an inverted file. They usually have two separate catalogues, an author catalogue and a subject catalogue. If we consider the author's name to be the primary key of the record (that is, the

FIGURE 11.10

Inverted file for bank account balance

balance range	account numbers
0- 99	10234, 23441, 45555,...
100-199	12345, 23455, 32111,...
200-299	34112, 42000, 56987,...

book or article), then the author catalogue is a simple directory that tells you where to find a book, if you know the author and title. The subject catalogue is an inverted file in which you can find books on specific topics. If you are interested, for example, in "existential philosophy," the subject catalogue can provide the locations of the books on this topic. It would be impossible to get such information from the author catalogue in any reasonable amount of time.

Files can be inverted according to any attribute, and the more inverted files there are, the easier it is to answer complicated questions about the data base. Even so, inverted files have to be constructed and stored. Every time a record is changed, added, or deleted, the inverted files have to be updated. All of this creates a significant overhead in processing and storage. To limit the number of inverted files that are constructed, we must predict the usage of the data base and find what attribute will give significant improvement for information retrieval.

All file organizations have both good features and problems. None is clearly superior to the others. We must think of them as structures that must be selected to serve the application. For this, it is necessary to know how the file will be searched, how frequent additions and deletions will be, and what kind of questions a user is likely to ask. In short, we must know the intended uses of a file or data base.

EXERCISES 11.5

1. As manager of a small bank, you have decided to automate all the bank's operations. As part of this, all account records are to be stored on a disk and made available to bank personnel through video terminals. For this purpose, you have acquired a disk with 1000 tracks of 100 sectors each. Each sector stores a single account record. Fast retrieval of the records is essential to aid the tellers in the completion of transactions. Your chief programmer approaches you with the following suggestion. Reassign all account numbers so that they will consist of five digits, the first three of which are the track and the last two the sector number where the record is stored. This allows for 100,000 accounts, more than the bank can be expected to have at any one time. The account number then is a perfect hashing function; because it is unique, no collisions can occur. Although there will be some initial work in reassigning all account numbers, this will pay off in the long run because record retrieval is very fast.

    Do you consider this a workable suggestion? Is it perfect, impossible, or promising but requiring some more thought?

2. Design a "mini information system" with data on the presidents of the United States. For each president, the data base should contain the name, years in office, birthplace, year of birth, and year of death.

a. Design a query language that allows (in some coded form) such questions as

Who was president in 1819?

How many presidents were born in Missouri?

How many presidents who were born in Ohio died in office?

b. Design a data base, using inverted files, so that the questions allowed by the query language can be answered efficiently. Implement this with sequential files. If direct access files are available to you, implement the information system with them.

3. In Exercise 2, what increase in storage is created by each additional inverted file?

further reading

Bartee, T. C. *Digital Computer Fundamentals,* 5th ed., Chapter 7. New York: McGraw-Hill, 1981.

Burch, J. G., Strater, F. R., and Grudnitski, G. *Information Systems: Theory and Practice,* 2d. ed., Appendix B. New York: John Wiley & Sons, 1979.

Standish, T. A. *Data Structure Techniques,* Chapter 9. Reading, Mass.: Addison-Wesley Publishing Co., 1980.

Chapter Twelve

algorithm design and analysis

A major step in programming is to find an algorithm to solve the problem under consideration. In most of our examples, we have approached the discovery of an algorithm in a somewhat informal fashion. A solution method suggested itself, and all we had to do was to make it precise. Stepwise refinement is a powerful method for translating our intuitive understanding into an unambiguous description. But matters are not always so easy. In some problems, it is very hard to find any algorithm at all. In other cases, several alternatives may be available, so that a rational choice has to be made. The design and selection of the algorithm is a crucial step in the programming process.

To determine the efficiency of a proposed algorithm, we must analyze it and predict its performance on given data. Algorithm analysis generally requires some mathematical reasoning. In this chapter, we will illustrate with a few examples the kinds of elementary arguments that can be made to evaluate algorithm efficiency. A more thorough and technical discussion of some important problems will be given in Chapter 13.

12.1

algorithm discovery

The discovery of algorithms is undoubtedly the most creative aspect of programming. It is also the most difficult to formalize. Like much of mathematical problem solving, finding good algorithms requires ingenuity and insight. There is no sure-fire technique that will always yield an algorithm for a given problem. We learn to discover algorithms mostly by experience. Starting with some simple problems, we gradually develop our skills until, after a period of time, we can tackle problems we once thought impossible to solve. However, as our abilities increase, so does the difficulty of the problems that we are asked to solve. Even for professional programmers, algorithm discovery remains an intellectual challenge.

Nonetheless, there are some well-defined and established ways to produce an algorithm. For example, in many business applications, the computer is used to automate existing manual operations, so that the computer algorithm can mimic what was previously done by people. In this case, the initial task of the programmer is to produce specifications that formalize accepted procedures to such a degree that they can be used for algorithm design and coding. This may expose some unexpected difficulties. When operations are done manually, exceptional cases are often left to the discretion of the person responsible for the job, and hence are neglected in the formal rules. It becomes the responsibility of the programmer to ferret out these troublesome cases and take them into account in choosing the algorithm. Also, the manual procedures may not be the most suitable for automation, so alternatives may have to be considered.

When no specific established procedures exist, new algorithms have to be designed. Many times, the solution is fairly obvious at the conceptual level. This is certainly true of most of our examples so far. As long as we are allowed to be sufficiently vague, we can describe the solution process without much trouble. The major difficulty lies in translating our intuitive understanding into a precise description. Stepwise refinement and top-down design help considerably, because they are in essence a sort of conditional implementation (or, alternatively, the creation of a very high-level language). What we are saying at the higher level is something like "if I had a procedure for doing such-and-such, then I would write the program in the following way." This allows us to think about the problem without worrying about the finer points, which often makes seemingly hard problems relatively easy.

In using a top-down design, you may find a need for subprograms that implement common tasks, for example, a sorting procedure. Sorting is so common that there will undoubtedly be several programmed procedures already available. You should use these. In fact, you should always see if your program can be designed to utilize available programs. It is your job as programmer to get things done, not to think up new ways to do routine computations. Utilizing existing routines not only saves work, but also cuts down on errors. If no program does exactly what you want, perhaps you can find a similar one that can be adapted to your needs easily (and hope that the original programmer used good techniques!).

Once in a while you will encounter a problem for which your experience does not immediately suggest a solution. The algorithm for the translation from infix to postfix in Example 9.3 is a good example. When this happens, you must first reach a good understanding of the problem in your own mind. Take a few cases and solve them, looking for patterns in the method. This will increase your understanding, and most of the time you will soon see what an algorithm might be.

At times you will be faced with problems for which the solution may not be obvious at all. Sometimes finding a good algorithm requires more mathematical knowledge than most programmers possess. Some examples are the solution of complicated algebraic equations, operations on tree structures, or scheduling and resource allocation strategies. This is the time to consult books, published articles, or experts in the area. Don't reinvent the wheel; use all available help.

Occasionally, you will get a problem that is truly difficult. If you are to have any chance at all to find an algorithm, you must understand the problem well enough to solve it yourself (ignoring, perhaps, practical limitations such as time). It does not follow, however, that if you know how to solve the problem you can eventually find an acceptable algorithm for it. We solve many problems intuitively, but when asked to say what steps we use in doing so, we have difficulty in expressing our method formally. For an example, consider the program GAME in Chapter 7, taking ticktacktoe as a specific case. To write the module COMPUTERMOVE, we need a formal strategy for playing a good game. Because the game is not particularly complex, most adults will know what move to make in any given situation. But writing down our strategy is not all that easy. In this instance, we get some insight into our own thought processes by playing a few games and writing down at each step what strategy we use. Actually, it is possible to design a strategy for ticktacktoe by considering all possible sequences of plays. There are nine possibilities for the opponent's first move; for each of these, we can make a unique response. For the second move, the opponent will have seven choices, so that there are $9 \times 7 = 63$ possible board positions to be considered for the computer's second move. By similar reasoning, we see that there are 315 positions at the third move and 945 positions at the fourth move. We could store all of the possible positions, say in an array of board positions, then search the array in an actual game for the correct next move. This strategy would result in a perfect game (provided that all positions are evaluated properly); the computer would never lose and could win against a careless opponent.

The actual coding for such an algorithm, however, would be quite tedious. One way to simplify and shorten the program is to notice that many positions are equivalent through symmetry. Thus, after the opponent's first move we need consider only three distinct cases (Figure 12.1); the others are effectively the same as one of these. In the same way, symmetry can be used to reduce the number of distinct positions later in the game. Using the symmetry allows a considerable reduction in the number of stored posi-

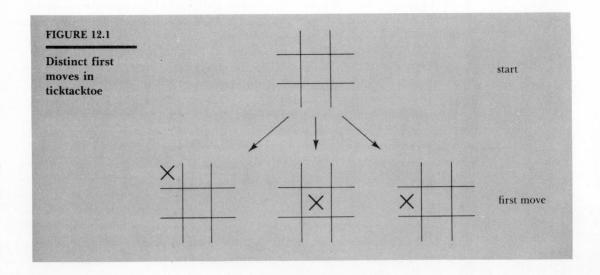

FIGURE 12.1

Distinct first moves in ticktacktoe

start

first move

tions, but the programmer will have to provide some procedures that can take an actual board position and determine its stored equivalent. While writing a perfect ticktacktoe program cannot be classified as difficult, it cannot be done in a few hours.

If we do not insist on a perfect game, but are willing to accept a strategy that occasionally loses, we might try the following algorithm:

1. If the computer has an immediate win, move into the appropriate position.
2. If the opponent threatens with an immediate win, block the move.
3. If neither the computer nor the opponent has an immediate win, choose an unoccupied position at random.

This strategy is typical of a child playing the game for the first time. It is easy for a good player to win against this algorithm.

heuristic

Solution methods like the last algorithm are sometimes called heuristics. A *heuristic* is a method for attacking the problem that yields a reasonable solution most of the time, but can fail occasionally. In ticktacktoe, we would use a heuristic only to save effort, because a perfect strategy is not too difficult to implement. Usually, heuristic methods are used when a perfect algorithm is either unknown, too tedious, or impractical.

In complicated games, such as chess, a similar introspection can be used to discover strategies. Chess, however, is exceedingly complex, and cataloguing of all possible board positions is completely out of the question (although most chess-playing programs have a catalogue of standard openings). Chess-playing programs rely heavily on heuristics, the quality of which determines the strength of the program. It takes a great deal of work and ingenuity to produce even a minimal program for chess.

artificial intelligence

Game-playing programs are typical of a class of problems for which algorithm discovery is very challenging. Although we have some understanding of how the solution is to be obtained, we find it difficult to give a precise description of our methods of deciding the moves. Other examples of this type are language translation, recognition of written and spoken words, and proving theorems in mathematics. Ability to perform such tasks is generally taken as a sign of intelligence; hence, the name *artificial intelligence* has been given to this aspect of computer science. The algorithms for most problems in artificial intelligence are complicated and not obvious. They generally require a deep understanding of our thought processes and often rely heavily on heuristics.

A good algorithm designer can use various sources to devise effective algorithms. These sources include existing programs, technical books and papers, and formalizing an intuitive understanding. Many times this will yield not only a single algorithm, but rather a number of possibilities from which the best one must be selected.

EXERCISES 12.1

1. Many systems contain a "library" of useful programs. Find out if your system has a library and, if so, what it contains.
2. Extend the heuristics given for ticktacktoe to produce a better strategy.
3. Without carrying out the details, investigate what might be involved in designing algorithms for
   a. Playing checkers.
   b. Recognizing printed letters.
   c. Translating from French into English.

12.2
efficiency of some algorithms

As we have mentioned, there are often a number of algorithms for solving a particular problem. Some important criteria for selecting among them are:

1. Simplicity and generality.
2. Memory and secondary storage requirements.
3. Required CPU time.

The last of these is particularly important for large and time-consuming problems. Before coding an algorithm, we should study whether it can in fact solve the given problem in a reasonable amount of time.

To evaluate the execution efficiency of an algorithm, we must predict how long the computations will take for specific cases. This means that we need to determine how many operations have to be performed. To do this exactly would be an extremely tedious undertaking even for moderately sized programs. Actually, exact predictions are rarely needed, so it is more profitable to start with some crude evaluations. These may give enough information to let us decide in favor of one or the other possibility. If not, we refine our study until we can make an informed decision. A few examples will illustrate this point.

EXAMPLE 12.1

SEARCHING

Searching for information is perhaps the most common process in computer application. We have already discussed information retrieval in Chapter 11, and we will study it further in Chapter 13. Here, let us consider a very simple setting to develop some initial understanding of what is involved.

Let us assume that we have stored in main memory an array of integer numbers NUMBER[1], NUMBER[2],...,NUMBER[N]. We are also given a value KEY, the search key, and want to find out if KEY occurs anywhere in the array NUMBER. If so, we want to find the smallest value I such that

NUMBER[I]=KEY

This is certainly a rather easy problem. Consecutive elements NUMBER[I] are compared against KEY until either a match is found or the end of the *sequential search* array is reached. The algorithm is called a **sequential search.** The code for it is simple:

```
FOUND:=false;
I:=0;
repeat
    I:=I+1;
    if NUMBER[I]=KEY
        then FOUND:=true
until FOUND or (I=N)
```

The search consists of a single loop in which NUMBER[I] is compared with KEY. In addition, there are some bookkeeping operations for controlling the loop. But all in all, the loop contains only a few simple instructions and a pass through it will require very little time.

To analyze the efficiency of the search, we have to determine how many times the loop is traversed. If KEY is not in the array, we have to do N comparisons before we find this out. If KEY is in the array, we may find a match on the first comparison, or we may have to search until we get to the last item. It is not unreasonable to think that on the average N/2 traversals of the loop will have to be made for a successful search.

Unless we are prepared to carry out a much more detailed study (taking properties of the machine and compiler into account), we cannot say exactly how long such a search will take. But what we have found gives us a fair amount of insight. Suppose N equals 10,000. On the average, 5000 loop traversals will have to be made to find an entry in the array. Even on a relatively slow computer, this can be done in a fraction of a second.

Nevertheless, even though sequential searching is feasible, it is not the most efficient approach. When data have to be searched repeatedly, even a fraction of a second may be too long. We can draw on everyday experience to find a better alternative. In looking for a number in the telephone directory, we certainly do not make a sequential search; if we did, the process would take a very long time. Rather, we might open the directory in the middle and check the names appearing there. This will tell us whether the name for which we are looking is in the first or the second half of the directory. We then repeat the process a few more times until we locate the right page. The algorithmic equivalent of this intuitive approach *binary search* is the **binary search.** This, as well as some other search techniques, will be discussed in Chapter 13. For the moment, it is important to realize that we can do better than a sequential search because the information in the telephone directory is organized, in this case alphabetically. Proper data organization is important for the design of efficient search methods as well as other algorithms.

EXAMPLE 12.2

SEARCHING WITH SEVERAL KEYS

For a somewhat more challenging problem, suppose we are given a text consisting of individual words WORD[1],...,WORD[M], and a set of key words KEY[1],...,KEY[N]. We want to find each occurrence of a key word in the text and delete it. Although this description is not very concrete, the problem is representative of a common data processing activity. For example, think of WORD[1],...,WORD[M] as a telephone directory and KEY[1],...,KEY[N] as the names of customers whose service has been discontinued.

A pseudolanguage code for this is

```
for I:=1 to N do
   for J:= 1 to M do
      if WORD[J]=KEY[I]
         then delete(WORD[J])
```

The time taken by this algorithm is proportional to the number of times the innermost loop is executed. Let us denote the time for one inner loop computation by t_L. Then the total time taken is approximately

$$T = NMt_L$$

This is not completely precise, because we are neglecting the computations done in the outer loop. But for the majority of cases it is quite adequate to look only at the inner loop, because most of the time is spent there. Without adding a great many details, we cannot get an exact number for t_L. However, for a computer in which arithmetic operations and comparisons can be done in a microsecond or so, a reasonable figure for t_L might be 10–100 microseconds. If we now have a case for which M equals 10,000 and N equals 100, then T will be of the order of 10–100 seconds—a significant amount of computer time.

To find a more efficient method, let us look a little more closely at what has been suggested. For each key word KEY[I], we search the whole text and delete all occurrences of the key word. If we had to do this without the aid of a computer, we would very likely use a different method based on introducing some organization into the data. For example, we could divide the key words into 26 categories according to the first letter. We could then take the first letter of each word and search only the corresponding key word category. It is not hard to implement this algorithm, but whether it will improve matters depends on the key words as well as the text. If all text words and key words start with the same letter, then nothing is gained. However, it is much more likely that the first letters are more uniformly distributed.

If the distribution of the first letters were completely uniform, each category would contain $N/26$ key words, so that

$$T = NMt_L/26$$

This is not completely realistic for texts in a natural language, because letters do not occur with equal frequency. Also, because the new algorithm will be more complicated than the first one, t_L for the new algorithm will be larger. On the whole, though, it would not be unreasonable to expect an improvement by perhaps a factor of five to ten.

This example demonstrates vividly the importance of finding efficient algorithms. There are still better ways to do searching, as we will see, but even relatively obvious modifications can result in considerable improvement.

EXAMPLE 12.3

SORTING

Another very common task for the computer is sorting data. For simplicity, let us assume that we have in main memory an array $\mathtt{NUMBER[1]},\ldots,$ $\mathtt{NUMBER[N]}$ of integers, which is to be sorted. In Section 5.3, we discussed one possible algorithm, the bubblesort. The bubblesort is fairly simple, but how good is it?

We can see from the program on page 112 that the main computations are carried out in a doubly nested loop. The inner loop consists of a comparison and a possible interchange, so that the inner loop time t_L is small, perhaps of the order of ten microseconds. For the $\mathtt{I}$th pass through the outer loop, the inner loop is executed $N-I$ times. Hence the total number of times the inner loop is traversed is

$$(N-1) + (N-2) + \cdots + 2 + 1$$

This sum can be computed for each N, but there is a formula for it:

$$(N-1) + (N-2) + \cdots + 2 + 1 = \frac{N(N-1)}{2}$$

The total time taken by the bubblesort to sort a list of N elements is then

$$T = \frac{N(N-1)}{2} t_L$$

If t_L equals ten microseconds, we get the following search times:

(N = 100)	T = 0.05 seconds
(N = 1000)	T = 5 seconds
(N = 10,000)	T = 500 seconds

While the bubblesort can handle arrays of several hundred entries with ease, when N is much larger than 1000 it is much slower. Data sets containing 10,000 or more items are not uncommon, so again we have to look for more efficient algorithms.

One possible improvement is based on the observation that the bubblesort always takes roughly the same amount of time, regardless of the initial order of the elements. When the algorithm is applied to an array that is already sorted, it will still perform all comparisons (of course, there will be no interchanges). One suggestion is then that we check to determine at what stage the array is sorted; if this happens before all $N(N-1)/2$ inner loop passes have been made, we can stop early. There is an easy way to find out when the array is sorted. If in one pass through the outer loop, all inner loop calculations are done without any interchange, the array must be in order. We can then use the following program, which is a direct modification of BUBBLESORT in Example 5.3:

```
procedure NEWBUBBLESORT(N:integer;
                        var NUMBER:INTEGERARRAY);
{ sort an array containing N items, stored in
  NUMBER[1]..NUMBER[N], in place, ascending order
  INTEGERARRAY must be type array[1..M] of integer.
  The algorithm is a modified bubblesort}
var I,J,TEMP:integer;
    SORTED:boolean;
begin
  I:=0;
  repeat
    I:=I+1;
    SORTED:=true;
    for J:=N-1 downto I do
      if NUMBER[J+1]<NUMBER[J]
        then begin
              TEMP:=NUMBER[J+1];
              NUMBER[J+1]:=NUMBER[J];
              NUMBER[J]:=TEMP;
              SORTED:=false
            end
  until SORTED or (I=N-1)
end
```

In this procedure, we use the boolean variable SORTED to check whether any interchanges have been made. Before entry to the inner loop, it is set to true; therefore, if it is true on exit the array is sorted and the algorithm terminates. For example, when this algorithm is applied to an array containing

    1 2 4 3 5

then one complete pass through the outer loop gives

    1 2 3 4 5

which is completely sorted. During the next pass through the outer loop, no interchanges are made, so that SORTED remains true and the procedure terminates. In this case, the algorithm requires only two passes through the outer loop instead of the four done by the original bubblesort.

Even though NEWBUBBLESORT represents only a minor modification of BUBBLESORT, it is much more difficult to determine its efficiency. First, note that the time required depends on the data to be sorted. If the data are very nearly in order, we can expect NEWBUBBLESORT to be quite efficient. On the other hand, if the sorting is not complete until all $N(N-1)/2$ passes have been made, it will be less efficient than BUBBLESORT, because there are extra steps in the inner loop. It is therefore necessary to consider some kind of "average" efficiency for NEWBUBBLESORT. In our subsequent discussion, we will see how such average behavior can be defined and sometimes computed. Here, however, this is surprisingly difficult, so we will not pursue the matter. We will just mention that evidence (theoretical and experimental) indicates that, except for nearly sorted arrays, NEWBUBBLESORT is not much better, and perhaps even worse, than BUBBLESORT.

More efficient methods for sorting will be discussed in Chapter 13; from this example, two points should be remembered. The first is that plausible modifications of an algorithm may not lead to any actual improvements. Either mathematical arguments or extensive testing is needed to substantiate any claims of increased efficiency. The second point is that the bubblesort and its variants, although effective for small amounts of data, are very inefficient for sorting long sequences.

EXAMPLE 12.4

PACKING OBJECTS INTO A BIN

For this example, we will assume that we have a set of positive integers x_1, $x_2, \ldots, x_N$, and a given positive number W. We are asked to pick a subset of the x_i so that their sum is as close as possible to W, but does not exceed it. For example, if

$$x_1 = 4$$
$$x_2 = 5$$
$$x_3 = 6$$
$$x_4 = 7$$
$$x_5 = 10$$

and $W = 24$, then for the solution we pick x_3, x_4, and x_5, the sum of which is 23. No other subset comes closer to W.

An algorithm for this problem is not hard to find. The sum of every possible selection can be written as

$$S = c_1x_1 + c_2x_2 + \cdots + c_Nx_N$$

where each c_i is either 0 or 1. To find the answer to our problem, all we need is to find S for all possible combinations of the c_i, then pick the one with the sum closest to W.

How feasible is such an algorithm? For c_1, we must take 0 and 1; for c_2, we must also consider 0 and 1, and so on. Therefore we must look at a total of 2^N combinations. Each case will require N additions, and we have

$$T = N2^N t_L$$

where t_L is essentially the time for one addition. If we take t_L to equal ten microseconds, we get

(N = 10)	T = 0.01 seconds
(N = 20)	T = 21 seconds
(N = 100)	T = 1.3×10^{32} seconds

The time for $N = 100$ is approximately 4×10^{24} years! Clearly, this algorithm cannot handle a very large value for N.

This example is much less artificial than might appear at first sight. It arises in computer science in several forms, and is called the *bin packing* problem. The origin of this name becomes clear if we consider the x_i to be the sizes of certain objects to be packed into a bin of capacity W. The bin is to be packed as fully as possible by putting in some of the available objects. In more practical settings, such problems arise in scheduling or resource allocation, making the algorithms of considerable importance.

As can be seen from these examples, to find out how long an algorithm will take, we must perform an analysis of its efficiency. In our examples, the discussion has been quite loose and intuitive, although we gained some valuable insights. However, whenever possible a more precise and mathematically rigorous study should be made.

EXERCISES 12.2

1. Write programs for both algorithms in Example 12.2.
2. Write a program for the algorithm in Example 12.4.
3. Consider sets implemented by
   a. Characteristic vectors.
   b. Linked lists.
   Make an analysis of the time required to compute the set union and intersection of two sets with N and M elements, respectively.
4. How much time will be taken to sort a list of 10,000 elements by the sorting method of Exercise 3 in Section 5.3?
5. Consider the following "solution" to the bin packing problem. Sort the x_i in decreasing order, then fill the bin, starting with the largest item. When one x_i does not fit, take the next smaller one until one does fit.
   a. Evaluate the effort required by this algorithm.
   b. Does the algorithm always solve the problem?

12.3

analysis of algorithms

In order to select the best algorithm, we must be able to predict the performance of the various alternatives. The selection of the most efficient algorithm is especially important for large problems, which are very time-consuming. The examples in the previous section show that some very innocent-looking problems can take a great deal of time if the wrong approach is used.

The time required for an algorithm depends most of all on the amount of data—that is, on the size of the problem. We will use the integer N to denote size, for example, the number of characters in a piece of text or the number of items in a list. Occasionally, as in Example 12.2, there will be more than one parameter characterizing size, in which case we will use N ,M ,, ,. The time required will be a function of the size, which in mathematical notation we write as T(N) or T(N ,M). In theoretical computer

complexity   science, this is called the time *complexity* or just complexity of the algorithm. (In everyday language, complexity essentially means "complicatedness." Here, however, the word takes on a technical meaning.) Complexity theory concerns itself with the study of T(N) for various problems and algorithms.

To make life a little easier, we can neglect some of the less important details. In Example 12.3, it was shown that for the bubblesort

$$T(N) = \frac{N(N-1)}{2} t_L$$

$$= \left(\frac{N^2}{2} - \frac{N}{2}\right) t_L$$

The inner loop time t_L is system dependent; in general, we can say little about it except to give its order of magnitude. But this is sufficient, because the main interest is to compare algorithms, not to find the exact time for one particular implementation. Also, a detailed analysis of an algorithm is usually of interest only for large problems; therefore terms involving N are much smaller than those involving N^2, and can be neglected. To indicate that an approximation has been made, we write

$$T(N) \simeq \frac{N^2}{2} t_L$$

which is to be read as "$T(N)$ is approximately $(N^2/2)t_L$." Even less precisely, we use

$$T(N) = O(N^2)$$

which is read as "T is of order N squared." This is mathematical notation expressing that for large N, T is essentially proportional to N^2, with the constant of proportionality unspecified.

order of magnitude O notation

This so-called *order of magnitude* or *O notation* is commonly used in mathematics. The order of magnitude of a function is the same as the order of that term which increases most rapidly with N. Thus, if

$$f(N) = N^3 + 10N^2 + 100N$$

we say that $f(N)$ is of order N^3 or $f(N)$ is $O(N^3)$, because for large enough N the term involving N^3 is always larger than those involving N^2 and N only. Similarly, if

$$f(N) = 2^N + N^3$$

then we write

$$f(N) = O(2^N)$$

because 2^N increases faster than N^3. Finally, the function

$$f(N) = 2 + \frac{1}{N}$$

is said to be of order unity, written as $O(1)$, because for large N it is essentially independent of N.

The O notation is useful when the behavior of a function for large values of a parameter is important. Because this is exactly what complexity analysis requires, the O notation is widely used in characterizing the complexity of algorithms.

Referring to the examples in the previous section, we see that the time required may depend on the specific data set; for example, NEWBUBBLESORT works best on nearly sorted data. To make complexity analysis useful, we must obtain a measure that is independent of the particulars of an individual data set. One way to achieve this is to consider the ***worst case complexity,*** that is, the most time that can ever be needed. The worst case may, however, occur so rarely that it would be unrealistic to use it as a characterization of the algorithm. More realistic may be the ***average*** or *expected complexity,* which we can think of as the average time taken when the algorithm is used over a long period. We will use $T_W(N)$ for the worst case complexity and $T_A(N)$ for the average complexity. In cases where it is immaterial or where we do not want to say which complexity, we will write $T(N)$.

worst case
complexity

average
complexity

Finding $T_W(N)$ involves identifying the set of data for which the algorithm is slowest. This is often relatively easy. The average complexity tends to be more troublesome, and its computation requires some familiarity with elementary probability theory. First, average complexity has to be defined precisely. The average or expected value of a variable is a statistical quantity, which for a given set of events depends on the probabilities of occurrence and values of the variable for each event. More formally, if $p_1, p_2, \ldots,$ p_n denote the probabilities of occurrence of events $e_1, e_2, \ldots, e_n$, and $v_1, v_2,$ $\ldots, v_n$ are the values associated with these events, then the average or expected value is

$$\bar{v} = p_1 v_1 + p_2 v_2 + \cdots + p_n v_n$$

A rather simple example is furnished by the throwing of a standard six-sided die. If the die is fair, each side is as likely to appear as any other. Therefore, the probability that any one face will appear is

$$p_1 = p_2 = p_3 = p_4 = p_5 = p_6 = \frac{1}{6}$$

and the average value is

$$\bar{v} = \frac{1}{6} \times 1 + \frac{1}{6} \times 2 + \frac{1}{6} \times 3 + \frac{1}{6} \times 4 + \frac{1}{6} \times 5 + \frac{1}{6} \times 6$$

$$= 3.5$$

If we were to throw the die many times, add all the face values, and divide by the number of throws, we would expect to get a value close to 3.5.

For the computation of $T_A(N)$, let us assume that $d_1, d_2, \ldots, d_n$ denote all the possible data sets of size N to which the algorithm might be applied, and let $p_1, p_2, \ldots, p_n$ be a set of probabilities, such that p_i is the probability that during some period of time the algorithm is used on d_i. The average complexity is then defined as

$$T_A(N) = p_1 T(d_1) + p_2 T(d_2) + \cdots + p_n T(d_n)$$

where $T(d_i)$ is the time taken for the algorithm to process the data set d_i.

The average complexity is often difficult to find. It is rare that the probabilities involved are known; even when they are available, the computation of $T_A(N)$ may be impossible. Nevertheless, the idea can give us a great deal of insight. In Chapter 13, we will see how both the worst case and the average complexity can be computed for some important algorithms. In general, though, a fair amount of mathematical knowledge is needed to make the necessary arguments. This is especially so for the computation of $T_A(N)$.

When a rigorous mathematical analysis for finding $T(N)$ is possible, it should be done. Unfortunately, it is not uncommon that the mathematics turn out to be too difficult. In that case, an experimental investigation of the algorithm should be carried out. Taking a variety of representative cases, we run the program and measure the time taken. This will give us some idea of $T_A(N)$ that can be used to select between competing algorithms.

EXERCISES 12.3

1. Find the order of magnitude of the following functions:
   a. $f(N) = N^3 + 100(N + 3)$.
   b. $f(N) = N! + N^2$.
   c. $f(N) = N + 1/N$.
   d. $f(N) = 1/(1 + N)$.
2. Characterize $T(N)$ using the $\simeq$ and O notation for all algorithms in Examples 12.1 to 12.4.
3. For which of the algorithms in Examples 12.2 and 12.3 are $T_W(N)$ and $T_A(N)$ equal? For which are they equal in order of magnitude?
4. Perform some experimental studies to compare the efficiency of the regular bubblesort with the modified algorithm suggested in Example 12.3.
5. For the bubblesort in its original and modified versions, are the worst case complexities of the same order of magnitude? If so, does this mean that the programs will take exactly the same amount of time in the worst case?
6. Find the worst case complexity for the set union and intersection algorithms in Exercise 3, Section 12.2.
7. What is needed to establish a $T_A(N)$ for the previous exercise?
8. In another version of the bin packing problem, we are given an unlimited number of bins. The requirement is that we distribute all the

objects into as many bins as needed, in such a way that the total number of bins used is as small as possible. Find an algorithm for this version of bin packing and determine its complexity.

9. Investigate the complexity of the function VALID in Example 6.5.

further reading

Baase, S. *Computer Algorithms: Introduction to Design and Analysis,* Chapter 1. Reading, Mass.: Addison-Wesley Publishing Co., 1978.

Horowitz, E., and Sahni, S. *Fundamentals of Computer Algorithms,* Chapter 1. Potomac, Md.: Computer Science Press, 1978.

Knuth, D. E. *The Art of Computer Programming, Vol. III, Sorting and Searching.* Reading, Mass.: Addison-Wesley Publishing Co., 1973.

Chapter Thirteen

some important algorithms

In this chapter, we will look at some specific problems to see how the general framework outlined in Chapter 12 can be applied to some practical problems. The algorithms discussed are among the most important in computer science. For example, searching and sorting occur so frequently in a multitude of applications that it is of utmost importance to find the most efficient algorithms. Much effort has been and still is being devoted to analyzing and extending the algorithms considered here. Our first topic concerns the processing of character strings.

13.1

string manipulation

The term "string" is used to denote an ordered sequence of characters of varying length. The processing of strings is an important topic, because much of the information in computers is stored in strings. In Section 5.4 we took a brief glimpse at string manipulation in Pascal. The language provides only minimal string handling. To extend these capabilities efficiently, we must design a variety of useful algorithms.

The most common operations on strings are the following.

1. Concatenation. Combine two strings to form a new one. If STRING1 is 'This is' and STRING2 is 'an example', then the concatenation of STRING1 and STRING2 is 'This isan example'.
2. Extracting substrings. Create a new string of length N, starting with the Ith character of the given string. If STRING has the value 'This isan example', then the substring of length four starting at the sixth character is 'isan'.
3. Pattern matching. Given one string, called the text string T, and another string, the pattern P, determine whether P is a substring of T. If T is 'This isan example' and P is 'isan', we have a match. If P is 'isany', we have no match.

The algorithms for these operations are conceptually simple, although pattern matching raises some interesting questions.

One question that does have to be considered in detail is how the implementation of strings affects the efficiency of the string-processing algorithms.

concatenation

The algorithms for concatenation are quite obvious, but the details depend on how the string is implemented. Take, for example, sequential allocation in a one-dimensional array. To concatenate two strings S and T, of length N and M respectively, we first copy S into a new array, then follow it with the elements of T. If a linked list implementation is used, we effectively follow

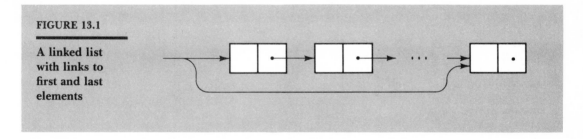

the same procedure, except that we also have to do the linking. In either case, we easily see that the complexity of the algorithm is

$$T(N,M) = O(N + M)$$

Because the new string contains $N + M$ characters, and all characters have to be copied, it is clear that one cannot expect to find an algorithm with a significantly lower complexity.

This conclusion holds only if we assume that the original strings S and T cannot be modified in forming their concatenation. If we relax this requirement, we have a somewhat different situation. With sequential allocation, not much can be done, because elements still have to be moved. For linked lists, if the location of the last element in S were known, concatenation could be done with a single linking. Therefore

$$T(N,M) = O(1)$$

that is, the complexity of concatenation is independent of the lengths of the strings. Unfortunately, in a simply linked list it will take $O(N)$ operations to find the last element of S, so not much is gained. If concatenation is a frequent operation, we might consider a somewhat different linking, such as the one shown in Figure 13.1, in which a list has links to both its initial and its final elements.

EXAMPLE 13.1

CONCATENATION WITH A SPECIAL LINKED LIST

An implementation of the linked structure shown in Figure 13.1 using Pascal pointers can be made with

```
type STRINGPTR=↑ELEMENT;
     ELEMENT=record
                VALUE:char;
                LINK:STRINGPTR
             end;
     STRING=record
                FRONT,BACK:STRINGPTR
             end
```

Suppose we now have

```
var ASTRING,BSTRING,CSTRING:STRING
```

and want to concatenate ASTRING with BSTRING to form CSTRING, setting ASTRING and BSTRING to the empty string. The algorithm involves linking ASTRING to BSTRING, pointing CSTRING to the front and back of the new string, and deleting ASTRING and BSTRING. The code for this is

```
ASTRING.BACK↑.LINK:=BSTRING.FRONT;
CSTRING.FRONT:=ASTRING.FRONT;
CSTRING.BACK:=BSTRING.BACK;
ASTRING.FRONT:=nil;
ASTRING.BACK:=nil;
BSTRING.FRONT:=nil;
BSTRING.BACK:=nil
```

The state of the strings before and after the concatenation is shown in Figure 13.2. The code makes it obvious that concatenation does not depend on the lengths of the strings.

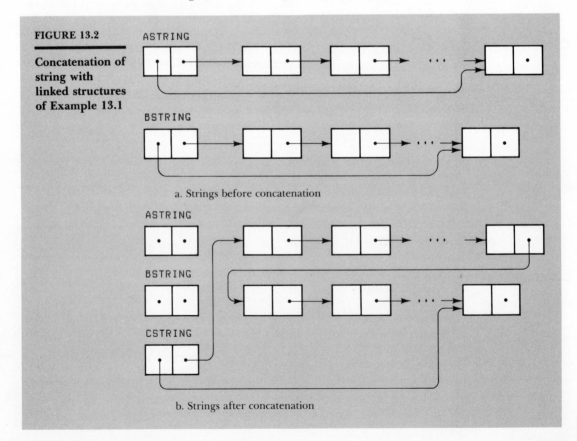

FIGURE 13.2

Concatenation of string with linked structures of Example 13.1

ASTRING

BSTRING

a. Strings before concatenation

ASTRING

BSTRING

CSTRING

b. Strings after concatenation

extracting substrings

Once the data structure implementation is chosen, writing a procedure for extracting a substring is simple. There are some minor differences in the complexity of the algorithms, depending on the representation used.

If sequential allocation is used, we simply copy a string of length N, starting with the Ith element, so that

$$T(N,I) = O(N)$$

If a simply linked list is used, we must first locate the Ith element by traversing the list from the beginning. Only after it is located can we proceed with the copying. Thus

$$T(N,I) = O(N + I)$$

For the extraction of short substrings from very long strings, the linked representation leads to somewhat less efficient algorithms than sequential allocation.

pattern matching

Pattern matching is a special case of the searching problem. It is done by a series of comparisons of text and pattern characters until either a match has been found or the text is exhausted. The algorithm is straightforward. Referring to Figure 13.3, we associate with the text T a text cursor, which marks the place in the text where matching is attempted. Comparison is done by comparing the text, starting from the cursor, with the pattern. When a mismatch on a character is found, the text cursor is moved to the next character and the comparison sequence restarted.

EXAMPLE 13.2

A PATTERN-MATCHING PROGRAM

  In this example, we write a boolean function MATCH for matching a pattern to a text. The value of MATCH will be true if a match is found anywhere in

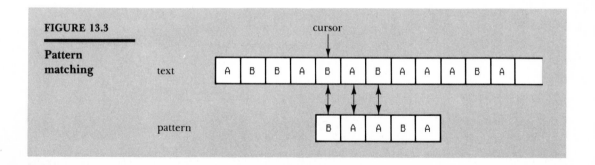

FIGURE 13.3

Pattern matching

the text, and false otherwise. The formal parameters for MATCH will be

1. TEXTSTR = name of text
2. PATTERN = name of pattern
3. N = length of TEXTSTR
4. M = length of PATTERN

N and M are integers, while TEXTSTR and PATTERN will be of type

```
type STRING=array[1..100] of char
```

The text is assumed to be stored in TEXTSTR[1] to TEXTSTR[N], while the pattern is in PATTERN[1] to PATTERN[M].

The algorithm is as described before. More formally, we use

1. CURSOR:=1; MATCH:=false.
2. While CURSOR<=N−M+1 do Steps 3 to 5.
3. Compare TEXTSTR[CURSOR] with PATTERN[1], TEXTSTR[CURSOR+1] with PATTERN[2], etc.
4. If there is a mismatch on Step 3, CURSOR:=CURSOR+1.
5. If in Step 3 all characters of PATTERN match, set MATCH to true and terminate.

```
function MATCH(TEXTSTR,PATTERN:STRING;
               N,M:integer):boolean;
{ this function tries to match PATTERN to
  TEXTSTR. Its value will be true if there
  is a match, false otherwise.
    N=length of TEXTSTR
    M=length of PATTERN }
var CURSOR,I:integer;
    MATCHED:boolean;
begin
  CURSOR:=0;
  repeat
    CURSOR:=CURSOR+1;
    I:=0;
    MATCHED:=true;
    repeat
      {compare each character of text with
       pattern until mismatch is found}
      I:=I+1;
      if PATTERN[I]<>TEXTSTR[CURSOR+I−1]
        then MATCHED:=false;
    until (MATCHED=false) or (I=M)
  until MATCHED or (CURSOR=N−M+1);
  MATCH:=MATCHED
end
```

This algorithm is not very sensitive to the data implementation. If linked lists had been used instead of sequential allocation, there would be little that is different.

The worst case complexity of MATCH is easily found. At most, M comparisons are made for each of the first N − M + 1 characters of the text, so there will never be more than M × N − M² + M total operations. Are there cases that actually require this many operations? The answer is yes, as we can see from the example

```
TEXT: AAA...A
PATTERN: AAA...AB
```

For each of the first N − M + 1 characters of TEXT, we have to check all M characters of PATTERN until we discover the mismatch. This is the worst case and we have

$$T_W(M,N) = O(M \times N - M^2 + M)$$

If N is much larger than M, then

$$T_W(M,N) = O(M \times N)$$

If the text is very long, say N = 10,000, and the pattern has length M = 100, then the work is considerable.

However, the worst case is rather unusual, and T_W is not at all representative of the efficiency of the algorithm. The average complexity, if we can compute it, will give more insight. To find T_A, we have to know the probabilities of occurrence of various text and pattern strings. This is not an easy matter unless some simplifying assumptions are made.

Consider the case where the text and the pattern consist of the 26 uppercase letters of the alphabet, with all letters occurring with equal probability. Also assume that the letters are uncorrelated; that is, that one letter is equally likely to be followed by any other. In this situation, we can make some relatively simple arguments to determine the expected number of comparisons per character of the text.

1. With probability 25/26, the first comparison will fail, so that only one comparison is needed.
2. With probability 1/26, the first comparison will succeed, while there is a probability of 25/26 that the second will fail. Thus, with probability 1/26 × 25/26, two comparisons will have to be made.

Continuing with the argument, we see that the average number of comparisons per character of the text is

$$a(M) = \frac{25}{26} + \frac{1}{26} \times \frac{25}{26} \times 2 + \left(\frac{1}{26}\right)^2 \times \frac{25}{26} \times 3 + \cdots + \left(\frac{1}{26}\right)^{M-1} \times M$$

A simple calculation shows that $a(M)$ is nearly independent of M, and

$$a(M) \simeq 1.054$$

Therefore, we expect that

$$T_A(M,N) \simeq 1.054N$$

which is much better than the worst case.

Objections to this simple analysis can be raised on the grounds that it is unrealistic. If the text is in any given language, programming or natural, not all strings are equally likely, and the computed T_A may be too optimistic. An analysis for, say, the English language is much too complicated, but we can use experimental observations for information. For example, we used MATCH on several passages in this book, using patterns such as `'then '`, `'programs'`, and `'This is a test'`. The observed average number of comparisons per character of the text was close to 1.10, not far from our optimistic value of 1.054. The conclusion is that MATCH is likely to be quite efficient, except for special cases that behave something like the worst case example.

Appreciation of the preceding arguments requires some knowledge of elementary probability, which is very useful for computer scientists (as well as for aspiring programmers). But even if you cannot completely follow the reasoning, you should remember two points from the example. The first is that the worst case behavior of an algorithm may be artificial and not at all representative of its behavior in real situations. The worst case complexity is important mainly where it is essential that the computation can always be completed within a limited time. In most cases, the average complexity is more useful for characterizing an algorithm. The second point of this discussion is that when mathematical arguments cannot be done, experimental measurements with some representative examples can give much valuable insight.

EXERCISES 13.1

1. Show how the linked list in Figure 13.1 can be implemented using arrays. For this implementation, write a procedure for concatenation similar to that in Example 13.1.
2. Write a procedure for concatenating strings as in Example 13.1; this procedure should not modify the original strings.
3. Run efficiency tests on MATCH using some of the Pascal programs in this book. Find patterns for which the algorithm is least efficient. To test the efficiency of MATCH, modify the function so that it counts the number of comparisons done on each call. Then write a driver program that will call MATCH repeatedly and print the length of the text, the length of the pattern, and the number of comparisons.

4. Rewrite function MATCH using a linked list structure implemented with pointers.
5. Write a procedure SUBSTITUTE that will replace the first (left-most) occurrence of a pattern in a text with a given string. Investigate how the representation (sequential or linked) affects the efficiency of the algorithm.
6. Write a procedure PARTIALMATCH in which the pattern (of length M) is considered to match if at least M − 1 characters match. Find the worst case and average complexities for your algorithm.

13.2
searching

Searching for information is an everyday activity; we look up words in the dictionary, numbers in the telephone directory, or go to the library to find books. As more and more information is stored in computers, the retrieval of such information becomes one of the main tasks of a computer system. While on the surface searching seems to be very simple, the need for high efficiency in retrieving stored information poses many difficult problems for the algorithm designer.

Here, we will consider the search of data consisting of a set of records, in other words, a file. However, to keep matters simple, we will consider only the case where the whole file can be stored in main memory. For large files that have to be stored in secondary storage, not all of the methods given here are suitable as described. Searching files in secondary storage is a more difficult matter, which we cannot pursue in this text beyond what was said in Chapter 11.

We assume that each record has one field that is its key. We are given a certain value, the search key, and need to find the record with its key matching the search key. For simplicity, we also assume that each record contains only a key (and no other information), that all keys are distinct, and that all keys are integers. The conclusions reached in this way have all the essential features of the more complicated practical cases.

sequential search

The sequential search algorithm has already been introduced in Example 12.1. The algorithm is quite simple and is affected very little by the choice of data structure. The discussion in Example 12.1 makes it clear that, for a file with N records, at most N comparisons have to be made. Therefore

$$T_W(N) = O(N)$$

If, over a period of use, all key values are sought an equal number of times, then on the average $N/2$ comparisons will have to be made before the record is located. It follows, then, that

$$T_A(N) \simeq \frac{T_W(N)}{2}$$

but $T_A(N)$ is still of order N. While a sequential search seems obvious and quite efficient, it is not optimal in many cases. As we will see, there is considerable room for improvement.

First, we may be incorrect in assuming that all keys are sought equally often. Suppose, for example, that the file contains a set of bank accounts that have to be updated whenever a transaction occurs. Very likely some of the accounts will be much more active than others and hence have much higher search probabilities. When this is the case, there is an obvious way of taking advantage of the situation. Because the file is searched from the beginning, we simply put the most active records at the front, arranged in order of decreasing probability. Because the inactive records are in the back, the whole file will have to be searched only on rare occasions.

This arrangement does not improve the worst case behavior of the sequential search, because we may occasionally need to retrieve the last record. But it can significantly affect the average complexity. If we let x_1, $x_2, \ldots, x_N$ be the key values, and if we denote the probability that the search key k is the key of the ith record by p_i, then the expected search time is

$$p_1 \times \text{time to find } x_1 + p_2 \times \text{time to find } x_2 + \cdots$$

But the time to find x_i is proportional to i, because i comparisons have to be made before we get to the ith record. Consequently,

$$T_A(N) = (p_1 + 2p_2 + 3p_3 + \cdots + Np_N) \times c$$

where c is some constant depending on the program and the computer. Whether this is much of an improvement over the unorganized file case depends on the probabilities p_i.

EXAMPLE 13.3

RETRIEVING RECORDS WITH DIFFERENT ACTIVITIES

Suppose we have 100 records, arranged in order of decreasing search probabilities. Twenty-five percent of the searches are for the first record, fifteen percent for the second record, and fifteen percent for the third. The rest of the time the fourth through last records are looked for with equal probability.

These stated probabilities tell us that $p_1 = 0.25$, $p_2 = p_3 = 0.15$. Assuming all searches are successful, the sum of all the probabilities must be one, and

$$p_4 = p_5 = \cdots = p_{100} = 0.45/97 = 0.00464$$

Then, with $c = 1$,

$$T_A = 0.25 + 2 \times 0.15 + 3 \times 0.15 + (4 + 5 + \cdots + 100) \times 0.00464$$
$$= 24.4$$

On the average, about 25 operations have to be performed to locate a record. If all probabilities were the same, the average would be 50.

Some improvement can be made in sequential searching if the relative activities of the records are known and the file can be arranged accordingly. This is intuitively obvious, although to predict how much time will be saved one needs to know the probabilities involved. As Example 13.3 indicates, a significant improvement is possible only if there are a few records with a much higher activity than the rest. To get better results for searching in general, a completely different approach is needed.

binary search

To see how to improve on the sequential search, let us ask whether it is possible to find a record without, in the worst case, having to look at every item in the file. The answer is no if the file is totally unorganized and the keys unrelated. Because no information, except whether or not the record was found, is obtained in one step, it may be necessary to look at every record in the file before finding the right one. For a more effective algorithm, the file must be organized in some way.

One way of organizing the file is to sort the records by their keys, say, in ascending order, so that

$$x_1 < x_2 < \cdots < x_N$$

To find a record whose key matches a search key K, we first look at the middle record with key $x_{N/2}$. If $K > x_{N/2}$, then the record sought is in the upper half of the file, while for $K < x_{N/2}$, it is in the lower half. In any case, we can ignore half of the file and repeat the process on the remaining half. Each comparison cuts the file in half; therefore the method is called a *binary search*.

Consider now what happens in successive comparisons. After one comparison, the file to be searched has length $N/2$, after the second it has length $N/4$, and so on. If initially the file length N is a power of two, then after p comparisons the file still to be searched has length $N/2^p$. Eventually, the file will have shrunk to one record, which must be the right one. Of course, we may have succeeded earlier if the search key matches one of the middle elements. But here we are concerned with the worst case, in which

TABLE 13.1

Table of $\log_2 N$

N	10^2	10^3	10^6	10^9
$\log_2 N$	6.7	10	20	30

p comparisons have to be made, with p such that

$$N/2^p = 1$$

or

$$p = \log_2 N$$

The worst case complexity of the binary search is then

$$T_W(N) = O(\log_2 N)$$

Table 13.1 demonstrates the effectiveness of the binary search by a comparison between N and $\log_2 N$. To search a list of 10^9 elements sequentially might take several hours, while a binary search can be done with about 30 comparisons—though very few computers have main memories capable of holding 10^9 records. To search a large file of a billion words is a lengthy task in any system. But the figure does illustrate the effectiveness of the binary search for large N.

EXAMPLE 13.4

RECURSIVE BINARY SEARCH

Let X be an array of type

```
type DATAFILE=array[1..N] of integer
```

and let KEY be the search key. Write a boolean function FOUND that will return the value true if KEY is in X, and false otherwise.

Rather than looking at this from the point of view described, that is, a consecutive splitting of the file, define FOUND by the following. FOUND, when applied to X[1..N], will be true if and only if either FOUND applied to X[1..N/2] is true or FOUND applied to X[N/2+1..N] is true. This is a recursive definition of FOUND, and the corresponding code is a straightforward recursive implementation of this definition.

```
function FOUND(X:DATAFILE;
              INIT,FINAL,KEY:integer):boolean;
{ this procedure performs a binary search on the
array X from X[INIT] to X[FINAL]. The value of
FOUND will be true if KEY is in the array, false
otherwise }
var MIDDLE:integer;
begin
```

```
{check for file with one entry, this
 provides escape from recursion}
if (INIT=FINAL)
   then if X[INIT]=KEY
           then FOUND:=true
           else FOUND:=false
   else begin
           {split file into two parts and apply
            FOUND to the part containing KEY}
           MIDDLE:=(INIT+FINAL) div 2;
           if X[MIDDLE]>=KEY
              then FOUND:=FOUND(X,INIT,
                                MIDDLE,KEY)
              else FOUND:=FOUND(X,MIDDLE+1,
                                FINAL,KEY)
        end
end
```

As with many recursive programs, the code is short and elegant. As a practical matter, though, one would rarely use it because of the computational inefficiency of recursion. A nonrecursive version of FOUND is not difficult to write, but the code will be a little longer.

As can be seen from the code for FOUND, binary search is not restricted to cases where N is a power of two. When N is not a perfect power of two, occasionally some subfiles will not be exactly of the same length. This does not matter for the algorithm or its efficiency.

While the binary search is very efficient, it does require that the middle element of a file be easily found. When we use sequential allocation, this is no problem, but with a linked list, the middle element cannot be found without traversing the whole list. Therefore, the simple binary search does not work well when the records are arranged in a linked list.

binary search trees

If a file can be structured as an ordered sequential list, then a binary search is extremely effective. In a completely static situation this structure is reasonable, but if frequent insertions and deletions have to be made, sequential allocation becomes very inefficient. In a changing situation, we prefer a dynamic representation. Let us now look at the possibility of extending the concept of a binary search to linked structures.

What makes the binary search work is the fact that each comparison divides the file into two parts of equal or nearly equal length, one of which is known not to contain the desired record. The algorithm cannot be applied to a linked list because it is too time-consuming to find the middle.

What is needed is a dynamic data structure with a middle element (and the middle of subsequent pieces) readily located. A binary tree is a possibility, because the tree can easily be divided at its root into two subtrees. If we can arrange the structure such that nodes are ordered in some way and such that the subtrees always have roughly the same number of nodes, we may have the answer to the problem. By such reasoning one is led to consider special kinds of binary trees, called *binary search trees*.

A binary search tree is a binary tree arranged as follows. Each node has as its label the key of a record. For any given node with label x_i, all nodes whose labels are less than x_i are in the left subtree, while those with labels greater than x_i are in the right subtree. A binary search tree for the set of keys

10 12 13 14 15 16 17 18 20 25 30 40

is shown in Figure 13.4. Actually, there is no unique binary tree for a given sequence. The above set of numbers can also be represented as the tree in Figure 13.5. To search a binary tree, we check each node value, starting with the root, against the search key k. If k is less than the node value, we descend into the left subtree; if k is larger than the node value, we go down the right subtree. This step is repeated until a match is found or, in the case of an unsuccessful search, we end in a leaf.

Insertions and deletions in a binary tree are easily made. Rather than describing the full algorithm, let us take a specific example, starting with Figure 13.4, and the value 22 to be added to the tree. First, proceed as if you were searching with a key of 22. This will eventually get you to the node labeled 25, with no left subtree. Because $k = 22$ is smaller than the node value, insert it as a left subtree. This will give the new tree shown in Figure 13.6.

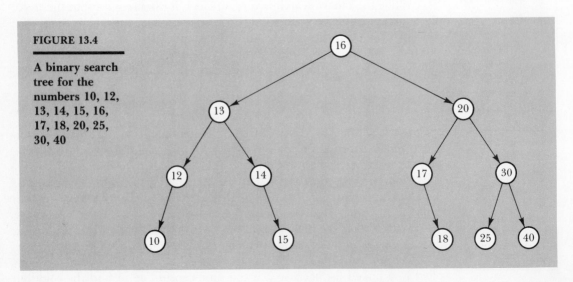

FIGURE 13.4

A binary search tree for the numbers 10, 12, 13, 14, 15, 16, 17, 18, 20, 25, 30, 40

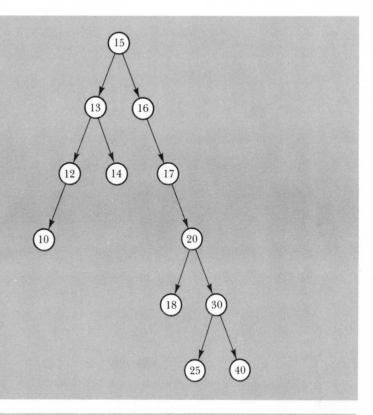

FIGURE 13.5

Another binary search tree for 10, 12, 13, 14, 15, 16, 17, 18, 20, 25, 30, 40

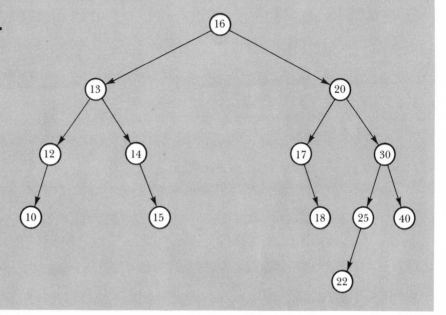

FIGURE 13.6

The binary search tree of Figure 13.4 after insertion of 22

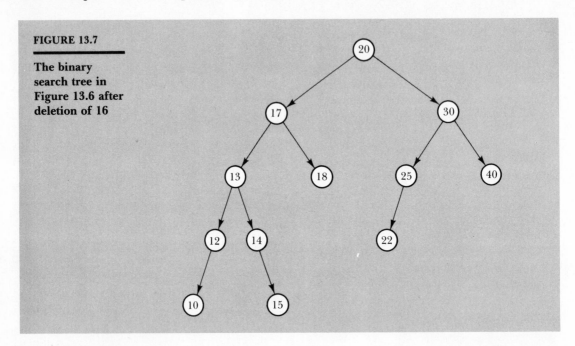

FIGURE 13.7

The binary
search tree in
Figure 13.6 after
deletion of 16

There are several methods for deleting a node, but all are somewhat less than obvious. Let us take one of the simpler ones and apply it to delete the node 16 (i.e., the root) in Figure 13.6. First, we find the node the label for which is the successor of 16, in this case the node labeled 17. This node has no left subtree so that we can make the left subtree of 16 the left subtree of 17. After that, we delete node 16, making its right child, node 20, the new root and giving Figure 13.7.

This can be made into a general algorithm. To delete a node with label x, we find its successor node with label y. Because y is the immediate successor to x, we know that

$$x < y$$

and that there is no label w such that

$$x < w < y$$

This shows that, unless y is the parent of x, it cannot have a left subtree. If it did, every node in it would have a label with value between x and y. Once y has been found, the left subtree of x is made the left subtree of y and x is removed. The right child z of x takes the place in the tree previously taken by x. All elements of the left subtree of z were either in the left subtree of x or in the left subtree of z. Therefore, the tree is still a binary search tree. The exceptional case when y is the parent of x is quite simple. We leave it as an exercise to formalize the algorithm and write programs for insertion and deletion.

The worst case complexity for searching a binary tree is proportional to the height of the tree. If we compare Figures 13.4 and 13.5, we see that the first is better because its height is three, while the height of the second is five. The tree in Figure 13.5 is said to be unbalanced, having a height greater than necessary. It is easy to show that a binary tree of height p has at most $2^{p+1} - 1$ nodes. Therefore, to store N keys, the tree must have at least height p, where p is the smallest integer such that

$$N \le 2^{p+1} - 1$$

For large N

$$p = O(\log_2 N)$$

Consequently, the worst case complexity for a search in a binary tree of minimal height is

$$T_W(N) = O(\log_2 N)$$

which is the same as for a binary search in a sequential file.

One difficulty with this approach is that, even if we start with a tree of minimal height, insertions and deletions soon destroy the balance and hence degrade the efficiency of the search. This implies that we need to restructure the file periodically to make it more balanced, or to rebalance after each insertion and deletion. There are effective algorithms for doing this, but they are a little complicated and not easy to visualize. Some of the books listed at the end of the chapter explore this subject in more detail.

hash addressing

Another way of structuring a file for quick access is to put each record in a place that depends, in some easily predictable fashion, on the value of the record key. If, for example, the keys are all positive numbers between 0 and 100, and the file is stored in a one-dimensional array DATAFILE, we put the record with key KEY into DATAFILE[KEY]. Retrieval is then a simple indexing operation and the search complexity is independent of the number of records in the file.

This is certainly direct and efficient, but not very practical for large files. If the keys were in the range 0–999999, we would need a main memory of a million words. Even if that much space is available, the method is quite wasteful. If only a limited amount of memory, say 1000 words, is available, one could use the lowest three digits in the six digit key as the index. Thus, 743134 would be sorted in DATAFILE[134], while 192374 would be put into DATAFILE[374]. Such a relation between the key and the memory address (index) is an example of a hashing function, introduced in Section 11.5. In this example, the hashing function is easily written down, namely

```
HASH(KEY) = KEY mod 1000
```

One problem in this scheme is immediately apparent; it frequently causes collisions. Suppose we have two keys, 720101 and 613101. Both of these should be put into DATAFILE[101]—obviously impossible. An elegant way of resolving such collisions is not to think of the hashing function as an index, but rather as a pointer to a linked list. This allows for a variable number of records in each list; when a collision occurs, we insert the new record by linking it to the ones already there. If, with the hashing function just given, we have keys

$$102001,304002,517999,527001,529001,742002$$

the file will look like Figure 13.8.

A somewhat subtler difficulty appears when we consider the complexity of the search in such a structure. Clearly, the worst case complexity is proportional to the maximum length of any list. Similarly, for the average complexity, if all the records are concentrated in a single list, then the average search time will be O(N), which is the same as for a sequential search. For maximum efficiency the records should be evenly distributed over all the lists. The hashing function just discussed is usually not very good. If the keys show little variability in the lower three digits, the organization is very inefficient. What is needed is a hashing function whose values are more or less random, destroying any possible pattern in the keys.

To get a better hashing function we need to take less obvious and sometimes rather strange functions. Consider for example the function

$$HASH(KEY)=(KEY \bmod 1001) \bmod 1000$$

Then

$$HASH(102001) = 900$$
$$HASH(527001) = 475$$

and the pattern in the lower digits has been removed. (The study of good hashing functions that distribute an arbitrary set of keys uniformly over a

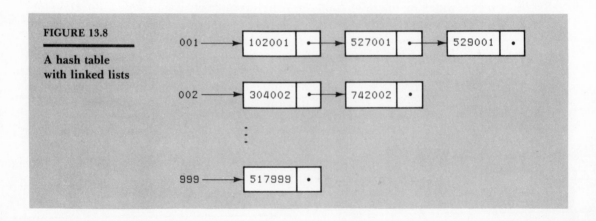

FIGURE 13.8

A hash table with linked lists

number of categories is of interest in computer science, but it is beyond the scope of our discussion.)

If the hashing function is a good one and distributes the records evenly, one can expect the search to be efficient. If N records are evenly distributed among p categories, and all search keys are equally probable, then hashing, followed by a sequential search, has average complexity

$$T_A(N) = O(N/2p)$$

If p is around 1000, the algorithm is significantly faster than sequential search on the whole file.

EXERCISES 13.2

1. Suppose that in Example 13.3, 50% of the searches are unsuccessful; 25% of the time we are looking for the first record; and the rest of the time we search for the other records with equal probability. What is $T_A(N)$?

2. Suppose we have a file consisting of 1000 records. Half of the time we search with equal probability for one of the first 100 records. The other half of the time we look for a record in the last 900, also with equal probability. Compute T_A for a sequential search.

3. Write a nonrecursive procedure for binary search using the same data structure as in Example 13.4.

4. Suppose a file of 10^7 records is stored on disk. Main memory has just enough space for 10^5 records at one time. Devise a method that utilizes the binary search method in this situation. Estimate the number of operations needed for such a search.

5. What is $T_A(N)$ for a binary search on a sequential list?

6. Write a procedure to determine whether a binary search tree is of minimal height.

7. Devise an algorithm for constructing a binary search tree from an unsorted file so that the tree is of minimal height. What is $T_W(N)$ for this algorithm?

8. Write recursive and nonrecursive procedures for searching a binary search tree. Use the implementation of binary trees described in Example 10.5.

9. Write procedures for inserting elements in and deleting elements from a binary search tree.

10. Show that the claim that a binary tree of height p cannot have more than $2^{p+1} - 1$ nodes is true for $p = 3$ and $p = 4$. Then give a proof for general p.

11. Design an implementation for the structure depicted in Figure 13.8. Then write a procedure to insert values into this structure using

```
HASH(KEY)=KEY mod 1000
```

12. Compute HASH(173002) using the hashing function

    HASH(KEY)=(KEY mod 1013) mod 1000

    Find two values of KEY that produce a collision.
13. Write a procedure to search for a key in the structure generated in Exercise 11.
14. Which of the search methods described do you use when you look up a word in the dictionary?
15. Consider the following function FOUND1, which is a different version of recursive binary search previously implemented as FOUND.

```
function FOUND1(X:LIST;
                INIT,FINAL,KEY:integer):boolean;
var MIDDLE:integer;
begin
  if (INIT=FINAL)
    then if X[INIT]=KEY
            then FOUND:=true
            else FOUND:=false
    else begin
            MIDDLE:=(INIT+FINAL) div 2;
            FOUND:=FOUND(X,INIT,MIDDLE,KEY) or
                   FOUND(X,MIDDLE+1,FINAL,KEY)
         end
end
```

Give reasons why FOUND is more efficient than FOUND1.

13.3

merging and sorting

Two problems of considerable practical importance are merging, in which the records in two different files are combined to form a new file, and sorting, which arranges a file so that the record keys are in some order. These two problems are very closely connected, as we will see. (We will restrict our discussion to files contained entirely in main memory.)

merging of two sorted files

Merging of two files can be done very efficiently if both files are sorted, say in ascending order. The two files are scanned simultaneously, and the appropriate element is inserted into a new file. Each file is controlled by a cursor; on each step the two current keys are compared and the smaller inserted into the new file. The cursor pointing to the smaller key and the one pointing to the merged file are advanced, while the third cursor remains fixed. Several steps in this process are depicted in Figure 13.9. The result is a new file, which is also sorted.

It is clear that in the algorithm each key is considered only once. Hence, the complexity of the algorithm has order of magnitude

$$T(N,M) = O(N + M)$$

where N and M are the lengths of the two files.

The Pascal code for the algorithm is easy enough. For the following procedure MERGE, the two files, FILEA and FILEB are of type INTFILE, where

```
type INTFILE=array[1..100] of integer
```

FIGURE 13.9

Several steps in merging two sorted files

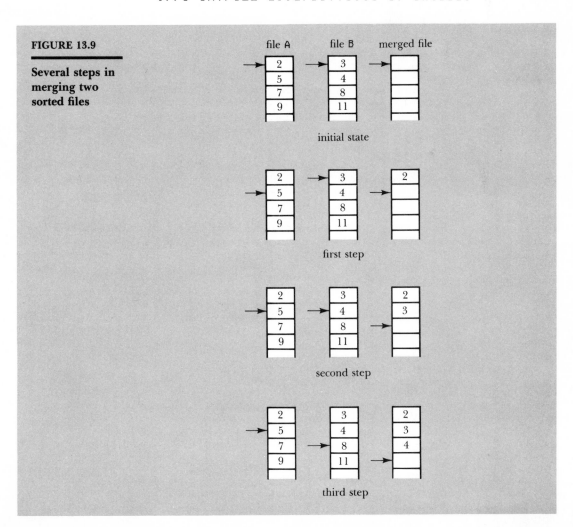

The merged file MERGEDFILE is also of this type.

```
Procedure MERGE(FILEA,FILEB:INTFILE;
                var MERGEDFILE:INTFILE;
                AINIT,AFINAL,BINIT,
                BFINAL,MINIT:integer);
{this Procedure merges two sorted files
 contained in FILEA[AINIT..AFINAL] and
 FILEB[BINIT..BFINAL] into MERGEDFILE starting
 at MINIT}
var I,CURSORA,CURSORB,CURSORM:integer;
    TEMP:INTFILE;
begin
   {initialize cursors}
   CURSORA:=AINIT;
   CURSORB:=BINIT;
   CURSORM:=1;
   { merge until one file is done
     on each step test which element
     is to be inserted in merged file
     and which cursor to advance}
   while (CURSORA<=AFINAL) and
         (CURSORB<=BFINAL) do
     begin
       if FILEA[CURSORA]<=FILEB[CURSORB]
         then begin
                TEMP[CURSORM]:=FILEA[CURSORA];
                CURSORA:=CURSORA+1
              end
         else begin
                TEMP[CURSORM]:=FILEB[CURSORB];
                CURSORB:=CURSORB+1
              end;
       CURSORM:=CURSORM+1
     end;
   { copy anything left in either file}
   for I:=0 to BFINAL-CURSORB do
     TEMP[CURSORM+I]:=FILEB[CURSORB+I];
   for I:=0 to AFINAL-CURSORA do
     TEMP[CURSORM+I]:=FILEA[CURSORA+I];
   { finally copy merged file from temporary
     space to MERGEDFILE] }
   for I:=1 to AFINAL-AINIT+BFINAL-BINIT+2 do
     MERGEDFILE[MINIT+I-1]:=TEMP[I]
end
```

The procedure uses a file TEMP to store the merged file temporarily. After completion of the merge, the results are transferred to MERGEDFILE. This makes it possible to merge when either AFILE or BFILE is the same as MERGEDFILE.

sorting

The one sorting algorithm we have discussed in some detail is the bubblesort. A program for it was given in Section 5.3, while in Example 12.3 we saw that

$$T\,(N) \simeq \frac{N^2}{2}\, t_L$$

The complexity of the algorithm is quadratic in the length of the file. For large N, the bubblesort method is very time-consuming.

Sometimes, when the complexity of an algorithm increases faster than the first power of the problem size, we can get increased efficiency if we can split the problem into parts and treat each part separately. It is not always easy to do this, but in sorting a way suggests itself without too much trouble. If we have a file of length N, we split it into two files FILE1 and FILE2, both of length N/2. We then sort both of them with the bubblesort. Finally, we merge the two parts to get a complete, sorted file. The work required is:

1. To sort FILE1 we need $(N/2)^2/2 = N^2/8$ operations.
2. To sort FILE2, we also need $N^2/8$ operations.
3. To merge the two files we need N operations.

The complexity of the complete algorithm is then

$$T(N) = \frac{N^2}{4} \times t_s + N \times t_M$$

$$\simeq \frac{N^2}{4} \times t_s$$

where t_s and t_M are inner loop times for the bubblesort and the merge, respectively. This is approximately half the amount of work that would have to be done if the whole file were sorted with the bubblesort directly.

We don't have to stop here. We can subdivide FILE1 and FILE2 again, getting four files, and so on. If we continue as far as possible, we end up with files all of length one. At this point, we begin merging, first taking pairs of elements to get sorted files of length two, then merging these into files of length four, and so on. The process is shown in Figure 13.10 for a specific case. When this is coded, there is no actual splitting of files. All that needs to be done is to merge subfiles of increasing length until the whole file is sorted. The algorithm is called the ***mergesort.***

mergesort

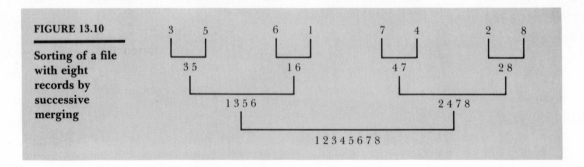

FIGURE 13.10

Sorting of a file with eight records by successive merging

How much work does the mergesort require? Again, for simplicity's sake, assume that N is a power of two, and that $N = 2^p$. In the first step, we merge N files of length one, so that the number of operations is N. In the next step, we merge N/2 files of length two, so that again the work required is proportional to N. In fact, the work required at each stage is proportional to N. But the number of stages is $p = \log_2 N$, because each stage reduces the number of files by two. Therefore,

$$T(N) = O(N\log_2 N)$$

To show how effective the mergesort is, look at Table 13.2, which gives a comparison of $N\log_2 N$ with $N^2/2$.

TABLE 13.2

Comparison of $N\log_2 N$ and $\frac{1}{2}N^2$

N	10	10^2	10^3	10^4	10^5
$N\log_2 N$	33	664	9965	132877	1.7×10^6
$\frac{1}{2}N^2$	50	5000	5×10^5	5×10^7	5×10^9

It is a reasonable undertaking to sort a list with 100,000 elements by the mergesort technique, while doing this problem with a bubblesort would take many hours even on a fast computer.

An implementation of the scheme shown in Figure 13.10 is reasonably easy. Actually, we can also look at the mergesort from a recursive point of view. A sorted list is constructed by merging two smaller sorted lists.

EXAMPLE 13.5

RECURSIVE MERGESORT

We assume that the file contains a sequence of integers, stored in the array X of type

```
type INTFILE=array[1..100] of integer
```

The file is to be sorted using the mergesort technique. The sorted file will replace the original values in X.

In pseudolanguage, the algorithm is

1. Split file into two parts, SUBFILE1 and SUBFILE2.
2. The sorted file is constructed by merging sorted SUBFILE1 and SUBFILE2.

This definition is recursive, and we must provide an escape.

3. If a file has one element, then it is sorted.

For the following procedure MERGESORT, the variable X is assumed to be global. For merging, the previously written procedure MERGE will be used.

```
Procedure MERGESORT(INIT,FINAL:integer);
{ merge sort to sort a file in place,
  ascending order. Original and sorted file
  will be in X[INIT..FINAL] }
var MIDDLE:integer;
begin
  if FINAL-INIT>0
    {if array has length greater than one, sort
     recursively. For lists of length one,
     do nothing }
    then begin
          MIDDLE:=(INIT+FINAL) div 2;
          MERGESORT(INIT,MIDDLE);
          MERGESORT(MIDDLE+1,FINAL);
          MERGE(X,X,X,INIT,MIDDLE,
                MIDDLE+1,FINAL,INIT)
         end
end
```

The recursive version of the mergesort is certainly shorter and more elegant than any corresponding nonrecursive procedure we might produce. Nevertheless, it is not recommended for practical use. For large N, many recursive calls to MERGESORT have to be made. This can be very inefficient. Furthermore, many systems have limits on the depth of recursion, so that the procedure may not even work for large N. Because the whole purpose of using a mergesort is efficiency, we must be concerned with efficiency of implementation. As a practical method, the nonrecursive mergesort is much more acceptable. We leave it as an exercise to produce such a code.

The mergesort is one of several approaches to sorting large files efficiently. Sorting is a topic of considerable interest, and much has been written on it. For further information, refer to the books listed at the end of this chapter.

bucket sort

There are some algorithms for sorting that do not rely entirely on successive comparisons of the keys, but use some properties of the keys to first distribute the records into a number of categories, or buckets. The distribution is made in such a way that, if the buckets are sorted individually, the complete sorted file is easily assembled (say, by copying the buckets in some order). If, for example, the keys are five-digit integer numbers, one can put all records with keys starting with one into one bucket, those whose keys start with two into another, and so on. Once the initial distribution has been made, the records in each category are sorted by some method, after which the buckets can be combined easily to get the complete sorted file.

EXAMPLE 13.6

COMPARISON OF VARIOUS SORTING METHODS

As a specific example, to compare methods and variations, take a file with 10,000 records. For the bucket sort assume that there are 100 buckets, and that after the initial distribution each bucket will contain roughly the same number of records. Consider the following four methods:

1. Sort the whole file with the bubblesort. The total number of operations will be approximately $(10^4)^2/2$, which equals 5×10^7.
2. Sort the whole file using the mergesort. The number of operations will be about $10^4 \times \log_2 10^4$, or approximately 130,000.
3. Distribute the file into the 100 buckets, sort each bucket using a bubblesort, then combine the buckets. The initial distribution takes about 10^4 operations. To sort each subfile, containing on the average 100 records, requires 5×10^3 operations. This must be done 100 times, so that this step takes roughly 5×10^5 operations. The final combining of the buckets involves copying them and will take about 10^4 operations. The total is, then, roughly 5×10^5 operations.
4. Divide the file into 100 buckets, then use a mergesort on each. A mergesort of 100 records takes 6×10^2 operations, so that the time required to sort 100 buckets is of the order of 6×10^4. Distributing and recombining records each take 10^4 operations, making the total operation count of the order of 8×10^4.

Method 4 takes less than 100,000 operations, while the most naive approach, Method 1, requires about 50 million. Proper algorithm selection is clearly of utmost importance.

EXERCISES 13.3

1. Write a nonrecursive procedure for mergesort.
2. What is $T_W(\mathbb{N})$ for the bucket sort?

3. Another popular method for sorting is called *quicksort*. In this algorithm we pick some key x_i, then generate two files FILE1 and FILE2 such that all elements of FILE1 have keys less than x_i, while all those in FILE2 have keys greater than x_i. The subfiles are sorted and then merged. To sort the subfiles, we again use the quicksort approach. Take an arbitrary key, separate into two smaller files, sort, and finally merge.
   a. Write a recursive procedure for quicksort.
   b. Write a nonrecursive procedure for it.
   c. Show that $T_W(N) = O(N^2)$.
   d. Carry out some experimental tests to estimate $T_A(N)$.
4. In Example 13.6, how much work is involved in Methods 3 and 4 if only ten buckets are used?
5. The selection sort method works as follows. Search the file for the smallest key. Insert it into a new file and remove it from the original one. Repeat this process to find the second smallest, and so on. Show that $T_W(N)$ is $O(N^2)$. Does the selection sort have any advantage over the bubblesort for sorting an array? What if the file is a linked list?
6. Given two unsorted files FILEA and FILEB with length N and M, respectively, and with M much smaller than N. A new file (not necessarily sorted) is to be constructed, which will contain all records either in FILEA or FILEB, but no duplicates. Design an efficient algorithm and find its complexity.

13.4

combinatorial problems

exhaustive search

Let us return to the bin packing problem in Example 12.4. This problem can be solved by evaluating S for all possible combinations of the c_i. Since each c can have values zero or one, we have a total of 2^N combinations. This problem is representative of a large class of problems of this type. They involve the evaluations of a number of possible combinations, and can, at least in principle, be solved by an **exhaustive search**, that is, by checking all possible combinations.

The only difficulty in writing a program for an exhaustive search is keeping track of all the combinations so that none are missed or repeated. This may seem quite trivial, but is actually a little harder than it appears. The trouble lies in the fact that N is not fixed. If N were fixed, then we could write for the bin packing problem

```
for C1:= 0 to 1 do
   for C2:= 0 to 1 do
      .
      .
      .
      for CN:= 0 to 1 do
         evaluate S(C1,C2,....,CN)
```

But it is not immediately clear how such a nested loop structure can be used when N is a variable.

It is more profitable to look at the computation as a sequence of two-way decisions, represented in Figure 13.11 by a tree. The interpretation of Figure 13.11 is that, if c_1 is zero, we go left from the root, if c_1 is one, we go to the right. Similarly, at any ith level node, we go to the left if c_i is zero and right if it is one. Following a path from the root to a leaf represents one possible combination of c. The complete tree includes all combinations.

If the decision tree were actually constructed, a procedure like PREPRINT in Example 10.1 could be used to traverse the tree and evaluate S for all paths. But this is unnecessary; by using the picture of the decision tree as a guide, we can construct a more direct algorithm. All we really need is a systematic method for traversing paths in a binary tree in which all interior nodes have exactly two branches.

The first path is generated by going down the tree, always bearing left. This ends at the left-most leaf, representing the uninteresting combination $0, 0, \ldots, 0$. The second path is obtained by backing up one level from the left-most leaf, then going right, giving the combination $0, 0, \ldots, 1$. Once more we back up, but this time we have to go up two levels to find a new combination. If you think about this for a minute, you will quickly see the pattern that must be followed to traverse the whole tree. We have here an

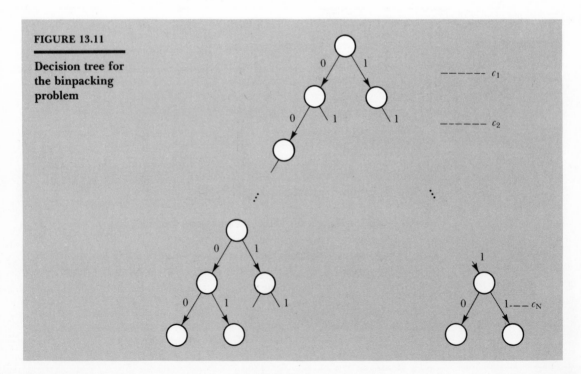

FIGURE 13.11

Decision tree for the binpacking problem

backtracking   application of a technique called **backtracking,** which is very useful in exhaustive search algorithms for combinatorial problems.

EXAMPLE 13.7

SOLUTION OF THE BIN PACKING PROBLEM

Given as input a sequence of integers $X[1], X[2], \ldots, X[N]$, terminated by the end of the file, write a program that will generate all possible combinations

$$S = c[1]*X[1]+c[2]*X[2]+\ldots+c[N]*X[N]$$

where each $c[i]$ takes on values zero and one.

As output, print N and $X[1], X[2], \ldots, X[N]$. For each combination, print the $c[i]$ and the corresponding value of S.

For the algorithm, we use the binary tree traversal and backtracking method just described. The precise description of backtracking for the bin packing problem is

1. If you come into a node from above, go down to the left.
2. If you back up to a node from the left branch, go down to the right.
3. If you back up to a node from a right branch, back up again.

We start at the root; when we back up to the root from the right, we are done.

To remember where we are in the tree we need to keep a list of the branches taken (that is, 0 or 1). When we back up, we return to the node most recently visited. This suggests that a stack is the right data structure for this problem.

In the program we will use a procedure NEXTCOMB, which, given any combination (represented by a stack with N zeros and ones), will generate the next combination, using the backtrack technique described. The main program BINPACK uses NEXTCOMB and evaluates S for each combination generated by NEXTCOMB. To manipulate the stack, the subprograms PUSH, POP, and EMPTY from Example 9.2 are used.

```
program BINPACK(input,output);
{ program to solve binpacking problem
    described in Example 12.4, using
    exhaustive search with backtracking}
const MAXLENGTH=20;
var N,I,TOP,TOPVALUE,SUM:integer;
    FINISHED:boolean;
    STACK:array[1..MAXLENGTH] of integer;
    X:array[1..MAXLENGTH] of integer;
```

```
function EMPTY:boolean;
{  boolean function which has value
   true if stack is empty}
begin
  if TOP=0
    then EMPTY:=true
    else EMPTY:=false
end;

procedure PUSH(NEWTOP:integer);
{  this procedure pushes NEWTOP
   onto stack. An overflow
   will give an error message}
begin
  if TOP>=MAXLENGTH
    then begin
            writeln(' error in PUSH');
            writeln(' stack overflow')
         end
    else begin
            TOP:=TOP+1;
            STACK[TOP]:=NEWTOP
         end
end;

procedure POP(var TOPVALUE:integer);
{  this procedure puts the value at the
   top of the stack into TOPVALUE and
   pops the stack. An empty stack will
   give an error message}
begin
  if EMPTY
    then begin
            writeln(' error in POP');
            writeln(' stack is empty')
         end
    else begin
            TOPVALUE:=STACK[TOP];
            TOP:=TOP-1
         end
end;

procedure NEXTCOMB;
{ given a binary string stored in STACK
   this procedure generates the next
   combination for bin packing problem}
```

```
var BACKUP:boolean;
begin
  FINISHED:=false;
  {since NEXTCOMB starts with a combination
   the first step is always a backup}
  BACKUP:=true;
  repeat
    if not BACKUP
      {go forward to left}
      then PUSH(0);
    if BACKUP
      then begin
              POP(TOPVALUE);
              if TOPVALUE=0
                {backing up from left, go right}
                then begin
                        PUSH(1);
                        BACKUP:=false
                     end
                {backing up from right, check
                 for completion}
                else if EMPTY
                        then FINISHED:=true
           end
  until FINISHED or (TOP=N)
end;

begin
  {read all data }
  N:=0;
  while not eof do
    begin
      N:=N+1;
      read(X[N]);
      if eoln
        then readln
    end;
  {print heading and echo input}
  writeln(' Bin Packing Problem' );
  writeln;
  writeln(' N= ',N:5);
  write(' X[I]        ');
  for I:=1 to N do
    write(X[I]:5);
  writeln;
  writeln;
```

```
      { initialize and set stack to
        all zeros giving combination 0,0,...,0}
      TOP:=0;
      for I:=1 to N do
        PUSH(0);
      FINISHED:=false;
      repeat
        write( 'combination');
        SUM:=0;
        {evaluate sum for latest combination}
        for I:= 1 to N do
          begin
            SUM:=SUM+X[I]*STACK[I];
            write(STACK[I]:5)
          end;
        writeln;
        writeln(' SUM=',SUM:5);
        {generate new combination}
        NEXTCOMB;
      until FINISHED
    end.
```

Sample input

```
    4 3 6
```

Output

```
Bin Packing Problem

N=        3
 X[I]              4     3     6

combination        0     0     0
 SUM=     0
combination        0     0     1
 SUM=     6
combination        0     1     0
 SUM=     3
combination        0     1     1
 SUM=     9
combination        1     0     0
 SUM=     4
combination        1     0     1
 SUM=    10
combination        1     1     0
 SUM=     7
combination        1     1     1
 SUM=    13
```

If W has the value 11, then the solution of the bin packing problem with these data is to take x_1 and x_3, because

$$x_1 + x_3 = 10$$

Another well-known combinatorial problem is the *traveling salesman problem*. Here we are given n cities $c_1, c_2, \ldots, c_n$ and positive numbers $d_{12}, d_{13}, \ldots,$ such that d_{ij} is the distance between c_i and c_j. A salesman is supposed to make a tour of all cities, starting at some arbitrary place, visiting each city once and only once and returning to the starting point. Two typical tours for a seven-city problem are shown in Figure 13.12. We are interested in finding the tour with the shortest length.

An exhaustive search solution to the problem is conceptually easy. Start, say, at c_1, then pick any of the remaining cities as the next stop. From there again pick a city not yet visited, and continue until all have been visited. It is a simple matter to compute the length for each tour; after all the tours have been made, pick the shortest one. The only challenge is to keep track of all the tours. The decision tree for the problem is a little more complicated, because it is not a binary tree. Figure 13.13 shows part of this tree for the seven-city problem of Figure 13.12.

The search and backtrack algorithm for the traveling salesman problem is similar to the bin packing algorithm. At each node we search the subtree, always taking the left-most branch not yet visited. Again, a stack can be used to remember where we are. Note, however, that not all subtrees look the same at different nodes. This is because at different nodes different cities will have been visited previously. This complicates the book-keeping operations somewhat, but does not change the basic principle. An algorithm along the lines of NEXTCOMB in the bin packing problem can be written here. We will leave this as an exercise.

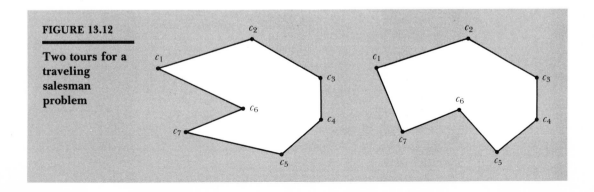

FIGURE 13.12

Two tours for a traveling salesman problem

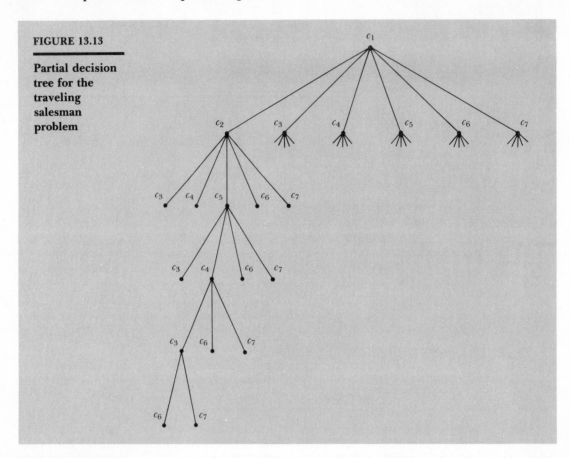

FIGURE 13.13

Partial decision tree for the traveling salesman problem

The exhaustive search method for the traveling salesman problem can be very time-consuming, because there are a very large number of possible tours. Once the starting city is chosen, there are $N - 1$ possibilities for the second city, $N - 2$ for the third, and so on. Therefore, there are a total of $(N-1)!$ tours and

$$T(N) = O((N-1)!)$$

The factorial function grows very rapidly with N as Table 13.3 demonstrates. It is not possible to solve the traveling salesman problem by exhaustive search for N larger than about 15 with present computer speeds or even with machines that we can expect to have in the foreseeable future.

TABLE 13.3

Table of factorials

N	5	10	12	15
N!	120	3.6×10^6	4.8×10^8	1.3×10^{12}

EXERCISES 13.4

1. In program B I NPACK there are some computations that do not access the stack through PUSH and POP, but take advantage of the fact that the stack is implemented as an array. Rewrite B I NPACK so that the stack is manipulated only through PUSH and POP.
2. Write an exhaustive search algorithm for the traveling salesman problem.
3. There are some algorithms for the traveling salesman problem which, although they do not give the shortest tour, tend to give reasonable answers. One is the so-called *greedy* method. This is a heuristic in which at each point we visit the nearest city not yet visited.
   a. Write a program for the greedy method.
   b. Compute T(N) for the greedy method.
   c. Show by example that the greedy method does not always give the shortest tour.

13.5

the complexity of problems

The complexities of the algorithms we have discussed vary over a wide range, from the very slowly increasing $\log_2 N$ of binary search to the extremely fast-growing N ! for the traveling salesman problem. We have also seen that, for a given problem, there are algorithms with quite different complexities. A complete understanding of a given situation requires that we not only be able to find the complexity of a prospective algorithm, but that we also find the most efficient algorithm. Thus, we are interested in the complexity of the problem, which is defined as the complexity of the best algorithm for the problem for large N. The study of the complexity of problems is not only challenging mathematically, but also of practical interest. It allows us to determine when we have found the best possible algorithm.

For most interesting problems, there are a large, if not an unlimited, number of algorithms, so it is not possible to find the complexity of a problem by examining all relevant algorithms. The complexity of a problem can only be found through general, mathematical arguments. This is not an easy matter. Theoretical computer scientists devote a great deal of effort to such questions. We can do no more here than outline some of the most elementary results.

Take the case of searching a file. Assume that the searching is done by successive comparisons of the keys, and that on this basis a two-way decision is made regarding where to look next. Both the sequential and the binary

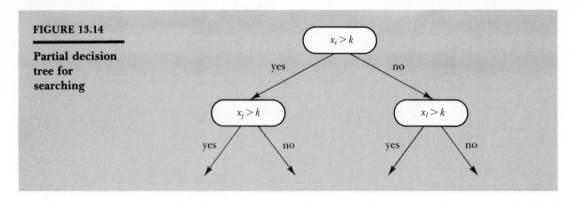

FIGURE 13.14

**Partial decision
tree for
searching**

search are in this class of algorithms. We can think of this process as a binary
decision tree (Figure 13.14). Each comparison takes us down one or the
other of the branches, depending on its outcome. In different branches
different comparisons are done. Comparisons are made until either the
record is found or it is known that the file does not contain it. The end of
an unsuccessful comparison sequence is a leaf of the tree. In the worst case,
we will have to follow the longest path from the root to a leaf, so that the
complexity of the algorithm is the height of the tree. Each key must occur
in at least one node; otherwise, it will never be examined. This implies that
the decision tree must have at least N nodes. The best we can do is make the
tree full, by which we mean that each interior node has exactly two children
and the leaves are all at the same height. In this case a tree of height p has
$2^{p+1} - 1$ nodes, and we must have

$$2^{p+1} = N + 1$$

$$p = O(\log_2 N)$$

showing that any algorithm in this class must have a decision tree of height
no less than $\log_2 N$ for the searching of a file with N records.

These somewhat loose arguments can be tightened to give a mathematical theorem stating that any search based on successive comparisons of
the search key with the record keys and a two-way decision must have a
worst case complexity no smaller than

$$T_W(N) = O(\log_2 N)$$

We can conclude from this that the binary search is about as efficient as can
be hoped.

This result does not apply to algorithms based on a different
principle—for example, algorithms that allow multi-way decisions on each
comparison. Searching in a hash table is an example of an algorithm that
can work faster than the $O(\log_2 N)$ limit.

Similarly, it can be shown that for sorting algorithms, based on successive comparisons of keys, the best one can do is

$$T_W(N) = O(Nlog_2N)$$

The mergesort that achieves this limit is among the optimal algorithms.

TABLE 13.4

Comparison of power and exponential functions

N	5	10	15	20
N^2	25	100	225	400
N^3	75	1000	3375	8000
2^N	32	1024	32768	1.0×10^6
$N!$	120	3.6×10^6	1.3×10^{12}	2.4×10^{18}

The exhaustive search algorithms for the bin packing and traveling salesman problems had complexities

$$T(N) = O(2^N)$$

and

$$T(N) = O(N!)$$

respectively. These complexities are said to be *exponential,* because the functions grow more rapidly than any power of N (see Table 13.4). Algorithms with exponential complexity are not useful for even moderately sized problems.

The interesting question is whether the difficulty in the bin packing and traveling salesman problems stems from the approach (the use of exhaustive search) or whether it is inherent in these problems. We could hope that, with enough ingenuity, we might be able to solve the bin packing and traveling salesman problems for N = 1000 or so. This is a question of the complexities of these problems. Is it in principle possible to find an algorithm for which

$$T(N) = O(N^p)$$

for some number p? If so, there is some hope of finding a reasonable algorithm. On the other hand, if the complexity of the problem is exponential, then nothing much can be done. It may be possible to make some minor efficiency improvements, but eventually the exponential complexity will make it impossible to solve large problems.

Unfortunately, the answer to this question is not known. So far, nobody has found an algorithm for either the bin packing or the traveling salesman problem with less than exponential complexity. Furthermore, it is known that both of them belong to a class called the ***N−P complete*** prob-

N − P complete

lems. If we could find one nonexponential algorithm for one $N - P$ complete problem, we could find such algorithms for all of them. In spite of continued efforts, no one has been able to find a good algorithm for any $N - P$ complete problem, so it is suspected that their complexities are exponential. Still, no mathematical proof of this conjecture exists, leaving us with a strong suspicion but no certainty.

EXERCISES 13.5

1. What is the smallest value of N (with N > 1) for which $2^N > N^5$?
2. Suppose you want to sort a file of N five digit positive integer numbers. Take an array X[1..99999] and initialize it to zero. Then put each item with value NUMBER into X[NUMBER]. Finally, pick up all nonzero entries in X, giving the sorted file. Show that the complexity of this algorithm is independent of N (at least for N < 10,000). Does this contradict the claim that the best algorithm for sorting has complexity $O(N\log_2 N)$?

---

further reading

Baase, S. *Computer Algorithms: Introduction to Design and Analysis,* Chapter 2. Reading, Mass.: Addison-Wesley Publishing Co., 1978.

Horowitz, E., and Sahni, S. *Fundamentals of Computer Algorithms,* Chapter 3. Potomac, Md.: Computer Science Press, 1978.

Knuth, D. E. *The Art of Computer Programming. Vol III, Sorting and Searching.* Reading, Mass.: Addison-Wesley Publishing Co., 1973.

Reingold, E. M., Nievergelt, J. and Deo, N. *Combinatorial Algorithms: Theory and Practice,* Chapters 6 and 7. Englewood Cliffs, N.J.: Prentice-Hall, 1977.

Wirth, N. *Algorithms + Data Structures = Programs,* Chapter 2. Englewood Cliffs, N.J.: Prentice-Hall, 1976.

Appendix

summary of pascal syntax

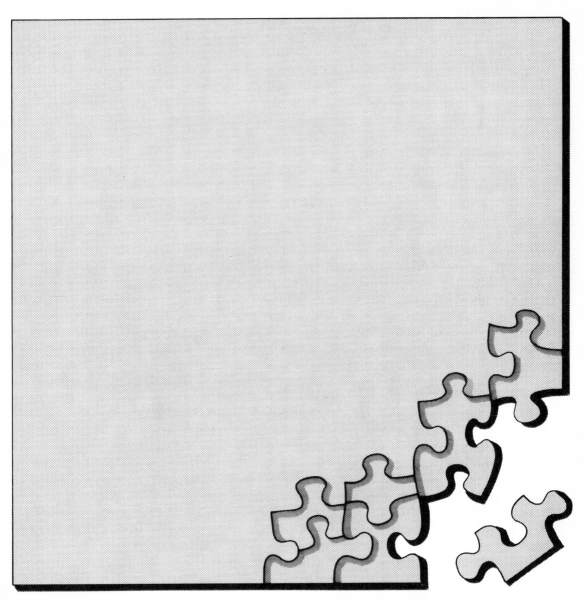

This appendix elaborates on some aspects of Pascal syntax that were not described explicitly in the main text. What is given here is limited to the subset of Pascal used in the book.

A
reserved words and standard identifiers

reserved words

and	function	program
array	goto	record
begin	if	repeat
case	in	set
const	label	then
div	mod	to
do	nil	type
downto	not	until
else	of	var
end	or	while
file	packed	with
for	procedure	

standard identifiers

abs	input	rewrite
arctan	integer	round
boolean	ln	sin
char	new	sqr
chr	odd	sqrt
cos	ord	text
dispose	output	true
eof	put	trunc
eoln	read	write
exp	readln	writeln
false	real	
get	reset	

B

operator precedence rules

In the following list, all operators on the same line have equal priority. All operators on one line have precedence over those on a lower line. In case of equal priority, evaluation in an expression is from left to right.

```
not
*, /, mod, div, and
+, -, or
<, <=, >, >=, =, <>, in
```

C

syntax charts

Syntax charts are a means for describing precisely what form a particular construct must have to be syntactically correct. The charts consist of three types of boxes, oblong, circular and rectangular, connected by lines and arrows. Oblong boxes contain reserved words or words with agreed-upon meanings, such as "digit." Circular boxes contain characters or character combinations with specific meaning (for example, := for assignment). In the rectangular boxes are the names of constructs that are explained in other syntax charts. By referring to a sequence of charts, each construct can be broken down into the elementary constituents of the language.

Syntax charts are read by starting at the upper-left-hand corner and going in the direction of the arrows in any way possible. Loops may be traversed as often as desired. Eventually, the exit is reached, signifying the end of the construct. For example, by looking at the chart for "compound statement" below, we see that a compound statement must start with the reserved word begin, that it consists of one or more statements separated by semicolons, and is terminated with the reserved word end. To find out what is meant by "statement," we must consider the syntax chart for it.

A construct can be syntactically correct only if it can be generated by a syntax chart. However, the converse is not true; not every construct generated by a syntax chart is necessarily acceptable. For example, the expression

```
A in B
```

can be produced by a syntax chart. But to be acceptable, B must be a set and A must be of the same type as the elements of B. Syntax charts do not include the rules for type compatibility. Another type of error not ruled out by the syntax charts is

```
var A:integer;
    B,A:real
```

although Pascal allows only one type declaration for each variable.

program

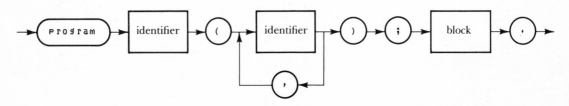

block

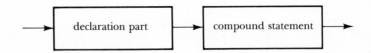

declaration part

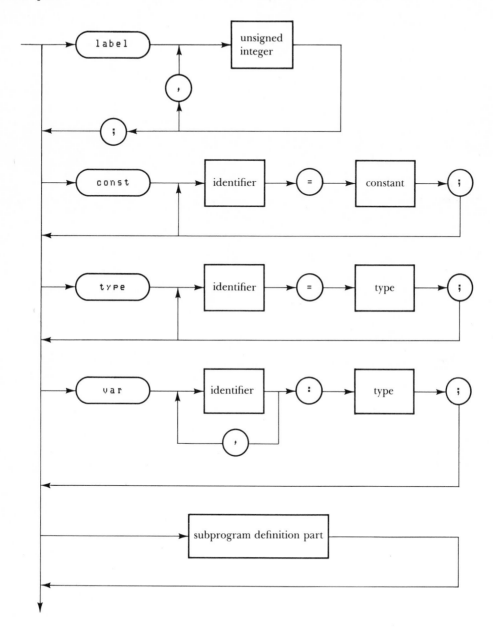

subprogram definition part

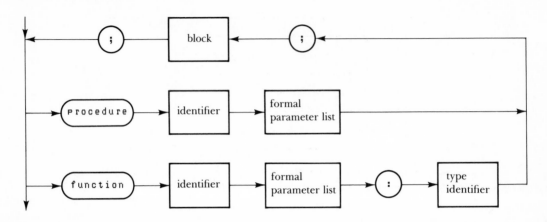

formal parameter list

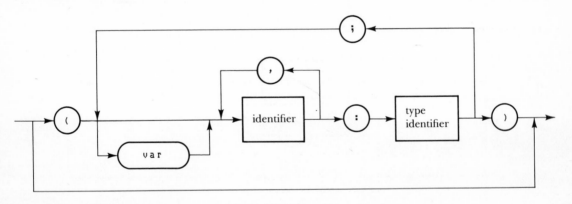

compound statement

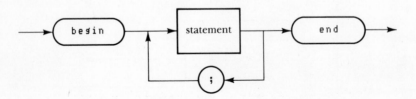

statement

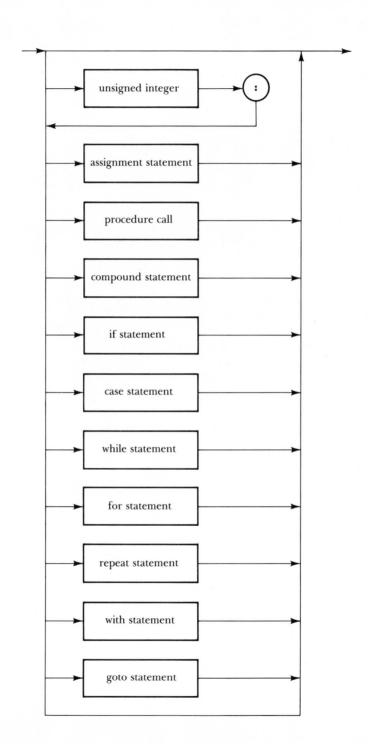

assignment statement

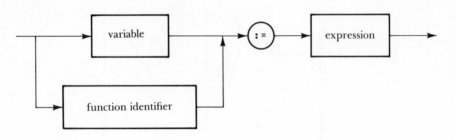

procedure call

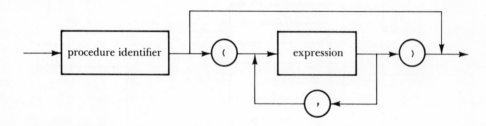

function call

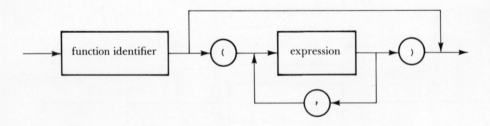

if statement

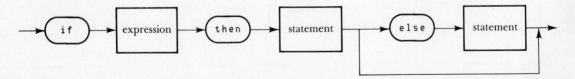

case statement

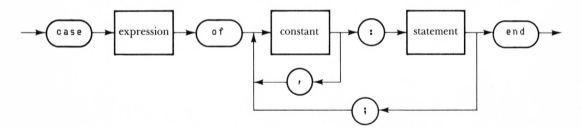

while statement

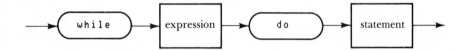

for statement

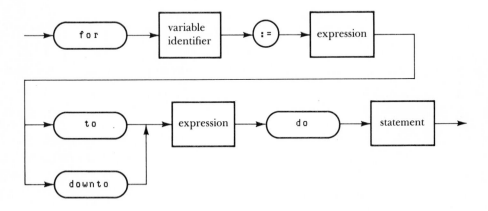

repeat statement

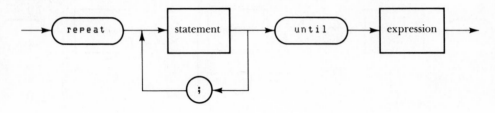

with statement

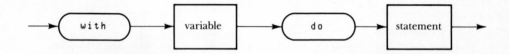

goto statement

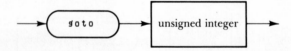

type

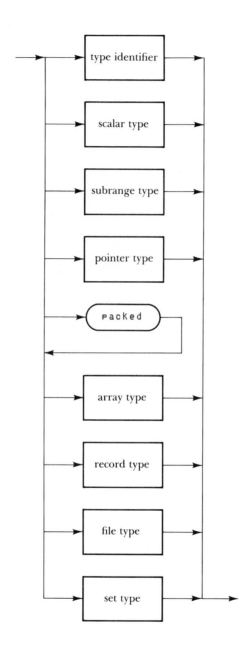

array type

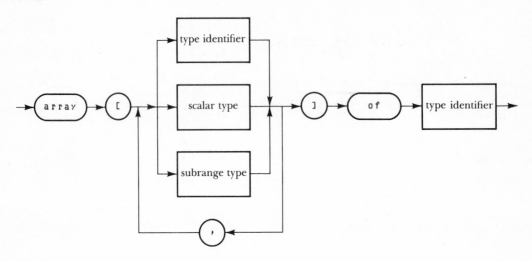

scalar type

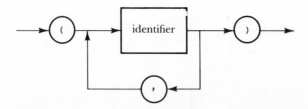

subrange type

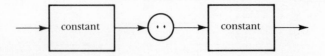

pointer type

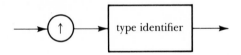

record type

file type

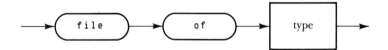

set type

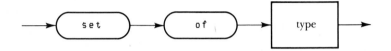

field list

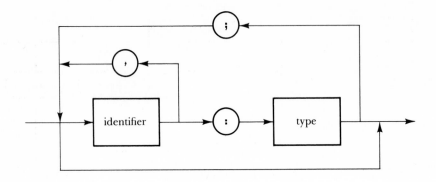

expression

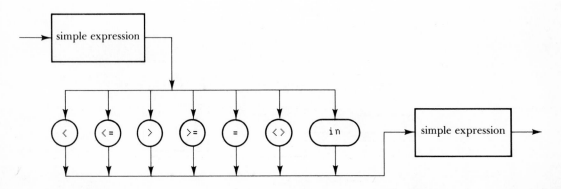

simple expression

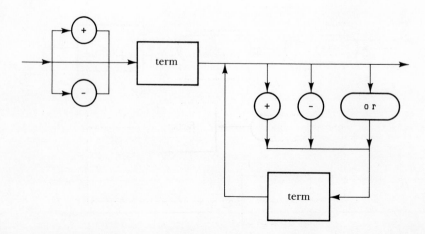

term

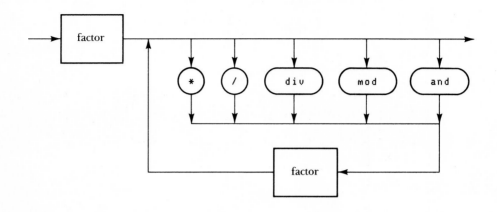

factor

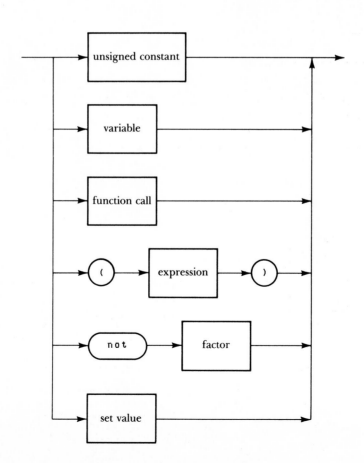

set value

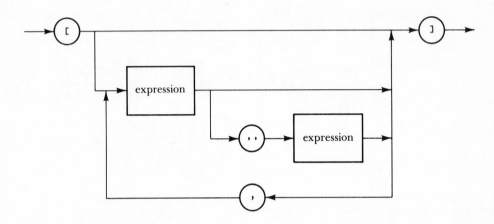

variable

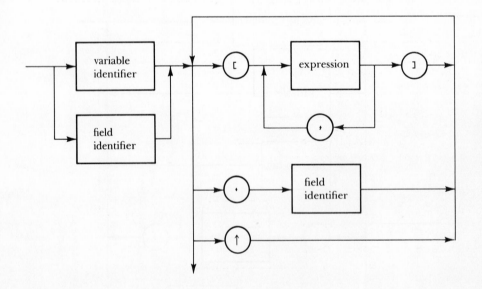

identifier

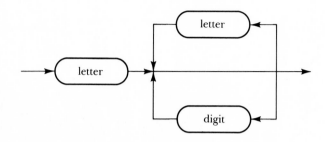

unsigned constant

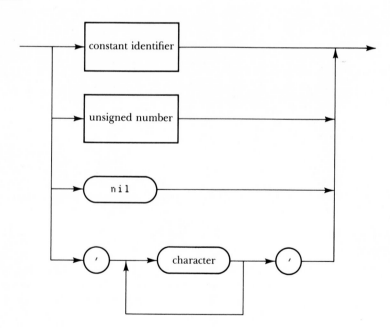

constant

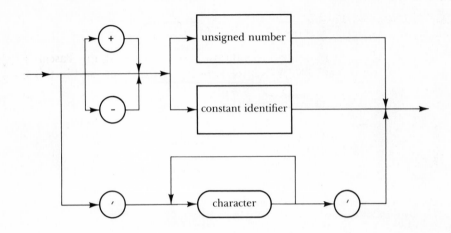

unsigned number

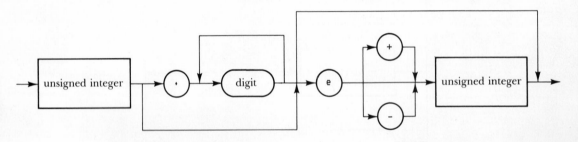

unsigned integer

D

an indentation convention

Conventions for indentation are not part of the Pascal language. For reference, we summarize here the conventions used in this book.

compound statement

```
begin
    statement1 ;
    statement2 ;
        .
        .
    statementn
end
```

if statements

```
if  condition
    then  statement1
    else  statement2
```

case statement

```
case expression of
    c1 : statement1 ;
    c2 : statement2 ;
        .
        .
    cn : statementn
end
```

while statement

```
while condition do
    statement
```

repeat statement

```
repeat
    statement1 ;
    statement2 ;
    .
    .
    statementn
until condition
```

for statement

```
for variable:=expr1 to expr2 do
    statement
```

with statement

```
with recordid do
    statement
```

index

abs, 42
access program, 275
access time, 14
accumulator, 13
address, 14
ALGOL, 21
algorithm, 24–26
　analysis, 321–324
　design, 35
　discovery, 310–313
alternative computations, 65–66
and, 43
arctan, 42
argument of a function, 135
array, 108
arrays, 107
　one-dimensional, 107
　multidimensional, 113
　two-dimensional, 113
artificial intelligence, 313
ASCII code, 12
assembler, 20
assembly language, 16
assignment operator, 27
assignment statement, 45–47

backtracking, 355
BASIC, 21
batch system, 19
begin, 59
bin packing problem, 319–320,
　355–359
binary, 7
　digit, 7
　number representation, 7
　point, 7
bistable circuit, 7
bit, 7
block, 144
blocking of a program, 95
boolean, 40
boolean
　expression, 43
　operators, 43
branch of a tree, 254

bubblesort, 111
　complexity, 322
　modified, 318
bucket sort, 352
buffer, 290
byte, 12

case, 72
case statement, 72
central processing unit, 4, 13
char, 40
character string, 118–120
chr, 119
COBOL, 21
coding, 35
collision, 304
comments, 58, 169–170
compiler, 18
complexity
　average or expected, 323
　of an algorithm, 321
　of a problem, 361–364
　worst case, 323
compound statement, 67
computer classification, 18
concatenation of strings, 328–329
const, 99
constants, 39–40
　boolean, 39
　character, 39
　integer, 39
　real, 39
　symbolic, 98
control flow, 92
conversion error, 9
correctness proving, 212
cos, 42
CPU, 4, 13

dangling else, 72
data, 3
　representation, 7–9
　storage, 9–10
　types, 98
data base, 300

data management, 282
data structures, 98, 220
  aggregate or compound, 220
  dynamic, 221
  implementation, 220–222
  selection, 275–276
  static, 221
debugging, 77, 209–212
decision tables, 94
declarations, 58
deque, 237
dispose, 268
directory, 302–303
  simple, 302
  multilevel, 303
div, 42
do, 81, 83
documentation, 197–198
  external, 197
  internal, 197
downto, 82

echoing of input, 63, 187
efficiency
  execution time, 191–195
  storage, 195
else, 66
end, 59
entry assertion, 212
enumerated data type, 100
eof, 49, 292
eoln, 49, 296
errors, 202–204
  due to incompleteness, 204
  execution, 203
  implementation, 204
  logic, 77
  specification, 202
  syntax, 77, 203
exit assertion, 212
exp, 42
exponent notation, 10
exponent overflow, 12
exponent underflow, 12

false, 40
Fibonacci numbers, 88
field list, 124
file, 291
file
  input, 48
  organization, 301–306
  processing, 282
  random access, 287
  sequential, 48, 287, 289–292

first-in-first-out store, 233
floating point representation, 10–12
  normalized, 10
floppy disk, 286
flowcharts, 27–31
for, 81
format description, 51
FORTRAN, 21
function, 136
functions, 135–137

get, 291
global identifier, 151
goto, 90
goto statement, 89–91

hardware, 4
hashing, 303, 343–345
heuristic, 313
higher level languages, 17

identifiers, 26
  in Pascal, 38
if, 66
if-then-else statement, 66
implementation
  of algorithms, 35
  of data structures, 220–222
in, 103
indentation, 170–171, 383–384
index, 107
  invalid, 108
indexed sequential organization,
  304–305
infix notation, 231
information, 3
information processing system, 3–4
information retrieval, 299–301
inorder traversal of a tree, 263
input, 58
input, 3, 48–50
  file, 50
  validation, 92
input-output
  design, 186–187
  devices, 5
insertion sort, 117
integer, 40
integer representation, 9
interactive system, 19
intrinsic functions in Pascal, 42, 136
inverted files, 305–306

key of a record, 287
key word, 301

`label`, 90
label declaration, 90
labeled statements, 89
last-in-first-out store, 222, 226
list, 237–244
    doubly linked, 244
    linked, 238
    sequential, 237
`ln`, 42
local identifier, 151
logic errors, 77
loop, 80–85
    conditional, 82
    counted, 80
    final-test, 82
    initial-test, 82
    variable, 80

machine language, 14–18
    instructions, 15
magnetic disk, 14, 284–286
magnetic drum, 286
magnetic tape, 14, 283–284
mainframe computer, 18
mantissa, 11
matrix, 113
    sparse, 249
    symmetric, 277
memory, 4
    dynamic allocation, 265–266
    location, 15
    main, 4
mergesort, 349
merging of files, 346–349
microcomputer, 18
minicomputer, 18
`mod`, 42
modular programming, 175
module, 175

`new`, 268
nesting
    of if statements, 70
    of loops, 85
`nil`, 268
nonlocal identifiers, 151
`not`, 43
N-P complete problems, 363

`odd`, 45
`of`, 72
O-notation, 322
operating system, 19
operators
    arithmetic, 41
    boolean, 43
    priority or precedence, 41, 367
    relational or comparison, 43
`output`, 58
output, 3, 50–54
    formatted, 50
    unformatted, 50

`packed`, 119
parameter
    actual, 143
    formal, 135
Pascal, 17, 21
pattern matching, 331–334
peripheral devices, 5
PL/I, 21
pointers, 266–269
polynomial representation, 246–247
postfix notation, 227
postorder traversal of a tree, 263
prefix notation, 236
preorder traversal of a tree,
    257–258
problem statement, 35
`procedure`, 140
procedures, 139–140
processor, 3
`program`, 58
program, 4
    debugging, 77, 209–212
    design, 177
    maintenance, 188
    modification, 188–190
    structure, 171–173
    testing, 77, 204–208
programming, 3
    defensive, 202
    languages, 20–21
    modular, 175
    structured, 164
    style, 165–166
prologue, 61
pseudolanguage, 26
push-down list, 223
`put`, 292

queue, 233–234
    circular, 234
quicksort, 353

`read`, 48
`readln`, 49
read-write head, 283, 284
`real`, 40
`record`, 124

records
  in Pascal, 123–127
  of a general file, 287
recursion, 155–160
reference parameter, 153
register, 13
repeat, 84
repeat statement, 84
reserved words, 37, 366
reset, 291
rewrite, 291
rotational delay, 285
round, 42
roundoff error, 12

scope of an identifier, 150–152
search
  binary, 337, 339
  complexity, 362
  exhaustive, 353
  sequential, 315, 335
searching, 314, 335
  examples, 314–317
secondary storage, 5, 14, 282–286
sectors of a disk, 284
seek time, 285
selection
  two-way, 66
  many-way, 70
set, 102
sets, 102
  operations, 102–103
simulation, 235
sin, 42
SNOBOL, 21
software, 4
sorting, 110–113, 317–319, 349–352
  comparison of methods, 352
  complexity, 363
sparse tables and matrices, 248
specification errors, 202
sqr, 42
sqrt, 42
stack, 222–224
  overflow, 223
standard identifiers, 37, 366
statements, 37, 58
stepwise refinement, 35
storage devices
  direct or random access, 285
  sequential, 284
straightline program, 17
string manipulation, 328–334
structured problem solving, 34–35
subprogram, 134

subrange type, 100
subscript notation, 107
syntax, 37
  charts, 38, 367–382
  error, 77
system software, 19–20

table, 113
  symmetric, 277
testing, 204–208
  bottom-up, 208
  top-down, 208
text, 296
text editing, 247–248, 278–279
text editor, 20
text file, 296
then, 66
time sharing, 19
to, 81
top-down design, 174
tracks of a disk, 284
traveling salesman problem, 359–360
tree
  height, 255
  label, 254
  leaves, 254
  node, 254
trees, 254–255
  binary, 255–257
  binary search, 339–343
  ternary, 265
true, 40
trunc, 42
type, 99
type
  declaration, 99
  error, 40

until, 84

value parameter, 153
var, 40
variables, 26
  with restricted range, 99–100

while, 83
while statement, 83
Wirth, N., 21
with, 126
with statement, 126
word in memory, 19
workspace, 237
  management, 240
write, 51
writeln, 52